FREE Study Skills DVD Offer

Dear Customer,

Thank you for your purchase from Mometrix! We consider it an honor and a privilege that you have purchased our product and we want to ensure your satisfaction.

As a way of showing our appreciation and to help us better serve you, we have developed a Study Skills DVD that we would like to give you for FREE. This DVD covers our *best practices* for getting ready for your exam, from how to use our study materials to how to best prepare for the day of the test.

All that we ask is that you email us with feedback that would describe your experience so far with our product. Good, bad, or indifferent, we want to know what you think!

To get your FREE Study Skills DVD, email freedvd@mometrix.com with *FREE STUDY SKILLS DVD* in the subject line and the following information in the body of the email:

- The name of the product you purchased.
- Your product rating on a scale of 1-5, with 5 being the highest rating.
- Your feedback. It can be long, short, or anything in between. We just want to know your impressions and experience so far with our product. (Good feedback might include how our study material met your needs and ways we might be able to make it even better. You could highlight features that you found helpful or features that you think we should add.)
- Your full name and shipping address where you would like us to send your free DVD.

If you have any questions or concerns, please don't hesitate to contact me directly.

Thanks again!

Sincerely,

Jay Willis
Vice President
jay.willis@mometrix.com
1-800-673-8175

TExES

Mathematics 7-12 (235)

SECRETS

Study Guide

Your Key to Exam Success

Written and edited by the Mometrix Texas Teacher Certification Test Team

Printed in the United States of America

This paper meets the requirements of ANSI/NISO Z39.48-1992 (Permanence of Paper).

Mometrix offers volume discount pricing to institutions. For more information or a price quote, please contact our sales department at sales@mometrix.com or 888-248-1219.

Paperback
ISBN 13: 978-1-63094-000-3
ISBN 10: 1-63094-000-3

Ebook
ISBN 13: 978-1-5167-0297-8
ISBN 10: 1-5167-0297-2

DEAR FUTURE EXAM SUCCESS STORY

First of all, **THANK YOU** for purchasing Mometrix study materials!

Second, congratulations! You are one of the few determined test-takers who are committed to doing whatever it takes to excel on your exam. **You have come to the right place.** We developed these study materials with one goal in mind: to deliver you the information you need in a format that's concise and easy to use.

In addition to optimizing your guide for the content of the test, we've outlined our recommended steps for breaking down the preparation process into small, attainable goals so you can make sure you stay on track.

We've also analyzed the entire test-taking process, identifying the most common pitfalls and showing how you can overcome them and be ready for any curveball the test throws you.

Standardized testing is one of the biggest obstacles on your road to success, which only increases the importance of doing well in the high-pressure, high-stakes environment of test day. Your results on this test could have a significant impact on your future, and this guide provides the information and practical advice to help you achieve your full potential on test day.

Your success is our success

We would love to hear from you! If you would like to share the story of your exam success or if you have any questions or comments in regard to our products, please contact us at **800-673-8175** or **support@mometrix.com**.

Thanks again for your business and we wish you continued success!

Sincerely,
The Mometrix Test Preparation Team

Table of Contents

Introduction

Thank you for purchasing this resource! You have made the choice to prepare yourself for a test that could have a huge impact on your future, and this guide is designed to help you be fully ready for test day. Obviously, it's important to have a solid understanding of the test material, but you also need to be prepared for the unique environment and stressors of the test, so that you can perform to the best of your abilities.

For this purpose, the first section that appears in this guide is the **Secret Keys**. We've devoted countless hours to meticulously researching what works and what doesn't, and we've boiled down our findings to the five most impactful steps you can take to improve your performance on the test. We start at the beginning with study planning and move through the preparation process, all the way to the testing strategies that will help you get the most out of what you know when you're finally sitting in front of the test.

We recommend that you start preparing for your test as far in advance as possible. However, if you've bought this guide as a last-minute study resource and only have a few days before your test, we recommend that you skip over the first two Secret Keys since they address a long-term study plan.

If you struggle with **test anxiety**, we strongly encourage you to check out our recommendations for how you can overcome it. Test anxiety is a formidable foe, but it can be beaten, and we want to make sure you have the tools you need to defeat it.

Secret Key #1 – Plan Big, Study Small

There's a lot riding on your performance. If you want to ace this test, you're going to need to keep your skills sharp and the material fresh in your mind. You need a plan that lets you review everything you need to know while still fitting in your schedule. We'll break this strategy down into three categories.

Information Organization

Start with the information you already have: the official test outline. From this, you can make a complete list of all the concepts you need to cover before the test. Organize these concepts into groups that can be studied together, and create a list of any related vocabulary you need to learn so you can brush up on any difficult terms. You'll want to keep this vocabulary list handy once you actually start studying since you may need to add to it along the way.

Time Management

Once you have your set of study concepts, decide how to spread them out over the time you have left before the test. Break your study plan into small, clear goals so you have a manageable task for each day and know exactly what you're doing. Then just focus on one small step at a time. When you manage your time this way, you don't need to spend hours at a time studying. Studying a small block of content for a short period each day helps you retain information better and avoid stressing over how much you have left to do. You can relax knowing that you have a plan to cover everything in time. In order for this strategy to be effective though, you have to start studying early and stick to your schedule. Avoid the exhaustion and futility that comes from last-minute cramming!

Study Environment

The environment you study in has a big impact on your learning. Studying in a coffee shop, while probably more enjoyable, is not likely to be as fruitful as studying in a quiet room. It's important to keep distractions to a minimum. You're only planning to study for a short block of time, so make the most of it. Don't pause to check your phone or get up to find a snack. It's also important to **avoid multitasking**. Research has consistently shown that multitasking will make your studying dramatically less effective. Your study area should also be comfortable and well-lit so you don't have the distraction of straining your eyes or sitting on an uncomfortable chair.

The time of day you study is also important. You want to be rested and alert. Don't wait until just before bedtime. Study when you'll be most likely to comprehend and remember. Even better, if you know what time of day your test will be, set that time aside for study. That way your brain will be used to working on that subject at that specific time and you'll have a better chance of recalling information.

Finally, it can be helpful to team up with others who are studying for the same test. Your actual studying should be done in as isolated an environment as possible, but the work of organizing the information and setting up the study plan can be divided up. In between study sessions, you can discuss with your teammates the concepts that you're all studying and quiz each other on the details. Just be sure that your teammates are as serious about the test as you are. If you find that your study time is being replaced with social time, you might need to find a new team.

Secret Key #2 – Make Your Studying Count

You're devoting a lot of time and effort to preparing for this test, so you want to be absolutely certain it will pay off. This means doing more than just reading the content and hoping you can remember it on test day. It's important to make every minute of study count. There are two main areas you can focus on to make your studying count:

Retention

It doesn't matter how much time you study if you can't remember the material. You need to make sure you are retaining the concepts. To check your retention of the information you're learning, try recalling it at later times with minimal prompting. Try carrying around flashcards and glance at one or two from time to time or ask a friend who's also studying for the test to quiz you.

To enhance your retention, look for ways to put the information into practice so that you can apply it rather than simply recalling it. If you're using the information in practical ways, it will be much easier to remember. Similarly, it helps to solidify a concept in your mind if you're not only reading it to yourself but also explaining it to someone else. Ask a friend to let you teach them about a concept you're a little shaky on (or speak aloud to an imaginary audience if necessary). As you try to summarize, define, give examples, and answer your friend's questions, you'll understand the concepts better and they will stay with you longer. Finally, step back for a big picture view and ask yourself how each piece of information fits with the whole subject. When you link the different concepts together and see them working together as a whole, it's easier to remember the individual components.

Finally, practice showing your work on any multi-step problems, even if you're just studying. Writing out each step you take to solve a problem will help solidify the process in your mind, and you'll be more likely to remember it during the test.

Modality

Modality simply refers to the means or method by which you study. Choosing a study modality that fits your own individual learning style is crucial. No two people learn best in exactly the same way, so it's important to know your strengths and use them to your advantage.

For example, if you learn best by visualization, focus on visualizing a concept in your mind and draw an image or a diagram. Try color-coding your notes, illustrating them, or creating symbols that will trigger your mind to recall a learned concept. If you learn best by hearing or discussing information, find a study partner who learns the same way or read aloud to yourself. Think about how to put the information in your own words. Imagine that you are giving a lecture on the topic and record yourself so you can listen to it later.

For any learning style, flashcards can be helpful. Organize the information so you can take advantage of spare moments to review. Underline key words or phrases. Use different colors for different categories. Mnemonic devices (such as creating a short list in which every item starts with the same letter) can also help with retention. Find what works best for you and use it to store the information in your mind most effectively and easily.

Secret Key #3 – Practice the Right Way

Your success on test day depends not only on how many hours you put into preparing, but also on whether you prepared the right way. It's good to check along the way to see if your studying is paying off. One of the most effective ways to do this is by taking practice tests to evaluate your progress. Practice tests are useful because they show exactly where you need to improve. Every time you take a practice test, pay special attention to these three groups of questions:

- The questions you got wrong
- The questions you had to guess on, even if you guessed right
- The questions you found difficult or slow to work through

This will show you exactly what your weak areas are, and where you need to devote more study time. Ask yourself why each of these questions gave you trouble. Was it because you didn't understand the material? Was it because you didn't remember the vocabulary? Do you need more repetitions on this type of question to build speed and confidence? Dig into those questions and figure out how you can strengthen your weak areas as you go back to review the material.

Additionally, many practice tests have a section explaining the answer choices. It can be tempting to read the explanation and think that you now have a good understanding of the concept. However, an explanation likely only covers part of the question's broader context. Even if the explanation makes sense, **go back and investigate** every concept related to the question until you're positive you have a thorough understanding.

As you go along, keep in mind that the practice test is just that: practice. Memorizing these questions and answers will not be very helpful on the actual test because it is unlikely to have any of the same exact questions. If you only know the right answers to the sample questions, you won't be prepared for the real thing. **Study the concepts** until you understand them fully, and then you'll be able to answer any question that shows up on the test.

It's important to wait on the practice tests until you're ready. If you take a test on your first day of study, you may be overwhelmed by the amount of material covered and how much you need to learn. Work up to it gradually.

On test day, you'll need to be prepared for answering questions, managing your time, and using the test-taking strategies you've learned. It's a lot to balance, like a mental marathon that will have a big impact on your future. Like training for a marathon, you'll need to start slowly and work your way up. When test day arrives, you'll be ready.

Start with the strategies you've read in the first two Secret Keys—plan your course and study in the way that works best for you. If you have time, consider using multiple study resources to get different approaches to the same concepts. It can be helpful to see difficult concepts from more than one angle. Then find a good source for practice tests. Many times, the test website will suggest potential study resources or provide sample tests.

Practice Test Strategy

When you're ready to start taking practice tests, follow this strategy:

Untimed and Open-Book Practice

Take the first test with no time constraints and with your notes and study guide handy. Take your time and focus on applying the strategies you've learned.

Timed and Open-Book Practice

Take the second practice test open-book as well, but set a timer and practice pacing yourself to finish in time.

Timed and Closed-Book Practice

Take any other practice tests as if it were test day. Set a timer and put away your study materials. Sit at a table or desk in a quiet room, imagine yourself at the testing center, and answer questions as quickly and accurately as possible.

Keep repeating timed and closed-book tests on a regular basis until you run out of practice tests or it's time for the actual test. Your mind will be ready for the schedule and stress of test day, and you'll be able to focus on recalling the material you've learned.

Secret Key #4 – Pace Yourself

Once you're fully prepared for the material on the test, your biggest challenge on test day will be managing your time. Just knowing that the clock is ticking can make you panic even if you have plenty of time left. Work on pacing yourself so you can build confidence against the time constraints of the exam. Pacing is a difficult skill to master, especially in a high-pressure environment, so **practice is vital**.

Set time expectations for your pace based on how much time is available. For example, if a section has 60 questions and the time limit is 30 minutes, you know you have to average 30 seconds or less per question in order to answer them all. Although 30 seconds is the hard limit, set 25 seconds per question as your goal, so you reserve extra time to spend on harder questions. When you budget extra time for the harder questions, you no longer have any reason to stress when those questions take longer to answer.

Don't let this time expectation distract you from working through the test at a calm, steady pace, but keep it in mind so you don't spend too much time on any one question. Recognize that taking extra time on one question you don't understand may keep you from answering two that you do understand later in the test. If your time limit for a question is up and you're still not sure of the answer, mark it and move on, and come back to it later if the time and the test format allow. If the testing format doesn't allow you to return to earlier questions, just make an educated guess; then put it out of your mind and move on.

On the easier questions, be careful not to rush. It may seem wise to hurry through them so you have more time for the challenging ones, but it's not worth missing one if you know the concept and just didn't take the time to read the question fully. Work efficiently but make sure you understand the question and have looked at all of the answer choices, since more than one may seem right at first.

Even if you're paying attention to the time, you may find yourself a little behind at some point. You should speed up to get back on track, but do so wisely. Don't panic; just take a few seconds less on each question until you're caught up. Don't guess without thinking, but do look through the answer choices and eliminate any you know are wrong. If you can get down to two choices, it is often worthwhile to guess from those. Once you've chosen an answer, move on and don't dwell on any that you skipped or had to hurry through. If a question was taking too long, chances are it was one of the harder ones, so you weren't as likely to get it right anyway.

On the other hand, if you find yourself getting ahead of schedule, it may be beneficial to slow down a little. The more quickly you work, the more likely you are to make a careless mistake that will affect your score. You've budgeted time for each question, so don't be afraid to spend that time. Practice an efficient but careful pace to get the most out of the time you have.

Secret Key #5 – Have a Plan for Guessing

When you're taking the test, you may find yourself stuck on a question. Some of the answer choices seem better than others, but you don't see the one answer choice that is obviously correct. What do you do?

The scenario described above is very common, yet most test takers have not effectively prepared for it. Developing and practicing a plan for guessing may be one of the single most effective uses of your time as you get ready for the exam.

In developing your plan for guessing, there are three questions to address:

- When should you start the guessing process?
- How should you narrow down the choices?
- Which answer should you choose?

When to Start the Guessing Process

Unless your plan for guessing is to select C every time (which, despite its merits, is not what we recommend), you need to leave yourself enough time to apply your answer elimination strategies. Since you have a limited amount of time for each question, that means that if you're going to give yourself the best shot at guessing correctly, you have to decide quickly whether or not you will guess.

Of course, the best-case scenario is that you don't have to guess at all, so first, see if you can answer the question based on your knowledge of the subject and basic reasoning skills. Focus on the key words in the question and try to jog your memory of related topics. Give yourself a chance to bring the knowledge to mind, but once you realize that you don't have (or you can't access) the knowledge you need to answer the question, it's time to start the guessing process.

It's almost always better to start the guessing process too early than too late. It only takes a few seconds to remember something and answer the question from knowledge. Carefully eliminating wrong answer choices takes longer. Plus, going through the process of eliminating answer choices can actually help jog your memory.

Summary: Start the guessing process as soon as you decide that you can't answer the question based on your knowledge.

How to Narrow Down the Choices

The next chapter in this book (**Test-Taking Strategies**) includes a wide range of strategies for how to approach questions and how to look for answer choices to eliminate. You will definitely want to read those carefully, practice them, and figure out which ones work best for you. Here though, we're going to address a mindset rather than a particular strategy.

Your chances of guessing an answer correctly depend on how many options you are choosing from.

How many choices you have	How likely you are to guess correctly
5	20%
4	25%
3	33%
2	50%
1	100%

You can see from this chart just how valuable it is to be able to eliminate incorrect answers and make an educated guess, but there are two things that many test takers do that cause them to miss out on the benefits of guessing:

- Accidentally eliminating the correct answer
- Selecting an answer based on an impression

We'll look at the first one here, and the second one in the next section.

To avoid accidentally eliminating the correct answer, we recommend a thought exercise called **the $5 challenge**. In this challenge, you only eliminate an answer choice from contention if you are willing to bet $5 on it being wrong. Why $5? Five dollars is a small but not insignificant amount of money. It's an amount you could afford to lose but wouldn't want to throw away. And while losing $5 once might not hurt too much, doing it twenty times will set you back $100. In the same way, each small decision you make—eliminating a choice here, guessing on a question there—won't by itself impact your score very much, but when you put them all together, they can make a big difference. By holding each answer choice elimination decision to a higher standard, you can reduce the risk of accidentally eliminating the correct answer.

The $5 challenge can also be applied in a positive sense: If you are willing to bet $5 that an answer choice *is* correct, go ahead and mark it as correct.

Summary: Only eliminate an answer choice if you are willing to bet $5 that it is wrong.

Which Answer to Choose

You're taking the test. You've run into a hard question and decided you'll have to guess. You've eliminated all the answer choices you're willing to bet $5 on. Now you have to pick an answer. Why do we even need to talk about this? Why can't you just pick whichever one you feel like when the time comes?

The answer to these questions is that if you don't come into the test with a plan, you'll rely on your impression to select an answer choice, and if you do that, you risk falling into a trap. The test writers know that everyone who takes their test will be guessing on some of the questions, so they intentionally write wrong answer choices to seem plausible. You still have to pick an answer though, and if the wrong answer choices are designed to look right, how can you ever be sure that you're not falling for their trap? The best solution we've found to this dilemma is to take the decision out of your hands entirely. Here is the process we recommend:

Once you've eliminated any choices that you are confident (willing to bet $5) are wrong, select the first remaining choice as your answer.

Whether you choose to select the first remaining choice, the second, or the last, the important thing is that you use some preselected standard. Using this approach guarantees that you will not be enticed into selecting an answer choice that looks right, because you are not basing your decision on how the answer choices look.

This is not meant to make you question your knowledge. Instead, it is to help you recognize the difference between your knowledge and your impressions. There's a huge difference between thinking an answer is right because of what you know, and thinking an answer is right because it looks or sounds like it should be right.

Summary: To ensure that your selection is appropriately random, make a predetermined selection from among all answer choices you have not eliminated.

Test-Taking Strategies

This section contains a list of test-taking strategies that you may find helpful as you work through the test. By taking what you know and applying logical thought, you can maximize your chances of answering any question correctly!

It is very important to realize that every question is different and every person is different: no single strategy will work on every question, and no single strategy will work for every person. That's why we've included all of them here, so you can try them out and determine which ones work best for different types of questions and which ones work best for you.

Question Strategies

Read Carefully

Read the question and answer choices carefully. Don't miss the question because you misread the terms. You have plenty of time to read each question thoroughly and make sure you understand what is being asked. Yet a happy medium must be attained, so don't waste too much time. You must read carefully, but efficiently.

Contextual Clues

Look for contextual clues. If the question includes a word you are not familiar with, look at the immediate context for some indication of what the word might mean. Contextual clues can often give you all the information you need to decipher the meaning of an unfamiliar word. Even if you can't determine the meaning, you may be able to narrow down the possibilities enough to make a solid guess at the answer to the question.

Prefixes

If you're having trouble with a word in the question or answer choices, try dissecting it. Take advantage of every clue that the word might include. Prefixes and suffixes can be a huge help. Usually they allow you to determine a basic meaning. Pre- means before, post- means after, pro - is positive, de- is negative. From prefixes and suffixes, you can get an idea of the general meaning of the word and try to put it into context.

Hedge Words

Watch out for critical hedge words, such as *likely*, *may*, *can*, *sometimes*, *often*, *almost*, *mostly*, *usually*, *generally*, *rarely*, and *sometimes*. Question writers insert these hedge phrases to cover every possibility. Often an answer choice will be wrong simply because it leaves no room for exception. Be on guard for answer choices that have definitive words such as *exactly* and *always*.

Switchback Words

Stay alert for *switchbacks*. These are the words and phrases frequently used to alert you to shifts in thought. The most common switchback words are *but*, *although*, and *however*. Others include *nevertheless, on the other hand, even though, while, in spite of, despite, regardless of.* Switchback words are important to catch because they can change the direction of the question or an answer choice.

Face Value

When in doubt, use common sense. Accept the situation in the problem at face value. Don't read too much into it. These problems will not require you to make wild assumptions. If you have to go beyond creativity and warp time or space in order to have an answer choice fit the question, then you should move on and consider the other answer choices. These are normal problems rooted in reality. The applicable relationship or explanation may not be readily apparent, but it is there for you to figure out. Use your common sense to interpret anything that isn't clear.

Answer Choice Strategies

Answer Selection

The most thorough way to pick an answer choice is to identify and eliminate wrong answers until only one is left, then confirm it is the correct answer. Sometimes an answer choice may immediately seem right, but be careful. The test writers will usually put more than one reasonable answer choice on each question, so take a second to read all of them and make sure that the other choices are not equally obvious. As long as you have time left, it is better to read every answer choice than to pick the first one that looks right without checking the others.

Answer Choice Families

An answer choice family consists of two (in rare cases, three) answer choices that are very similar in construction and cannot all be true at the same time. If you see two answer choices that are direct opposites or parallels, one of them is usually the correct answer. For instance, if one answer choice says that quantity *x* increases and another either says that quantity *x* decreases (opposite) or says that quantity *y* increases (parallel), then those answer choices would fall into the same family. An answer choice that doesn't match the construction of the answer choice family is more likely to be incorrect. Most questions will not have answer choice families, but when they do appear, you should be prepared to recognize them.

Eliminate Answers

Eliminate answer choices as soon as you realize they are wrong, but make sure you consider all possibilities. If you are eliminating answer choices and realize that the last one you are left with is also wrong, don't panic. Start over and consider each choice again. There may be something you missed the first time that you will realize on the second pass.

Avoid Fact Traps

Don't be distracted by an answer choice that is factually true but doesn't answer the question. You are looking for the choice that answers the question. Stay focused on what the question is asking for so you don't accidentally pick an answer that is true but incorrect. Always go back to the question and make sure the answer choice you've selected actually answers the question and is not merely a true statement.

Extreme Statements

In general, you should avoid answers that put forth extreme actions as standard practice or proclaim controversial ideas as established fact. An answer choice that states the "process should be used in certain situations, if…" is much more likely to be correct than one that states the "process should be discontinued completely." The first is a calm rational statement and doesn't even make a definitive, uncompromising stance, using a hedge word *if* to provide wiggle room, whereas the second choice is a radical idea and far more extreme.

Benchmark

As you read through the answer choices and you come across one that seems to answer the question well, mentally select that answer choice. This is not your final answer, but it's the one that will help you evaluate the other answer choices. The one that you selected is your benchmark or standard for judging each of the other answer choices. Every other answer choice must be compared to your benchmark. That choice is correct until proven otherwise by another answer choice beating it. If you find a better answer, then that one becomes your new benchmark. Once you've decided that no other choice answers the question as well as your benchmark, you have your final answer.

Predict the Answer

Before you even start looking at the answer choices, it is often best to try to predict the answer. When you come up with the answer on your own, it is easier to avoid distractions and traps because you will know exactly what to look for. The right answer choice is unlikely to be word-for-word what you came up with, but it should be a close match. Even if you are confident that you have the right answer, you should still take the time to read each option before moving on.

General Strategies

Tough Questions

If you are stumped on a problem or it appears too hard or too difficult, don't waste time. Move on! Remember though, if you can quickly check for obviously incorrect answer choices, your chances of guessing correctly are greatly improved. Before you completely give up, at least try to knock out a couple of possible answers. Eliminate what you can and then guess at the remaining answer choices before moving on.

Check Your Work

Since you will probably not know every term listed and the answer to every question, it is important that you get credit for the ones that you do know. Don't miss any questions through careless mistakes. If at all possible, try to take a second to look back over your answer selection and make sure you've selected the correct answer choice and haven't made a costly careless mistake (such as marking an answer choice that you didn't mean to mark). This quick double check should more than pay for itself in caught mistakes for the time it costs.

Pace Yourself

It's easy to be overwhelmed when you're looking at a page full of questions; your mind is confused and full of random thoughts, and the clock is ticking down faster than you would like. Calm down and maintain the pace that you have set for yourself. Especially as you get down to the last few minutes of the test, don't let the small numbers on the clock make you panic. As long as you are on track by monitoring your pace, you are guaranteed to have time for each question.

Don't Rush

It is very easy to make errors when you are in a hurry. Maintaining a fast pace in answering questions is pointless if it makes you miss questions that you would have gotten right otherwise. Test writers like to include distracting information and wrong answers that seem right. Taking a little extra time to avoid careless mistakes can make all the difference in your test score. Find a pace that allows you to be confident in the answers that you select.

KEEP MOVING

Panicking will not help you pass the test, so do your best to stay calm and keep moving. Taking deep breaths and going through the answer elimination steps you practiced can help to break through a stress barrier and keep your pace.

Final Notes

The combination of a solid foundation of content knowledge and the confidence that comes from practicing your plan for applying that knowledge is the key to maximizing your performance on test day. As your foundation of content knowledge is built up and strengthened, you'll find that the strategies included in this chapter become more and more effective in helping you quickly sift through the distractions and traps of the test to isolate the correct answer.

Now it's time to move on to the test content chapters of this book, but be sure to keep your goal in mind. As you read, think about how you will be able to apply this information on the test. If you've already seen sample questions for the test and you have an idea of the question format and style, try to come up with questions of your own that you can answer based on what you're reading. This will give you valuable practice applying your knowledge in the same ways you can expect to on test day.

Good luck and good studying!

Number Concepts

Classifications of Numbers

Numbers are the basic building blocks of mathematics. Specific features of numbers are identified by the following terms:

Integer – any positive or negative whole number, including zero. Integers do not include fractions $\left(\frac{1}{3}\right)$, decimals (0.56), or mixed numbers $\left(7\frac{3}{4}\right)$.

Prime number – any whole number greater than 1 that has only two factors, itself and 1; that is, a number that can be divided evenly only by 1 and itself.

Composite number – any whole number greater than 1 that has more than two different factors; in other words, any whole number that is not a prime number. For example: The composite number 8 has the factors of 1, 2, 4, and 8.

Even number – any integer that can be divided by 2 without leaving a remainder. For example: 2, 4, 6, 8, and so on.

Odd number – any integer that cannot be divided evenly by 2. For example: 3, 5, 7, 9, and so on.

Decimal number – any number that uses a decimal point to show the part of the number that is less than one. Example: 1.234.

Decimal point – a symbol used to separate the ones place from the tenths place in decimals or dollars from cents in currency.

Decimal place – the position of a number to the right of the decimal point. In the decimal 0.123, the 1 is in the first place to the right of the decimal point, indicating tenths; the 2 is in the second place, indicating hundredths; and the 3 is in the third place, indicating thousandths.

The **decimal**, or base 10, system is a number system that uses ten different digits (0, 1, 2, 3, 4, 5, 6, 7, 8, 9). An example of a number system that uses something other than ten digits is the **binary**, or base 2, number system, used by computers, which uses only the numbers 0 and 1. It is thought that the decimal system originated because people had only their 10 fingers for counting.

Rational numbers include all integers, decimals, and fractions. Any terminating or repeating decimal number is a rational number.

Irrational numbers cannot be written as fractions or decimals because the number of decimal places is infinite and there is no recurring pattern of digits within the number. For example, pi (π) begins with 3.141592 and continues without terminating or repeating, so pi is an irrational number.

Real numbers are the set of all rational and irrational numbers.

Review Video: Numbers and Their Classifications
Visit mometrix.com/academy and enter code: 461071

Place Value

Write the place value of each digit in the following number: 14,059.826

1: ten-thousands
4: thousands
0: hundreds
5: tens
9: ones
8: tenths
2: hundredths
6: thousandths

Review Video: Number Place Value
Visit mometrix.com/academy and enter code: 205433

Writing Numbers in Word Form

Example 1

Write each number in words.

29: twenty-nine
478: four hundred seventy-eight
9,435: nine thousand four hundred thirty-five
98,542: ninety-eight thousand five hundred forty-two
302, 876: three hundred two thousand eight hundred seventy-six

Example 2

Write each decimal in words.

0.06: six hundredths
0.6: six tenths
6.0: six
0.009: nine thousandths
0.113: one hundred thirteen thousandths
0.901: nine hundred one thousandths

Rounding and Estimation

Rounding is reducing the digits in a number while still trying to keep the value similar. The result will be less accurate, but will be in a simpler form, and will be easier to use. Whole numbers can be rounded to the nearest ten, hundred or thousand.

Example 1

Round each number:

1. Round each number to the nearest ten: 11, 47, 118
2. Round each number to the nearest hundred: 78, 980, 248
3. Round each number to the nearest thousand: 302, 1274, 3756

ANSWER

1. Remember, when rounding to the nearest ten, anything ending in 5 or greater rounds up. So, 11 rounds to 10, 47 rounds to 50, and 118 rounds to 120.
2. Remember, when rounding to the nearest hundred, anything ending in 50 or greater rounds up. So, 78 rounds to 100, 980 rounds to 1000, and 248 rounds to 200.
3. Remember, when rounding to the nearest thousand, anything ending in 500 or greater rounds up. So, 302 rounds to 0, 1274 rounds to 1000, and 3756 rounds to 4000.

When you are asked to estimate the solution a problem, you will need to provide only an approximate figure or **estimation** for your answer. In this situation, you will need to round each number in the calculation to the level indicated (nearest hundred, nearest thousand, etc.) or to a level that makes sense for the numbers involved. When estimating a sum **all numbers must be rounded to the same level**. You cannot round one number to the nearest thousand while rounding another to the nearest hundred.

EXAMPLE 2

Estimate the solution to 345,932 + 96,369 *by rounding each number to the nearest ten thousand.*

Start by rounding each number to the nearest ten thousand: 345,932 becomes 350,000, and 96,369 becomes 100,000.

Then, add the rounded numbers: 350,000 + 100,000 = 450,000. So, the answer is approximately 450,000.

The exact answer would be 345,932 + 96,369 = 442,301. So, the estimate of 450,000 is a similar value to the exact answer.

EXAMPLE 3

A runner's heart beats 422 times over the course of six minutes. About how many times did the runner's heart beat during each minute?

"About how many" indicates that you need to estimate the solution. In this case, look at the numbers you are given. 422 can be rounded down to 420, which is easily divisible by 6. A good estimate is $420 \div 6 = 70$ beats per minute. More accurately, the patient's heart rate was just over 70 beats per minute since his heart actually beat a little more than 420 times in six minutes.

Review Video: Rounding and Estimation
Visit mometrix.com/academy and enter code: 126243

MEASUREMENT CONVERSION

When going from a larger unit to a smaller unit, multiply the number of the known amount by the **equivalent amount**. When going from a smaller unit to a larger unit, divide the number of the known amount by the equivalent amount.

Also, you can set up conversion fractions. In these fractions, one fraction is the **conversion factor**. The other fraction has the unknown amount in the numerator. So, the known value is placed in the denominator. Sometimes the second fraction has the known value from the problem in the numerator, and the unknown in the denominator. Multiply the two fractions to get the converted measurement.

Conversion Units

Metric Conversions

1000 mcg (microgram)	1 mg
1000 mg (milligram)	1 g
1000 g (gram)	1 kg
1000 kg (kilogram)	1 metric ton
1000 mL (milliliter)	1 L
1000 um (micrometer)	1 mm
1000 mm (millimeter)	1 m
100 cm (centimeter)	1 m
1000 m (meter)	1 km

U.S. and Metric Equivalents

Unit	U.S. equivalent	Metric equivalent
Inch	1 inch	2.54 centimeters
Foot	12 inches	0.305 meters
Yard	3 feet	0.914 meters
Mile	5280 feet	1.609 kilometers

Capacity Measurements

Unit	U.S. equivalent	Metric equivalent
Ounce	8 drams	29.573 milliliters
Cup	8 ounces	0.237 liter
Pint	16 ounces	0.473 liter
Quart	2 pints	0.946 liter
Gallon	4 quarts	3.785 liters

Weight Measurements

Unit	U.S. equivalent	Metric equivalent
Ounce	16 drams	28.35 grams
Pound	16 ounces	453.6 grams
Ton	2,000 pounds	907.2 kilograms

Fluid Measurements

Unit	English equivalent	Metric equivalent
1 tsp	1 fluid dram	5 milliliters
3 tsp	4 fluid drams	15 or 16 milliliters
2 tbsp	1 fluid ounce	30 milliliters
1 glass	8 fluid ounces	240 milliliters

Measurement Conversion Practice Problems

Example 1

a. Convert 1.4 meters to centimeters.
b. Convert 218 centimeters to meters.

Example 2

a. Convert 42 inches to feet.
b. Convert 15 feet to yards.

Example 3

a. How many pounds are in 15 kilograms?
b. How many pounds are in 80 ounces?

Example 4

a. How many kilometers are in 2 miles?
b. How many centimeters are in 5 feet?

Example 5

a. How many gallons are in 15.14 liters?
b. How many liters are in 8 quarts?

Example 6

a. How many grams are in 13.2 pounds?
b. How many pints are in 9 gallons?

Measurement Conversion Practice Solutions

Example 1

Write ratios with the conversion factor $\frac{100 \text{ cm}}{1 \text{ m}}$. Use proportions to convert the given units.

a. $\frac{100 \text{ cm}}{1 \text{ m}} = \frac{x \text{ cm}}{1.4 \text{ m}}$. Cross multiply to get $x = 140$. So, 1.4 m is the same as 140 cm.

b. $\frac{100 \text{ cm}}{1 \text{ m}} = \frac{218 \text{ cm}}{x \text{ m}}$. Cross multiply to get $100x = 218$, or $x = 2.18$. So, 218 cm is the same as 2.18 m.

Example 2

Write ratios with the conversion factors $\frac{12 \text{ in}}{1 \text{ ft}}$ and $\frac{3 \text{ ft}}{1 \text{ yd}}$. Use proportions to convert the given units.

a. $\frac{12 \text{ in}}{1 \text{ ft}} = \frac{42 \text{ in}}{x \text{ ft}}$. Cross multiply to get $12x = 42$, or $x = 3.5$. So, 42 inches is the same as 3.5 feet.

b. $\frac{3 \text{ ft}}{1 \text{ yd}} = \frac{15 \text{ ft}}{x \text{ yd}}$. Cross multiply to get $3x = 15$, or $x = 5$. So, 15 feet is the same as 5 yards.

Example 3

a. $15 \text{ kilograms} \times \frac{2.2 \text{ pounds}}{1 \text{ kilogram}} = 33 \text{ pounds}$

b. $80 \text{ ounces} \times \frac{1 \text{ pound}}{16 \text{ ounces}} = 5 \text{ pounds}$

Example 4

a. $2 \text{ miles} \times \frac{1.609 \text{ kilometers}}{1 \text{ mile}} = 3.218 \text{ kilometers}$

b. $5 \text{ feet} \times \frac{12 \text{ inches}}{1 \text{ foot}} \times \frac{2.54 \text{ centimeters}}{1 \text{ inch}} = 152.4 \text{ centimeters}$

Example 5

a. $15.14 \text{ liters } \times \frac{1 \text{ gallon}}{3.785 \text{ liters}} = 4 \text{ gallons}$

b. $8 \text{ quarts } \times \frac{1 \text{ gallon}}{4 \text{ quarts}} \times \frac{3.785 \text{ liters}}{1 \text{ gallon}} = 7.57 \text{ liters}$

Example 6

a. $13.2 \text{ pounds } \times \frac{1 \text{ kilogram}}{2.2 \text{ pounds}} \times \frac{1000 \text{ grams}}{1 \text{ kilogram}} = 6000 \text{ grams}$

b. $9 \text{ gallons } \times \frac{4 \text{ quarts}}{1 \text{ gallon}} \times \frac{2 \text{ pints}}{1 \text{ quarts}} = 72 \text{ pints}$

Operations

There are four basic mathematical operations:

Addition and Subtraction

Addition increases the value of one quantity by the value of another quantity. Example: $2 + 4 = 6$; $8 + 9 = 17$. The result is called the **sum**. With addition, the order does not matter. $4 + 2 = 2 + 4$.

Subtraction is the opposite operation to addition; it decreases the value of one quantity by the value of another quantity. Example: $6 - 4 = 2$; $17 - 8 = 9$. The result is called the **difference**. Note that with subtraction, the order does matter. $6 - 4 \neq 4 - 6$.

Review Video: Addition and Subtraction
Visit mometrix.com/academy and enter code: 521157

Multiplication and Division

Multiplication can be thought of as repeated addition. One number tells how many times to add the other number to itself. Example: 3×2 (three times two) $= 2 + 2 + 2 = 6$. With multiplication, the order does not matter. $2 \times 3 = 3 \times 2$ or $3 + 3 = 2 + 2 + 2$.

Division is the opposite operation to multiplication; one number tells us how many parts to divide the other number into. Example: $20 \div 4 = 5$; if 20 is split into 4 equal parts, each part is 5. With division, the order of the numbers does matter. $20 \div 4 \neq 4 \div 20$.

Review Video: Multiplication and Division
Visit mometrix.com/academy and enter code: 643326

Order of Operations

Order of operations is a set of rules that dictates the order in which we must perform each operation in an expression so that we will evaluate it accurately. If we have an expression that includes multiple different operations, order of operations tells us which operations to do first. The most common mnemonic for order of operations is **PEMDAS**, or "Please Excuse My Dear Aunt Sally." PEMDAS stands for parentheses, exponents, multiplication, division, addition, and subtraction. It is important to understand that multiplication and division have equal precedence, as do addition and subtraction, so those pairs of operations are simply worked from left to right in order.

Example: Evaluate the expression $5 + 20 \div 4 \times (2 + 3) - 6$ using the correct order of operations.

- **P:** Perform the operations inside the parentheses: $(2 + 3) = 5$
- **E:** Simplify the exponents.
    - The equation now looks like this: $5 + 20 \div 4 \times 5 - 6$
- **MD:** Perform multiplication and division from left to right: $20 \div 4 = 5$; then $5 \times 5 = 25$
    - The equation now looks like this: $5 + 25 - 6$
- **AS:** Perform addition and subtraction from left to right: $5 + 25 = 30$; then $30 - 6 = 24$

Review Video: Order of Operations
Visit mometrix.com/academy and enter code: 259675

Subtraction with Regrouping

Example 1

Demonstrate how to subtract 189 from 525 using regrouping.

First, set up the subtraction problem:

$$\begin{array}{r} 525 \\ -\ 189 \\ \hline \end{array}$$

Notice that the numbers in the ones and tens columns of 525 are smaller than the numbers in the ones and tens columns of 189. This means you will need to use regrouping to perform subtraction:

$$\begin{array}{rrrr} & 5 & 2 & 5 \\ - & 1 & 8 & 9 \\ \hline \end{array}$$

To subtract 9 from 5 in the ones column you will need to borrow from the 2 in the tens columns:

$$\begin{array}{rrrr} & 5 & 1 & 15 \\ - & 1 & 8 & 9 \\ \hline & & & 6 \end{array}$$

Next, to subtract 8 from 1 in the tens column you will need to borrow from the 5 in the hundreds column:

$$\begin{array}{rrrr} & 4 & 11 & 15 \\ - & 1 & 8 & 9 \\ \hline & & 3 & 6 \end{array}$$

Last, subtract the 1 from the 4 in the hundreds column:

$$\begin{array}{rrrr} & 4 & 11 & 15 \\ - & 1 & 8 & 9 \\ \hline & 3 & 3 & 6 \end{array}$$

Example 2

Demonstrate how to subtract 477 from 620 using regrouping.

First, set up the subtraction problem:

$$\begin{array}{r} 620 \\ -\ 477 \\ \hline \end{array}$$

Notice that the numbers in the ones and tens columns of 620 are smaller than the numbers in the ones and tens columns of 477. This means you will need to use regrouping to perform subtraction:

$$\begin{array}{rccc} & 6 & 2 & 0 \\ - & 4 & 7 & 7 \\ \hline \end{array}$$

To subtract 7 from 0 in the ones column you will need to borrow from the 2 in the tens column:

$$\begin{array}{rccc} & 6 & 1 & 10 \\ - & 4 & 7 & 7 \\ \hline & & & 3 \end{array}$$

Next, to subtract 7 from the 1 that's still in the tens column you will need to borrow from the 6 in the hundreds column:

$$\begin{array}{rccc} & 5 & 11 & 10 \\ - & 4 & 7 & 7 \\ \hline & & 4 & 3 \end{array}$$

Lastly, subtract 4 from the 5 remaining in the hundreds column:

$$\begin{array}{rccc} & 5 & 11 & 10 \\ - & 4 & 7 & 7 \\ \hline & 1 & 4 & 3 \end{array}$$

Real World One or Multi-Step Problems with Rational Numbers

Example 1

A woman's age is thirteen more than half of 60. How old is the woman?

"More than" indicates addition, and "of" indicates multiplication. The expression can be written as $\frac{1}{2}(60) + 13$. So, the woman's age is equal to $\frac{1}{2}(60) + 13 = 30 + 13 = 43$. The woman is 43 years old.

Example 2

A patient was given pain medicine at a dosage of 0.22 grams. The patient's dosage was then increased to 0.80 grams. By how much was the patient's dosage increased?

The first step is to determine what operation (addition, subtraction, multiplication, or division) the problem requires. Notice the keywords and phrases "by how much" and "increased." "Increased" means that you go from a smaller amount to a larger amount. This change can be found by subtracting the smaller amount from the larger amount: $0.80 \text{ grams} - 0.22 \text{ grams} = 0.58 \text{ grams}$.

Remember to line up the decimal when subtracting:

$$\begin{array}{r} 0.80 \\ -\ 0.22 \\ \hline 0.58 \end{array}$$

EXAMPLE 3

At a hotel, $\frac{3}{4}$ of the 100 rooms are occupied today. Yesterday, $\frac{4}{5}$ of the 100 rooms were occupied. On which day were more of the rooms occupied and by how much more?

First, find the number of rooms occupied each day. To do so, multiply the fraction of rooms occupied by the number of rooms available:

$$\text{Number occupied} = \text{Fraction occupied} \times \text{Total number}$$

Today:

$$\text{Number of rooms occupied today} = \frac{3}{4} \times 100 = 75$$

Today, 75 rooms are occupied.

Yesterday:

$$\text{Number of rooms occupied} = \frac{4}{5} \times 100 = 80$$

Yesterday, 80 rooms were occupied.

The difference in the number of rooms occupied is

$$80 - 75 = 5 \text{ rooms}$$

Therefore, five more rooms were occupied yesterday than today.

Review Video: Rational Numbers
Visit mometrix.com/academy and enter code: 280645

EXAMPLE 4

At a school, 40% of the teachers teach English. If 20 teachers teach English, how many teachers work at the school?

To answer this problem, first think about the number of teachers that work at the school. Will it be more or less than the number of teachers who work in a specific department such as English? More teachers work at the school, so the number you find to answer this question will be greater than 20.

40% of the teachers are English teachers. "Of" indicates multiplication, and words like "is" and "are" indicate equivalence. Translating the problem into a mathematical sentence gives $40\% \times t = 20$, where t represents the total number of teachers. Solving for t gives $t = \frac{20}{40\%} = \frac{20}{0.40} = 50$. Fifty teachers work at the school.

EXAMPLE 5

A patient was given blood pressure medicine at a dosage of 2 grams. The patient's dosage was then decreased to 0.45 grams. By how much was the patient's dosage decreased?

The decrease is represented by the difference between the two amounts:

$$2 \text{ grams} - 0.45 \text{ grams} = 1.55 \text{ grams}.$$

Remember to line up the decimal point before subtracting.

$$\begin{array}{r} 2.00 \\ -\ \ 0.45 \\ \hline 1.55 \end{array}$$

EXAMPLE 6

Two weeks ago, $\frac{2}{3}$ of the 60 customers at a skate shop were male. Last week, $\frac{3}{6}$ of the 80 customers were male. During which week were there more male customers?

First, you need to find the number of male customers that were in the skate shop each week. You are given this amount in terms of fractions. To find the actual number of male customers, multiply the fraction of male customers by the number of customers in the store.

Actual number of male customers = fraction of male customers × total number of customers.

Number of male customers two weeks ago $= \frac{2}{3} \times 60 = \frac{120}{3} = 40.$

Number of male customers last week $= \frac{3}{6} \times 80 = \frac{1}{2} \times 80 = \frac{80}{2} = 40.$

The number of male customers was the same both weeks.

EXAMPLE 7

Jane ate lunch at a local restaurant. She ordered a $4.99 appetizer, a $12.50 entrée, and a $1.25 soda. If she wants to tip her server 20%, how much money will she spend in all?

To find total amount, first find the sum of the items she ordered from the menu and then add 20% of this sum to the total.

$$\begin{aligned} &\$4.99 + \$12.50 + \$1.25 = \$18.74 \\ &\$18.74 \times 20\% = (0.20)(\$18.74) = \$3.748 \approx \$3.75 \\ &\text{Total} = \$18.74 + \$3.75 = \$22.49. \end{aligned}$$

Another way to find this sum is to multiply 120% by the cost of the meal.

$$\$18.74(120\%) = \$18.74(1.20) = \$22.49.$$

PARENTHESES

Parentheses are used to designate which operations should be done first when there are multiple operations. Example: $4 - (2 + 1) = 1$; the parentheses tell us that we must add 2 and 1, and then subtract the sum from 4, rather than subtracting 2 from 4 and then adding 1 (this would give us an answer of 3).

Review Video: Mathematical Parentheses
Visit mometrix.com/academy and enter code: 978600

EXPONENTS

An **exponent** is a superscript number placed next to another number at the top right. It indicates how many times the base number is to be multiplied by itself. Exponents provide a shorthand way to write what would be a longer mathematical expression. Example: $a^2 = a \times a$; $2^4 = 2 \times 2 \times 2 \times 2$. A number with an exponent of 2 is said to be "squared," while a number with an exponent of 3 is said to be "cubed." The value of a number raised to an exponent is called its power. So, 8^4 is read as "8 to the 4th power," or "8 raised to the power of 4." A negative exponent is the same as the **reciprocal** of a positive exponent. Example: $a^{-2} = \frac{1}{a^2}$.

Review Video: Exponents
Visit mometrix.com/academy and enter code: 600998

ROOTS

A **root**, such as a square root, is another way of writing a fractional exponent. Instead of using a superscript, roots use the radical symbol ($\sqrt{\ }$) to indicate the operation. A radical will have a number underneath the bar, and may sometimes have a number in the upper left: $\sqrt[n]{a}$, read as "the nth root of a." The relationship between radical notation and exponent notation can be described by this equation: $\sqrt[n]{a} = a^{\frac{1}{n}}$. The two special cases of $n = 2$ and $n = 3$ are called square roots and cube roots. If there is no number to the upper left, it is understood to be a square root ($n = 2$). Nearly all of the roots you encounter will be square roots. A square root is the same as a number raised to the one-half power. When we say that a is the square root of b ($a = \sqrt{b}$), we mean that a multiplied by itself equals b: ($a \times a = b$).

Review Video: Roots
Visit mometrix.com/academy and enter code: 795655

Review Video: Square Root and Perfect Square
Visit mometrix.com/academy and enter code: 648063

A **perfect square** is a number that has an integer for its square root. There are 10 perfect squares from 1 to 100: 1, 4, 9, 16, 25, 36, 49, 64, 81, 100 (the squares of integers 1 through 10).

ABSOLUTE VALUE

A precursor to working with negative numbers is understanding what **absolute values** are. A number's absolute value is simply the distance away from zero a number is on the number line. The absolute value of a number is always positive and is written $|x|$.

Example

Show that $|3| = |-3|$.

The absolute value of 3, written as $|3|$, is 3 because the distance between 0 and 3 on a number line is three units. Likewise, the absolute value of -3, written as $|-3|$, is 3 because the distance between 0 and -3 on a number line is three units. So, $|3| = |-3|$.

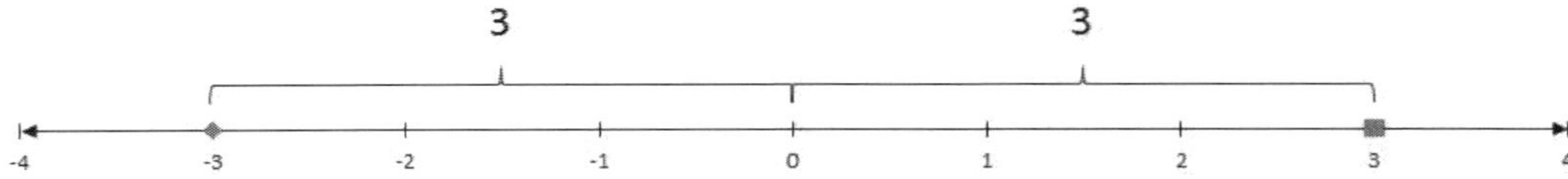

Review Video: Absolute Value
Visit mometrix.com/academy and enter code: 314669

Operations with Positive and Negative Numbers

Addition

When adding signed numbers, if the signs are the same simply add the absolute values of the addends and apply the original sign to the sum. For example, $(+4) + (+8) = +12$ and $(-4) + (-8) = -12$. When the original signs are different, take the absolute values of the addends and subtract the smaller value from the larger value, then apply the original sign of the larger value to the difference. For instance, $(+4) + (-8) = -4$ and $(-4) + (+8) = +4$.

Subtraction

For subtracting signed numbers, change the sign of the number after the minus symbol and then follow the same rules used for addition. For example, $(+4) - (+8) = (+4) + (-8) = -4$.

Multiplication

If the signs are the same the product is positive when multiplying signed numbers. For example, $(+4) \times (+8) = +32$ and $(-4) \times (-8) = +32$. If the signs are opposite, the product is negative. For example, $(+4) \times (-8) = -32$ and $(-4) \times (+8) = -32$. When more than two factors are multiplied together, the sign of the product is determined by how many negative factors are present. If there are an odd number of negative factors then the product is negative, whereas an even number of negative factors indicates a positive product. For instance, $(+4) \times (-8) \times (-2) = +64$ and $(-4) \times (-8) \times (-2) = -64$.

Division

The rules for dividing signed numbers are similar to multiplying signed numbers. If the dividend and divisor have the same sign, the quotient is positive. If the dividend and divisor have opposite signs, the quotient is negative. For example, $(-4) \div (+8) = -0.5$.

The Number Line

A number line is a graph to see the distance between numbers. Basically, this graph shows the relationship between numbers. So, a number line may have a point for zero and may show negative numbers on the left side of the line. Also, any positive numbers are placed on the right side of the line.

<u>EXAMPLE</u>

Name each point on the number line below:

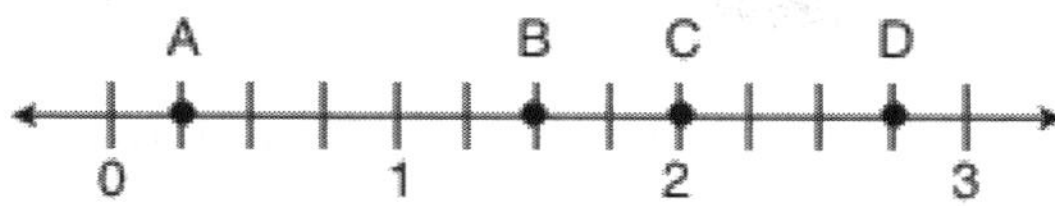

Use the dashed lines on the number line to identify each point. Each dashed line between two whole numbers is $\frac{1}{4}$. The line halfway between two numbers is $\frac{1}{2}$.

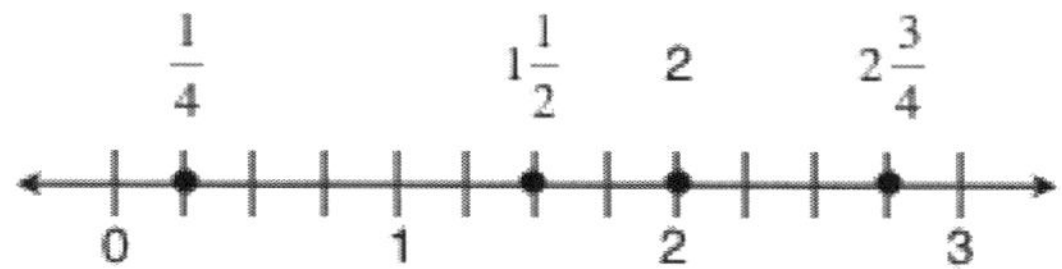

Review Video: Negative and Positive Number Line
Visit mometrix.com/academy and enter code: 816439

FRACTIONS

A **fraction** is a number that is expressed as one integer written above another integer, with a dividing line between them $\left(\frac{x}{y}\right)$. It represents the **quotient** of the two numbers "x divided by y." It can also be thought of as x out of y equal parts.

The top number of a fraction is called the **numerator**, and it represents the number of parts under consideration. The 1 in $\frac{1}{4}$ means that 1 part out of the whole is being considered in the calculation. The bottom number of a fraction is called the **denominator**, and it represents the total number of equal parts. The 4 in $\frac{1}{4}$ means that the whole consists of 4 equal parts. A fraction cannot have a denominator of zero; this is referred to as "*undefined*."

Fractions can be manipulated, without changing the value of the fraction, by multiplying or dividing (but not adding or subtracting) both the numerator and denominator by the same number. If you divide both numbers by a common factor, you are **reducing** or simplifying the fraction. Two fractions that have the same value but are expressed differently are known as **equivalent fractions**. For example, $\frac{2}{10}, \frac{3}{15}, \frac{4}{20}$, and $\frac{5}{25}$ are all equivalent fractions. They can also all be reduced or simplified to $\frac{1}{5}$.

When two fractions are manipulated so that they have the same denominator, this is known as finding a **common denominator**. The number chosen to be that common denominator should be the least common multiple of the two original denominators. Example: $\frac{3}{4}$ and $\frac{5}{6}$; the least common multiple of 4 and 6 is 12. Manipulating to achieve the common denominator: $\frac{3}{4} = \frac{9}{12}; \frac{5}{6} = \frac{10}{12}$.

PROPER FRACTIONS AND MIXED NUMBERS

A fraction whose denominator is greater than its numerator is known as a **proper fraction**, while a fraction whose numerator is greater than its denominator is known as an **improper fraction**. Proper fractions have values *less than one* and improper fractions have values *greater than one*.

A **mixed number** is a number that contains both an integer and a fraction. Any improper fraction can be rewritten as a mixed number. Example: $\frac{8}{3} = \frac{6}{3} + \frac{2}{3} = 2 + \frac{2}{3} = 2\frac{2}{3}$. Similarly, any mixed number can be rewritten as an improper fraction. Example: $1\frac{3}{5} = 1 + \frac{3}{5} = \frac{5}{5} + \frac{3}{5} = \frac{8}{5}$.

Review Video: Proper and Improper Fractions and Mixed Numbers
Visit mometrix.com/academy and enter code: 211077

Review Video: Fractions
Visit mometrix.com/academy and enter code: 262335

DECIMALS

DECIMAL ILLUSTRATION

USE A MODEL TO REPRESENT THE DECIMAL: 0.24. WRITE 0.24 AS A FRACTION.

The decimal 0.24 is twenty-four hundredths. One possible model to represent this fraction is to draw 100 pennies, since each penny is worth one-hundredth of a dollar. Draw one hundred circles to represent one hundred pennies. Shade 24 of the pennies to represent the decimal twenty-four hundredths.

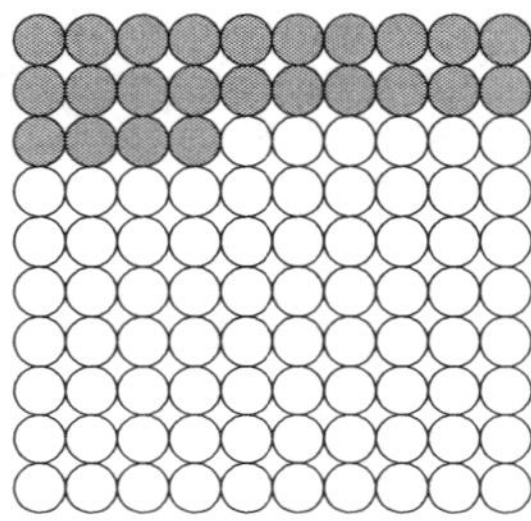

To write the decimal as a fraction, write a fraction: $\frac{\#\text{ shaded spaces}}{\#\text{ total spaces}}$. The number of shaded spaces is 24, and the total number of spaces is 100, so as a fraction 0.24 equals $\frac{24}{100}$. This fraction can then be reduced to $\frac{6}{25}$.

Review Video: Decimals
Visit mometrix.com/academy and enter code: 837268

PERCENTAGES

Percentages can be thought of as fractions that are based on a whole of 100; that is, one whole is equal to 100%. The word **percent** means "per hundred." Fractions can be expressed as a percentage by finding equivalent fractions with a denomination of 100. Example: $\frac{7}{10} = \frac{70}{100} = 70\%$; $\frac{1}{4} = \frac{25}{100} = 25\%$.

To express a *percentage as a fraction*, divide the percentage number by 100 and reduce the fraction to its simplest possible terms. Example: $60\% = \frac{60}{100} = \frac{3}{5}$; $96\% = \frac{96}{100} = \frac{24}{25}$.

Review Video: Percentages
Visit mometrix.com/academy and enter code: 141911

Real World Problems with Percentages

A percentage problem can be presented three main ways: (1) Find what percentage of some number another number is. Example: What percentage of 40 is 8? (2) Find what number is some percentage of a given number. Example: What number is 20% of 40? (3) Find what number another number is a given percentage of. Example: What number is 8 20% of?

The three components in all of these cases are the same: a **whole** (W), a **part** (P), and a **percentage** (%). These are related by the equation: $\boldsymbol{P} = \boldsymbol{W} \times \%$. This is the form of the equation you would use to solve problems of type (2). To solve types (1) and (3), you would use these two forms:

$$\% = \frac{P}{W} \text{ and } W = \frac{P}{\%}$$

The thing that frequently makes percentage problems difficult is that they are most often also word problems, so a large part of solving them is figuring out which quantities are what. Example: In a school cafeteria, 7 students choose pizza, 9 choose hamburgers, and 4 choose tacos. Find the percentage that chooses tacos. To find the whole, you must first add all of the parts: $7 + 9 + 4 = 20$. The percentage can then be found by dividing the part by the whole ($\% = \frac{P}{W}$): $\frac{4}{20} = \frac{20}{100} = 20\%$.

Example 1

What is 30% of 120?

The word *of* indicates multiplication, so 30% of 120 is found by multiplying 120 by 30%. Change 30% to a fraction or decimal, then multiply:

$$30\% = \frac{30}{100} = 0.3$$

$$120 \times 0.3 = 36$$

Review Video: Finding Percentage of Number Given Whole
Visit mometrix.com/academy and enter code: 932623

Example 2

What is 150% of 20?

The word *of* indicates multiplication, so 150% of 20 is found by multiplying 20 by 150%. Change 150% to a fraction or decimal, then multiply:

$$150\% = \frac{150}{100} = 1.5$$

$$20 \times 1.5 = 30$$

Notice that 30 is greater than the original number of 20. This makes sense because you are finding a number that is more than 100% of the original number.

EXAMPLE 3

What is 14.5% of 96?

Change 14.5% to a decimal before multiplying. $0.145 \times 96 = 13.92$. Notice that 13.92 is much smaller than the original number of 96. This makes sense because you are finding a small percentage of the original number.

EXAMPLE 4

According to a survey, about 82% of engineers were highly satisfied with their job. If 145 engineers were surveyed, how many reported that they were highly satisfied?

$$82\% \text{ of } 145 = 0.82 \times 145 = 118.9$$

Because you can't have 0.9 of a person, we must round up to say that 119 engineers reported that they were highly satisfied with their jobs.

EXAMPLE 5

On Monday, Lucy spent 5 hours observing sales, 3 hours working on advertising, and 4 hours doing paperwork. On Tuesday, she spent 4 hours observing sales, 6 hours working on advertising, and 2 hours doing paperwork. What was the percent change for time spent on each task between the two days?

The three tasks are observing sales, working on advertising, and doing paperwork. To find the amount of change, compare the first amount with the second amount for each task. Then, write this difference as a percentage compared to the initial amount.

Amount of change for observing sales:

$$5 \text{ hours} - 4 \text{ hours} = 1 \text{ hour}$$

The percent of change is

$$\frac{\text{amount of change}}{\text{original amount}} \times 100\%. \frac{1 \text{ hour}}{5 \text{ hours}} \times 100\% = 20\%.$$

Lucy spent 20% less time observing sales on Tuesday than she did on Monday.

Amount of change for working on advertising:

$$6 \text{ hours} - 3 \text{ hours} = 3 \text{ hours}$$

The percent of change is

$$\frac{\text{amount of change}}{\text{original amount}} \times 100\%. \frac{3 \text{ hours}}{3 \text{ hours}} \times 100\% = 100\%.$$

Lucy spent 100% more time (or twice as much time) working on advertising on Tuesday than she did on Monday.

Amount of change for doing paperwork:

$$4 \text{ hours} - 2 \text{ hours} = 2 \text{ hours}$$

The percent of change is

$$\frac{\text{amount of change}}{\text{original amount}} \times 100\%. \frac{2 \text{ hours}}{4 \text{ hours}} \times 100\% = 50\%.$$

Lucy spent 50% less time (or half as much time) working on paperwork on Tuesday than she did on Monday.

EXAMPLE 6

A patient was given 40 mg of a certain medicine. Later, the patient's dosage was increased to 45 mg. What was the percent increase in his medication?

To find the percent increase, first compare the original and increased amounts. The original amount was 40 mg, and the increased amount is 45 mg, so the dosage of medication was increased by 5 mg ($45 - 40 = 5$). Note, however, that the question asks not by how much the dosage increased but by what percentage it increased. Percent increase $= \frac{\text{new amount}-\text{original amount}}{\text{original amount}} \times 100\%$.

$$\frac{45 \text{ mg} - 40 \text{ mg}}{40 \text{ mg}} \times 100\% = \frac{5}{40} \times 100\% = 0.125 \times 100\% = 12.5\%$$

The percent increase is 12.5%.

EXAMPLE 7

A patient was given 100 mg of a certain medicine. The patient's dosage was later decreased to 88 mg. What was the percent decrease?

The medication was decreased by 12 mg:

$$(100 \text{ mg} - 88 \text{ mg} = 12 \text{ mg})$$

To find by what percent the medication was decreased, this change must be written as a percentage when compared to the original amount.

In other words, $\frac{\text{new amount} - \text{original amount}}{\text{original amount}} \times 100\% = \text{percent change}$

So $\frac{12 \text{ mg}}{100 \text{ mg}} \times 100\% = 0.12 \times 100\% = 12\%$.

The percent decrease is 12%.

EXAMPLE 8

A barista used 125 units of coffee grounds to make a liter of coffee. The barista later reduced the amount of coffee to 100 units. By what percentage was the amount of coffee grounds reduced?

In this problem you must determine which information is necessary to answer the question. The question asks by what percentage the coffee grounds were reduced. Find the two amounts and perform subtraction to find their difference. The first pot of coffee used 125 units. The second time, the barista used 100 units. Therefore, the difference is 125 units − 100 units = 25 units. The percentage reduction can then be calculated as:

$$\frac{\text{change}}{\text{original}} = \frac{25}{125} = \frac{1}{5} = 20\%$$

EXAMPLE 9

In a performance review, an employee received a score of 70 for efficiency and 90 for meeting project deadlines. Six months later, the employee received a score of 65 for efficiency and 96 for meeting project deadlines. What was the percent change for each score on the performance review?

To find the percent change, compare the first amount with the second amount for each score; then, write this difference as a percentage of the initial amount.

Percent change for efficiency score:

$$70 - 65 = 5;\ \frac{5}{70} \approx 7.1\%$$

The employee's efficiency decreased by about 7.1%.

Percent change for meeting project deadlines score:

$$96 - 90 = 6;\ \frac{6}{90} \approx 6.7\%$$

The employee increased his ability to meet project deadlines by about 6.7%.

SIMPLIFY

EXAMPLE 1

Simplify the following expression:

$$\frac{\frac{2}{5}}{\frac{4}{7}}$$

Dividing a fraction by a fraction may appear tricky, but it's not if you write out your steps carefully. Follow these steps to divide a fraction by a fraction.

Step 1: Rewrite the problem as a multiplication problem. Dividing by a fraction is the same as multiplying by its **reciprocal**, also known as its **multiplicative inverse**. The product of a number and its reciprocal is 1. Because $\frac{4}{7}$ times $\frac{7}{4}$ is 1, these numbers are reciprocals. Note that reciprocals can be found by simply interchanging the numerators and denominators. So, rewriting the problem as a multiplication problem gives $\frac{2}{5} \times \frac{7}{4}$.

Step 2: Perform multiplication of the fractions by multiplying the numerators by each other and the denominators by each other. In other words, multiply across the top and then multiply across the bottom.

$$\frac{2}{5} \times \frac{7}{4} = \frac{2 \times 7}{5 \times 4} = \frac{14}{20}$$

Step 3: Make sure the fraction is reduced to lowest terms. Both 14 and 20 can be divided by 2.

$$\frac{14}{20}=\frac{14\div 2}{20\div 2}=\frac{7}{10}$$

The answer is $\frac{7}{10}$.

EXAMPLE 2

Simplify the following expression:

$$\frac{1}{4}+\frac{3}{6}$$

Fractions with common denominators can be easily added or subtracted. Recall that the denominator is the bottom number in the fraction and that the numerator is the top number in the fraction.

The denominators of $\frac{1}{4}$ and $\frac{3}{6}$ are 4 and 6, respectively. The lowest common denominator of 4 and 6 is 12 because 12 is the least common multiple of 4 (multiples 4, 8, 12, 16, ...) and 6 (multiples 6, 12, 18, 24, ...). Convert each fraction to its equivalent with the newly found common denominator of 12.

$$\frac{1\times 3}{4\times 3}=\frac{3}{12};\ \frac{3\times 2}{6\times 2}=\frac{6}{12}$$

Now that the fractions have the same denominator, you can add them.

$$\frac{3}{12}+\frac{6}{12}=\frac{9}{12}$$

Be sure to write your answer in lowest terms. Both 9 and 12 can be divided by 3, so the answer is $\frac{3}{4}$.

EXAMPLE 3

Simplify the following expression:

$$\frac{7}{8}-\frac{8}{16}$$

The denominators of $\frac{7}{8}$ and $\frac{8}{16}$ are 8 and 16, respectively. The lowest common denominator of 8 and 16 is 16 because 16 is the least common multiple of 8 (multiples 8, 16, 24 ...) and 16 (multiples 16, 32, 48, ...). Convert each fraction to its equivalent with the newly found common denominator of 16.

$$\frac{7\times 2}{8\times 2}=\frac{14}{16};\ \frac{8\times 1}{16\times 1}=\frac{8}{16}$$

Now that the fractions have the same denominator, you can subtract them.

$$\frac{14}{16}-\frac{8}{16}=\frac{6}{16}$$

Be sure to write your answer in lowest terms. Both 6 and 16 can be divided by 2, so the answer is $\frac{3}{8}$.

EXAMPLE 4

Simplify the following expression:

$$\frac{1}{2} + \left(3\left(\frac{3}{4}\right) - 2\right) + 4$$

When simplifying expressions, first perform operations within groups. Within the set of parentheses are multiplication and subtraction operations. Perform the multiplication first to get $\frac{1}{2} + \left(\frac{9}{4} - 2\right) + 4$. Then, subtract two to obtain $\frac{1}{2} + \frac{1}{4} + 4$. Finally, perform addition from left to right:

$$\frac{1}{2} + \frac{1}{4} + 4 = \frac{2}{4} + \frac{1}{4} + \frac{16}{4} = \frac{19}{4}$$

EXAMPLE 5

Simplify the following expression:

$$0.22 + 0.5 - (5.5 + 3.3 \div 3)$$

First, evaluate the terms in the parentheses $(5.5 + 3.3 \div 3)$ using order of operations. $3.3 \div 3 = 1.1$, and $5.5 + 1.1 = 6.6$.

Next, rewrite the problem: $0.22 + 0.5 - 6.6$.

Finally, add and subtract from left to right: $0.22 + 0.5 = 0.72$; $0.72 - 6.6 = -5.88$. The answer is -5.88.

EXAMPLE 6

Simplify the following expression:

$$\frac{3}{2} + (4(0.5) - 0.75) + 2$$

First, simplify within the parentheses:

$$\frac{3}{2} + (2 - 0.75) + 2 =$$
$$\frac{3}{2} + 1.25 + 2$$

Finally, change the fraction to a decimal and perform addition from left to right:

$$1.5 + 1.25 + 2 = 4.75$$

EXAMPLE 7

Simplify the following expression:

$$1.45 + 1.5 + (6 - 9 \div 2) + 45$$

First, evaluate the terms in the parentheses using proper order of operations.

$$1.45 + 1.5 + (6 - 4.5) + 45$$
$$1.45 + 1.5 + 1.5 + 45$$

Finally, add from left to right.

$$1.45 + 1.5 + 1.5 + 45 = 49.45$$

Converting Percentages, Fractions, and Decimals

Converting decimals to percentages and percentages to decimals is as simple as moving the decimal point. To *convert from a decimal to a percentage*, move the decimal point **two places to the right**. To *convert from a percentage to a decimal*, move it **two places to the left**. Example: $0.23 = 23\%$; $5.34 = 534\%$; $0.007 = 0.7\%$; $700\%\ 7.00$; $86\% = 0.86$; $0.15\% = 0.0015$.

It may be helpful to remember that the percentage number will always be larger than the equivalent decimal number.

Review Video: Converting Decimals to Fractions and Percentages
Visit mometrix.com/academy and enter code: 986765

Example 1

Convert 15% to both a fraction and a decimal.

First, write the percentage over 100 because percent means "per one hundred." So, 15% can be written as $\frac{15}{100}$. Fractions should be written in the simplest form, which means that the numbers in the numerator and denominator should be reduced if possible. Both 15 and 100 can be divided by 5:

$$\frac{15 \div 5}{100 \div 5} = \frac{3}{20}$$

As before, write the percentage over 100 because percent means "per one hundred." So, 15% can be written as $\frac{15}{100}$. Dividing a number by a power of ten (10, 100, 1000, etc.) is the same as moving the decimal point to the left by the same number of spaces that there are zeros in the divisor. Since 100 has 2 zeros, move the decimal point two places to the left:

$$15\% = 0.15$$

In other words, when converting from a percentage to a decimal, drop the percent sign and move the decimal point two places to the left.

Example 2

Write 24.36% as a fraction and then as a decimal. Explain how you made these conversions.

24.36% written as a fraction is $\frac{24.36}{100}$, or $\frac{2436}{10{,}000}$, which reduces to $\frac{609}{2500}$. 24.36% written as a decimal is 0.2436. Recall that dividing by 100 moves the decimal two places to the left.

Review Video: Converting Percentages to Decimals and Fractions
Visit mometrix.com/academy and enter code: 287297

Example 3

Convert $\frac{4}{5}$ to a decimal and to a percentage.

To convert a fraction to a decimal, simply divide the numerator by the denominator in the fraction. The numerator is the top number in the fraction and the denominator is the bottom number in a fraction.

$$\frac{4}{5} = 4 \div 5 = 0.80 = 0.8$$

Percent means "per hundred."

$$\frac{4 \times 20}{5 \times 20} = \frac{80}{100} = 80\%$$

Example 4

Convert $3\frac{2}{5}$ *to a decimal and to a percentage.*

The mixed number $3\frac{2}{5}$ has a whole number and a fractional part. The fractional part $\frac{2}{5}$ can be written as a decimal by dividing 5 into 2, which gives 0.4. Adding the whole to the part gives 3.4. Alternatively, note that $3\frac{2}{5} = 3\frac{4}{10} = 3.4$

To change a decimal to a percentage, multiply it by 100.

$$3.4(100) = 340\%$$

Notice that this percentage is greater than 100%. This makes sense because the original mixed number $3\frac{2}{5}$ is greater than 1.

Review Video: Converting Fractions to Percentages and Decimals
Visit mometrix.com/academy and enter code: 306233

Scientific Notation

Scientific notation is a way of writing large numbers in a shorter form. The form $a \times 10^n$ is used in scientific notation, where a is greater than or equal to 1, but less than 10, and n is the number of places the decimal must move to get from the original number to a. Example: The number 230,400,000 is cumbersome to write. To write the value in scientific notation, place a decimal point between the first and second numbers, and include all digits through the last non-zero digit ($a = 2.304$). To find the appropriate power of 10, count the number of places the decimal point had to move ($n = 8$). The number is positive if the decimal moved to the left, and negative if it moved to the right. We can then write 230,400,000 as 2.304×10^8. If we look instead at the number 0.00002304, we have the same value for a, but this time the decimal moved 5 places to the right ($n = -5$). Thus, 0.00002304 can be written as 2.304×10^{-5}. Using this notation makes it simple to compare very large or very small numbers. By comparing exponents, it is easy to see that 3.28×10^4 is smaller than 1.51×10^5, because 4 is less than 5.

Review Video: Scientific Notation
Visit mometrix.com/academy and enter code: 976454

Operations with Decimals

Adding and Subtracting Decimals

When adding and subtracting decimals, the decimal points must always be aligned. Adding decimals is just like adding regular whole numbers. Example: $4.5 + 2 = 6.5$.

If the problem-solver does not properly align the decimal points, an incorrect answer of 4.7 may result. An easy way to add decimals is to align all of the decimal points in a vertical column visually. This will allow one to see exactly where the decimal should be placed in the final answer. Begin adding from right to left. Add each column in turn, making sure to carry the number to the left if a column adds up to more than 9. The same rules apply to the subtraction of decimals.

Review Video: Adding and Subtracting Decimals
Visit mometrix.com/academy and enter code: 381101

Multiplying Decimals

A simple multiplication problem has two components: a **multiplicand** and a **multiplier**. When multiplying decimals, work as though the numbers were whole rather than decimals. Once the final product is calculated, count the number of places to the right of the decimal in both the multiplicand and the multiplier. Then, count that number of places from the right of the product and place the decimal in that position.

For example, 12.3×2.56 has three places to the right of the respective decimals. Multiply 123×256 to get 31488. Now, beginning on the right, count three places to the left and insert the decimal. The final product will be 31.488.

Review Video: Multiplying Decimals
Visit mometrix.com/academy and enter code: 731574

Dividing Decimals

Every division problem has a **divisor** and a **dividend**. The dividend is the number that is being divided. In the problem $14 \div 7$, 14 is the dividend and 7 is the divisor. In a division problem with decimals, the divisor must be converted into a whole number. Begin by moving the decimal in the divisor to the right until a whole number is created. Next, move the decimal in the dividend the same number of spaces to the right. For example, 4.9 into 24.5 would become 49 into 245. The decimal was moved one space to the right to create a whole number in the divisor, and then the same was done for the dividend. Once the whole numbers are created, the problem is carried out normally: $245 \div 49 = 5$.

Review Video: Dividing Decimals
Visit mometrix.com/academy and enter code: 560690

Operations with Fractions

Adding and Subtracting Fractions

If two fractions have a common denominator, they can be added or subtracted simply by adding or subtracting the two numerators and retaining the same denominator. Example: $\frac{1}{2} + \frac{1}{4} = \frac{2}{4} + \frac{1}{4} = \frac{3}{4}$. If the two fractions do not already have the same denominator, one or both of them must be manipulated to achieve a common denominator before they can be added or subtracted.

Review Video: Adding and Subtracting Fractions
Visit mometrix.com/academy and enter code: 378080

Multiplying Fractions

Two fractions can be multiplied by multiplying the two numerators to find the new numerator and the two denominators to find the new denominator. Example: $\frac{1}{3} \times \frac{2}{3} = \frac{1 \times 2}{3 \times 3} = \frac{2}{9}$.

Review Video: Multiplying Fractions
Visit mometrix.com/academy and enter code: 638849

Dividing Fractions

Two fractions can be divided by flipping the numerator and denominator of the second fraction and then proceeding as though it were a multiplication. Example: $\frac{2}{3} \div \frac{3}{4} = \frac{2}{3} \times \frac{4}{3} = \frac{8}{9}$.

Review Video: Dividing Fractions
Visit mometrix.com/academy and enter code: 300874

Rational Numbers from Least to Greatest

Example

Order the following rational numbers from least to greatest: 0.55, 17%, $\sqrt{25}$, $\frac{64}{4}$, $\frac{25}{50}$, 3.

Recall that the term **rational** simply means that the number can be expressed as a ratio or fraction. The set of rational numbers includes integers and decimals. Notice that each of the numbers in the problem can be written as a decimal or integer:

$$17\% = 0.1717$$
$$\sqrt{25} = 5$$
$$\frac{64}{4} = 16$$
$$\frac{25}{50} = \frac{1}{2} = 0.5$$

So, the answer is 17%, $\frac{25}{50}$, 0.55, 3, $\sqrt{25}$, $\frac{64}{4}$.

Rational Numbers from Greatest to Least

Example

Order the following rational numbers from greatest to least: 0.3, 27%, $\sqrt{100}$, $\frac{72}{9}$, $\frac{1}{9}$, 4.5

$$27\% = 0.27$$
$$\sqrt{100} = 10$$
$$\frac{72}{9} = 8$$
$$\frac{1}{9} \approx 0.11$$

So, the answer is $\sqrt{100}$, $\frac{72}{9}$, 4.5, 0.3, 27%, $\frac{1}{9}$.

Review Video: Ordering Rational Numbers
Visit mometrix.com/academy and enter code: 419578

Factors and Greatest Common Factor

Factors are numbers that are multiplied together to obtain a **product**. For example, in the equation $2 \times 3 = 6$, the numbers 2 and 3 are factors. A **prime number** has only two factors (1 and itself), but other numbers can have many factors.

A **common factor** is a number that divides exactly into two or more other numbers. For example, the factors of 12 are 1, 2, 3, 4, 6, and 12, while the factors of 15 are 1, 3, 5, and 15. The common factors of 12 and 15 are 1 and 3.

A **prime factor** is also a prime number. Therefore, the prime factors of 12 are 2 and 3. For 15, the prime factors are 3 and 5.

Review Video: Factors
Visit mometrix.com/academy and enter code: 920086

The **greatest common factor** (**GCF**) is the largest number that is a factor of two or more numbers. For example, the factors of 15 are 1, 3, 5, and 15; the factors of 35 are 1, 5, 7, and 35. Therefore, the greatest common factor of 15 and 35 is 5.

Review Video: Greatest Common Factor (GCF)
Visit mometrix.com/academy and enter code: 838699

Multiples and Least Common Multiple

The least common multiple (**LCM**) is the smallest number that is a multiple of two or more numbers. For example, the multiples of 3 include 3, 6, 9, 12, 15, etc.; the multiples of 5 include 5, 10, 15, 20, etc. Therefore, the least common multiple of 3 and 5 is 15.

Review Video: Multiples
Visit mometrix.com/academy and enter code: 626738

Review Video: Multiples and Least Common Multiple (LCM)
Visit mometrix.com/academy and enter code: 520269

Patterns and Algebra

Proportions and Ratios

Proportions

A proportion is a relationship between two quantities that dictates how one changes when the other changes. A **direct proportion** describes a relationship in which a quantity increases by a set amount for every increase in the other quantity, or decreases by that same amount for every decrease in the other quantity. Example: Assuming a constant driving speed, the time required for a car trip increases as the distance of the trip increases. The distance to be traveled and the time required to travel are directly proportional.

Inverse proportion is a relationship in which an increase in one quantity is accompanied by a decrease in the other, or vice versa. Example: the time required for a car trip decreases as the speed increases, and increases as the speed decreases, so the time required is inversely proportional to the speed of the car.

Review Video: Proportions
Visit mometrix.com/academy and enter code: 505355

Ratios

A **ratio** is a comparison of two quantities in a particular order. Example: If there are 14 computers in a lab, and the class has 20 students, there is a student to computer ratio of 20 to 14, commonly written as 20:14. Ratios are normally reduced to their smallest whole number representation, so 20:14 would be reduced to 10:7 by dividing both sides by 2.

Review Video: Ratios
Visit mometrix.com/academy and enter code: 996914

Real World Problems with Proportions and Ratios

Example 1

A child was given 100 mg of chocolate every two hours. How much chocolate will the child receive in five hours?

Using proportional reasoning, since five hours is two and a half times as long as two hours, the child will receive two and a half times as much chocolate, $2.5 \times 100\text{ mg} = 250\text{ mg}$, in five hours.

To compute the answer methodically, first write the amount of chocolate per 2 hours as a ratio.

$$\frac{100\text{ mg}}{2\text{ hours}}$$

Next create a proportion to relate the different time increments of 2 hours and 5 hours.

$\frac{100\text{ mg}}{2\text{ hours}} = \frac{x\text{ mg}}{5\text{ hours}}$, where x is the amount of chocolate the child receives in five hours. Make sure to keep the same units in either the numerator or denominator. In this case the numerator units must be mg for both ratios and the denominator units must be hours for both ratios.

Use cross multiplication and division to solve for x:

$$\frac{100 \text{ mg}}{2 \text{ hours}} = \frac{x \text{ mg}}{5 \text{ hours}}$$
$$100(5) = 2(x)$$
$$500 = 2x$$
$$500 \div 2 = 2x \div 2$$
$$250 = x$$

Therefore, the child receives 250 mg every five hours.

Review Video: Proportions in the Real World
Visit mometrix.com/academy and enter code: 221143

EXAMPLE 2

At a school, for every 20 female students there are 15 male students. This same student ratio happens to exist at another school. If there are 100 female students at the second school, how many male students are there?

One way to find the number of male students is to set up and solve a proportion.

$$\frac{\text{number of female students}}{\text{number of male students}} = \frac{20}{15} = \frac{100}{\text{number of male students}}$$

Represent the unknown number of male students as the variable x.

$$\frac{20}{15} = \frac{100}{x}$$

Cross multiply and then solve for x:

$$20x = 15 \times 100 = 1500$$
$$x = \frac{1500}{20} = 75$$

Alternatively, notice that: $\frac{20 \times 5}{15 \times 5} = \frac{100}{75}$, so $x = 75$.

EXAMPLE 3

In a hospital emergency room, there are 4 nurses for every 12 patients. What is the ratio of nurses to patients? If the nurse-to-patient ratio remains constant, how many nurses must be present to care for 24 patients?

The ratio of nurses to patients can be written as 4 to 12, 4:12, or $\frac{4}{12}$. Because four and twelve have a common factor of four, the ratio should be reduced to 1:3, which means that there is one nurse present for every three patients. If this ratio remains constant, there must be eight nurses present to care for 24 patients.

EXAMPLE 4

In a bank, the banker-to-customer ratio is 1:2. If seven bankers are on duty, how many customers are currently in the bank?

Use proportional reasoning or set up a proportion to solve. Because there are twice as many customers as bankers, there must be fourteen customers when seven bankers are on duty. Setting up and solving a proportion gives the same result:

$$\frac{\text{number of bankers}}{\text{number of customers}} = \frac{1}{2} = \frac{7}{\text{number of customers}}$$

Represent the unknown number of patients as the variable x.

$$\frac{1}{2} = \frac{7}{x}$$

To solve for x, cross multiply:

$1 \times x = 7 \times 2$, so $x = 14$.

Constant of Proportionality

When two quantities have a proportional relationship, there exists a **constant of proportionality** between the quantities; the product of this constant and one of the quantities is equal to the other quantity. For example, if one lemon costs \$0.25, two lemons cost \$0.50, and three lemons cost \$0.75, there is a proportional relationship between the total cost of lemons and the number of lemons purchased. The constant of proportionality is the **unit price**, namely \$0.25/lemon. Notice that the total price of lemons, t, can be found by multiplying the unit price of lemons, p, and the number of lemons, n: $t = pn$.

Slope

On a graph with two points, (x_1, y_1) and (x_2, y_2), the **slope** is found with the formula $m = \frac{y_2 - y_1}{x_2 - x_1}$; where $x_1 \neq x_2$ and m stands for slope. If the value of the slope is **positive**, the line has an *upward direction* from left to right. If the value of the slope is **negative**, the line has a *downward direction* from left to right.

Unit Rate as the Slope

A new book goes on sale in bookstores and online stores. In the first month, 5,000 copies of the book are sold. Over time, the book continues to grow in popularity. The data for the number of copies sold is in the table below.

# of Months on Sale	1	2	3	4	5
# of Copies Sold (In Thousands)	5	10	15	20	25

So, the number of copies that are sold and the time that the book is on sale is a proportional relationship. In this example, an equation can be used to show the data: $y = 5x$, where x is the number of months that the book is on sale. Also, y is the number of copies sold. So, the slope is $\frac{\text{rise}}{\text{run}} = \frac{5}{1}$. This can be reduced to 5.

Review Video: Finding the Slope of a Line
Visit mometrix.com/academy and enter code: 766664

Work/Unit Rate

Unit rate expresses a quantity of one thing in terms of one unit of another. For example, if you travel 30 miles every two hours, a unit rate expresses this comparison in terms of one hour: in one hour you travel 15 miles, so your unit rate is 15 miles per hour. Other examples are how much one ounce of food costs (price per ounce) or figuring out how much one egg costs out of the dozen (price per 1 egg, instead of price per 12 eggs). The denominator of a unit rate is always 1. Unit rates are used to compare different situations to solve problems. For example, to make sure you get the best deal when deciding which kind of soda to buy, you can find the unit rate of each. If Soda #1 costs $1.50 for a 1-liter bottle, and soda #2 costs $2.75 for a 2-liter bottle, it would be a better deal to buy Soda #2, because its unit rate is only $1.375 per 1-liter, which is cheaper than Soda #1. Unit rates can also help determine the length of time a given event will take. For example, if you can paint 2 rooms in 4.5 hours, you can determine how long it will take you to paint 5 rooms by solving for the unit rate per room and then multiplying that by 5.

Review Video: Rates and Unit Rates
Visit mometrix.com/academy and enter code: 185363

Example 1

Janice made $40 during the first 5 hours she spent babysitting. She will continue to earn money at this rate until she finishes babysitting in 3 more hours. Find how much money Janice earned babysitting and how much she earns per hour.

Janice will earn $64 babysitting in her 8 total hours (adding the first 5 hours to the remaining 3 gives the 8 hour total). This can be found by setting up a proportion comparing money earned to babysitting hours. Since she earns $40 for 5 hours and since the rate is constant, she will earn a proportional amount in 8 hours: $\frac{40}{5} = \frac{x}{8}$. Cross multiplying will yield $5x = 320$, and division by 5 shows that $x = 64$.

Janice earns $8 per hour. This can be found by taking her total amount earned, $64, and dividing it by the total number of hours worked, 8. Since $\frac{64}{8} = 8$, Janice makes $8 in one hour. This can also be found by finding the unit rate, money earned per hour: $\frac{64}{8} = \frac{x}{1}$. Since cross multiplying yields $8x = 64$, and division by 8 shows that $x = 8$, Janice earns $8 per hour.

Example 2

The McDonalds are taking a family road trip, driving 300 miles to their cabin. It took them 2 hours to drive the first 120 miles. They will drive at the same speed all the way to their cabin. Find the speed at which the McDonalds are driving and how much longer it will take them to get to their cabin.

The McDonalds are driving 60 miles per hour. This can be found by setting up a proportion to find the unit rate, the number of miles they drive per one hour: $\frac{120}{2} = \frac{x}{1}$. Cross multiplying yields $2x = 120$ and division by 2 shows that $x = 60$.

Since the McDonalds will drive this same speed, it will take them another 3 hours to get to their cabin. This can be found by first finding how many miles the McDonalds have left to drive, which is $300 - 120 = 180$. The McDonalds are driving at 60 miles per hour, so a proportion can be set up to determine how many hours it will take them to drive 180 miles: $\frac{180}{x} = \frac{60}{1}$. Cross multiplying yields $60x = 180$, and division by 60 shows that $x = 3$. This can also be found by using the formula $D = r \times t$ (or Distance = rate × time), where $180 = 60 \times t$, and division by 60 shows that $t = 3$.

EXAMPLE 3

It takes Andy 10 minutes to read 6 pages of his book. He has already read 150 pages in his book that is 210 pages long. Find how long it takes Andy to read 1 page and also find how long it will take him to finish his book if he continues to read at the same speed.

It takes Andy 1 minute and 40 seconds to read one page in his book. This can be found by finding the unit rate per one page, by dividing the total time it takes him to read 6 pages by 6. Since it takes him 10 minutes to read 6 pages, $\frac{10}{6} = 1\frac{2}{3}$ minutes, which is 1 minute and 40 seconds.

It will take Andy another 100 minutes, or 1 hour and 40 minutes to finish his book. This can be found by first figuring out how many pages Andy has left to read, which is $210 - 150 = 60$. Since it is now known that it takes him $1\frac{2}{3}$ minutes to read each page, then that rate must be multiplied by however many pages he has left to read (60) to find the time he'll need: $60 \times 1\frac{2}{3} = 100$, so it will take him 100 minutes, or 1 hour and 40 minutes, to read the rest of his book.

FUNCTION AND RELATION

When expressing functional relationships, the **variables** x and y are typically used. These values are often written as the **coordinates** (x, y). The x-value is the independent variable and the y-value is the dependent variable. A **relation** is a set of data in which there is not a unique y-value for each x-value in the dataset. This means that there can be two of the same x-values assigned to different y-values. A relation is simply a relationship between the x and y-values in each coordinate but does not apply to the relationship between the values of x and y in the data set. A **function** is a relation where one quantity depends on the other. For example, the amount of money that you make depends on the number of hours that you work. In a function, each x-value in the data set has one unique y-value because the y-value depends on the x-value.

Review Video: Definition of a Function
Visit mometrix.com/academy and enter code: 784611

FUNCTIONS

A **function** is an equation that has exactly one value of **output variable** (dependent variable) for each value of the **input variable** (independent variable). The set of all values for the input variable (here assumed to be x) is the domain of the function, and the set of all corresponding values of output variable (here assumed to be y) is the range of the function. When looking at a graph of an equation, the easiest way to determine if the equation is a function or not is to conduct the vertical line test. If a vertical line drawn through any value of x crosses the graph in more than one place, the equation is not a function.

DETERMINING A FUNCTION

You can determine whether an equation is a **function** by substituting different values into the equation for x. These values are called input values. All possible input values are referred to as the **domain**. The result of substituting these values into the equation is called the output, or **range**. You can display and organize these numbers in a data table. A **data table** contains the values for x and y, which you can also list as coordinates. In order for a function to exist, the table cannot contain any repeating x-values that correspond with different y-values. If each x-coordinate has a unique y-coordinate, the table contains a function. However, there can be repeating y-values that correspond with different x-values. An example of this is when the function contains an exponent. For example, if $x^2 = y$, $2^2 = 4$, and $(-2)^2 = 4$.

Review Video: Basics of Functions
Visit mometrix.com/academy and enter code: 822500

Properties of Functions

In functions with the notation f(x), the value substituted for x in the equation is called the argument. The domain is the set of all values for x in a function. Unless otherwise given, assume the domain is the set of real numbers that will yield real numbers for the range. This is the domain of definition.

The graph of a function is the set of all ordered pairs (x, y) that satisfy the equation of the function. The points that have zero as the value for y are called the zeros of the function. These are also the x-intercepts, because that is the point at which the graph crosses, or intercepts, the x-axis. The points that have zero as the value for x are the y-intercepts because that is where the graph crosses the y-axis.

Writing a Function Rule Using a Table

If given a set of data, place the corresponding x and y-values into a table and analyze the relationship between them. Consider what you can do to each x-value to obtain the corresponding y-value. Try adding or subtracting different numbers to and from x and then try multiplying or dividing different numbers to and from x. If none of these **operations** give you the y-value, try combining the operations. Once you find a rule that works for one pair, make sure to try it with each additional set of ordered pairs in the table. If the same operation or combination of operations satisfies each set of coordinates, then the table contains a function. The rule is then used to write the equation of the function in "y =" form.

Equations and Graphing

When algebraic functions and equations are shown graphically, they are usually shown on a *Cartesian coordinate plane*. The Cartesian coordinate plane consists of two number lines placed perpendicular to each other, and intersecting at the zero point, also known as the origin. The horizontal number line is known as the x-axis, with positive values to the right of the origin, and negative values to the left of the origin. The vertical number line is known as the y-axis, with positive values above the origin, and negative values below the origin. Any point on the plane can be identified by an ordered pair in the form (x,y), called coordinates. The x-value of the coordinate is called the abscissa, and the y-value of the coordinate is called the ordinate. The two number lines divide the plane into *four quadrants*: I, II, III, and IV.

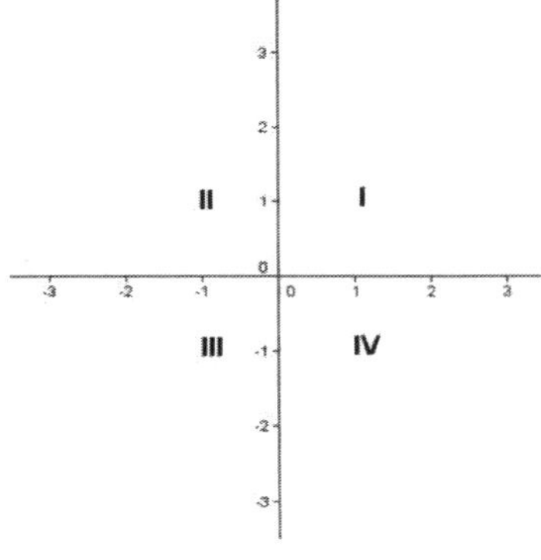

Before learning the different forms in which equations can be written, it is important to understand some terminology. A ratio of the change in the vertical distance to the change in horizontal distance is called the *slope*. On a graph with two points, (x_1, y_1) and (x_2, y_2), the slope is represented by the formula $s = \frac{y_2 - y_1}{x_2 - x_1}; x_1 \neq x_2$. If the value of the slope is positive, the line slopes upward from left to right. If the value of the slope is negative, the line slopes downward from left to right. If the *y*-coordinates are the same for both points, the slope is 0 and the line is a *horizontal line*. If the *x*-coordinates are the same for both points, there is no slope and the line is a *vertical line*. Two or more lines that have equal slopes are *parallel lines*. *Perpendicular lines* have slopes that are negative reciprocals of each other, such as $\frac{a}{b}$ and $\frac{-b}{a}$.

Review Video: Graphs of Functions
Visit mometrix.com/academy and enter code: 492785

Equations are made up of monomials and polynomials. A *monomial* is a single variable or product of constants and variables, such as *x*, 2*x*, or $\frac{2}{x}$. There will never be addition or subtraction symbols in a monomial. Like monomials have like variables, but they may have different coefficients. *Polynomials* are algebraic expressions which use addition and subtraction to combine two or more monomials. Two terms make a binomial; three terms make a trinomial; etc.. The d*egree of a monomial* is the sum of the exponents of the variables. The *degree of a polynomial* is the highest degree of any individual term.

As mentioned previously, equations can be written many ways. Below is a list of the many forms equations can take.

- Standard Form: $Ax + By = C$; the slope is $\frac{-A}{B}$ and the y-intercept is $\frac{C}{B}$
- *Slope Intercept Form*: $y = mx + b$, where m is the slope and b is the y-intercept
- Point-Slope Form: $y - y_1 = m(x - x_1)$, where m is the slope and (x_1, y_1) is a point on the line
- Two-Point Form: $\frac{y - y_1}{x - x_1} = \frac{y_2 - y_1}{x_2 - x_1}$, where (x_1, y_1) and (x_2, y_2) are two points on the given line
- *Intercept Form*: $\frac{x}{x_1} + \frac{y}{y_1} = 1$, where $(x_1, 0)$ is the point at which a line intersects the *x*-axis, and $(0, y_1)$ is the point at which the same line intersects the *y*-axis

Review Video: Slope-Intercept and Point-Slope Forms
Visit mometrix.com/academy and enter code: 113216

Equations can also be written as $ax + b = 0$, where $a \neq 0$. These are referred to as **one variable linear equations**. A solution to such an equation is called a **root**. In the case where we have the equation $5x + 10 = 0$, if we solve for x we get a solution of $x = -2$. In other words, the root of the equation is -2. This is found by first subtracting 10 from both sides, which gives $5x = -10$. Next, simply divide both sides by the coefficient of the variable, in this case 5, to get $x = -2$. This can be checked by plugging -2 back into the original equation $(5)(-2) + 10 = -10 + 10 = 0$.

The **solution set** is the set of all solutions of an equation. In our example, the solution set would simply be -2. If there were more solutions (there usually are in multivariable equations) then they would also be included in the solution set. When an equation has no true solutions, this is referred to as an **empty set**. Equations with identical solution sets are ***equivalent equations***. An **identity** is a term whose value or determinant is equal to 1.

Solving One-Variable Linear Equations

Multiply all terms by the lowest common denominator to eliminate any fractions. Look for addition or subtraction to undo so you can isolate the variable on one side of the equal sign. Divide both sides by the coefficient of the variable. When you have a value for the variable, substitute this value into the original equation to make sure you have a true equation.

Manipulation of Functions

Horizontal and vertical shift occur when values are added to or subtracted from the *x* or *y* values, respectively.

If a constant is added to the *y* portion of each point, the graph shifts up. If a constant is subtracted from the *y* portion of each point, the graph shifts down. This is represented by the expression $f(x) \pm k$, where k is a constant.

If a constant is added to the x portion of each point, the graph shifts left. If a constant is subtracted from the x portion of each point, the graph shifts right. This is represented by the expression $f(x \pm k)$, where k is a constant.

Stretch, compression, and reflection occur when different parts of a function are multiplied by different groups of constants. If the function as a whole is multiplied by a real number constant greater than 1, $(k \times f(x))$, the graph is stretched vertically. If *k* in the previous equation is greater than zero but less than 1, the graph is compressed vertically. If *k* is less than zero, the graph is reflected about the *x*-axis, in addition to being either stretched or compressed vertically if *k* is less than or greater than -1, respectively. If instead, just the *x*-term is multiplied by a constant greater than 1 $(f(k \times x))$, the graph is compressed horizontally. If *k* in the previous equation is greater than zero but less than 1, the graph is stretched horizontally. If *k* is less than zero, the graph is reflected about the *y*-axis, in addition to being either stretched or compressed horizontally if *k* is greater than or less than -1, respectively.

Classification of Functions

There are many different ways to classify functions based on their structure or behavior. Listed here are a few common classifications.

Constant functions are given by the equation *y*=b or $f(x) = b$, where b is a real number. There is no independent variable present in the equation, so the function has a constant value for all *x*. The graph of a constant function is a horizontal line of slope 0 that is positioned *b* units from the *x*-axis. If *b* is positive, the line is above the *x*-axis; if *b* is negative, the line is below the *x*-axis.

Identity functions are identified by the equation *y=x* or $f(x) = x$, where every value of *y* is equal to its corresponding value of *x*. The only zero is the point (0, 0). The graph is a diagonal line with slope 1.

In **linear functions**, the value of the function changes in direct proportion to *x*. The rate of change,represented by the slope on its graph, is constant throughout. The standard form of a linear equation is $ax + by = c$, where a, b, and c are real numbers. As a function, this equation is commonly written as $y = mx + b$ or $f(x) = mx + b$. This is known as the slope-intercept form, because the coefficients give the slope of the graphed function (m) and its *y*-intercept (b). Solve the equation $mx + b = 0$ for *x* to get $x = -\frac{b}{m}$, which is the only zero of the function. The domain and range are both the set of all real numbers.

A **polynomial function** is a function with multiple terms and multiple powers of x, such as:

$$f(x) = a_n x^n + a_{n-1} x^{n-1} + a_{n-2} x^{n-2} + \cdots + a_1 x + a_0$$

where n is a non-negative integer that is the highest exponent in the polynomial, and $a_n \neq 0$. The domain of a polynomial function is the set of all real numbers. If the greatest exponent in the polynomial is even, the polynomial is said to be of even degree and the range is the set of real numbers that satisfy the function. If the greatest exponent in the polynomial is odd, the polynomial is said to be odd and the range, like the domain, is the set of all real numbers.

Review Video: Simplifying Rational Polynomial Functions
Visit mometrix.com/academy and enter code: 351038

A **quadratic function** is a polynomial function that follows the equation pattern $y = ax^2 + bx + c$, or $f(x) = ax^2 + bx + c$, where a, b, and c are real numbers and $a \neq 0$. The domain of a quadratic function is the set of all real numbers. The range is also real numbers, but only those in the subset of the domain that satisfy the equation. The root(s) of any quadratic function can be found by plugging the values of a, b, and c into the **quadratic formula**:

$$x = \frac{-b \pm \sqrt{b^2 - 4ac}}{2a}$$

If the expression $b^2 - 4ac$ is negative, you will instead find complex roots.

A quadratic function has a parabola for its graph. In the equation $f(x) = ax^2 + bx + c$, if a is positive, the parabola will open upward. If a is negative, the parabola will open downward. The axis of symmetry is a vertical line that passes through the vertex. To determine whether or not the parabola will intersect the x-axis, check the number of real roots. An equation with two real roots will cross the x-axis twice. An equation with one real root will have its vertex on the x-axis. An equation with no real roots will not contact the x-axis.

Review Video: Deriving the Quadratic Formula
Visit mometrix.com/academy and enter code: 317436

Review Video: Using the Quadratic Formula
Visit mometrix.com/academy and enter code: 163102

Review Video: Changing Constants in Graphs of Functions: Quadratic Equations
Visit mometrix.com/academy and enter code: 476276

A **rational function** is a function that can be constructed as a ratio of two polynomial expressions: $f(x) = \frac{p(x)}{q(x)}$, where $p(x)$ and $q(x)$ are both polynomial expressions and $q(x) \neq 0$. The domain is the set of all real numbers, except any values for which $q(x) = 0$. The range is the set of real numbers that satisfies the function when the domain is applied. When you graph a rational function, you will have vertical asymptotes wherever $q(x) = 0$. If the polynomial in the numerator is of lesser degree than the polynomial in the denominator, the x-axis will also be a horizontal asymptote. If the numerator and denominator have equal degrees, there will be a horizontal asymptote not on the x-axis. If the degree of the numerator is exactly one greater than the degree of the denominator, the graph will have an oblique, or diagonal, asymptote. The asymptote will be along the line $y =$

$\frac{p_n}{q_{n-1}}x + \frac{p_{n-1}}{q_{n-1}}$, where p_n and q_{n-1} are the coefficients of the highest degree terms in their respective polynomials.

A **square root function** is a function that contains a radical and is in the format $f(x) = \sqrt{ax + b}$. The domain is the set of all real numbers that yields a positive radicand or a radicand equal to zero. Because square root values are assumed to be positive unless otherwise identified, the range is all real numbers from zero to infinity. To find the zero of a square root function, set the radicand equal to zero and solve for x. The graph of a square root function is always to the right of the zero and always above the x-axis.

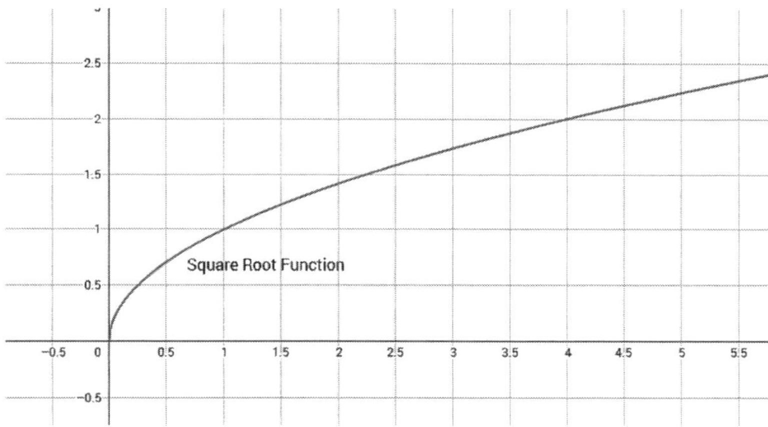

An **absolute value function** is in the format $f(x) = |ax + b|$. Like other functions, the domain is the set of all real numbers. However, because absolute value indicates positive numbers, the range is limited to positive real numbers. To find the zero of an absolute value function, set the portion inside the absolute value sign equal to zero and solve for x.

An absolute value function is also known as a piecewise function because it must be solved in pieces – one for if the value inside the absolute value sign is positive, and one for if the value is negative. The function can be expressed as

$$f(x) = \begin{cases} ax + b \text{ if } ax + b \geq 0 \\ -(ax + b) \text{ if } ax + b < 0 \end{cases}$$

This will allow for an accurate statement of the range.

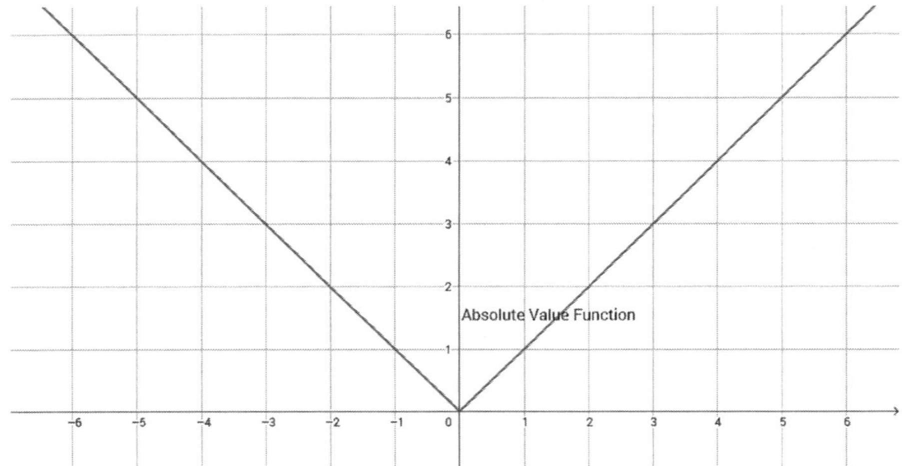

Exponential functions are equations that have the format $y = b^x$, where base $b > 0$ and $b \neq 1$. The exponential function can also be written $f(x) = b^x$.

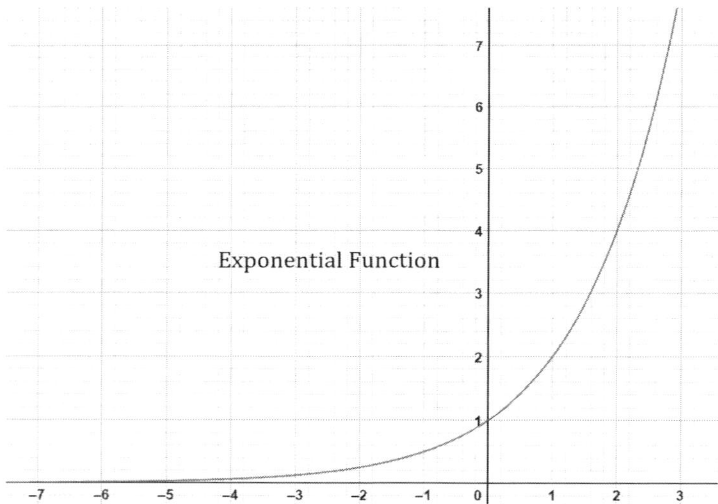

Logarithmic functions are equations that have the format $y = \log_b x$ or $f(x) = \log_b x$. The base b may be any number except one; however, the most common bases for logarithms are base 10 and base *e*. The log base *e* is known the natural logarithm, or *ln*, expressed by the function $f(x) = \ln x$.

Any logarithm that does not have an assigned value of b is assumed to be base 10: $\log x = \log_{10} x$. Exponential functions and logarithmic functions are related in that one is the inverse of the other. If $f(x) = b^x$, then $f^{-1}(x) = \log_b x$. This can perhaps be expressed more clearly by the two equations: $y = b^x$ and $x = \log_b y$.

The following properties apply to logarithmic expressions:

$$\log_b 1 = 0$$
$$\log_b b = 1$$
$$\log_b b^p = p$$
$$\log_b MN = \log_b M + \log_b N$$
$$\log_b \frac{M}{N} = \log_b M - \log_b N$$
$$\log_b M^p = p \log_b M$$

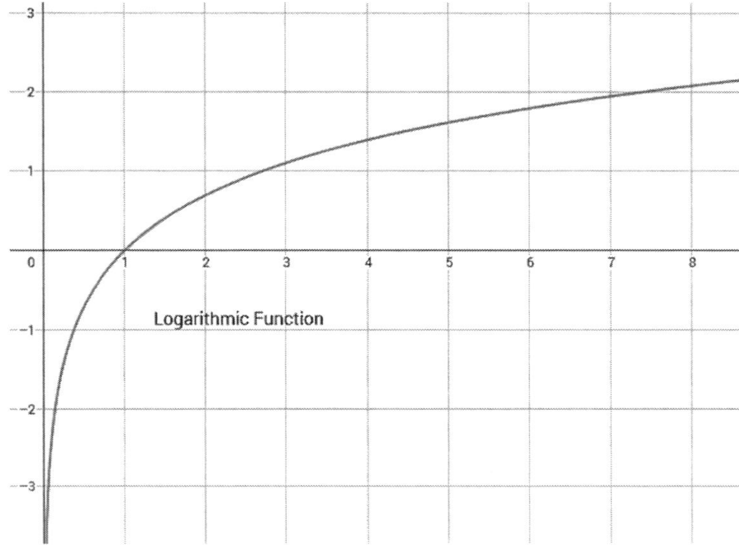

In a **one-to-one function**, each value of x has exactly one value for y (this is the definition of a function) *and* each value of y has exactly one value for x. While the vertical line test will determine if a graph is that of a function, the horizontal line test will determine if a function is a one-to-one function. If a horizontal line drawn at any value of y intersects the graph in more than one place, the graph is not that of a one-to-one function. Do not make the mistake of using the horizontal line test exclusively in determining if a graph is that of a one-to-one function. A one-to-one function must pass both the vertical line test and the horizontal line test. One-to-one functions are also **invertible functions**.

A **monotone function** is a function whose graph either constantly increases or constantly decreases. Examples include the functions $f(x) = x$, $f(x) = -x$, or $f(x) = x^3$.

An **even function** has a graph that is symmetric with respect to the y-axis and satisfies the equation $f(x) = f(-x)$. Examples include the functions $f(x) = x^2$ and $f(x) = ax^n$, where a is any real number and n is a positive even integer.

An **odd function** has a graph that is symmetric with respect to the origin and satisfies the equation $f(x) = -f(-x)$. Examples include the functions $f(x) = x^3$ and $f(x) = ax^n$, where a is any real number and n is a positive odd integer.

Algebraic functions are those that exclusively use polynomials and roots. These would include polynomial functions, rational functions, square root functions, and all combinations of these functions, such as polynomials as the radicand. These combinations may be joined by addition, subtraction, multiplication, or division, but may not include variables as exponents.

Transcendental functions are all functions that are non-algebraic. Any function that includes logarithms, trigonometric functions, variables as exponents, or any combination that includes any of these is not algebraic in nature, even if the function includes polynomials or roots.

Related Concepts

According to the **fundamental theorem of algebra**, every non-constant, single variable polynomial has exactly as many roots as the polynomial's highest exponent. For example, if x^4 is the largest exponent of a term, the polynomial will have exactly 4 roots. However, some of these roots may have multiplicity or be non-real numbers. For instance, in the polynomial function $f(x) = x^4 - 4x + 3$, the only real roots are 1 and -1. The root 1 has multiplicity of 2 and there is one non-real root $(-1 - \sqrt{2}i)$.

The **remainder theorem** is useful for determining the remainder when a polynomial is divided by a binomial. The Remainder Theorem states that if a polynomial function $f(x)$ is divided by a binomial $x - a$, where a is a real number, the remainder of the division will be the value of $f(a)$. If $f(a) = 0$, then a is a root of the polynomial.

The **factor theorem** is related to the Remainder Theorem and states that if $f(a) = 0$ then $(x - a)$ is a factor of the function.

According to the **rational root theorem,** any rational root of a polynomial function $f(x) = a_nx^n + a_{n-1}x^{n-1} + \cdots + a_1x + a_0$ with integer coefficients will, when reduced to its lowest terms, be a positive or negative fraction such that the numerator is a factor of a_0 and the denominator is a factor of a_n. For instance, if the polynomial function $f(x) = x^3 + 3x^2 - 4$ has any rational roots, the numerators of those roots can only be factors of 4 (1, 2, 4), and the denominators can only be factors of 1 (1). The function in this example has roots of 1 $\left(\text{or } \frac{1}{1}\right)$ and -2 $\left(\text{or } -\frac{2}{1}\right)$.

Variables that vary directly are those that either both increase at the same rate or both decrease at the same rate. For example, in the functions $f(x) = kx$ or $f(x) = kx^n$, where k and n are positive, the value of $f(x)$ increases as the value of x increases and decreases as the value of x decreases.

Variables that vary inversely are those where one increases while the other decreases. For example, in the functions $f(x) = \frac{k}{x}$ or $f(x) = \frac{k}{x^n}$ where k is a positive constant, the value of y increases as the value of x decreases, and the value of y decreases as the value of x increases.

In both cases, k is the constant of variation.

Applying the Basic Operations to Functions

For each of the basic operations, we will use these functions as examples: $f(x) = x^2$ and $g(x) = x$.

To find the sum of two functions f and g, assuming the domains are compatible, simply add the two functions together: $(f + g)(x) = f(x) + g(x) = x^2 + x$

To find the difference of two functions f and g, assuming the domains are compatible, simply subtract the second function from the first: $(f - g)(x) = f(x) - g(x) = x^2 - x$.

To find the product of two functions f and g, assuming the domains are compatible, multiply the two functions together: $(f \cdot g)(x) = f(x) \cdot g(x) = x^2 \cdot x = x^3$.

To find the quotient of two functions *f* and *g*, assuming the domains are compatible, divide the first function by the second: $\frac{f}{g}(x) = \frac{f(x)}{g(x)} = \frac{x^2}{x} = x\,; x \neq 0$.

The example given in each case is fairly simple, but on a given problem, if you are looking only for the value of the sum, difference, product or quotient of two functions at a particular *x*-value, it may be simpler to solve the functions individually and then perform the given operation using those values.

The composite of two functions *f* and *g*, written as $(f \circ g)(x)$ simply means that the output of the second function is used as the input of the first. This can also be written as $f\big(g(x)\big)$. In general, this can be solved by substituting $g(x)$ for all instances of *x* in $f(x)$ and simplifying. Using the example functions $f(x) = x^2 - x + 2$ and $g(x) = x + 1$, we can find that $(f \circ g)(x)$ or $f\big(g(x)\big)$ is equal to $f(x + 1) = (x + 1)^2 - (x + 1) + 2$, which simplifies to $x^2 + x + 2$.

It is important to note that $(f \circ g)(x)$ is not necessarily the same as $(g \circ f)(x)$. The process is not commutative like addition or multiplication expressions. If $(f \circ g)(x)$ does equal $(g \circ f)(x)$, the two functions are inverses of each other.

SOLVE EQUATIONS IN ONE VARIABLE

MANIPULATING EQUATIONS

Sometimes you will have variables missing in equations. So, you need to find the missing variable. To do this, you need to remember one important thing: *whatever you do to one side of an equation, you need to do to the other side.* If you subtract 100 from one side of an equation, you need to subtract 100 from the other side of the equation. This will allow you to change the form of the equation to find missing values.

EXAMPLE

Ray earns \$10 an hour at his job. Write an equation for his earnings as a function of time spent working. Determine how long Ray has to work in order to earn \$360.

The number of dollars that Ray earns is dependent on the number of hours he works, so earnings will be represented by the dependent variable *y* and hours worked will be represented by the independent variable *x*. He earns 10 dollars per hour worked, so his earning can be calculated as

$$y = 10x$$

To calculate the number of hours Ray must work in order to earn \$360, plug in 360 for *y* and solve for *x*:

$$360 = 10x$$

$$x = \frac{360}{10} = 36$$

So, Ray must work 36 hours in order to earn \$360.

Review Video: Dependent and Independent Variables and Inverting Functions
Visit mometrix.com/academy and enter code: 704764

Solving One Variable Linear Equations

Another way to write an equation is $ax + b = 0$ where $a \neq 0$. This is known as a **one-variable linear equation**. A solution to an equation is called a **root**. Consider the following equation:

$$5x + 10 = 0$$

If we solve for x, the solution is $x = -2$. In other words, the root of the equation is –2.

The first step is to subtract 10 from both sides. This gives $5x = -10$.

Next, divide both sides by the **coefficient** of the variable. For this example, that is 5. So, you should have $x = -2$. You can make sure that you have the correct answer by substituting –2 back into the original equation. So, the equation now looks like this: $(5)(-2) + 10 = -10 + 10 = 0$.

Example 1

Solve for x.

$$\frac{45\%}{12\%} = \frac{15\%}{x}$$

First, cross multiply; then, solve for x:

$$45x = 12 \times 15 = 180$$
$$x = \frac{180}{45} = 4\%$$

Alternatively, notice that $\frac{45\% \div 3}{12\% \div 3} = \frac{15\%}{4\%}$, so $x = 4\%$.

Example 2

Solve for x in the following equation:

$$\frac{0.50}{2} = \frac{1.50}{x}$$

First, cross multiply; then, solve for x:

$$0.5x = 1.5 \times 2 = 3$$
$$x = \frac{3}{0.5} = 3 \times 2 = 6$$

Alternatively, notice that $\frac{0.50 \times 3}{2 \times 3} = \frac{1.50}{6}$, so $x = 6$.

Example 3

Solve for x in the following equation:

$$\frac{40}{8} = \frac{x}{24}$$

First, cross multiply; then, solve for x:

$$8x = 40 \times 24 = 960$$
$$x = \frac{960}{8} = 120$$

Alternatively, notice that $\frac{40 \times 3}{8 \times 3} = \frac{120}{24}$, so $x = 120$.

Other Important Concepts

Commonly in algebra and other upper-level fields of math you find yourself working with mathematical expressions that do not equal each other. The statement comparing such expressions with symbols such as < (less than) or > (greater than) is called an *inequality*. An example of an inequality is $7x > 5$. To solve for x, simply divide both sides by 7 and the solution is shown to be $x > \frac{5}{7}$. Graphs of the solution set of inequalities are represented on a number line. Open circles are used to show that an expression approaches a number but is never quite equal to that number.

Review Video: Inequalities
Visit mometrix.com/academy and enter code: 347842

Conditional inequalities are those with certain values for the variable that will make the condition true and other values for the variable where the condition will be false. **Absolute inequalities** can have any real number as the value for the variable to make the condition true, while there is no real number value for the variable that will make the condition false. Solving inequalities is done by following the same rules as for solving equations with the exception that when multiplying or dividing by a negative number the direction of the inequality sign must be flipped or reversed. **double inequalities** are situations where two inequality statements apply to the same variable expression. An example of this is $-c < ax + b < c$.

A **weighted mean**, or weighted average, is a mean that uses "weighted" values. The formula is weighted mean $= \frac{w_1x_1+w_2x_2+w_3x_3...+w_nx_n}{w_1+w_2+w_3+\cdots+w_n}$. Weighted values, such as $w_1, w_2, w_3, ... w_n$ are assigned to each member of the set $x_1, x_2, x_3, ... x_n$. If calculating weighted mean, make sure a weight value for each member of the set is used.

Graphing Inequalities

Graph the inequality $10 > -2x + 4$.

In order to **graph the inequality** $10 > -2x + 4$, you must first solve for x. The opposite of addition is subtraction, so subtract 4 from both sides. This results in $6 > -2x$. Next, the opposite of multiplication is division, so divide both sides by -2. Don't forget to flip the inequality symbol since you are dividing by a negative number. This results in $-3 < x$. You can rewrite this as $x > -3$. To graph an inequality, you create a number line and put a circle around the value that is being compared to x. If you are graphing a greater than or less than inequality, as the one shown, the circle remains open. This represents all of the values excluding -3. If the inequality happens to be a greater than or equal to or less than or equal to, you draw a closed circle around the value. This would represent all of the values including the number. Finally, take a look at the values that the solution represents and shade the number line in the appropriate direction. You are graphing all of the values greater than -3 and since this is all of the numbers to the right of -3, shade this region on the number line.

Determining Solutions to Inequalities

Determine whether $(-2, 4)$ is a solution of the inequality $y \geq -2x + 3$.

To determine whether a coordinate is a **solution of an inequality**, you can either use the inequality or its graph. Using $(-2, 4)$ as (x, y), substitute the values into the inequality to see if it makes a true statement. This results in $4 \geq -2(-2) + 3$. Using the integer rules, simplify the right side of the inequality by multiplying and then adding. The result is $4 \geq 7$, which is a false statement. Therefore, the coordinate is not a solution of the inequality. You can also use the **graph** of an inequality to see if a coordinate is a part of the solution. The graph of an inequality is shaded over the section of the coordinate grid that is included in the solution. The graph of $y \geq -2x + 3$ includes the solid line $y = -2x + 3$ and is shaded to the right of the line, representing all of the points greater than and including the points on the line. This excludes the point $(-2, 4)$, so it is not a solution of the inequality.

Calculations Using Points

Sometimes you need to perform calculations using only points on a graph as input data. Using points, you can determine what the **midpoint** and **distance** are. If you know the equation for a line you can calculate the distance between the line and the point.

To find the **midpoint** of two points (x_1, y_1) and (x_2, y_2), average the x-coordinates to get the x-coordinate of the midpoint, and average the y-coordinates to get the y-coordinate of the midpoint. The formula is Midpoint $= \left(\frac{x_1+x_2}{2}, \frac{y_1+y_2}{2}\right)$.

The **distance** between two points is the same as the length of the hypotenuse of a right triangle with the two given points as endpoints, and the two sides of the right triangle parallel to the x-axis and y-axis, respectively. The length of the segment parallel to the x-axis is the difference between the x-coordinates of the two points. The length of the segment parallel to the y-axis is the difference between the y-coordinates of the two points. Use the Pythagorean theorem $a^2 + b^2 = c^2$ or $c = \sqrt{a^2 + b^2}$ to find the distance. The formula is distance $= \sqrt{(x_2 - x_1)^2 + (y_2 - y_1)^2}$.

When a line is in the format $Ax + By + C = 0$, where A, B, and C are coefficients, you can use a point (x_1, y_1) not on the line and apply the formula $d = \frac{|Ax_1+By_1+C|}{\sqrt{A^2+B^2}}$ to find the distance between the line and the point (x_1, y_1).

Example

Find the distance and midpoint between points (2, 4) and (8,6).

Midpoint

$$\text{Midpoint} = \left(\frac{x_1+x_2}{2}, \frac{y_1+y_2}{2}\right)$$
$$\text{Midpoint} = \left(\frac{2+8}{2}, \frac{4+6}{2}\right)$$
$$\text{Midpoint} = \left(\frac{10}{2}, \frac{10}{2}\right)$$
$$\text{Midpoint} = (5,5)$$

DISTANCE

$$\text{Distance} = \sqrt{(x_2 - x_1)^2 + (y_2 - y_1)^2}$$
$$\text{Distance} = \sqrt{(8 - 2)^2 + (6 - 4)^2}$$
$$\text{Distance} = \sqrt{(6)^2 + (2)^2}$$
$$\text{Distance} = \sqrt{36 + 4}$$
$$\text{Distance} = \sqrt{40} \text{ or } 2\sqrt{10}$$

SYSTEMS OF EQUATIONS

Systems of equations are a set of simultaneous equations that all use the same variables. A solution to a system of equations must be true for each equation in the system. *Consistent systems* are those with at least one solution. *Inconsistent systems* are systems of equations that have no solution.

Review Video: Systems of Equations
Visit mometrix.com/academy and enter code: 658153

SUBSTITUTION

To solve a system of linear equations by *substitution*, start with the easier equation and solve for one of the variables. Express this variable in terms of the other variable. Substitute this expression in the other equation and solve for the other variable. The solution should be expressed in the form (x, y). Substitute the values into both of the original equations to check your answer. Consider the following problem.

Solve the system using substitution:

$$x + 6y = 15$$
$$3x - 12y = 18$$

Solve the first equation for x:

$$x = 15 - 6y$$

Substitute this value in place of x in the second equation, and solve for y:

$$3(15 - 6y) - 12y = 18$$
$$45 - 18y - 12y = 18$$
$$30y = 27$$
$$y = \frac{27}{30} = \frac{9}{10} = 0.9$$

Plug this value for y back into the first equation to solve for x:

$$x = 15 - 6(0.9) = 15 - 5.4 = 9.6$$

Check both equations if you have time:

$$9.6 + 6(0.9) = 9.6 + 5.4 = 15$$
$$3(9.6) - 12(0.9) = 28.8 - 10.8 = 18$$

Therefore, the solution is $(9.6, 0.9)$.

ELIMINATION

To solve a system of equations using *elimination*, begin by rewriting both equations in standard form $Ax + By = C$. Check to see if the coefficients of one pair of like variables add to zero. If not, multiply one or both of the equations by a non-zero number to make one set of like variables add to zero. Add the two equations to solve for one of the variables. Substitute this value into one of the original equations to solve for the other variable. Check your work by substituting into the other equation. Next, we will solve the same problem as above, but using the addition method.

Solve the system using elimination:

$$x + 6y = 15$$
$$3x - 12y = 18$$

If we multiply the first equation by 2, we can eliminate the y terms:

$$2x + 12y = 30$$
$$3x - 12y = 18$$

Add the equations together and solve for x:

$$5x = 48$$
$$x = \frac{48}{5} = 9.6$$

Plug the value for x back into either of the original equations and solve for y:

$$9.6 + 6y = 15$$
$$y = \frac{15 - 9.6}{6} = 0.9$$

Check both equations if you have time:

$$9.6 + 6(0.9) = 9.6 + 5.4 = 15$$
$$3(9.6) - 12(0.9) = 28.8 - 10.8 = 18$$

Therefore, the solution is (9.6, 0.9).

GRAPHICALLY

To solve a system of linear equations **graphically**, plot both equations on the same graph. The solution of the equations is the point where both lines cross. If the lines do not cross (are parallel), then there is **no solution**.

For example, consider the following system of equations:

$$y = 2x + 7$$
$$y = -x + 1$$

Since these equations are given in slope-intercept form, they are easy to graph; the y intercepts of the lines are $(0, 7)$ and $(0, 1)$. The respective slopes are 2 and –1, thus the graphs look like this:

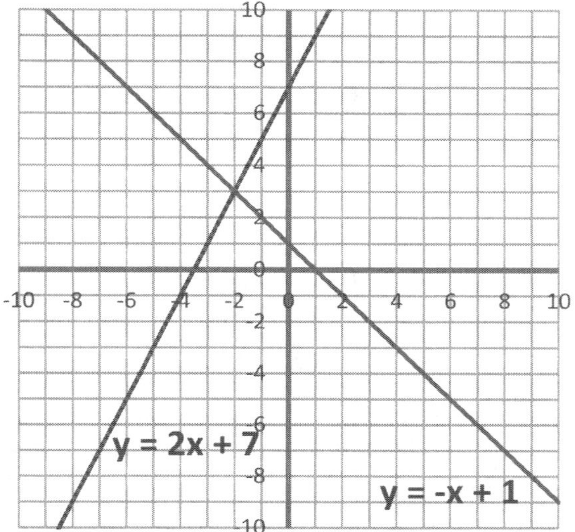

The two lines intersect at the point $(-2, 3)$, thus this is the solution to the system of equations.

Solving a system graphically is generally only practical if both coordinates of the solution are integers; otherwise the intersection will lie between gridlines on the graph and the coordinates will be difficult or impossible to determine exactly. It also helps if, as in this example, the equations are in slope-intercept form or some other form that makes them easy to graph. Otherwise, another method of solution (by substitution or elimination) is likely to be more useful.

Solving Systems of Equations Using the Trace Feature

Using the **trace feature** on a calculator requires that you rewrite each equation, isolating the y-variable on one side of the equal sign. Enter both equations in the graphing calculator and plot the graphs simultaneously. Use the trace cursor to find where the two lines cross. Use the zoom feature if necessary to obtain more accurate results. Always check your answer by substituting into the original equations. The trace method is likely to be less accurate than other methods due to the resolution of graphing calculators, but is a useful tool to provide an approximate answer.

Solving a System of Equations Consisting of a Linear Equation and a Quadratic Equation

Algebraically

Generally, the simplest way to solve a system of equations consisting of a linear equation and a quadratic equation algebraically is through the method of **substitution**. One possible strategy is to solve the linear equation for y and then substitute that expression into the quadratic equation. After expansion and combining like terms, this will result in a new quadratic equation for x which, like all quadratic equations, may have zero, one, or two solutions. Plugging each solution for x back into one of the original equations will then produce the corresponding value of y.

For example, consider the following system of equations:

$$x + y = 1$$
$$y = (x + 3)^2 - 2$$

We can solve the linear equation for y to yield $y = -x + 1$.

Substituting this expression into the quadratic equation produces $-x + 1 = (x + 3)^2 - 2$

We can simplify this equation:

$$-x + 1 = (x + 3)^2 - 2$$
$$-x + 1 = x^2 + 6x + 9 - 2$$
$$-x + 1 = x^2 + 6x + 7$$
$$x^2 + 7x + 6 = 0$$

This quadratic equation can be factored as $(x + 1)(x + 6) = 0$. It therefore has two solutions: $x_1 = -1$ and $x_2 = -6$. Plugging each of these back into the original linear equation yields $y_1 = -x_1 + 1 = -(-1) + 1 = 2$ and $y_2 = -x_2 + 1 = -(-6) + 1 = 7$. Thus this system of equations has two solutions, $(-1, 2)$ and $(-6, 7)$.

It may help to check your work by putting each x and y value back into the original equations and verifying that they do provide a solution.

GRAPHICALLY

To solve a system of equations consisting of a linear equation and a quadratic equation **graphically**, plot both equations on the same graph. The linear equation will of course produce a straight line, while the quadratic equation will produce a parabola. These two graphs will intersect at zero, one, or two points; each point of intersection is a solution of the system.

For example, consider the following system of equations:

$$y = -2x + 2$$
$$y = -2x^2 + 4x + 2$$

The linear equation describes a line with a y-intercept of $(0, 2)$ and a slope of -2.

To graph the quadratic equation, we can first find the vertex of the parabola: the x-coordinate of the vertex is $h = -\frac{b}{2a} = -\frac{4}{2(-2)} = 1$, and the y coordinate is $k = -2(1)^2 + 4(1) + 2 = 4$. Thus, the vertex lies at $(1, 4)$. To get a feel for the rest of the parabola, we can plug in a few more values of x to find more points; by putting in $x = 2$ and $x = 3$ in the quadratic equation, we find that the points $(2, 2)$ and $(3, -4)$ lie on the parabola; by symmetry thus do $(0, 2)$ and $(-1, -4)$. We can now plot both equations:

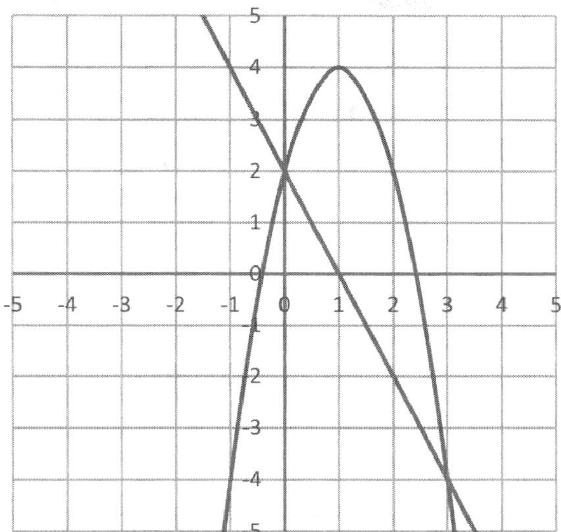

These two curves intersect at the points $(0, 2)$ and $(3, -4)$, thus these are the solutions of the equation.

POLYNOMIAL ALGEBRA

To multiply two binomials, follow the **FOIL** method. FOIL stands for:

- First: Multiply the first term of each binomial
- Outer: Multiply the outer terms of each binomial
- Inner: Multiply the inner terms of each binomial
- Last: Multiply the last term of each binomial

Using FOIL $(Ax + By)(Cx + Dy) = ACx^2 + ADxy + BCxy + BDy^2$.

EXAMPLE

Use the FOIL method on binomials $(x + 2)$ and $(x - 3)$.

$$\begin{aligned}
&\text{First: } (x + 2)(x - 3) = (x)(x) = x^2 \\
&\text{Outer: } (x + 2)\,(x - 3) = (x)(-3) = -3x \\
&\text{Inner: } (x + 2)\,(x - 3) = (2)(x) = 2x \\
&\text{Last: } (x + 2)(x - 3) = (2)(-3) = -6
\end{aligned}$$

Combine like Terms:

$$(x^2) + (-3x) + (2x) + (-6) = x^2 - x - 6$$

Review Video: Multiplying Terms Using the FOIL Method
Visit mometrix.com/academy and enter code: 854792

To divide polynomials, begin by arranging the terms of each polynomial in order of one variable. You may arrange in ascending or descending order, but make sure to be consistent with both polynomials. To get the first term of the quotient, divide the first term of the dividend by the first term of the divisor. Multiply the first term of the quotient by the entire divisor and subtract that product from the dividend. Repeat for the second and successive terms until you either get a remainder of zero or a remainder whose degree is less than the degree of the divisor. If the quotient has a remainder, write the answer as a mixed expression in the form: quotient $+\frac{\text{remainder}}{\text{divisor}}$.

Rational expressions are fractions with polynomials in both the numerator and the denominator; the value of the polynomial in the denominator cannot be equal to zero. To add or subtract rational expressions, first find the common denominator, then rewrite each fraction as an equivalent fraction with the common denominator. Finally, add or subtract the numerators to get the numerator of the answer, and keep the common denominator as the denominator of the answer. When multiplying rational expressions factor each polynomial and cancel like factors (a factor which appears in both the numerator and the denominator). Then, multiply all remaining factors in the numerator to get the numerator of the product, and multiply the remaining factors in the denominator to get the denominator of the product. Remember – cancel entire factors, not individual terms. To divide rational expressions, take the reciprocal of the divisor (the rational expression you are dividing by) and multiply by the dividend.

Review Video: Simplifying Rational Polynomial Functions
Visit mometrix.com/academy and enter code: 351038

Below are patterns of some special products to remember: *perfect trinomial squares*, the *difference between two squares*, the *sum and difference of two cubes*, and *perfect cubes*.

- Perfect trinomial squares: $x^2 + 2xy + y^2 = (x + y)^2$ or $x^2 - 2xy + y^2 = (x - y)^2$
- Difference between two squares: $x^2 - y^2 = (x + y)(x - y)$
- Sum of two cubes: $x^3 + y^3 = (x + y)(x^2 - xy + y^2)$
- Note: the second factor is *not* the same as a perfect trinomial square, so do not try to factor it further.
- Difference between two cubes: $x^3 - y^3 = (x - y)(x^2 + xy + y^2)$
- Again, the second factor is *not* the same as a perfect trinomial square.
- Perfect cubes: $x^3 + 3x^2y + 3xy^2 + y^3 = (x + y)^3$ and $x^3 - 3x^2y + 3xy^2 - y^3 = (x - y)^3$

In order to **factor a polynomial**, first check for a common monomial factor. When the greatest common monomial factor has been factored out, look for patterns of special products: differences of two squares, the sum or difference of two cubes for binomial factors, or perfect trinomial squares for trinomial factors. If the factor is a trinomial but not a perfect trinomial square, look for a factorable form, such as $x^2 + (a + b)x + ab = (x + a)(x + b)$ or$(ac)x^2 + (ad + bc)x + bd = (ax + b)(cx + d)$. For factors with four terms, look for groups to factor. Once you have found the factors, write the original polynomial as the product of all the factors. Make sure all of the polynomial factors are prime. Monomial factors may be prime or composite. Check your work by multiplying the factors to make sure you get the original polynomial.

Solving Quadratic Equations

The **quadratic formula** is used to solve quadratic equations when other methods are more difficult. To use the quadratic formula to solve a quadratic equation, begin by rewriting the equation in standard form $ax^2 + bx + c = 0$, where a, b, and c are coefficients. Once you have identified the values of the coefficients, substitute those values into the quadratic formula $x = \frac{-b\pm\sqrt{b^2-4ac}}{2a}$. Evaluate the equation and simplify the expression. Again, check each root by substituting into the original equation. In the quadratic formula, the portion of the formula under the radical ($b^2 - 4ac$) is called the **discriminant**. If the discriminant is zero, there is only one root: $-\frac{b}{2a}$. If the discriminant is positive, there are two different real roots. If the discriminant is negative, there are no real roots.

To solve a quadratic equation by factoring, begin by rewriting the equation in standard form, if necessary. Factor the side with the variable then set each of the factors equal to zero and solve the resulting linear equations. Check your answers by substituting the roots you found into the original equation. If, when writing the equation in standard form, you have an equation in the form $x^2 + c = 0$ or $x^2 - c = 0$, set $x^2 = -c$ or $x^2 = c$ and take the square root of c. If $c = 0$, the only real root is zero. If c is positive, there are two real roots—the positive and negative square root values. If c is negative, there are no real roots because you cannot take the square root of a negative number.

Review Video: Factoring Quadratic Equations
Visit mometrix.com/academy and enter code: 336566

To solve a quadratic equation by **completing the square**, rewrite the equation so that all terms containing the variable are on the left side of the equal sign, and all the constants are on the right side of the equal sign. Make sure the coefficient of the squared term is 1. If there is a coefficient with the squared term, divide each term on both sides of the equal side by that number. Next, work with the coefficient of the single-variable term. Square half of this coefficient and add that value to both sides. Now you can factor the left side (the side containing the variable) as the square of a binomial. $x^2 + 2ax + a^2 = C \Rightarrow (x + a)^2 = C$, where x is the variable, and a and C are constants. Take the square root of both sides and solve for the variable. Substitute the value of the variable in the original problem to check your work.

Quadratic Function

A *quadratic function* is a function in the form $y = ax^2 + bx + c$, where a does not equal 0. While a linear function forms a line, a quadratic function forms a **parabola**, which is a u-shaped figure that either opens upward or downward. A parabola that opens upward is said to be a **positive quadratic function** and a parabola that opens downward is said to be a **negative quadratic function**. The shape of a parabola can differ, depending on the values of a, b, and c. All parabolas contain a **vertex**, which is the highest possible point, the **maximum**, or the lowest possible point, the **minimum**. This is the point where the graph begins moving in the opposite direction. A quadratic function can have zero, one, or two solutions, and therefore, zero, one, or two x-intercepts. Recall that the x-intercepts are referred to as the zeros, or roots, of a function. A quadratic function will have only one y-intercept. Understanding the basic components of a quadratic function can give you an idea of the shape of its graph.

Example graph of a positive quadratic function:

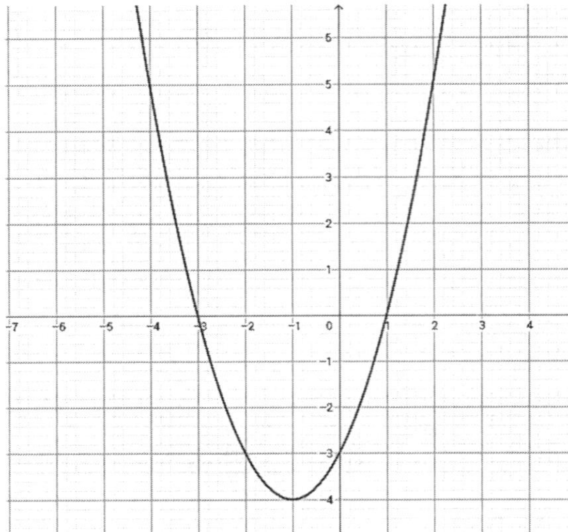

SIMPLIFYING POLYNOMIAL EXPRESSIONS

A polynomial is a group of monomials added or subtracted together. Simplifying polynomials requires combining like terms. The like terms in a polynomial expression are those that have the same variable raised to the same power. It is often helpful to connect the like terms with arrows or lines in order to separate them from the other monomials. Once you have determined the like terms, you can rearrange the polynomial by placing them together. Remember to include the sign that is in front of each term. Once the like terms are placed together, you can apply each operation and simplify. When adding and subtracting polynomials, only add and subtract the **coefficient**, or the number part; the variable and exponent stay the same.

POSITION OF PARABOLA

A **quadratic function** is written in the form $y = ax^2 + bx + c$. Changing the leading coefficient, a, in the equation changes the direction of the parabola. If the value of a is **positive**, the graph opens upward. The vertex of this parabola is the **minimum** value of the graph. If the value of a is **negative**, the graph opens downward. The vertex of this parabola is the **maximum** value of the graph. The leading coefficient, a, also affects the width of the parabola. The closer a is to 0, the wider the parabola will be. The values of b and c both affect the position of the parabola on the graph. The effect from changing b depends on the sign of a. If a is negative, increasing the value of b moves the parabola to the right and decreasing the value of b moves it to the left. If a is positive, changes to b have the opposite effect. The value of c in the quadratic equation represents the y-intercept and therefore, moves the parabola up and down the y-axis. The larger the c-value, the higher the parabola is on the graph.

FINDING ROOTS

Find the roots of $y = x^2 + 6x - 16$ and explain why these values are important.

The **roots** of a quadratic equation are the solutions when $ax^2 + bx + c = 0$. To find the roots of a quadratic equation, first replace y with 0. If $0 = x^2 + 6x - 16$, then to find the values of x, you can factor the equation if possible. When factoring a quadratic equation where $a = 1$, find the factors of c that add up to b. That is the factors of -16 that add up to 6. The factors of -16 include, -4 and 4, -8 and 2 and -2 and 8. The factors that add up to equal 6 are -2 and 8. Write these factors as the product of two binomials, $0 = (x - 2)(x + 8)$. You can verify that these are the correct factors by using FOIL to multiply them together. Finally, since these binomials multiply together to equal zero, set them each equal to zero and solve for x. This results in $x - 2 = 0$, which simplifies to $x = 2$ and $x + 8 = 0$, which simplifies to $x = -8$. Therefore, the roots of the equation are 2 and -8. These values are important because they tell you where the graph of the equation crosses the x-axis. The points of intersection are $(2, 0)$ and $(-8, 0)$.

Review Video: Finding the Missing Roots
Visit mometrix.com/academy and enter code: 198376

Solving Quadratic Equations

Methods

One way to find the solution or solutions of a quadratic equation is to use its **graph**. The solution(s) of a quadratic equation are the values of x when $y = 0$. On the graph, $y = 0$ is where the parabola crosses the x-axis, or the x-intercepts. This is also referred to as the **roots**, or zeros of a function. Given a graph, you can locate the x-intercepts to find the solutions. If there are no x-intercepts, the function has no solution. If the parabola crosses the x-axis at one point, there is one solution and if it crosses at two points, there are two solutions. Since the solutions exist where $y = 0$, you can also solve the equation by substituting 0 in for y. Then, try factoring the equation by finding the factors of ac that add up to equal b. You can use the guess and check method, the box method, or grouping. Once you find a pair that works, write them as the product of two binomials and set them equal to zero. Finally, solve for x to find the solutions. The last way to solve a quadratic equation is to use the **quadratic formula**. The quadratic formula is $x = \frac{-b \pm \sqrt{b^2 - 4ac}}{2a}$. Substitute the values of a, b, and c into the formula and solve for x. Remember that ± refers to two different solutions. Always check your solutions with the original equation to make sure they are valid.

Example

List the steps used in solving $y = 2x^2 + 8x + 4$.

First, substitute 0 in for y in the quadratic equation:

$$0 = 2x^2 + 8x + 4$$

Next, try to factor the quadratic equation. If $a \neq 1$, list the factors of ac, or 8:

$$(1, 8), (-1, -8), (2, 4), (-2, -4)$$

Look for the factors of ac that add up to b, or 8. Since none do, the equation cannot be factored with whole numbers. Substitute the values of a, b, and c into the quadratic formula, $x = \frac{-b \pm \sqrt{b^2 - 4ac}}{2a}$:

$$x = \frac{-8 \pm \sqrt{8^2 - 4(2)(4)}}{2(2)}$$

Use the order of operations to simplify:

$$x = \frac{-8 \pm \sqrt{64 - 32}}{4}$$
$$x = \frac{-8 \pm \sqrt{32}}{4}$$

Reduce and simplify:

$$x = \frac{-8 \pm \sqrt{(16)(2)}}{4}$$
$$x = \frac{-8 \pm 4\sqrt{2}}{4}$$
$$x = -2 \pm \sqrt{2}$$
$$x = -2 + \sqrt{2} \text{ and}$$
$$x = -2 - \sqrt{2}$$

Check both solutions with the original equation to make sure they are valid.

Simplify the square roots and round to two decimal places.

$$x = -3.41 \text{ and } x = -0.586$$

Laws of Exponents

Multiply $(2x^4)^2(xy)^4 \cdot 4y^3$ using the **laws of exponents**.

According the order of operations, the first step in simplifying expressions is to evaluate within the parentheses. Moving from left to right, the first set of parentheses contains a power raised to a power. The rules of exponents state that when a power is raised to a power, you *multiply* the exponents. Since $4 \times 2 = 8$, $(2x^4)^2$ can be written as $4x^8$. The second set of parentheses raises a product to a power. The **rules of exponents** state that you raise every value within the parentheses to the given power. Therefore, $(xy)^4$ can be written as x^4y^4. Combining these terms with the last term gives you, $4x^8 \cdot x^4y^4 \cdot 4y^3$. In this expression, there are powers with the same base. The rules of exponents state that you *add* powers with the same base, while multiplying the coefficients. You can group the expression as $(4x^8 \cdot x^4) \cdot (y^4 \cdot 4y^3)$ to organize the values with the same base. Then, using this rule add the exponents. The result is $4x^{12} \cdot 4y^7$, or $16x^{12}y^7$.

Review Video: Laws of Exponents
Visit mometrix.com/academy and enter code: 532558

Using Given Roots to Find Quadratic Equation

Example

Find a quadratic equation whose real roots are $x = 2$ and $x = -1$.

One way to find the roots of a quadratic equation is to factor the equation and use the **zero product property**, setting each factor of the equation equal to zero to find the corresponding root. We can use this technique in reverse to find an equation given its roots. Each root corresponds to a linear equation which in turn corresponds to a factor of the quadratic equation.

For example, the root x=2 corresponds to the equation $x - 2 = 0$, and the root $x = -1$ corresponds to the equation $x + 1 = 0$.

These two equations correspond to the factors (x - 2) and (x+1), from which we can derive the equation $(x - 2)(x + 1) = 0$, or $x^2 - x - 2 = 0$.

Any integer multiple of this entire equation will also yield the same roots, as the integer will simply cancel out when the equation is factored. For example, $2x^2 - 2x - 4 = 0$ factors as

$2(x - 2)(x + 1) = 0$.

SIMPLIFYING RATIONAL EXPRESSIONS

To *simplify a rational expression*, factor the numerator and denominator completely. Factors that are the same and appear in the numerator and denominator have a ratio of 1. The denominator, $(1 - x^2)$, is a difference of squares. It can be factored as $(1 - x)(1 + x)$. The factor $1 - x$ and the numerator $x - 1$ are opposites and have a ratio of −1. Rewrite the numerator as $-1(1 - x)$. So, the rational expression can be simplified as follows:

$$\frac{x-1}{1-x^2} = \frac{-1(1-x)}{(1-x)(1+x)} = \frac{-1}{1+x}$$

(Note that since the original expression is defined for $x \neq \{-1,1\}$, the simplified expression has the same restrictions.)

Review Video: Reducing Rational Expressions
Visit mometrix.com/academy and enter code: 788868

MATRIX BASICS

A **matrix** (plural: matrices) is a rectangular array of numbers or variables, often called **elements**, which are arranged in columns and rows. A matrix is generally represented by a capital letter, with its elements represented by the corresponding lowercase letter with two subscripts indicating the row and column of the element. For example, n_{ab} represents the element in row *a* column *b* of matrix *N*.

$$N = \begin{bmatrix} n_{11} & n_{12} & n_{13} \\ n_{21} & n_{22} & n_{23} \end{bmatrix}$$

A matrix can be described in terms of the number of rows and columns it contains in the format $a \times b$, where a is the number of rows and b is the number of columns. The matrix shown above is a 2×3 matrix. Any $a \times b$ matrix where $a = b$ is a square matrix. A **vector** is a matrix that has exactly one column (**column vector**) or exactly one row (**row vector**).

The **main diagonal** of a matrix is the set of elements on the diagonal from the top left to the bottom right of a matrix. Because of the way it is defined, only square matrices will have a main diagonal. For the matrix shown below, the main diagonal consists of the elements $n_{11}, n_{22}, n_{33}, n_{44}$.

$$\begin{bmatrix} n_{11} & n_{12} & n_{13} & n_{14} \\ n_{21} & n_{22} & n_{23} & n_{24} \\ n_{31} & n_{32} & n_{33} & n_{34} \\ n_{41} & n_{42} & n_{43} & n_{44} \end{bmatrix}$$

A 3×4 matrix such as the one shown below would not have a main diagonal because there is no straight line of elements between the top left corner and the bottom right corner that joins the elements.

$$\begin{bmatrix} n_{11} & n_{12} & n_{13} & n_{14} \\ n_{21} & n_{22} & n_{23} & n_{24} \\ n_{31} & n_{32} & n_{33} & n_{34} \end{bmatrix}$$

A **diagonal matrix** is a square matrix that has a zero for every element in the matrix except the elements on the main diagonal. All the elements on the main diagonal must be nonzero numbers.

$$\begin{bmatrix} n_{11} & 0 & 0 & 0 \\ 0 & n_{22} & 0 & 0 \\ 0 & 0 & n_{33} & 0 \\ 0 & 0 & 0 & n_{44} \end{bmatrix}$$

If every element on the main diagonal of a diagonal matrix is equal to one, the matrix is called an **identity matrix**. The identity matrix is often represented by the letter *I*.

$$I = \begin{bmatrix} 1 & 0 & 0 & 0 \\ 0 & 1 & 0 & 0 \\ 0 & 0 & 1 & 0 \\ 0 & 0 & 0 & 1 \end{bmatrix}$$

A **zero matrix** is a matrix that has zero as the value for every element in the matrix.

$$\begin{bmatrix} 0 & 0 & 0 & 0 \\ 0 & 0 & 0 & 0 \\ 0 & 0 & 0 & 0 \\ 0 & 0 & 0 & 0 \end{bmatrix}$$

The zero matrix is the *identity for matrix addition*. Do not confuse the zero matrix with the identity matrix.

The **negative of a matrix** is also known as the additive inverse of a matrix. If matrix *N* is the given matrix, then matrix –*N* is its negative. This means that every element n_{ab} is equal to $-n_{ab}$ in the negative. To find the negative of a given matrix, change the sign of every element in the matrix and keep all elements in their original corresponding positions in the matrix.

If two matrices have the same order and all corresponding elements in the two matrices are the same, then the two matrices are **equal matrices**.

A matrix *N* may be **transposed** to matrix N^T by changing all rows into columns and changing all columns into rows. The easiest way to accomplish this is to swap the positions of the row and column notations for each element. For example, suppose the element in the second row of the third column of matrix *N* is $n_{23} = 6$. In the transposed matrix N^T, the transposed element would be $n_{32} = 6$, and it would be placed in the third row of the second column.

$$N = \begin{bmatrix} 1 & 2 & 3 \\ 4 & 5 & 6 \end{bmatrix}; \; N^T = \begin{bmatrix} 1 & 4 \\ 2 & 5 \\ 3 & 6 \end{bmatrix}$$

To quickly transpose a matrix by hand, begin with the first column and rewrite a new matrix with those same elements in the same order in the first row. Write the elements from the second column of the original matrix in the second row of the transposed matrix. Continue this process until all columns have been completed. If the original matrix is identical to the transposed matrix, the matrices are symmetric.

The **determinant** of a matrix is a scalar value that is calculated by taking into account all the elements of a square matrix. A determinant only exists for square matrices. Finding the determinant of a 2×2 matrix is as simple as remembering a simple equation. For a 2×2 matrix

$M = \begin{bmatrix} m_{11} & m_{12} \\ m_{21} & m_{22} \end{bmatrix}$, the determinant is obtained by the equation $|M| = m_{11}m_{22} - m_{12}m_{21}$. Anything larger than 2×2 requires multiple steps. Take matrix $N = \begin{bmatrix} a & b & c \\ d & e & f \\ g & h & j \end{bmatrix}$. The determinant of N is calculated as $|N| = a\begin{vmatrix} e & f \\ h & j \end{vmatrix} - b\begin{vmatrix} d & f \\ g & j \end{vmatrix} + c\begin{vmatrix} d & e \\ g & h \end{vmatrix}$ or $|N| = a(ej - fh) - b(dj - fg) + c(dh - eg)$.

There is a shortcut for 3×3 matrices: add the products of each unique set of elements diagonally left-to-right and subtract the products of each unique set of elements diagonally right-to-left. In matrix N, the left-to-right diagonal elements are (a, e, j), (b, f, g), and (c, d, h). The right-to-left diagonal elements are (a, f, h), (b, d, j), and (c, e, g). $\det(N) = aej + bfg + cdh - afh - bdj - ceg$.

Calculating the determinants of matrices larger than 3×3 is rarely, if ever, done by hand.

The **inverse** of a matrix M is the matrix that, when multiplied by matrix M, yields a product that is the identity matrix. Multiplication of matrices will be explained in greater detail shortly. Not all matrices have inverses. Only a square matrix whose determinant is not zero has an inverse. If a matrix has an inverse, that inverse is unique to that matrix. For any matrix M that has an inverse, the inverse is represented by the symbol M^{-1}. To calculate the inverse of a 2×2 square matrix, use the following pattern:

$$M = \begin{bmatrix} m_{11} & m_{12} \\ m_{21} & m_{22} \end{bmatrix}; \; M^{-1} = \begin{bmatrix} \frac{m_{22}}{|M|} & \frac{-m_{12}}{|M|} \\ \frac{-m_{21}}{|M|} & \frac{m_{11}}{|M|} \end{bmatrix}$$

Another way to find the inverse of a matrix by hand is use an augmented matrix and elementary row operations. An **augmented matrix** is formed by appending the entries from one matrix onto the end of another. For example, given a 2×2 invertible matrix $N = \begin{bmatrix} a & b \\ c & d \end{bmatrix}$, you can find the inverse N^{-1} by creating an augmented matrix by appending a 2×2 identity matrix: $\left[\begin{array}{cc|cc} a & b & 1 & 0 \\ c & d & 0 & 1 \end{array}\right]$. To find the inverse of the original 2×2 matrix, perform elementary row operations to convert the original matrix on the left to an identity matrix: $\left[\begin{array}{cc|cc} 1 & 0 & e & f \\ 0 & 1 & g & h \end{array}\right]$.

Elementary row operations include multiplying a row by a non-zero scalar, adding scalar multiples of two rows, or some combination of these. For instance, the first step might be to multiply the second row by $\frac{b}{d}$ and then subtract it from the first row to make its second column a zero. The end result is that the 2×2 section on the right will become the inverse of the original matrix: $N^{-1} = \begin{bmatrix} e & f \\ g & h \end{bmatrix}$.

Calculating the inverse of any matrix larger than 2×2 is cumbersome and using a graphing calculator is recommended.

Basic Operations with Matrices

There are two categories of basic operations with regard to matrices: operations between a matrix and a scalar, and operations between two matrices.

Scalar Operations

A scalar being added to a matrix is treated as though it were being added to each element of the matrix:

$$M+4=\begin{bmatrix} m_{11}+4 & m_{12}+4 \\ m_{21}+4 & m_{22}+4 \end{bmatrix}$$

The same is true for the other three operations.

Subtraction:

$$M-4=\begin{bmatrix} m_{11}-4 & m_{12}-4 \\ m_{21}-4 & m_{22}-4 \end{bmatrix}$$

Multiplication:

$$M\times 4=\begin{bmatrix} m_{11}\times 4 & m_{12}\times 4 \\ m_{21}\times 4 & m_{22}\times 4 \end{bmatrix}$$

Division:

$$M\div 4=\begin{bmatrix} m_{11}\div 4 & m_{12}\div 4 \\ m_{21}\div 4 & m_{22}\div 4 \end{bmatrix}$$

Matrix Addition and Subtraction

All four of the basic operations can be used with operations between matrices (although division is usually discarded in favor of multiplication by the inverse), but there are restrictions on the situations in which they can be used. Matrices that meet all the qualifications for a given operation are called **conformable matrices**. However, conformability is specific to the operation; two matrices that are conformable for addition are not necessarily conformable for multiplication.

For two matrices to be conformable for addition or subtraction, they must be of the same dimension; otherwise the operation is not defined. If matrix M is a 3×2 matrix and matrix N is a 2×3 matrix, the operations $M+N$ and $M-N$ are meaningless. If matrices M and N are the same size, the operation is as simple as adding or subtracting all of the corresponding elements:

$$\begin{bmatrix} m_{11} & m_{12} \\ m_{21} & m_{22} \end{bmatrix}+\begin{bmatrix} n_{11} & n_{12} \\ n_{21} & n_{22} \end{bmatrix}=\begin{bmatrix} m_{11}+n_{11} & m_{12}+n_{12} \\ m_{21}+n_{21} & m_{22}+n_{22} \end{bmatrix}$$

$$\begin{bmatrix} m_{11} & m_{12} \\ m_{21} & m_{22} \end{bmatrix}-\begin{bmatrix} n_{11} & n_{12} \\ n_{21} & n_{22} \end{bmatrix}=\begin{bmatrix} m_{11}-n_{11} & m_{12}-n_{12} \\ m_{21}-n_{21} & m_{22}-n_{22} \end{bmatrix}$$

The result of addition or subtraction is a matrix of the same dimension as the two original matrices involved in the operation.

Matrix Multiplication

The first thing it is necessary to understand about matrix multiplication is that it is not commutative. In scalar multiplication, the operation is commutative, meaning that $a\times b=b\times a$. For matrix multiplication, this is not the case: $A\times B\neq B\times A$. The terminology must be specific when describing matrix multiplication. The operation $A\times B$ can be described as A multiplied (or **post-multiplied**) by B, or B **pre-multiplied** by A.

For two matrices to be conformable for multiplication, they need not be of the same dimension, but specific dimensions must correspond. Taking the example of two matrices M and N to be multiplied $M\times N$, matrix M must have the same number of columns as matrix N has rows. Put another way, if matrix M has the dimensions $a \times b$ and matrix N has the dimensions $c \times d$, b must equal c if the two matrices are to be conformable for this multiplication. The matrix that results from the multiplication will have the dimensions $a \times d$. If a and d are both equal to 1, the product is simply a scalar. Square matrices of the same dimensions are always conformable for multiplication, and their product is always a matrix of the same size.

The simplest type of matrix multiplication is a 1×2 matrix (a row vector) times a 2×1 matrix (a column vector). These will multiply in the following way:

$$\begin{bmatrix} m_{11} & m_{12} \end{bmatrix} \times \begin{bmatrix} n_{11} \\ n_{21} \end{bmatrix} = m_{11}n_{11} + m_{12}n_{21}$$

The two matrices are conformable for multiplication because matrix M has the same number of columns as matrix N has rows. Because the other dimensions are both 1, the result is a scalar. Expanding our matrices to 1×3 and 3×1, the process is the same:

$$\begin{bmatrix} m_{11} & m_{12} & m_{13} \end{bmatrix} \times \begin{bmatrix} n_{11} \\ n_{21} \\ n_{31} \end{bmatrix} = m_{11}n_{11} + m_{12}n_{21} + m_{13}n_{31}$$

Once again, the result is a scalar. This type of basic matrix multiplication is the building block for the multiplication of larger matrices.

To multiply larger matrices, treat each **row from the first matrix** and each **column from the second matrix** as individual vectors and follow the pattern for multiplying vectors. The scalar value found from multiplying the first-row vector by the first column vector is placed in the first row, first column of the new matrix. The scalar value found from multiplying the second-row vector by the first column vector is placed in the second row, first column of the new matrix. Continue this pattern until each row of the first matrix has been multiplied by each column of the second vector.

Below is an example of the multiplication of a 3×2 matrix and a 2×3 matrix.

$$\begin{bmatrix} m_{11} & m_{12} \\ m_{21} & m_{22} \\ m_{31} & m_{32} \end{bmatrix} \times \begin{bmatrix} n_{11} & n_{12} & n_{13} \\ n_{21} & n_{22} & n_{23} \end{bmatrix} = \begin{bmatrix} m_{11}n_{11} + m_{12}n_{21} & m_{11}n_{12} + m_{12}n_{22} & m_{11}n_{13} + m_{12}n_{23} \\ m_{21}n_{11} + m_{22}n_{21} & m_{21}n_{12} + m_{22}n_{22} & m_{21}n_{13} + m_{22}n_{23} \\ m_{31}n_{11} + m_{32}n_{21} & m_{31}n_{12} + m_{32}n_{22} & m_{31}n_{13} + m_{32}n_{23} \end{bmatrix}$$

This process starts by taking the first column of the second matrix and running it through each row of the first matrix. Removing all but the first M row and first N column, we would see only the following:

$$[m_{11} \;\; m_{12}] \times \begin{bmatrix} n_{11} \\ n_{21} \end{bmatrix}$$

The first product would then be $m_{11}n_{11} + m_{12}n_{21}$. This process will be continued for each column of the N matrix to find the first full row of the product matrix, as shown below.

$$[m_{11} \;\; m_{12}] \times \begin{bmatrix} n_{11} \\ n_{21} \end{bmatrix} = [m_{11}n_{11} + m_{12}n_{21} \quad m_{11}n_{12} + m_{12}n_{22} \quad m_{11}n_{13} + m_{12}n_{23}]$$

After completing the first row, the next step would be to simply move to the second row of the M matrix and repeat the process until all of the rows have been finished. The result is a 3×3 matrix.

$$\begin{bmatrix} m_{11} & m_{12} \\ m_{21} & m_{22} \\ m_{31} & m_{32} \end{bmatrix} \times \begin{bmatrix} n_{11} & n_{12} & n_{13} \\ n_{21} & n_{22} & n_{23} \end{bmatrix} = \begin{bmatrix} m_{11}n_{11} + m_{12}n_{21} & m_{11}n_{12} + m_{12}n_{22} & m_{11}n_{13} + m_{12}n_{23} \\ m_{21}n_{11} + m_{22}n_{21} & m_{21}n_{12} + m_{22}n_{22} & m_{21}n_{13} + m_{22}n_{23} \\ m_{31}n_{11} + m_{32}n_{21} & m_{31}n_{12} + m_{32}n_{22} & m_{31}n_{13} + m_{32}n_{23} \end{bmatrix}$$

If the operation were done in reverse $(N \times M)$, the result would be a 2×2 matrix.

$$\begin{bmatrix} n_{11} & n_{12} & n_{13} \\ n_{21} & n_{22} & n_{23} \end{bmatrix} \times \begin{bmatrix} m_{11} & m_{12} \\ m_{21} & m_{22} \\ m_{31} & m_{32} \end{bmatrix} = \begin{bmatrix} m_{11}n_{11} + m_{21}n_{12} + m_{31}n_{13} & m_{12}n_{11} + m_{22}n_{12} + m_{32}n_{13} \\ m_{11}n_{21} + m_{21}n_{22} + m_{31}n_{23} & m_{12}n_{21} + m_{22}n_{22} + m_{32}n_{23} \end{bmatrix}$$

Example

A sporting-goods store sells baseballs, volleyballs, and basketballs.

Baseballs	\$3 each
Volleyballs	\$8 each
Basketballs	\$15 each

Here are the same store's sales numbers for one weekend:

	Baseballs	**Volleyballs**	**Basketballs**
Friday	5	4	4
Saturday	7	3	10
Sunday	4	3	6

Find the total sales for each day by multiplying matrices.

The first table can be represented by the following column-vector:

$$\begin{bmatrix} 3 \\ 8 \\ 15 \end{bmatrix}$$

And the second table can be represented by this matrix:

$$\begin{bmatrix} 5 & 4 & 4 \\ 7 & 3 & 10 \\ 4 & 3 & 6 \end{bmatrix}$$

Multiplying the second matrix by the first will result in a column vector showing the total sales for each day:

$$\begin{bmatrix} 5 & 4 & 4 \\ 7 & 3 & 10 \\ 4 & 3 & 6 \end{bmatrix} \times \begin{bmatrix} 3 \\ 8 \\ 15 \end{bmatrix} = \begin{bmatrix} 3 \times 5 + 8 \times 4 + 15 \times 4 \\ 3 \times 7 + 8 \times 3 + 15 \times 10 \\ 3 \times 4 + 8 \times 3 + 15 \times 6 \end{bmatrix} = \begin{bmatrix} 15 + 32 + 60 \\ 21 + 24 + 150 \\ 12 + 24 + 90 \end{bmatrix} = \begin{bmatrix} 107 \\ 195 \\ 126 \end{bmatrix}$$

From this, we can see that Friday's sales were $107, Saturday's sales were $195, and Sunday's sales were $126.

Solving Systems of Equations

Matrices can be used to represent the coefficients of a system of linear equations and can be very useful in solving those systems. Take for instance three equations with three variables:

$$a_1x + b_1y + c_1z = d_1$$
$$a_2x + b_2y + c_2z = d_2$$
$$a_3x + b_3y + c_3z = d_3$$

where all a, b, c, and d are known constants.

To solve this system, define three matrices:

$$A = \begin{bmatrix} a_1 & b_1 & c_1 \\ a_2 & b_2 & c_2 \\ a_3 & b_3 & c_3 \end{bmatrix}; \; D = \begin{bmatrix} d_1 \\ d_2 \\ d_3 \end{bmatrix}; \; X = \begin{bmatrix} x \\ y \\ z \end{bmatrix}$$

The three equations in our system can be fully represented by a single matrix equation:

$$AX = D$$

We know that the identity matrix times X is equal to X, and we know that any matrix multiplied by its inverse is equal to the identity matrix.

$$A^{-1}AX = IX = X; \text{thus } X = A^{-1}D$$

Our goal then is to find the inverse of A, or A^{-1}. Once we have that, we can pre-multiply matrix D by A^{-1} (post-multiplying here is an undefined operation) to find matrix X.

Systems of equations can also be solved using the transformation of an augmented matrix in a process similar to that for finding a matrix inverse. Begin by arranging each equation of the system in the following format:

$$a_1x + b_1y + c_1z = d_1$$
$$a_2x + b_2y + c_2z = d_2$$
$$a_3x + b_3y + c_3z = d_3$$

Define matrices A and D and combine them into augmented matrix A_a:

$$A = \begin{bmatrix} a_1 & b_1 & c_1 \\ a_2 & b_2 & c_2 \\ a_3 & b_3 & c_3 \end{bmatrix};\ D = \begin{bmatrix} d_1 \\ d_2 \\ d_3 \end{bmatrix};A_a = \begin{bmatrix} a_1 & b_1 & c_1 & d_1 \\ a_2 & b_2 & c_2 & d_2 \\ a_3 & b_3 & c_3 & d_3 \end{bmatrix}$$

To solve the augmented matrix and the system of equations, use elementary row operations to form an identity matrix in the first 3×3 section. When this is complete, the values in the last column are the solutions to the system of equations:

$$\begin{bmatrix} 1 & 0 & 0 & x \\ 0 & 1 & 0 & y \\ 0 & 0 & 1 & z \end{bmatrix}$$

If an identity matrix is not possible, the system of equations has no unique solution. Sometimes only a partial solution will be possible. The following are partial solutions you may find:

$\begin{bmatrix} 1 & 0 & k_1 & x_0 \\ 0 & 1 & k_2 & y_0 \\ 0 & 0 & 0 & 0 \end{bmatrix}$ gives the non-unique solution $x = x_0 - k_1z;\ y = y_0 - k_2z$

$\begin{bmatrix} 1 & j_1 & k_1 & x_0 \\ 0 & 0 & 0 & 0 \\ 0 & 0 & 0 & 0 \end{bmatrix}$ gives the non-unique solution $x = x_0 - j_1y - k_1z$

This process can be used to solve systems of equations with any number of variables, but three is the upper limit for practical purposes. Anything more ought to be done with a graphing calculator.

Geometric Transformations

The four *geometric transformations* are **translations**, **reflections**, **rotations**, and **dilations**. When geometric transformations are expressed as matrices, the process of performing the transformations is simplified. For calculations of the geometric transformations of a planar figure, make a $2 \times n$ matrix, where n is the number of vertices in the planar figure. Each column represents the rectangular coordinates of one vertex of the figure, with the top row containing the values of the x-coordinates and the bottom row containing the values of the y-coordinates. For example, given a planar triangular figure with coordinates (x_1, y_1), (x_2, y_2), and (x_3, y_3), the corresponding matrix is $\begin{bmatrix} x_1 & x_2 & x_3 \\ y_1 & y_2 & y_3 \end{bmatrix}$. You can then perform the necessary transformations on this matrix to determine the coordinates of the resulting figure.

Translation

A **translation** moves a figure along the x-axis, the y-axis, or both axes without changing the size or shape of the figure. To calculate the new coordinates of a planar figure following a translation, set up a matrix of the coordinates and a matrix of the translation values and add the two matrices.

$$\begin{bmatrix} h & h & h \\ v & v & v \end{bmatrix} + \begin{bmatrix} x_1 & x_2 & x_3 \\ y_1 & y_2 & y_3 \end{bmatrix} = \begin{bmatrix} h + x_1 & h + x_2 & h + x_3 \\ v + y_1 & v + y_2 & v + y_3 \end{bmatrix}$$

where h is the number of units the figure is moved along the x-axis (horizontally) and v is the number of units the figure is moved along the y-axis (vertically).

Reflection

To find the **reflection** of a planar figure over the x-axis, set up a matrix of the coordinates of the vertices and pre-multiply the matrix by the 2×2 matrix $\begin{bmatrix} 1 & 0 \\ 0 & -1 \end{bmatrix}$ so that $\begin{bmatrix} 1 & 0 \\ 0 & -1 \end{bmatrix} \begin{bmatrix} x_1 & x_2 & x_3 \\ y_1 & y_2 & y_3 \end{bmatrix} = \begin{bmatrix} x_1 & x_2 & x_3 \\ -y_1 & -y_2 & -y_3 \end{bmatrix}$. To find the reflection of a planar figure over the y-axis, set up a matrix of the coordinates of the vertices and pre-multiply the matrix by the 2×2 matrix $\begin{bmatrix} -1 & 0 \\ 0 & 1 \end{bmatrix}$ so that $\begin{bmatrix} -1 & 0 \\ 0 & 1 \end{bmatrix} \begin{bmatrix} x_1 & x_2 & x_3 \\ y_1 & y_2 & y_3 \end{bmatrix} = \begin{bmatrix} -x_1 & -x_2 & -x_3 \\ y_1 & y_2 & y_3 \end{bmatrix}$. To find the reflection of a planar figure over the line $y = x$, set up a matrix of the coordinates of the vertices and pre-multiply the matrix by the 2×2 matrix $\begin{bmatrix} 0 & 1 \\ 1 & 0 \end{bmatrix}$ so that $\begin{bmatrix} 0 & 1 \\ 1 & 0 \end{bmatrix} \begin{bmatrix} x_1 & x_2 & x_3 \\ y_1 & y_2 & y_3 \end{bmatrix} = \begin{bmatrix} y_1 & y_2 & y_3 \\ x_1 & x_2 & x_3 \end{bmatrix}$. Remember that the order of multiplication is important when multiplying matrices. The commutative property does not apply.

Rotation

To find the coordinates of the figure formed by rotating a planar figure about the origin θ degrees in a counterclockwise direction, set up a matrix of the coordinates of the vertices and pre-multiply the matrix by the 2×2 matrix $\begin{bmatrix} \cos\theta & \sin\theta \\ -\sin\theta & \cos\theta \end{bmatrix}$. For example, if you want to rotate a figure 90° clockwise around the origin, you would have to convert the degree measure to 270° counterclockwise and solve the 2×2 matrix you have set as the pre-multiplier: $\begin{bmatrix} \cos 270° & \sin 270° \\ -\sin 270° & \cos 270° \end{bmatrix} = \begin{bmatrix} 0 & -1 \\ 1 & 0 \end{bmatrix}$. Use this as the pre-multiplier for the matrix $\begin{bmatrix} x_1 & x_2 & x_3 \\ y_1 & y_2 & y_3 \end{bmatrix}$ and solve to find the new coordinates.

Dilation

To find the **dilation** of a planar figure by a scale factor of k, set up a matrix of the coordinates of the vertices of the planar figure and pre-multiply the matrix by the 2×2 matrix $\begin{bmatrix} k & 0 \\ 0 & k \end{bmatrix}$ so that $\begin{bmatrix} k & 0 \\ 0 & k \end{bmatrix} \begin{bmatrix} x_1 & x_2 & x_3 \\ y_1 & y_2 & y_3 \end{bmatrix} = \begin{bmatrix} kx_1 & kx_2 & kx_3 \\ ky_1 & ky_2 & ky_3 \end{bmatrix}$. This is effectively the same as multiplying the matrix by the scalar k, but the matrix equation would still be necessary if the figure were being dilated by different factors in vertical and horizontal directions. The scale factor k will be greater than 1 if the figure is being enlarged, and between 0 and 1 if the figure is being shrunk. Again, remember that when multiplying matrices, the order of the matrices is important. The commutative property does not apply, and the matrix with the coordinates of the figure must be the second matrix.

Reduced Row-Echelon Forms

When a system of equations has a solution, finding the transformation of the augmented matrix will result in one of three reduced row-echelon forms. Only one of these forms will give a unique solution to the system of equations, however. The following examples show the solutions indicated by particular results:

$\begin{bmatrix} 1 & 0 & 0 & x_0 \\ 0 & 1 & 0 & y_0 \\ 0 & 0 & 1 & z_0 \end{bmatrix}$ gives the unique solution $x = x_0;\ y = y_0;\ z = z_0$

$\begin{bmatrix} 1 & 0 & k_1 & x_0 \\ 0 & 1 & k_2 & y_0 \\ 0 & 0 & 0 & 0 \end{bmatrix}$ gives a non-unique solution $x = x_0 - k_1 z;\ y = y_0 - k_2 z$

$\begin{bmatrix} 1 & j_1 & k_1 & x_0 \\ 0 & 0 & 0 & 0 \\ 0 & 0 & 0 & 0 \end{bmatrix}$ gives a non-unique solution $x = x_0 - j_1 y - k_1 z$

Basic Trigonometric Functions

The three basic trigonometric functions are sine, cosine, and tangent.

Sine

The **sine** (sin) function has a period of 360° or 2π radians. This means that its graph makes one complete cycle every 360° or 2π. Because $\sin 0 = 0$, the graph of $y = \sin x$ begins at the origin, with the x-axis representing the angle measure, and the y-axis representing the sine of the angle. The graph of the sine function is a smooth curve that begins at the origin, peaks at the point $\left(\frac{\pi}{2}, 1\right)$, crosses the x-axis at $(\pi, 0)$, has its lowest point at $\left(\frac{3\pi}{2}, -1\right)$, and returns to the x-axis to complete one cycle at $(2\pi, 0)$.

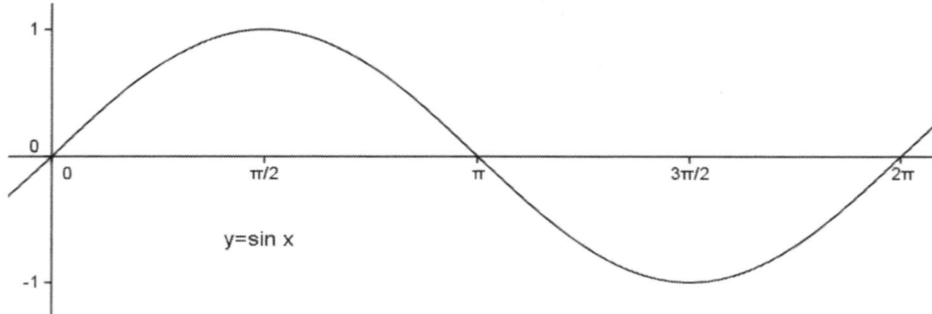

Cosine

The **cosine** (cos) function also has a period of 360° or 2π radians, which means that its graph also makes one complete cycle every 360° or 2π. Because $\cos 0° = 1$, the graph of $y = \cos x$ begins at the point $(0, 1)$, with the x-axis representing the angle measure, and the y-axis representing the cosine of the angle. The graph of the cosine function is a smooth curve that begins at the point $(0, 1)$, crosses the x-axis at the point $\left(\frac{\pi}{2}, 0\right)$, has its lowest point at $(\pi, -1)$, crosses the x-axis again at the point $\left(\frac{3\pi}{2}, 0\right)$, and returns to a peak at the point $(2\pi, 1)$ to complete one cycle.

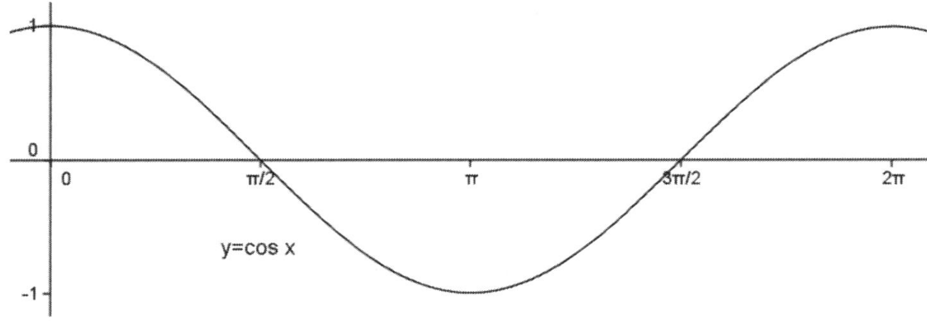

Review Video: Cosine
Visit mometrix.com/academy and enter code: 361120

TANGENT

The **tangent** (tan) function has a period of 180° or π radians, which means that its graph makes one complete cycle every 180° or π radians. The x-axis represents the angle measure, and the y-axis represents the tangent of the angle. The graph of the tangent function is a series of smooth curves that cross the x-axis at every 180° or π radians and have an asymptote every $k \cdot 90°$ or $\frac{k\pi}{2}$ radians, where k is an odd integer. This can be explained by the fact that the tangent is calculated by dividing the sine by the cosine, since the cosine equals zero at those asymptote points.

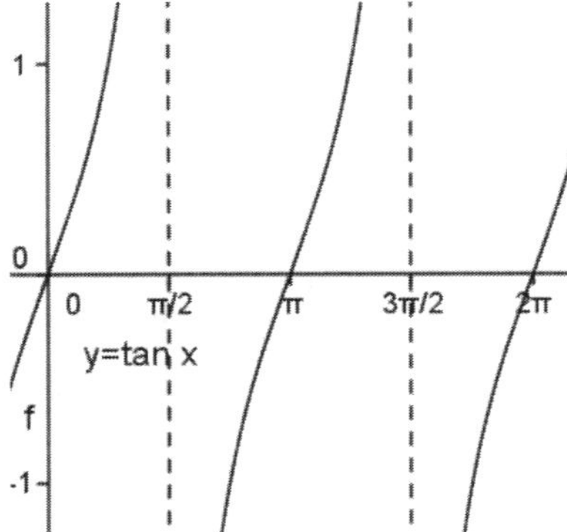

Review Video: Finding Tangent
Visit mometrix.com/academy and enter code: 947639

DEFINED AND RECIPROCAL FUNCTIONS

The tangent function is defined as the ratio of the sine to the cosine:

TANGENT (TAN):

$$\tan x = \frac{\sin x}{\cos x}$$

To take the reciprocal of a number means to place that number as the denominator of a fraction with a numerator of 1. The reciprocal functions are thus defined quite simply.

COSECANT (CSC):

$$\csc x = \frac{1}{\sin x}$$

SECANT (SEC):

$$\sec x = \frac{1}{\cos x}$$

COTANGENT (COT):

$$\cot x = \frac{1}{\tan x}$$

It is important to know these reciprocal functions, but they are not as commonly used as the three basic functions.

Review Video: Defined and Reciprocal Functions
Visit mometrix.com/academy and enter code: 996431

INVERSE FUNCTIONS

Each of the trigonometric functions accepts an angular measure, either degrees or radians, and gives a numerical value as the output. The inverse functions do the opposite; they accept a numerical value and give an angular measure as the output. The inverse sine, or arcsine, commonly written as either $\sin^{-1} x$ or $\arcsin x$, gives the angle whose sine is x. Similarly:

The inverse of $\cos x$ is written as $\cos^{-1} x$ or $\arccos x$ and means the angle whose cosine is x.
The inverse of $\tan x$ is written as $\tan^{-1} x$ or $\arctan x$ and means the angle whose tangent is x.
The inverse of $\csc x$ is written as $\csc^{-1} x$ or $\text{arccsc}\, x$ and means the angle whose cosecant is x.
The inverse of $\sec x$ is written as $\sec^{-1} x$ or $\text{arcsec}\, x$ and means the angle whose secant is x.
The inverse of $\cot x$ is written as $\cot^{-1} x$ or $\text{arccot}\, x$ and means the angle whose cotangent is x.

Review Video: Inverse of a Cosine
Visit mometrix.com/academy and enter code: 156054

Review Video: Inverse of a Tangent
Visit mometrix.com/academy and enter code: 229055

IMPORTANT NOTE ABOUT SOLVING TRIGONOMETRIC EQUATIONS

Trigonometric and algebraic equations are solved following the same rules, but while algebraic expressions have one unique solution, trigonometric equations could have multiple solutions, and you must find them all. When solving for an angle with a known trigonometric value, you must consider the sign and include all angles with that value. Your calculator will probably only give one value as an answer, typically in the following ranges:

For the inverse sine function, $\left[-\frac{\pi}{2}, \frac{\pi}{2}\right]$ or $[-90°, 90°]$

For the inverse cosine function, $[0, \pi]$ or $[0°, 180°]$

For the inverse tangent function, $\left[-\frac{\pi}{2}, \frac{\pi}{2}\right]$ or $[-90°, 90°]$

It is important to determine if there is another angle in a different quadrant that also satisfies the problem. To do this, find the other quadrant(s) with the same sign for that trigonometric function and find the angle that has the same reference angle. Then check whether this angle is also a solution.

In the first quadrant, all six trigonometric functions are positive (sin, cos, tan, csc, sec, cot).

In the second quadrant, sin and csc are positive.

In the third quadrant, tan and cot are positive.

In the fourth quadrant, cos and sec are positive.

If you remember the phrase, "ALL Students Take Classes," you will be able to remember the sign of each trigonometric function in each quadrant. ALL represents all the signs in the first quadrant. The "S" in "Students" represents the sine function and its reciprocal in the second quadrant. The "T" in "Take" represents the tangent function and its reciprocal in the third quadrant. The "C" in "Classes" represents the cosine function and its reciprocal.

Domain, Range, and Asymptotes in Trigonometry

The domain is the set of all possible real number values of x on the graph of a trigonometric function. Some graphs will impose limits on the values of x.

The range is the set of all possible real number values of y on the graph of a trigonometric function. Some graphs will impose limits on the values of y.

Asymptotes are lines which the graph of a trigonometric function approaches but never reaches. Asymptotes exist for values of x in the graphs of the tangent, cotangent, secant, and cosecant. The sine and cosine graphs do not have any asymptotes.

Domain, Range, and Asymptotes of the Six Trigonometric Functions

The domain, range, and asymptotes for each of the trigonometric functions are as follows:

- In the **sine** function, the domain is all real numbers, the range is $-1 \le y \le 1$, and there are no asymptotes.
- In the **cosine** function, the domain is all real numbers; the range is $-1 \le y \le 1$, and there are no asymptotes.
- In the **tangent** function, the domain is $x \in$ all real numbers; $x \neq \frac{\pi}{2} + k\pi$, the range is all real numbers; and the asymptotes are the lines $x = \frac{\pi}{2} + k\pi$.
- In the **cosecant** function, the domain is $x \in$ all real numbers; $x \neq k\pi$, the range is $(-\infty, -1] \cup [1, \infty)$, and the asymptotes are the lines $x = k\pi$.
- In the **secant** function, the domain is $x \in$ all real numbers; $x \neq \frac{\pi}{2} + k\pi$, the range is $(-\infty, 1] \cup [1, \infty)$, and the asymptotes are the lines $x = \frac{\pi}{2} + k\pi$.
- In the **cotangent** function, the domain is $x \in$ all real numbers; $x \neq k\pi$, the range is all real numbers, and the asymptotes are the lines $x = k\pi$.

In each of the above cases, k represents any integer.

Trigonometric Identities

Sum and Difference

To find the sine, cosine, or tangent of the sum or difference of two angles, use one of the following formulas:

$$\sin(\alpha \pm \beta) = \sin\alpha\cos\beta \pm \cos\alpha\sin\beta$$
$$\cos(\alpha \pm \beta) = \cos\alpha\cos\beta \mp \sin\alpha\sin\beta$$
$$\tan(\alpha \pm \beta) = \frac{\tan\alpha \pm \tan\beta}{1 \mp \tan\alpha\tan\beta}$$

where α and β are two angles with known sine, cosine, or tangent values as needed.

Half Angle

To find the sine or cosine of half of a known angle, use the following formulas:

$$\sin\frac{\theta}{2} = \pm\sqrt{\frac{1 - cos\theta}{2}}$$
$$\cos\frac{\theta}{2} = \pm\sqrt{\frac{1 + \cos\theta}{2}}$$

where θ is an angle with a known exact cosine value.

To determine the sine of the answer, you must recognize which quadrant the given angle is in and apply the correct sign for the trigonometric function you are using. If you need to find the exact sine or cosine of an angle that you do not know, such as sine 22.5°, you can rewrite the given angle as a half angle, such as sine $\frac{45°}{2}$, and use the formula above.

To find the tangent or cotangent of half of a known angle, use the following formulas:

$$\tan\frac{\theta}{2} = \frac{sin\theta}{1 + \cos\theta}$$
$$\cot\frac{\theta}{2} = \frac{\sin\theta}{1 - \cos\theta}$$

where θ is an angle with known exact sine and cosine values.

These formulas will work for finding the tangent or cotangent of half of any angle unless the cosine of θ happens to make the denominator of the identity equal to 0.

Double Angles

In each case, use one of the double angle formulas. To find the sine or cosine of twice a known angle, use one of the following formulas:

$$\sin(2\theta) = 2\sin\theta\cos\theta$$
$$\cos(2\theta) = \cos^2\theta - \sin^2\theta \text{ or}$$
$$\cos(2\theta) = 2\cos^2\theta - 1 \text{ or}$$
$$\cos(2\theta) = 1 - 2\sin^2\theta$$

To find the tangent or cotangent of twice a known angle, use the formulas:

$$\tan(2\theta) = \frac{2\tan\theta}{1 - \tan^2\theta}$$

$$\cot(2\theta) = \frac{\cot\theta - \tan\theta}{2}$$

In each case, θ is an angle with known exact sine, cosine, tangent, and cotangent values.

Products

To find the product of the sines and cosines of two different angles, use one of the following formulas:

$$\sin\alpha\sin\beta = \frac{1}{2}[\cos(\alpha - \beta) - \cos(\alpha + \beta)]$$
$$\cos\alpha\cos\beta = \frac{1}{2}[\cos(\alpha + \beta) + \cos(\alpha - \beta)]$$
$$\sin\alpha\cos\beta = \frac{1}{2}[\sin(\alpha + \beta) + \sin(\alpha - \beta)]$$
$$\cos\alpha\sin\beta = \frac{1}{2}[\sin(\alpha + \beta) - \sin(\alpha - \beta)]$$

where α and β are two unique angles.

Complementary

The trigonometric cofunction identities use the trigonometric relationships of complementary angles (angles whose sum is 90°). These are:

$$\cos x = \sin(90° - x)$$
$$\csc x = \sec(90° - x)$$
$$\cot x = \tan(90° - x)$$

Review Video: Complementary Angles
Visit mometrix.com/academy and enter code: 919405

Pythagorean Theorem

The Pythagorean theorem states that $a^2 + b^2 = c^2$ for all right triangles. The trigonometric identity that derives from this principle is stated in this way:

$$\sin^2\theta + \cos^2\theta = 1$$

Dividing each term by either $\sin^2\theta$ or $\cos^2\theta$ yields two other identities, respectively:

$$1 + \cot^2\theta = \csc^2\theta$$
$$\tan^2\theta + 1 = \sec^2\theta$$

Unit Circle

Recall that the standard equation for a circle is $(x - h)^2 + (y - k)^2 = r^2$. A unit circle is a circle with a radius of 1 ($r = 1$) that has its center at the origin ($h = 0, k = 0$). Thus, the equation for the unit circle simplifies from the standard equation down to $x^2 + y^2 = 1$.

Standard position is the position of an angle of measure θ whose vertex is at the origin, the initial side crosses the unit circle at the point $(1, 0)$, and the terminal side crosses the unit circle at some other point (a, b). In the standard position, $\sin\theta = b$, $\cos\theta = a$, and $\tan\theta = \frac{b}{a}$.

Review Video: Unit Circles and Standard Position
Visit mometrix.com/academy and enter code: 333922

Rectangular coordinates are those that lie on the square grids of the Cartesian plane. They should be quite familiar to you. The polar coordinate system is based on a circular graph, rather than the square grid of the Cartesian system. Points in the polar coordinate system are in the format (r, θ), where r is the distance from the origin (think radius of the circle) and θ is the smallest positive angle (moving counterclockwise around the circle) made with the positive horizontal axis.

Review Video: Rectangular and Polar Coordinate System
Visit mometrix.com/academy and enter code: 694585

To convert a point from rectangular (x, y) format to polar (r, θ) format, use the formula (x, y) to $(r, \theta) \Rightarrow r = \sqrt{x^2 + y^2}; \theta = \arctan\frac{y}{x}$ when $x \neq 0$

Review Video: Converting Between Polar and Rectangular Formats
Visit mometrix.com/academy and enter code: 281325

If x is positive, use the positive square root value for r. If x is negative, use the negative square root value for r.

If $x = 0$, use the following rules:
If $x = 0$ and $y = 0$, then $\theta = 0$
If $x = 0$ and $y > 0$, then $\theta = \frac{\pi}{2}$
If $x = 0$ and $y < 0$, then $\theta = \frac{3\pi}{2}$

To convert a point from polar (r, θ) format to rectangular (x, y) format, use the formula (r, θ) to $(x, y) \Rightarrow x = r\cos\theta\,; y = r\sin\theta$

TABLE OF COMMONLY ENCOUNTERED ANGLES

$0° = 0$ radians, $30° = \frac{\pi}{6}$ radians, $45° = \frac{\pi}{4}$ radians, $60° = \frac{\pi}{3}$ radians, and $90° = \frac{\pi}{2}$ radians

$\sin 0° = 0$	$\cos 0° = 1$	$\tan 0° = 0$
$\sin 30° = \frac{1}{2}$	$\cos 30° = \frac{\sqrt{3}}{2}$	$\tan 30° = \frac{\sqrt{3}}{3}$
$\sin 45° = \frac{\sqrt{2}}{2}$	$\cos 45° = \frac{\sqrt{2}}{2}$	$\tan 45° = 1$
$\sin 60° = \frac{\sqrt{3}}{2}$	$\cos 60° = \frac{1}{2}$	$\tan 60° = \sqrt{3}$
$\sin 90° = 1$	$\cos 90° = 0$	$\tan 90° =$ undefined
$\csc 0° =$ undefined	$\sec 0° = 1$	$\cot 0° =$ undefined
$\csc 30° = 2$	$\sec 30° = \frac{2\sqrt{3}}{3}$	$\cot 30° = \sqrt{3}$
$\csc 45° = \sqrt{2}$	$\sec 45° = \sqrt{2}$	$\cot 45° = 1$
$\csc 60° = \frac{2\sqrt{3}}{3}$	$\sec 60° = 2$	$\cot 60° = \frac{\sqrt{3}}{3}$
$\csc 90° = 1$	$\sec 90° =$ undefined	$\cot 90° = 0$

The values in the upper half of this table are values you should have memorized or be able to find quickly.

Review Video: Commonly Encountered Angles
Visit mometrix.com/academy and enter code: 204098

DE MOIVRE'S THEOREM

De Moivre's Theorem is used to find the powers of complex numbers (numbers that contain the imaginary number *i*) written in polar form. Given a trigonometric expression that contains *i*, such as $z = r\cos x + ir\sin x$, where *r* is a real number and *x* is an angle measurement in polar form, use the formula $z^n = r^n(\cos nx + i\sin nx)$, where *r* and *n* are real numbers, *x* is the angle measure in polar form, and *i* is the imaginary number $i = \sqrt{-1}$. The expression $\cos x + i\sin x$ can be written cis *x*, making the formula appear in the format $z^n = r^n \text{ cis } nx$.

Note that De Moivre's Theorem is only for angles in polar form. If you are given an angle in degrees, you must convert to polar form before using the formula.

CALCULUS

Calculus, also called analysis, is the branch of mathematics that studies the length, area, and volume of objects, and the rate of change of quantities (which can be expressed as slopes of curves). The two principal branches of calculus are differential and integral. Differential calculus is based on derivatives and takes the form,

$$\frac{d}{dx}f(x)$$

Integral calculus is based on integrals and takes the form,

$$\int f(x)dx$$

Some of the basic ideas of calculus were utilized as far back in history as Archimedes. However, its modern forms were developed by Newton and Leibniz.

LIMITS

The **limit of a function** is represented by the notation $\lim_{x \to a} f(x)$. It is read as "the limit of f of x as x approaches a." In many cases, $\lim_{x \to a} f(x)$ will simply be equal to $f(a)$, but not always. Limits are important because some functions are not defined or are not easy to evaluate at certain values of x.

The limit at the point is said to exist only if the limit is the same when approached from the right side as from the left: $\lim_{x \to a^+} f(x) = \lim_{x \to a^-} f(x)$). Notice the symbol by the a in each case. When x approaches a from the right, it approaches from the positive end of the number line. When x approaches a from the left, it approaches from the negative end of the number line.

If the limit as x approaches a differs depending on the direction from which it approaches, then the limit does not exist at a. In other words, if $\lim_{x \to a^+} f(x)$ does not equal $\lim_{x \to a^-} f(x)$, then the limit does not exist at a. The limit also does not exist if either of the one-sided limits does not exist.

Situations in which the limit does not exist include a function that jumps from one value to another at a, one that oscillates between two different values as x approaches a, or one that increases or decreases without bounds as x approaches a. If the limit you calculate has a value of $\frac{c}{0}$, where c is any constant, this means the function goes to infinity and the limit does not exist.

It is possible for two functions that do not have limits to be multiplied to get a new function that does have a limit. Just because two functions do not have limits, do not assume that the product will not have a limit.

DIRECT SUBSTITUTION

The first thing to try when looking for a limit is direct substitution. To find the limit of a function $\lim_{x \to a} f(x)$ by direct substitution, substitute the value of a for x in the function and solve. The following patterns apply to finding the limit of a function by direct substitution:

$\lim_{x \to a} b = b$, where b is any real number

$\lim_{x \to a} x = a$

$\lim_{x \to a} x^n = a^n$, where n is any positive integer

$\lim_{x \to a} \sqrt{x} = \sqrt{a}; a > 0$

$\lim_{x \to a} \sqrt[n]{x} = \sqrt[n]{a}$, where n is a positive integer and $a > 0$ for all even values of n

$$\lim_{x \to a} \frac{1}{x} = \frac{1}{a}; a \neq 0$$

You can also use substitution for finding the limit of a trigonometric function, a polynomial function, or a rational function. Be sure that in manipulating an expression to find a limit that you do not divide by terms equal to zero.

In finding the limit of a composite function, begin by finding the limit of the innermost function. For example, to find $\lim_{x \to a} f(g(x))$, first find the value of $\lim_{x \to a} g(x)$. Then substitute this value for x in $f(x)$ and solve. The result is the limit of the original problem.

SAMPLE PROBLEMS

1. *Evaluate the following limits:*

a. $\lim_{x \to 4} 7$

b. $\lim_{x \to 4} \frac{x-4}{x^2-16}$

c. $\lim_{x \to 4} f(x)$, where $f(x) = \begin{cases} x+1, \text{when } x < 4 \\ x-1, \text{when } x \geq 4 \end{cases}$

SOLUTIONS

a. 7 is a constant function, so therefore, $\lim_{x \to 4} 7 = 7$

b. $\lim_{x \to 4} \frac{x-4}{x^2-16}$ can be simplified by factoring.

$$\frac{x-4}{x^2-16} = \frac{x-4}{(x+4)(x-4)} = \frac{1}{x+4}$$

Thus,

$$\lim_{x \to 4} \frac{x-4}{x^2-16} = \lim_{x \to 4} \frac{1}{x+4} = \frac{1}{8}$$

c. $\lim_{x \to 4} f(x)$, when $f(x) = x + 1$ for $x < 4$ and $f(x) = x - 1$ for $x \geq 4$

$$\lim_{x \to 4^+} f(x) = x - 1 = 4 - 1 = 3$$
$$\lim_{x \to 4^-} f(x) = x + 1 = 4 + 1 = 5$$

Therefore, $\lim_{x \to 4} f(x)$, does not exist.

2. *Given that* $\lim_{x \to 3} f(x) = 2$, $\lim_{x \to 3} g(x) = 6$, *and* $k = 5$, *solve the following:*

a. $\lim_{x \to 3} kg(x)$
b. $\lim_{x \to 3} (f(x) + g(x))$
c. $\lim_{x \to 3} f(x) \cdot g(x)$
d. $\lim_{x \to 3} g(x) \div f(x)$
e. $\lim_{x \to 3} [f(x)]^n = C^n$, where $n = 3$

SOLUTIONS

a. $\lim_{x \to a} kf(x) = kC$, where k is a constant, so $\lim_{x \to 3} kg(x) = 5 \cdot 6 = 30$
b. $\lim_{x \to a} (f(x) \pm g(x)) = C \pm D$, so $\lim_{x \to 3} \big(f(x) + g(x)\big) = 2 + 6 = 8$
c. $\lim_{x \to a} f(x) \cdot g(x) = C \cdot D$, so $\lim_{x \to 3} f(x) \times g(x) = 2 \times 6 = 12$

d. $\lim_{x \to a} f(x) \div g(x) = C \div D$, if $D \neq 0$, so $\lim_{x \to 3} \frac{g(x)}{f(x)} = \frac{6}{2} = 3$
e. $\lim_{x \to a} [f(x)]^n = C^n$, so $\lim_{x \to 3} [f(x)]^n = C^n = 2^3 = 8$

L'HÔPITAL'S RULE

Sometimes solving $\lim_{x \to a} \frac{f(x)}{g(x)}$ by the direct substitution method will result in the numerator and denominator both being equal to zero, or both being equal to infinity. This outcome is called an indeterminate form. The limit cannot be directly found by substitution in these cases. L'Hôpital's rule is a useful method for finding the limit of a problem in the indeterminate form. L'Hôpital's rule allows you to find the limit using derivatives. Assuming both the numerator and denominator are differentiable, and that both are equal to zero when the direct substitution method is used, take the derivative of both the numerator and the denominator and then use the direct substitution method. For example, if $\lim_{x \to a} \frac{f(x)}{g(x)} = \frac{0}{0}$, take the derivatives of $f(x)$ and $g(x)$ and then find $\lim_{x \to a} \frac{f'(x)}{g'(x)}$. If $g'(x) \neq 0$, then you have found the limit of the original function. If $g'(x) = 0$ and $f'(x) = 0$, L'Hôpital's rule may be applied to the function $\frac{f'(x)}{g'(x)}$, and so on until either a limit is found, or it can be determined that the limit does not exist.

When finding the limit of the sum or difference of two functions, find the limit of each individual function and then add or subtract the results. For example, $\lim_{x \to a} [f(x) \pm g(x)] = \lim_{x \to a} f(x) \pm \lim_{x \to a} g(x)$.

To find the limit of the product or quotient of two functions, find the limit of each individual function and then multiply or divide the results. For example, $\lim_{x \to a} [f(x) \cdot g(x)] = \lim_{x \to a} f(x) \cdot \lim_{x \to a} g(x)$ and $\lim_{x \to a} \frac{f(x)}{g(x)} = \frac{\lim_{x \to a} f(x)}{\lim_{x \to a} g(x)}$, where $g(x) \neq 0$ and $\lim_{x \to a} g(x) \neq 0$. When finding the quotient of the limits of two functions, make sure the denominator is not equal to zero. If it is, use differentiation or L'Hôpital's rule to find the limit.

To find the limit of a power of a function or a root of a function, find the limit of the function and then raise the limit to the original power or take the root of the limit. For example, $\lim_{x \to a} [f(x)]^n = \left[\lim_{x \to a} f(x)\right]^n$ and $\lim_{x \to a} \sqrt[n]{f(x)} = \sqrt[n]{\lim_{x \to a} f(x)}$, where n is a positive integer and $\lim_{x \to a} f(x) > 0$ for all even values of n.

To find the limit of a function multiplied by a scalar, find the limit of the function and multiply the result by the scalar. For example, $\lim_{x \to a} kf(x) = k \lim_{x \to a} f(x)$, where k is a real number.

SQUEEZE THEOREM

The squeeze theorem is known by many names, including the sandwich theorem, the sandwich rule, the squeeze lemma, the squeezing theorem, and the pinching theorem. No matter what you call it, the principle is the same. To prove the limit of a difficult function exists, find the limits of two functions, one on either side of the unknown, that are easy to compute. If the limits of these functions are equal, then that is also the limit of the unknown function. In mathematical terms, the theorem is:

If $g(x) \leq f(x) \leq h(x)$ for all values of x where $f(x)$ is the function with the unknown limit, and if $\lim_{x \to a} g(x) = \lim_{x \to a} h(x)$, then this limit is also equal to $\lim_{x \to a} f(x)$.

To find the limit of an expression containing an absolute value sign, take the absolute value of the limit. If $\lim_{n\to\infty} a_n = L$, where L is the numerical value for the limit, then $\lim_{n\to\infty} |a_n| = |L|$. Also, if $\lim_{n\to\infty} |a_n| = 0$, then $\lim_{n\to\infty} a_n = 0$. The trick comes when you are asked to find the limit as n approaches from the left. Whenever the limit is being approached from the left, it is being approached from the negative end of the domain. The absolute value sign makes everything in the equation positive, essentially eliminating the negative side of the domain. In this case, rewrite the equation without the absolute value signs and add a negative sign in front of the expression. For example, $\lim_{n\to 0^-} |x|$ becomes $\lim_{n\to 0^-} (-x)$.

Derivatives

The derivative of a function is a measure of how much that function is changing at a specific point, and is the slope of a line tangent to a curve at the specific point. The derivative of a function $f(x)$ is written $f'(x)$, and read, "f prime of x." Other notations for the derivative include $D_x f(x)$, y', $D_x y$, $\frac{dy}{dx}$, and $\frac{d}{dx} f(x)$. The definition of the derivative of a function is $f'(x) = \lim_{h\to 0} \frac{f(x+h)-f(x)}{h}$. However, this formula is rarely used.

There is a simpler method you can use to find the derivative of a polynomial. Given a function $f(x) = a_n x^n + a_{n-1}x^{n-1} + a_{n-2}x^{n-2} + \cdots + a_1 x + a_0$, multiply each exponent by its corresponding coefficient to get the new coefficient and reduce the value of the exponent by one. Coefficients with no variable are dropped. This gives $f'(x) = na_n x^{n-1} + (n-1)a_{n-1}x^{n-2} + \cdots + a_1$, a pattern that can be repeated for each successive derivative.

Differentiable functions are functions that have a derivative. Some basic rules for finding derivatives of functions are:

$f(x) = c \Rightarrow f'(x) = 0$; where c is a constant

$$f(x) = x \Rightarrow f'(x) = 1$$

$\left(cf(x)\right)' = cf'(x)$; where c is a constant

$f(x) = x^n \Rightarrow f'(x) = nx^{n-1}$; where n is a real number

$$(f+g)'(x) = f'(x) + g'(x)$$
$$(fg)'(x) = f(x)g'(x) + f'(x)g(x)$$
$$\left(\frac{f}{g}\right)'(x) = \frac{f'(x)g(x) - f(x)g'(x)}{[g(x)]^2}$$
$$(f \circ g)'(x) = f'\left(g(x)\right) \cdot g'(x)$$

This last formula is also known as the Chain Rule. If you are finding the derivative of a polynomial that is raised to a power, let the polynomial be represented by $g(x)$ and use the Chain Rule. The chain rule is one of the most important concepts to grasp in the early stages of learning calculus. Many other rules and shortcuts are based upon the chain rule.

These rules may also be used to take multiple derivatives of the same function. The derivative of the derivative is called the second derivative and is represented by the notation $f''(x)$. Taking one more derivative, if possible, gives the third derivative and is represented by the notation $f'''(x)$ or $f^{(3)}(x)$.

Review Video: Definition of a Derivative
Visit mometrix.com/academy and enter code: 787269

Review Video: Derivative Properties and Formulas
Visit mometrix.com/academy and enter code: 735227

Review Video: Derivatives of Trigonometry Functions
Visit mometrix.com/academy and enter code: 132724

Rules of Operations with the Derivative

Many of the rules of operations with limits apply to operations with derivatives since the derivative is a limit.

Addition: The derivative of a sum of two functions is equal to the sum of the individual derivatives.
Constant multiplication: $(cf(x))' = c(f'(x))$, where c is a constant.
The derivative of a constant times a function is equal to the product of the constant times the derivative of the function.
Multiplication by another derivative: $(fg)' = f'g + g'f$, where f and g are both differentiable functions.
Division by another derivative: $\left(\frac{f}{g}\right)' = \frac{(f'g-fg')}{g^2}$ where f and g are both differentiable functions.

Difference Quotient and Derivative

A *secant* is a line that connects two points on a curve. The difference quotient gives the slope of an arbitrary secant line that connects the point $(x, f(x))$ with a nearby point $(x + h, f(x + h))$ on the graph of the function f. The difference quotient is the same formula that is always used to determine a slope—the change in y divided by the change in x. It is written as $\frac{f(x+h)-f(x)}{h}$.

A *tangent* is a line that touches a curve at one point. The tangent and the curve have the same slope at the point where they touch. The derivative is the function that gives the slope of both the tangent and the curve of the function at that point. The derivative is written as the limit of the difference quotient, or:

$$\lim_{h\to 0}\frac{f(x+h)-f(x)}{h}$$

If the function is f, the derivative is denoted as $f'(x)$, and it is the slope of the function f at point $(x, f(x))$. It is expressed as:

$$f'(x) = \lim_{h\to 0}\frac{f(x+h)-f(x)}{h}$$

Other Derivative Functions

An implicit function is one where it is impossible, or very difficult, to express one variable in terms of another by normal algebraic methods. This would include functions that have both variables raised to a power greater than 1, functions that have two variables multiplied by each other, or a combination of the two. To differentiate such a function with respect to x, take the derivate of each term that contains a variable, either x or y. When differentiating a term with y, use the chain rule, first taking the derivative with respect to y, and then multiplying by $\frac{dy}{dx}$. If a term contains both x and y, you will have to use the product rule as well as the chain rule. Once the derivative of each individual term has been found, use the rules of algebra to solve for $\frac{dy}{dx}$ to get the final answer.

Example:

Find $\frac{dy}{dx}$ given the equation $xy^2 = 3y + 2x$. Take the derivative of each term with respect to x: $y^2 + 2xy\frac{dy}{dx} = 3\frac{dy}{dx} + 2$. Note that the first term in the original equation required the use of the product rule and the chain rule. Using algebra, isolate $\frac{dy}{dx}$ on one side of the equation to yield $\frac{dy}{dx} = \frac{y^2-2}{3-2xy}$.

Trigonometric functions are any functions that include one of the six trigonometric expressions. The following rules for derivatives apply for all trigonometric differentiation:

$\frac{d}{dx}(\sin x) = \cos x, \frac{d}{dx}(\cos x) = -\sin x, \frac{d}{dx}(\tan x) = \sec^2 x$

For functions that are a combination of trigonometric and algebraic expressions, use the chain rule:

$$\frac{d}{dx}(\sin u) = \cos u \frac{du}{dx}$$
$$\frac{d}{dx}(\cos u) = -\sin u \frac{du}{dx}$$
$$\frac{d}{dx}(\tan u) = \sec^2 u \frac{du}{dx}$$
$$\frac{d}{dx}(\sec u) = \tan u \sec u \frac{du}{dx}$$
$$\frac{d}{dx}(\csc u) = -\csc u \cot u \frac{du}{dx}$$
$$\frac{d}{dx}(\cot u) = -\csc^2 u \frac{du}{dx}$$

Functions involving the inverses of the trigonometric functions can also be differentiated.

$$\frac{d}{dx}(\sin^{-1} u) = \frac{1}{\sqrt{1-u^2}}\frac{du}{dx}$$
$$\frac{d}{dx}(\cos^{-1} u) = \frac{-1}{\sqrt{1-u^2}}\frac{du}{dx}$$
$$\frac{d}{dx}(\tan^{-1} u) = \frac{1}{1+u^2}\frac{du}{dx}$$
$$\frac{d}{dx}(\csc^{-1} u) = \frac{-1}{u\sqrt{u^2-1}}\frac{du}{dx}$$
$$\frac{d}{dx}(\sec^{-1} u) = \frac{1}{u\sqrt{u^2-1}}\frac{du}{dx}$$
$$\frac{d}{dx}(\cot^{-1} u) = \frac{-1}{1+u^2}\frac{du}{dx}$$

In each of the above expressions, u represents a differentiable function. Also, the value of u must be such that the radicand, if applicable, is a positive number. Remember the expression $\frac{du}{dx}$ means to take the derivative of the function u with respect to the variable x.

Exponential functions are in the form e^x, which has itself as its derivative: $\frac{d}{dx}\, e^x = e^x$. For functions that have a function as the exponent rather than just an x, use the formula $\frac{d}{dx}\, e^u = e^u \frac{du}{dx}$.

The inverse of the exponential function is the **natural logarithm**. To find the derivative of the natural logarithm, use the formula $\frac{d}{dx} \ln u = \frac{1}{u} \frac{du}{dx}$.

If you are trying to solve an expression with a variable in the exponent, use the formula $a^x = e^{x \ln a}$, where a is a positive real number and x is any real number. To find the derivative of a function in this format, use the formula $\frac{d}{dx} a^x = a^x \ln a$. If the exponent is a function rather than a single variable x, use the formula $\frac{d}{dx} a^u = a^u \ln a \frac{du}{dx}$.

If you are trying to solve an expression involving a logarithm, use the formula $\frac{d}{dx}(\log_a x) = \frac{1}{x \ln a}$ or $\frac{d}{dx}(\log_a |u|) = \frac{1}{u \ln a} \frac{du}{dx}; u \neq 0$.

Continuity

A function can be either continuous or discontinuous. A conceptual way to describe continuity is this: A function is continuous if its graph can be traced with a pen without lifting the pen from the page. In other words, there are no breaks or gaps in the graph of the function. However, this is only a description, not a technical definition. A function is continuous at the point $x = a$ if the three following conditions are met:

1. $f(a)$ is defined
2. $\lim_{x \to a} f(x)$ exists
3. $\lim_{x \to a} f(x) = f(a)$

If any of these conditions are not met, the function is discontinuous at the point $x = a$.

A function can be continuous at a point, continuous over an interval, or continuous everywhere. The above rules define continuity at a point. A function that is continuous over an interval $[a,b]$ is continuous at the points a and b and at every point between them. A function that is continuous everywhere is continuous for every real number, that is, for all points in its domain.

Discontinuity

Discontinuous functions are categorized according to the type or cause of discontinuity. Three examples are point, infinite, and jump discontinuity. A function with a point discontinuity has one value of x for which it is not continuous. A function with infinite discontinuity has a vertical asymptote at $x = a$ and $f(a)$ is undefined. It is said to have an infinite discontinuity at x=a. A function with jump discontinuity has one-sided limits from the left and from the right, but they are not equal to one another, that is, $\lim_{x \to a^-} f(x) \neq \lim_{x \to a^+} f(x)$. It is said to have a jump discontinuity at $x = a$.

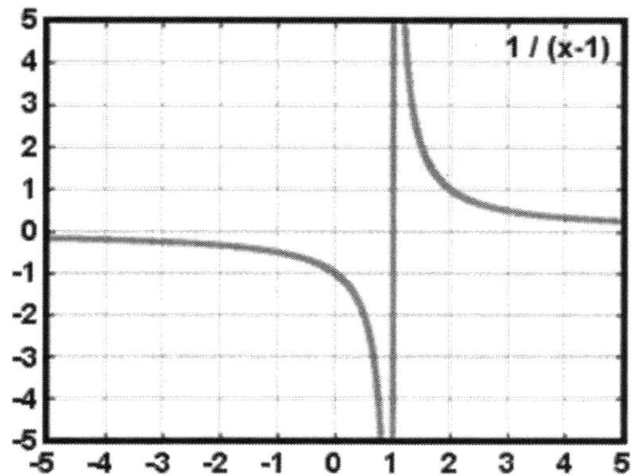

The function plotted in the graph has an infinite discontinuity. It has a vertical asymptote at $x = 1$ because $f(x) = \frac{1}{x-1}$ is undefined at $x = 1$.

SAMPLE PROBLEM

Identify the discontinuity in the graph of the function $f(x) = x$ for $x < 0$ *and* $f(x) = x + 1$ for $x \geq 0$

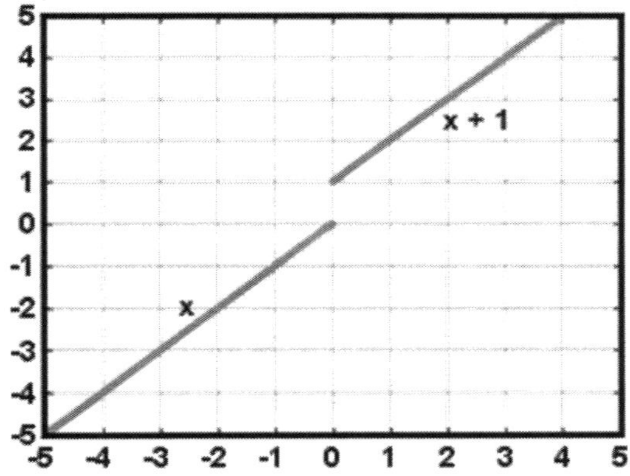

The function $f(x) = x$ for $x < 0$, $f(x) = x + 1$ for $x \geq 0$ has a jump discontinuity (also known as a gap discontinuity) at $x = 0$. It has one-sided limits from the left:

$$\lim_{x \to a^-} f(x) = 0$$

and from the right:

$$\lim_{x \to a^+} f(x) = 1$$

but they are not equal to one another. That is:

$$\lim_{x \to a^-} f(x) \neq \lim_{x \to a^+} f(x)$$

DIFFERENTIABILITY

A function is said to be differentiable at point $x = a$ if it has a derivative at that point, that is, if $f'(a)$ exists. For a function to be differentiable, it must be continuous because the slope cannot be defined at a point of discontinuity. Furthermore, for a function to be differentiable, its graph must not have any sharp turn for which it is impossible to draw a tangent line. The sine function is an example of a differentiable function. It is continuous, and a tangent line can be drawn anywhere along its graph.

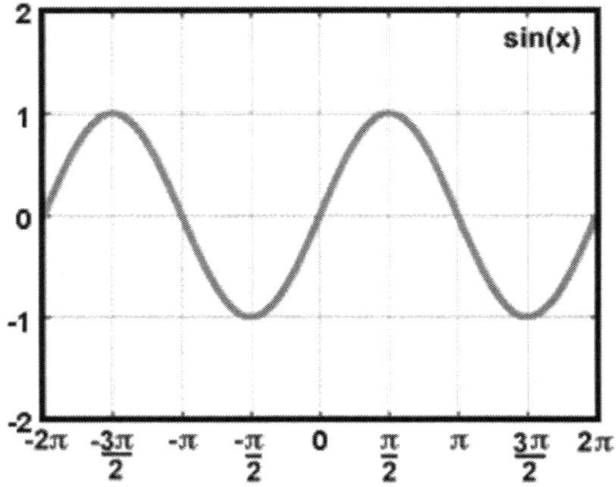

The function $f(x) = |x|$ is an example of a function that is not differentiable:

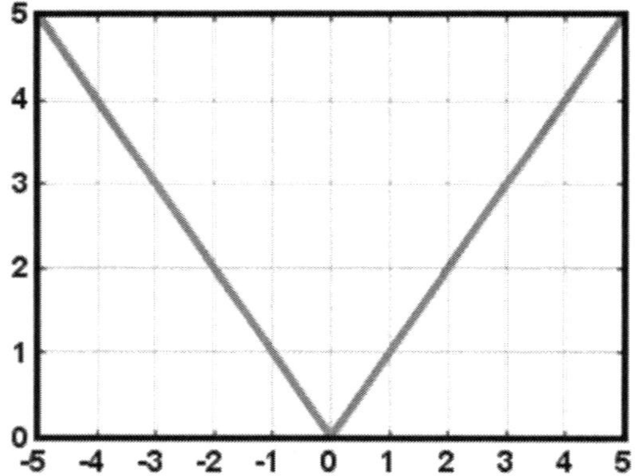

It is continuous, but it has a sharp turn at $x = 0$ which prohibits the drawing of a tangent at that point. All differentiable functions are continuous, but not all continuous functions are differentiable, as the absolute value function demonstrates.

The function $f(x) = \frac{1}{x-1}$ is not differentiable because it is not continuous. It has a discontinuity at $x = 1$. Therefore, a tangent could not be drawn at that point.

SAMPLE PROBLEMS

1. *Find $f'(x)$ for the function $f(x) = 3x$ and $f'(x)$ for the function $f(x) = x^2$.*

Using the formula $f'(x) = \lim_{h \to 0} \frac{f(x+h)-f(x)}{h}$,

$$\begin{aligned} f'(x) &= \lim_{h \to 0} \frac{3x + 3h - 3x}{h} \\ &= \lim_{h \to 0} \frac{3h}{h} \\ &= \lim_{h \to 0} 3 \\ &= 3 \end{aligned}$$

The derivative, and thus the slope of the function, is 3.

Using the formula $f'(x) = \lim_{h \to 0} \frac{f(x+h)-f(x)}{h}$

The derivative, and thus the slope of the function, is 2x.

2. *Find $f'(3)$ for $f(x) = x^2$*

To find the derivative of a function at a single point only, the value of the point can be substituted into the difference quotient $\frac{\lim_{h \to 0}(f(x+h)-f(x))}{h}$. Thus, for the function $f(x) = x^2$ and the value $x = 3$, the difference quotient becomes:

$$\begin{aligned} &= \lim_{h \to 0} \frac{\left(f(3+h) - f(3)\right)}{h} \\ &= \lim_{h \to 0} \frac{(3+h)^2 - 3^2}{h} \\ &= \lim_{h \to 0} \frac{9 + 6h + h^2 - 9}{h} \\ &= \lim_{h \to 0} \frac{h(6+h)}{h} \\ &= \lim_{h \to 0} 6 + h \\ &= 6 \end{aligned}$$

Thus, $f'(3) = 6$.

3. *Explain the power rule of differentiation and its usage and use it to differentiate $f(x) = 4x^2$, $f(x) = x^4$ and $f(x) = 3x^2 - 5x + 6$.*

The power rule is useful for finding the derivative of polynomial functions. It states that the derivative of $x^n = nx^{n-1}$.

By applying it to $f(x) = 4x^2$, we obtain

$$f'(x) = 2 \times 4x^2 - 1 = 8x$$

By applying it to $f(x) = x^4$, we obtain

$$f'(x) = 4 \times x^{4-1} = 4x^3$$

By applying it to $f(x) = 3x^2 - 5x + 6$, we obtain

$$f'(x) = 2 \times 3x^{2-1} - 1 \times 5x^{1-1} = 6x - 5$$

Approximating a Derivative From a Table of Values

The **derivative** of a function at a particular point is equal to the slope of the graph of the function at that point. For a nonlinear function, it can be thought of as the limit of the slope of a line drawn between two other points on the function as those points become closer to the point in question. Such a line drawn through two points on the function is called a **secant** of the function.

This definition of the derivative in terms of the secant allows us to approximate the derivative of a function at a point from a table of values: we take the slope of the line through the points on either side. That is, if the point lies between (x_1, y_1) and (x_2, y_2), the slope of the secant—the approximate derivative—is $\frac{y_2 - y_1}{x_2 - x_1}$. (This is also equal to the average slope over the interval $[x_1, x_2]$.)

For example, consider the function represented by the following table:

x	0	2	4	6	8	10
y	1	5	8	9	7	4

Suppose we want to know the derivative of the function when $x = 3$. This lies between the points $(2, 5)$ and $(4, 8)$; the approximate derivative is $\frac{8-5}{4-2} = \frac{3}{2}$.

Computing the Area Under a Curve

The common methods for *computing the area under a curve* include Riemann sums and the trapezoid rule. Riemann sums is a method in which the area under a curve is divided into narrow rectangles and then the individual areas of the rectangles are added together to obtain the total area. There are several variations on this method, including the left-hand approximation, the midpoint approximation, and the right-hand approximation. In left-hand approximation, the value of the function at the left endpoint of each equal width rectangle is used as the height of the rectangle. In the midpoint approximation, the value of the function at the midpoint of each equal width rectangle is used as the height of the rectangle. In right-hand approximation, the value of the function at the right endpoint of each equal width rectangle is used as the height of the rectangle. The trapezoid rule divides the area under a curve into narrow trapezoids, using the value of the function at the right and left endpoints of each section to determine the height of the two uneven corners of the trapezoid. Their areas are then summed to approximate the total area under the curve. For all of the above methods, the greater the number of subdivisions into which the area is divided, the greater the accuracy of the approximation.

Sample Problems

1. *Using right-hand approximation with six subdivisions, calculate the area under the curve of the function $f(x) = x^2 + 3$ on the interval [2,5].*

To solve the problem, first divide the interval [2,5] by the number of subdivisions, 6.

$$\Delta x = \frac{b-a}{n} = \frac{5-2}{6} = 0.5$$

Each rectangle has a width of 0.5.

The height of the right-hand side of each rectangle is given by the value of the function at the points $x = 2.5, 3, 3.5, 4, 4.5, 5$. Summing these heights and multiplying by the width of each rectangle gives the approximate total area under the curve.

$$= 0.5\big(f(2.5) + f(3) + f(3.5) + f(4) + f(4.5) + f(5)\big)$$

$$= 0.5(9.25 + 12 + 15.25 + 19 + 23.25 + 28) = 53.375$$

The total area under the curve of the function $f(x) = x^2 + 3$ on the interval [2,5], calculated using right-hand approximation, is found to be approximately 53.375.

2. *Using left-hand approximation with three subdivisions, calculate the area under the curve of the function $f(x) = x^2 + 3$ on the interval [2,5].*

To solve the problem, first divide the interval [2,5] by the number of subdivisions, 3.

$$\Delta x = \frac{b-a}{n} = \frac{5-2}{3} = 1$$

Each rectangle has a width of 1.

The height of the left-hand side of each rectangle is given by the value of the function at $x = 2, 3, 4$. Summing these heights and multiplying by the width of each rectangle gives the approximate area under the curve.

$$1(f(2) + f(3) + f(4)) = (7 + 12 + 19) = 38$$

The total area under the curve of the function $f(x) = x^2 + 3$ on the interval [2,5], calculated using left-hand approximation, is found to be approximately 38.

Position, Velocity, and Acceleration

Velocity is a specific type of rate of change. It refers to the rate of change of the position of an object with relation to a reference frame. Acceleration is the rate of change of velocity.

Average velocity over a period of time is found using the formula $\bar{v} = \frac{s(t_2)-s(t_1)}{t_2-t_1}$, where t_1 and t_2 are specific points in time and $s(t_1)$ and $s(t_2)$ are the distances traveled at those points in time.

Instantaneous velocity at a specific time is found using the formula $v = \lim\limits_{h\to 0}\frac{s(t+h)-s(t)}{h}$, or $v = s'(t)$.

Remember that velocity at a given point is found using the first derivative, and acceleration at a given point is found using the second derivative. Therefore, the formula for acceleration at a given point in time is found using the formula $a(t) = v'(t) = s''(t)$, where a is acceleration, v is velocity, and s is distance or location.

Scalar quantities express only magnitude. Vector quantities have both a magnitude and a direction. For example, speed is a scalar quantity. It is never negative and has no relation to direction. On the other hand, velocity is a vector quantity that expresses not only the speed, but also the direction of travel. It can be positive, as in the case of forward movement, or negative, as in the case of backward movement.

Sample Problems

1. *Suppose that the function $s(t) = t^2 + 4t + 5$ represents the position of a train that begins moving in a straight line (in units of meters and seconds). Find its position, velocity, and acceleration at the end of three seconds.*

The position function is $s(t) = t^2 + 4t + 5$. Therefore,

$$s(3) = 3^2 + 4(3) + 5 = 26\ m$$

At the end of three seconds, it has moved forward 26 meters.

The instantaneous velocity function is $v(t) = s'(t) = 2t + 4$.

$$v(3) = 2(3) + 4 = 10\frac{m}{s}$$

At the end of three seconds, it is moving at a velocity of 10 meters per second.

The acceleration function is $a(t) = v'(t) = 2$.

$$a(3) = 2\ \frac{m}{s^2}$$

At the end of three seconds, it is accelerating, or its velocity is increasing, at a rate of 2 meters per second per second.

2. *State the derivative relationship between the general equations for motion (position, velocity, and acceleration) and use this relationship to formulate the velocity and acceleration equations for the position equation $s(t) = t^2 + 4t - 7$.*

The relationship among the three functions is one of rate of change. Velocity is the rate of change of position, and acceleration is the rate of change of velocity. Therefore, one is the derivative of another.

If $s(t)$ is the function that represents the position of an object where t is the time, then:

$$v(t) = s'(t)$$

or, in word form, the instantaneous velocity is equal to the derivative of the position function.

$$a(t) = v'(t)$$

or, in word form, the acceleration is equal to the derivative of the instantaneous velocity function.

By applying this relationship to the position function $s(t) = t^2 + 4t - 7$, we obtain the following equations of velocity and acceleration.

$$v(t) = s'(t) = 2t + 4$$

$$a(t) = v'(t) = 2$$

3. *Suppose that the function $s(t) = t^3$ represents the position of a car that begins moving in a straight line (in units of feet and seconds). Find its position, velocity, and acceleration at the end of four seconds.*

The position function is $s(t) = t^3$. Therefore,

$$s(4) = 4^3 = 64 \text{ feet}$$

At the end of four seconds, it has moved forward 64 feet.

The instantaneous velocity function is $v(t) = s'(t) = 3t^2$

$$v(4) = 3(4)^2 = 48\frac{\text{ft}}{\text{s}}$$

At the end of four seconds, it is moving at a velocity of 48 feet per second.

The acceleration function is $a(t) = v'(t) = 6t$

$$a(4) = 6(4) = 24\frac{\text{ft}}{\text{s}^2}$$

At the end of four seconds, it is accelerating, or its velocity is increasing, at a rate of 24 feet per second per second.

4. *Suppose that the function $s(t) = 4t^3$ represents the position of a rocket that has been fired in a straight line. The position is measured in feet, and t is the time in seconds that has elapsed since its motion started. Determine the instantaneous rate of change of $s(t)$ at the time of $t =$ 3.*

The instantaneous rate of change measures the slope of a function at a certain point. Therefore, the instantaneous rate of change is expressed by the derivative. For this problem, the position of the rocket is given by the equation $s(t) = 4t^3$. Using the power rule for differentiation, the equation for velocity is obtained.

$$\begin{aligned} s'(t) &= 3 \times 4t^{3-1} \\ &= 12t^2 \\ s'(3) &= 12(3)^2 \\ &= 108\frac{\text{ft}}{\text{s}} \end{aligned}$$

108 feet per second is the instantaneous velocity of the rocket at an elapsed time of 3 seconds.

Using First and Second Derivatives

The **first derivative** of a function is equal to the **rate of change** of the function. The sign of the rate of change shows whether the value of the function is **increasing** or **decreasing**. A positive rate of change—and therefore a positive first derivative—represents that the function is increasing at that point. A negative rate of change represents that the function is decreasing. If the rate of change is zero, the function is not changing, i.e. it is constant.

For example, consider the function $f(x) = x^3 - 6x^2 - 15x + 12$. The derivative of this function is $f'(x) = 3x^2 - 12x - 15 = 3(x^2 - 4x - 5) = 3(x - 5)(x + 1)$. This derivative is a quadratic function with zeroes at $x = 5$ and $x = -1$; by plugging in points in each interval we can find that

$f'(x)$ is positive when $x < -1$ and when $x > 5$ and negative when $-1 < x < 5$. Thus $f(x)$ is increasing in the interval $(-\infty, -1) \cup (5, \infty)$ and decreasing in the interval $(-1, 5)$.

EXTREMA

The **maximum** and **minimum** of a function are collectively called the **extrema** of the function. Both maxima and minima can be local, also known as relative, or absolute. A local maximum or minimum refers to the value of a function near a certain value of *x*. An absolute maximum or minimum refers to the value of a function on a given interval.

The local maximum of a function is the largest value that the function attains near a certain value of *x*. For example, function *f* has a local maximum at $x = b$ if $f(b)$ is the largest value that *f* attains as it approaches *b*.

Conversely, the local minimum is the smallest value that the function attains near a certain value of *x*. In other words, function *f* has a local minimum at $x = b$ if $f(b)$ is the smallest value that f attains as it approaches *b*.

The absolute maximum of a function is the largest value of the function over a certain interval. The function f has an absolute maximum at $x = b$ if $f(b) \geq f(x)$ for all *x* in the domain of *f*.

The absolute minimum of a function is the smallest value of the function over a certain interval. The function *f* has an absolute minimum at $x = b$ if $f(b) \leq f(x)$ for all *x* in the domain of *f*.

CRITICAL POINTS

Remember Rolle's Theorem, which states that if two points have the same value in the range that there must be a point between them where the slope of the graph is zero. This point is located at a peak or valley on the graph. A **peak** is a maximum point, and a **valley** is a minimum point. The relative minimum is the lowest point on a graph for a given section of the graph. It may or may not be the same as the absolute minimum, which is the lowest point on the entire graph. The relative maximum is the highest point on one section of the graph. Again, it may or may not be the same as the absolute maximum. A relative extremum (plural extrema) is a relative minimum or relative maximum point on a graph.

A **critical point** is a point (*x*, *f(x)*) that is part of the domain of a function, such that either $f'(x) = 0$ or $f'(x)$ does not exist. If either of these conditions is true, then *x* is either an inflection point or a point at which the slope of the curve changes sign. If the slope changes sign, then a relative minimum or maximum occurs.

In graphing an equation with relative extrema, use a sign diagram to approximate the shape of the graph. Once you have determined the relative extrema, calculate the sign of a point on either side of each critical point. This will give a general shape of the graph, and you will know whether each critical point is a relative minimum, a relative maximum, or a point of inflection.

FIRST DERIVATIVE TEST

Remember that critical points occur where the slope of the curve is 0. Also remember that the **first derivative** of a function gives the slope of the curve at a particular point on the curve. Because of this property of the first derivative, the first derivative test can be used to determine if a critical point is a minimum or maximum. If $f'(x)$ is negative at a point to the left of a critical number and $f'(x)$ is positive at a point to the right of a critical number, then the critical number is a relative minimum. If $f'(x)$ is positive to the left of a critical number and $f'(x)$ is negative to the right of a critical number, then the critical number is a relative maximum. If $f'(x)$ has the same sign on both sides, then the critical number is a point of inflection.

Second Derivative Test

The **second derivative**, designated by $f''(x)$, is helpful in determining whether the relative extrema of a function are relative maximums or relative minimums. If the second derivative at the critical point is greater than zero, the critical point is a relative minimum. If the second derivative at the critical point is less than zero, the critical point is a relative maximum. If the second derivative at the critical point is equal to zero, you must use the first derivative test to determine whether the point is a relative minimum or a relative maximum.

There are a couple of ways to determine the concavity of the graph of a function. To test a portion of the graph that contains a point with domain *p*, find the second derivative of the function and evaluate it for *p*. If $f''(p) > 0$, then the graph is concave upward at that point. If $f''(p) < 0$, then the graph is concave downward at that point.

The **point of inflection** on the graph of a function is the point at which the concavity changes from concave downward to concave upward or from concave upward to concave downward. The easiest way to find the points of inflection is to find the second derivative of the function and then solve the equation $f''(x) = 0$. Remember that if $f''(p) > 0$, the graph is concave upward, and if $f''(p) < 0$, the graph is concave downward. Logically, the concavity changes at the point when

$$f''(p) = 0$$

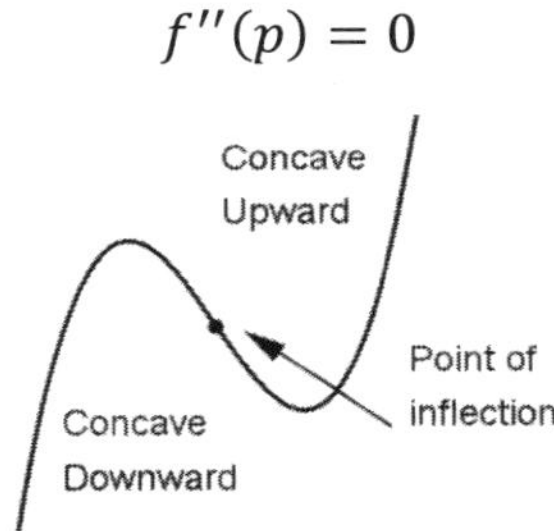

The derivative tests that have been discussed thus far can help you get a rough picture of what the graph of an unfamiliar function looks like. Begin by solving the equation $f(x) = 0$ to find all the zeros of the function, if they exist. Plot these points on the graph. Then, find the first derivative of the function and solve the equation $f'(x) = 0$ to find the critical points. Remember the numbers obtained here are the *x* portions of the coordinates. Substitute these values for *x* in the original function and solve for *y* to get the full coordinates of the points. Plot these points on the graph. Take the second derivative of the function and solve the equation $f''(x) = 0$ to find the points of inflection. Substitute in the original function to get the coordinates and graph these points. Test points on both sides of the critical points to test for concavity and draw the curve.

Derivative Problems

A **derivative** represents the **rate of change** of a function, thus derivatives are a useful tool for solving any problem that involves finding the rate at which a function is changing. In its simplest form, such a problem might provide a formula for a quantity as a function of time and ask for its rate of change at a particular time.

If the temperature in a chamber in degrees Celsius is equal to $T(t) = 20 + e^{-t/2}$, where *t* is the time in seconds, then the derivative of the function represents the *rate of change of the temperature over time*. The rate of change is equal to $\frac{dT}{dt} = \frac{d}{dt}\left(20 + e^{-t/2}\right) = -\frac{1}{2}e^{-t/2}$, and the initial rate of change is $T'(0) = -\frac{1}{2}e^{-0/2} = -\frac{1}{2}\frac{°C}{s}$.

Suppose we are told that the net profit that a small company makes when it produces and sells x units of a product is equal to $P(x) = 200x - 20000$. The derivative of this function would be the *additional profit for each additional unit sold*, a quantity known as the marginal profit. The marginal profit in this case is $P'(x) = 200$.

Solving Related Rates Problems

A *related rate problem* is one in which one variable has a relation with another variable, and the rate of change of one of the variables is known. With that information, the rate of change of the other variable can be determined. The first step in solving related rates problems is defining the known rate of change. Then, determine the relationship between the two variables, then the derivatives (the rates of change), and finally substitute the problem's specific values.

Sample Problem

Use the method to solve the following problem: the side of a cube is increasing at a rate of 2 feet per second. Determine the rate at which the volume of the cube is increasing when the side of the cube is 4 feet long.

For the problem in question, the known rate of change can be expressed as $s'(t) = 2\frac{\text{ft}}{\text{s}}$, where s is the length of the side and t is the elapsed time in seconds. The relationship between the two variables of the cube is $v = s^3$, where v is the volume of the cube and s is the length of the side. The unknown rate of change to determine is the volume. As both v and s change with time,

$$v = s^3 \text{ becomes } v(t) = [s(t)]^3$$

Now, the chain rule is applied to differentiate both sides of the equation with respect to t.

$$d\frac{v(t)}{dt} = \frac{d[s(t)]^3}{dt}; \frac{dv}{dt} = \frac{(2[s(t)]^2)ds}{dt}$$

Finally, the specific value of $s = 4$ feet is substituted, and the equation is evaluated.

$$\begin{aligned}\frac{dv}{dt} &= \frac{(2[s(t)]^2)ds}{dt} \\ &= 2(4)^2 \times 2 = 64\frac{\text{ft}^3}{\text{s}} \\ &= 64 \text{ cubic}\frac{\text{ft}}{\text{s}}\end{aligned}$$

Therefore, when a side of the cube is 4 feet long, the volume of the cube is increasing at a rate of 64 cubic feet/second .

Solving Optimization Problems

An **optimization problem** is a problem in which we are asked to find the value of a variable that maximizes or minimizes a particular value. Because the maximum or maximum occurs at a critical point, and because the critical point occurs when the derivative of the function is zero, we can solve an optimization problem by setting the derivative of the function to zero and solving for the desired variable.

For example, suppose a farmer has 720 m of fencing, and wants to use it to fence in a 2 by 3 block of identical rectangular pens. What dimensions of the pens will maximize their area?

We can draw a diagram:

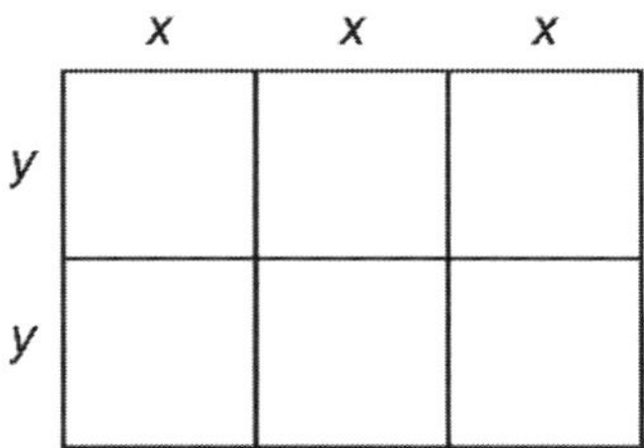

We want to maximize the area of the pens, $A(x, y) = xy$. However, we have the additional constraint that the farmer has only 720 m of fencing. In terms of x and y the total amount of fencing required will be $9x + 8y$. Our constraint becomes $9x + 8y = 720$; solving for y yields $y = -\frac{9}{8}x + 90$. We can substitute that into the area equation to get $A(x) = x\left(-\frac{9}{8}x + 90\right) = -\frac{9}{8}x^2 + 90x$. Taking the derivative yields $A'(x) = -\frac{9}{4}x + 90$; setting that to zero and solving for x yields $x = 40$. $y = -\frac{9}{8}(40) + 90 = 45$, thus, the maximum dimensions of the pen are 40 by 45 meters.

Characteristics of Functions (Using Calculus)

Rolle's Theorem states that if a differentiable function has two different values in the domain that correspond to a single value in the range, then the function must have a point between them where the slope of the tangent to the graph is zero. This point will be a maximum or a minimum value of the function between those two points. The maximum or minimum point is the point at which $f'(c) = 0$, where c is within the appropriate interval of the function's domain. The following graph shows a function with one maximum in the second quadrant and one minimum in the fourth quadrant.

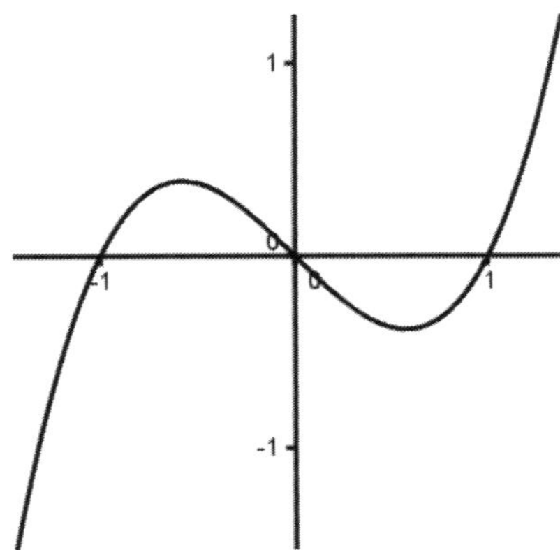

Mean Value Theorem

According to the Mean Value Theorem, between any two points on a curve, there exists a tangent to the curve whose slope is parallel to the chord formed by joining those two points. Remember the formula for slope: $m = \frac{\Delta x}{\Delta y}$. In a function, $f(x)$ represents the value for y. Therefore, if you have two points on a curve, m and n, the corresponding points are $(m, f(m))$ and $(n, f(n))$. Assuming $m < n$, the formula for the slope of the chord joining those two points is $\frac{f(n)-f(m)}{n-m}$. This must also be the slope of a line parallel to the chord, since parallel lines have equal slopes. Therefore, there must be a value p between m and n such that $f'(p) = \frac{f(n)-f(m)}{n-m}$.

For a function to have continuity, its graph must be an unbroken curve. That is, it is a function that can be graphed without having to lift the pencil to move it to a different point. To say a function is continuous at point p, you must show the function satisfies three requirements. First, $f(p)$ must exist. If you evaluate the function at p, it must yield a real number. Second, there must exist a relationship such that $\lim_{x \to p} f(x) = f(p)$. Finally, the following relationship must be true:

$$\lim_{x \to p^+} F(x) = \lim_{x \to p^-} F(x) = F(p)$$

If all three of these requirements are met, a function is considered continuous at p. If any one of them is not true, the function is not continuous at p.

Tangents

Tangents are lines that touch a curve in exactly one point and have the same slope as the curve at that point. To find the slope of a curve at a given point and the slope of its tangent line at that point, find the derivative of the function of the curve. If the slope is undefined, the tangent is a vertical line. If the slope is zero, the tangent is a horizontal line.

A line that is normal to a curve at a given point is perpendicular to the tangent at that point. Assuming $f'(x) \neq 0$, the equation for the normal line at point (a, b) is: $y - b = -\frac{1}{f'(a)}(x - a)$. The easiest way to find the slope of the normal is to take the negative reciprocal of the slope of the tangent. If the slope of the tangent is zero, the slope of the normal is undefined. If the slope of the tangent is undefined, the slope of the normal is zero.

Antiderivatives (Integrals)

The antiderivative of a function is the function whose first derivative is the original function. Antiderivatives are typically represented by capital letters, while their first derivatives are represented by lower case letters. For example, if $F' = f$, then F is the antiderivative of f. Antiderivatives are also known as indefinite integrals. When taking the derivative of a function, any constant terms in the function are eliminated because their derivative is 0. To account for this possibility, when you take the indefinite integral of a function, you must add an unknown constant C to the end of the function. Because there is no way to know what the value of the original constant was when looking just at the first derivative, the integral is indefinite.

To find the indefinite integral, reverse the process of differentiation. Below are the formulas for constants and powers of x.

$$\int 0\,dx = C$$

$$\int k\,dx = kx + C$$

$$\int x^n\,dx = \frac{x^{n+1}}{n+1} + C, \text{ where } n \neq -1$$

Recall that in the differentiation of powers of x, you multiplied the coefficient of the term by the exponent of the variable and then reduced the exponent by one. In integration, the process is reversed: add one to the value of the exponent, and then divide the coefficient of the term by this number to get the integral. Because you do not know the value of any constant term that might have been in the original function, add C to the end of the function once you have completed this process for each term.

Review Video: Indefinite Integrals
Visit mometrix.com/academy and enter code: 541913

Finding the integral of a function is the opposite of finding the derivative of the function. Where possible, you can use the trigonometric or logarithmic differentiation formulas in reverse, and add C to the end to compensate for the unknown term. In instances where a negative sign appears in the differentiation formula, move the negative sign to the opposite side (multiply both sides by -1) to reverse for the integration formula. You should end up with the following formulas:

$$\int \cos x \ dx = \sin x + C$$
$$\int \sec x \tan x \ dx = \sec x + C$$
$$\int \sin x \ dx = -\cos x + C$$
$$\int \csc x \cot x \ dx = -\csc x + C$$
$$\int \sec^2 x \ dx = \tan x + C$$
$$\int \csc^2 x \ dx = -\cot x + C$$
$$\int \frac{1}{x} \ dx = \ln |x| + C$$
$$\int e^x \ dx = e^x + C$$

Integration by substitution is the integration version of the chain rule for differentiation. The formula for integration by substitution is given by the equation

$$f\big(g(x)\big)g'(x)dx = \int f(u)du \, ; u = g(x) \text{ and } du = g'(x)dx.$$

When a function is in a format that is difficult or impossible to integrate using traditional integration methods and formulas due to multiple functions being combined, use the formula shown above to convert the function to a simpler format that can be integrated directly.

Integration by parts is the integration version of the product rule for differentiation. Whenever you are asked to find the integral of the product of two different functions or parts, integration by parts can make the process simpler. Recall for differentiation $(fg)'(x) = f(x)g'(x) + g(x)f'(x)$. This can also be written $\frac{d}{dx}(u \cdot v) = u\frac{dv}{dx} + v\frac{du}{dx}$, where $u = f(x)$ and $v = g(x)$. Rearranging to integral form gives the formula:

$$\int u \ dv = uv - \int v \ du$$

which can also be written as:

$$\int f(x)g'(x)\,dx = f(x)g(x) - \int f'(x)g(x)\,dx$$

When using integration by parts, the key is selecting the best functions to substitute for u and v so that you make the integral easier to solve and not harder.

While the indefinite integral has an undefined constant added at the end, the definite integral can be calculated as an exact real number. To find the definite integral of a function over a closed interval, use the formula

$$\int_n^m f(x)\,dx = F(m) - F(n)$$

where F is the integral of f. Because you have been given the boundaries of n and m, no undefined constant C is needed.

First Fundamental Theorem of Calculus

The First Fundamental Theorem of Calculus shows that the process of indefinite integration can be reversed by finding the first derivative of the resulting function. It also gives the relationship between differentiation and integration over a closed interval of the function. For example, assuming a function is continuous over the interval $[m, n]$, you can find the definite integral by using the formula $\int_m^n f(x)\,dx = F(n) - F(m)$. Many times the notation $\int_m^n f(x)\,dx = F(x)\,\big|_m^n = F(n) - F(m)$ is also used to represent the Fundamental Theorem of Calculus. To find the average value of the function over the given interval, use the formula $\frac{1}{n-m}\int_m^n f(x)\,dx$.

Sample Problem

Use the First Fundamental Theorem of Calculus to evaluate:

$\int_0^1 (x^3 + 2x)dx$ and $\int_{-1}^0 (3x^3 + 2)dx$

The First Fundamental Theorem of Calculus states that if F is an antiderivative of f, then:

$$\int_a^b f(x)dx = F(b) - F(a)$$

Therefore,

$$\int_0^1 (x^3 + 2x)dx = \frac{x^4}{4} + x^2\Bigg|_{x=0}^{1} = \frac{(1)^4}{4} + (1)^2 - \left(\frac{(0)^4}{4} + (0)^2\right)$$
$$= \frac{5}{4} - 0 = \frac{5}{4}$$

Likewise,

$$\int_{-1}^0 (3x^2 + 2)dx = x^3 + 2x\Bigg|_{x=-1}^{0} = (0)^3 + 2(0) - \left((-1)^3 + 2(-1)\right)$$
$$= 0 - (-3) = 3$$

Second Fundamental Theorem of Calculus

The Second Fundamental Theorem of Calculus is related to the first. This theorem states that, assuming the function is continuous over the interval you are considering, taking the derivative of the integral of a function will yield the original function. The general format for this theorem is $\frac{d}{dx}\int_c^x f(x)\,dx = f(x)$ for any point having a domain value equal to c in the given interval.

For each of the following properties of integrals of function f, the variables m, n, and p represent values in the domain of the given interval of $f(x)$. The function is assumed to be integrable across all relevant intervals.

$$\int_n^n f(x)\,dx = 0$$
$$\int_m^n f(x)\,dx = -\int_n^m f(x)\,dx$$
$$\int_m^n kf(x)dx = k\int_m^n f(x)\,dx$$
$$\int_m^n f(x)\,dx = \int_m^p f(x)\,dx + \int_p^n f(x)\,dx$$

If $f(x)$ is an even function, then

$$\int_{-m}^m f(x)\,dx = 2\int_0^m f(x)\,dx$$

If $f(x)$ is an odd function, then

$$\int_{-m}^m f(x)\,dx = 0$$

Matching Functions to Derivatives or Accumulations

Derivatives

We can use what we know about the meaning of a **derivative** to match the graph of a function with a graph of its derivative. For one thing, we know that where the function has a critical point, the derivative is zero. Therefore, at every x value at which the graph of a function has a maximum or minimum, the derivative must cross the x axis—and conversely, everywhere the graph of the derivative crosses the x axis, the function must have a critical point: either a maximum, a minimum, or an inflection point. If this is still not enough to identify the correct match, we can also use the fact that the sign of the derivative corresponds to whether the function is increasing or decreasing: everywhere the graph of the derivative is above the x axis, the function must be increasing (its slope is positive), and everywhere the graph of the derivative is below the x axis, the function must be decreasing (its slope is negative).

For example, below are graphs of the function and its derivative. The maxima and minima of the function (left) are circled, and the zeroes of the derivative (right) are circled.

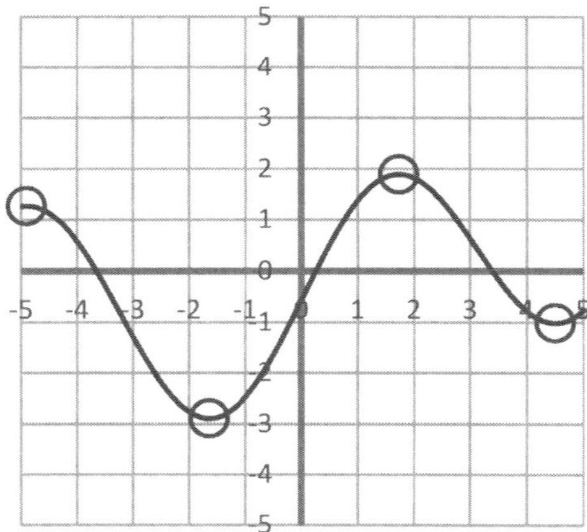

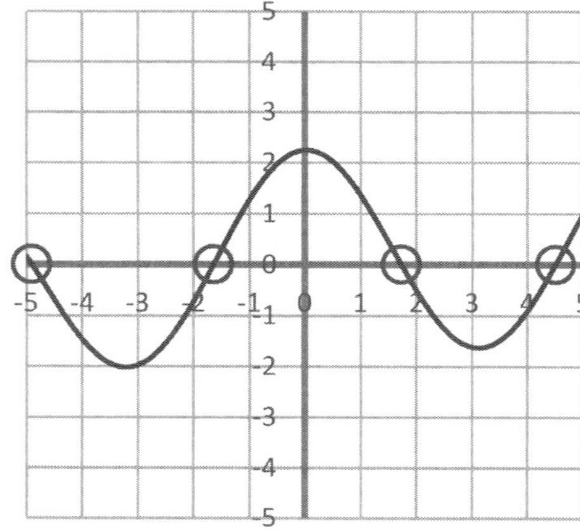

ACCUMULATIONS

The **accumulation** of a function is another name for its **antiderivative**, or **integral**. We can use the relationship between a function and its antiderivative to match the corresponding graphs. For example, we know that where the graph of the function is above the x axis, the function is positive, thus the accumulation must be increasing (its slope is positive); where the graph of the function is below the x axis, the accumulation must be decreasing (its slope is negative). It follows that where the function changes from positive to negative—where the graph crosses the x axis with a negative slope—, its accumulation changes from increasing to decreasing—so the accumulation has a local maximum. Where the function changes from negative to positive—where its graph crosses the x axis with a positive slope—, the accumulation has a local minimum.

For example, below are graphs of a function and its accumulation. The points on the function (left) where the graph crosses the x axis are circled; the local minima and maxima of the accumulation (right) are circled.

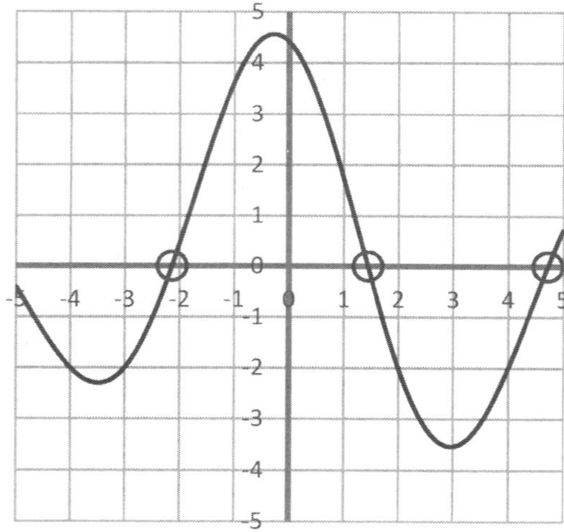

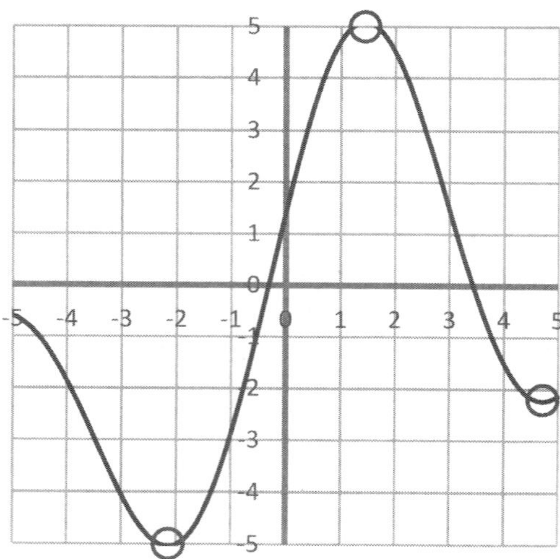

Mean Value Theorem of Integrals

For a discrete function with finitely many points, the **average value** of a function is simply the sum of all the values of the function, divided by the number of values. In the case of a continuous function, the definition is analogous: the average value of a function over an interval is equal to the **definite integral** of the function over that interval, divided by the **width** of the interval (that is, the difference between the endpoints of the interval).

For example, suppose we are told that the temperature in a chamber changes over time according to the function $T(t) = 10(t+1)e^{-t}$, where t is the time in minutes and T is the temperature in degrees Celsius, and we are asked to find the average temperature in the chamber during the first three minutes. We can find the integral of this function using integration by parts: $e^{-t} = \frac{d}{dt}(-e^{-t})$, thus: $\int 10(t+1)e^{-t}\,dt = 10\int (t+1)\frac{d}{dt}(-e^{-t})dt = 10(t+1)(-e^{-t}) - 10\int \frac{d}{dt}(t+1)(-e^{-t})dt = -10(t+1)e^{-t} - 10\int (1)(-e^{-t})dt = -10(t+1)e^{-t} - 10e^{-t} = -10(t+2)e^{-t}$.

Now, the definite integral of $T(t)$ over the interval $[0,3]$ is $\int_0^3 (-10(t+1)e^{-t})dt = [-10(t+2)e^{-t}]_0^3 = -10(3+2)e^{-3} - (-10(0+2)e^{-0}) = 17.511$. The average value of the function in this interval is just this value divided by the width of the interval: $\frac{17.511}{3-0} = 5.837$ °C.

Riemann Sums

A **Riemann sum** is a sum used to approximate the definite integral of a function over a particular interval by dividing the area under the function into vertical rectangular strips and adding the areas of the strips. The height of each strip is equal to the value of the function at some point within the interval covered by the strip. Formally, if we divide the interval over which we are finding the area into n intervals bounded by the $n+1$ points $\{x_i\}$ (where x_0 and x_n are the left and right bounds of the interval), then the Riemann sum is $\sum_{i=1}^{n} f(x_i^*)\Delta x_i$, where $\Delta x_i = x_i - x_{i-1}$ and x_i^* is some point in the interval $[x_{i-1}, x_i]$. In principle, any point in the interval can be chosen, but common choices include the left endpoint of the interval (yielding the **left Riemann sum**), the right endpoint (yielding the **right Riemann sum**), and the midpoint of the interval (the basis of the **midpoint rule**). Usually it is convenient to set all the intervals to the same width, although the definition of the Riemann sum does not require this.

The following graphic shows the rectangular strips used for one possible Riemann sum of a particular function:

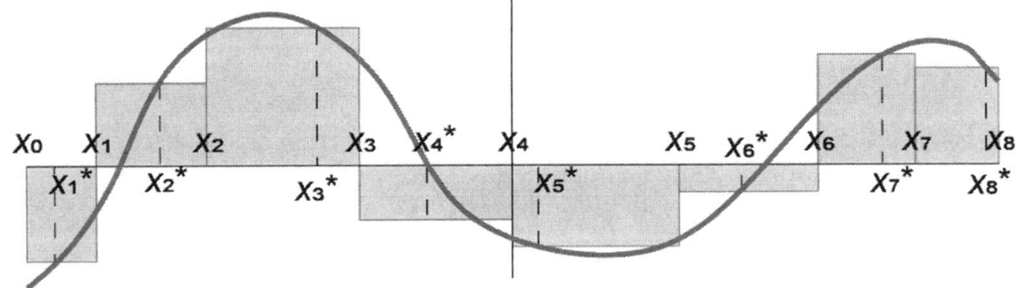

Left and Right Riemann Sums

A **Riemann sum** is an approximation to the definite integral of a function over a particular interval performed by dividing it into smaller intervals and summing the products of the width of each interval and the value of the function evaluated at some point within the interval. The **left Riemann**

sum is a Riemann sum in which the function is evaluated at the *left* endpoint of each interval. In the **right Riemann sum**, the function is evaluated at the *right* endpoint of each interval.

When the function is *increasing*, the left Riemann sum will always *underestimate* the function. This is because we are evaluating the function at the *minimum* point within each interval; the integral of the function in the interval will be larger than the estimate. Conversely, the right Riemann sum is evaluating the function at the *maximum* point within each interval, thus it will always *overestimate* the function. Consider the following diagrams, in which the area under the same increasing function is shown approximated by a left Riemann sum and a right Riemann sum:

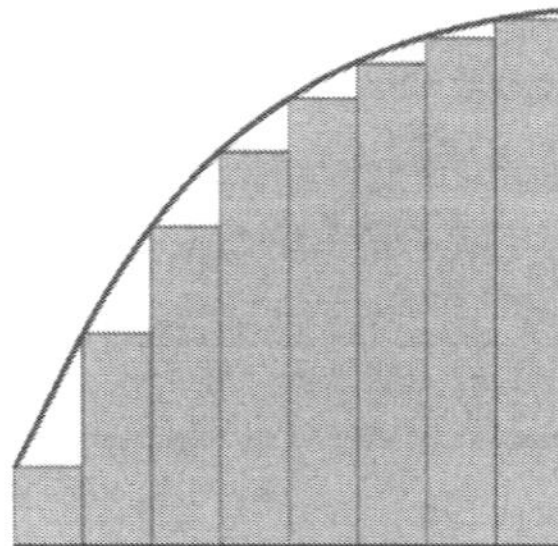

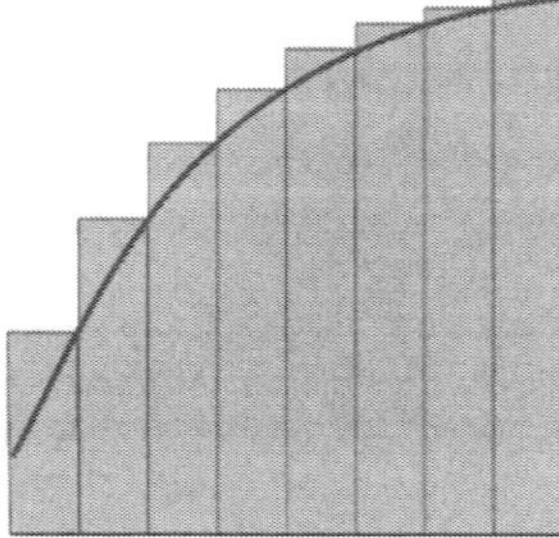

For a *de*creasing function these considerations are reversed: a left Riemann sum will overestimate the integral, and a right Riemann sum will underestimate it.

MIDPOINT RULE

The **midpoint rule** is a way of approximating the definite integral of a function over an interval by dividing the interval into smaller sub-intervals, multiplying the width of each sub-interval by the value of the function at the midpoint of the sub-interval, and then summing these products. This is a special case of the **Riemann sum**, specifying the midpoint of the interval as the point at which the function is to be evaluated. The approximation found using the midpoint rule is usually more accurate than that found using the left or right Riemann sum, though as the number of intervals becomes very large the difference becomes negligible.

For example, suppose we are asked to estimate by the midpoint rule the integral of $f(x) = \frac{1}{x}$ in the interval [2, 4]. We can divide this interval into four intervals of width $\frac{1}{2}$: [2, 2.5], [2.5, 3], [3, 3.5], and [3.5, 4]. (The more intervals, the more accurate the estimate, but we'll use a small number of intervals in this example to keep it simple.) The midpoint rule then gives an estimate of $\frac{1}{2}\left(f(2.25)\right) + \frac{1}{2}\left(f(2.75)\right) + \frac{1}{2}\left(f(3.25)\right) + \frac{1}{2}\left(f(3.75)\right) = \frac{1}{2}\left(\frac{4}{9}\right) + \frac{1}{2}\left(\frac{4}{11}\right) + \frac{1}{2}\left(\frac{4}{13}\right) + \frac{1}{2}\left(\frac{4}{15}\right) \approx 0.691$, not far from the actual value of $\int_2^4 \frac{1}{x}dx = [\ln x]_2^4 \approx 0.693$.

TRAPEZOID RULE

The **trapezoid rule** is a method of approximating the definite integral of a function by dividing the area under the function into a series of trapezoidal strips, the upper corners of the trapezoid touching the function, and adding the areas of the strips. The following diagram shows the use of the trapezoid rule to estimate the integral of the function $y = 2^x$ in the interval $[0, 3]$:

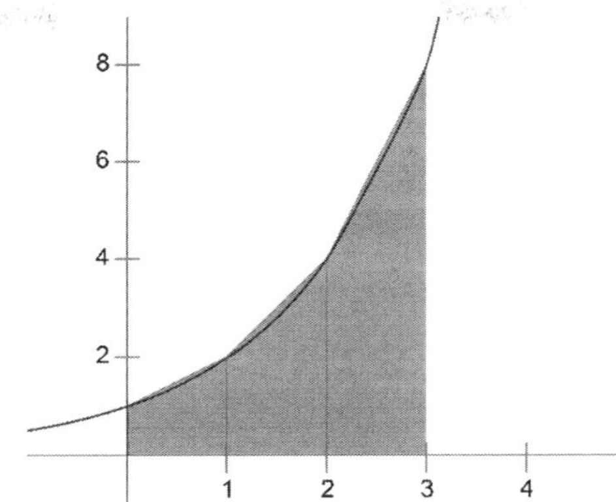

Mathematically, if we define the endpoints of the n subdivisions to be $\{x_i\}$, where x_0 and x_n are the endpoints of the entire interval over which we are estimating the integral, then the result of the application of the trapezoid rule is equal to $\sum_{i=1}^{n}\left(\frac{x_{i-1}+x_i}{2}\right)(x_i - x_{i-1})$. For the example shown above, that yields $\left(\frac{2^1+2^0}{2}\right)(1-0) + \left(\frac{2^2+2^1}{2}\right)(2-1) + \left(\frac{2^3+2^2}{2}\right)(3-2) = \frac{21}{2}$, or 10.5—not far from the actual value of $\int_0^3 2^x dx = \int_0^3 e^{x\ln 2}\,dx = \left[\frac{2^x}{\ln 2}\right]_0^3 \approx 10.1$. (Of course, we could have achieved more accuracy by using smaller subdivisions.)

The trapezoid rule is related to the Riemann sum, but usually gives more accurate results than the left or right Riemann sum for the same number of intervals. In fact, it isn't hard to prove that the answer given by the trapezoid rule is equal to the average of the left and right Riemann sums using the same partition.

Limit of Riemann Sums

As the number of sub-intervals becomes larger, and the width of each sub-interval becomes smaller, the approximation becomes increasingly accurate, and at the limit as the number of sub-intervals approaches infinity and their width approaches zero, the value becomes exact. In fact, the definite integral is often *defined* as a limit of Riemann sums.

It's possible to find the definite integral by this method. Suppose we want to find the integral of $f(x) = x^2$ over the interval $[0, 2]$. We'll divide this interval into n sub-intervals of equal width and evaluate the function at the right endpoint of each sub-interval. (This choice is arbitrary; at the limit the answer would be the same if we chose the left endpoint, or any other point within the interval.) Our Riemann sum becomes $\sum_{i=1}^{n}\frac{2}{n}\left(\frac{2}{n}i\right)^2 = \frac{8}{n^3}\sum_{i=1}^{n} i^2 . \sum_{i=1}^{n} i^2 = \frac{1}{6}n(n+1)(2n+1)$, thus this becomes $\frac{8}{n^3}\cdot\frac{1}{6}n(n+1)(2n+1) = \frac{4}{3}\left(1+\frac{1}{n}\right)\left(2+\frac{1}{n}\right)$. At the limit as $n \to \infty$, this becomes $\frac{4}{3}(1)(2) = \frac{8}{3}$. This is the same result as we get by integrating directly: $\int_0^2 x^2 dx = \left[\frac{1}{3}x^3\right]_0^2 = \frac{1}{3}2^3 - \frac{1}{3}0^3 = \frac{8}{3}$.

Integration Techniques

Accumulation Processes

The definite integral of a function represents the accumulated value of the function over an interval. Therefore, given a function representing a process that has a cumulative value, we can find that cumulative value by taking the definite integral of the function and adding the initial value. (This last step is important, and often forgotten—since the definite integral is the *change* in the accumulated value over the interval, it is necessary to add the initial value to find the final value of the **accumulation**.)

For example, suppose that we're told that the amount of water flowing into a basin is represented by the equation $q(t) = \frac{10t}{(t+1)^2}$, where t is the time in hours and $q(t)$ is the amount of water in liters per hour. The basin initially contains 20 liters, and we want to know how much it contains after one day. We can find this by taking the definite integral of the rate of flow: $\int_0^{24} \frac{10t}{(t+1)^2} = 10\int_0^{24}\left(\frac{t+1}{(t+1)^2} - \frac{1}{(t+1)^2}\right)dt = \int_0^{24}\frac{1}{t+1}dt - \int_0^{24}\frac{1}{(t+1)^2}dt = 10\left[\ln(t+1) + \frac{1}{t+1}\right]_0^{24} \approx 22.6$ liters. This is the *change* in the amount of water; we can find the final *amount* of water by adding the initial amount: 20 liters + 22.6 liters = 42.6 liters.

Calculating Areas

One way to calculate the area of an irregular shape is to find a formula for the width of the shape along the *x* direction as a function of the *y* coordinate, and then integrate over *y*, or vice versa. Effectively, what this amounts to is dividing the area into thin strips and adding the areas of the strips—and then taking the limit as the width of the strips approaches zero.

For example, suppose we want to find the area enclosed by the functions $y_1 = x^2$ and $y_2 = (2 - x^2)$. The height of this enclosure is equal to $y_2 - y_1 = 2 - 2x^2$; we can find the area by integrating this height over *x*. The two shapes intersect at the points $(1, 1)$ and $(-1, 1)$, thus our limits of integration are –1 and 1. Thus the area can be found as $\int_{-1}^{1}(2 - 2x^2)dx = \left[2x - \frac{2}{3}x^3\right]_{-1}^{1} = \left(2 - \frac{2}{3}\right) - \left(-2 + \frac{2}{3}\right) = \frac{8}{3}$.

Calculating Volumes

One way to calculate the **volume** of a three-dimensional shape is to find a formula for its cross-sectional area perpendicular to some axis and then integrate over that axis. Effectively, what this amounts to is dividing the shape into thin, flat slices and adding the volumes of the slices—and then taking the limit as the thickness of the slices approaches zero.

For example, suppose we want to find the area of the ellipsoid $4x^2 + 4y^2 + z^2 = 36$. If we take a cross-section parallel to the *z* axis, this has the formula $4x^2 + 4y^2 = 36 - z^2$, or $x^2 + y^2 = 9 - \frac{z^2}{4}$; this is the formula of a circle with a radius of $\sqrt{9 - \frac{z^2}{4}}$, and thus has an area of $\pi\left(9 - \frac{z^2}{4}\right)$. To find the volume, we integrate this formula over *z*. The maximum and minimum values of *z* occur when $x = y = 0$, and then $z^2 = 36$, thus $z = \pm 6$; these are our limits of integration. Thus, the volume is $\int_{-6}^{6}\pi\left(9 - \frac{z^2}{4}\right)dz = \pi\left[9z - \frac{z^3}{12}\right]_{-6}^{6} = 72\pi \approx 226.2$.

Calculating Distances

When given the velocity of an object over time, it's possible to find a **distance** by **integration**. The velocity is the rate of change of the position, therefore the distance is the accumulation of the velocity: that is, the integral of the velocity is the distance. However, if asked to find the total distance traveled (as opposed to the displacement), it's important to take the sign into account: we must integrate not just the velocity, but the *absolute value* of the velocity, which essentially means integrating separately over each interval in which the velocity has a different sign.

For example, suppose we're asked to find the total distance traveled from $t = 0$ to $t = 8$ by an object moving with a velocity in meters per second given by the equation $v(t) = 2\sqrt{t} - t$. This function is zero when $2\sqrt{t} - t = 0 \Rightarrow \sqrt{t}(2 - \sqrt{t}) = 0 \Rightarrow t = 0$ or 4. $v(t)$ is positive when $0 < t < 4$ and negative when $t > 4$. Thus the distance travelled is $\int_0^8 |v(t)|dt = \int_0^8 |2\sqrt{t} - t|dt = \int_0^4 (2\sqrt{t} - t)dt - \int_4^8 (2\sqrt{t} - t)dt = \left[\frac{4}{3}t^{3/2} - \frac{1}{2}t^2\right]_0^4 - \left[\frac{4}{3}t^{3/2} - \frac{1}{2}t^2\right]_4^8 = \frac{8}{3} - \frac{8}{3}(8\sqrt{2} - 13) \approx$ 7.16 meters.

Discrete Mathematics

Among mathematicians, there is not an agreed-upon definition of discrete math. What is agreed upon is the fact that discrete math deals with processes that use a finite, or countable, number of elements. In discrete math, the elements will be discontinuous, as this branch of mathematics does not involve the continuity that processes of calculus do. Generally, discrete math uses countable sets of rational numbers, although they do not use the set of all real numbers, as that would then make the math continuous and put it in the category of algebra or calculus. Discrete math has numerous applications in the fields of computer science and business.

Factorials

The **factorial** is a function that can be performed on any **non-negative integer**. It is represented by the ! sign written after the integer on which it is being performed. The factorial of an integer is the product of all positive integers less than or equal to the number. For example, 4! (read "4 factorial") is calculated as $4 \times 3 \times 2 \times 1 = 24$.

Since 0 is not itself a positive integer, nor does it have any positive integers less than it, 0! cannot be calculated using this method. Instead, 0! is defined by convention to equal 1. This makes sense if you consider the pattern of descending factorials:

$$5! = 120$$
$$4! = \frac{5!}{5} = 24$$
$$3! = \frac{4!}{4} = 6$$
$$2! = \frac{3!}{3} = 2$$
$$1! = \frac{2!}{2} = 1$$
$$0! = \frac{1!}{1} = 1$$

Permutations and Combinations

Permutations

For any given set of data, the individual elements in the set may be arranged in different groups containing different numbers of elements arranged in different orders. For example, given the set of integers from one to three, inclusive, the elements of the set are 1, 2, and 3: written as {1, 2, 3}. They may be arranged as follows: 1, 2, 3, 12, 21, 13, 31, 23, 32, 123, 132, 213, 231, 312, and 321. These ordered sequences of elements from the given set of data are called **permutations**. It is important to note that in permutations, the order of the elements in the sequence is important. The sequence 123 is not the same as the sequence 213. Also, no element in the given set may be used more times as an element in a permutation than it appears as an element in the original set. For example, 223 is not a permutation in the above example because the number 2 only appears one time in the given set.

To find the number of permutations of *r* items from a set of *n* items, use the formula ${}_nP_r = \frac{n!}{(n-r)!}$. When using this formula, each element of *r* must be unique. Also, this assumes that different arrangements of the same set of elements yields different outcomes. For example, 123 is not the same as 321; order is important.

A special case arises while finding the number of possible permutations of *n* items from a set of *n* items. Because $n = r$, the equation for the number of permutations becomes simply $P = n!$.

If a set contains one or more groups of **indistinguishable or interchangeable elements** (e.g., the set {1, 2, 3, 3}, which has a group of two indistinguishable 3's), there is a different formula for finding distinct permutations of all *n* elements. Use the formula $P = \frac{n!}{m_1!m_2!...m_k!}$, where *P* is the number of permutations, *n* is the total number of elements in the set, and m_1 through m_k are the number of identical elements in each group (e.g., for the set {1, 1, 2, 2, 2, 3, 3}, $m_1 = 2$, $m_2 = 3$, and $m_3 = 2$). It is important to note that each repeated number is counted as its own element for the purpose of defining *n* (e.g., for the set {1, 1, 2, 2, 2, 3, 3}, $n = 7$, not 3).

To find the number of possible permutations of **any number of elements** in a set of unique elements, you must apply the permutation formulas multiple times. For example, to find the total number of possible permutations of the set {1, 2, 3} first apply the permutation formula for situations where $n = r$ as follows: $P = n! = 3! = 6$. This gives the number of permutations of the three elements when all three elements are used. To find the number of permutations when only two of the three elements are used, use the formula ${}_nP_r = \frac{n!}{(n-r)!}$, where *n* is 3 and *r* is 2.

$${}_nP_r = \frac{n!}{(n-r)!} \Rightarrow {}_3P_2 = \frac{3!}{(3-2)!} = \frac{6}{1} = 6$$

To find the number of permutations when one element is used, use the formula ${}_nP_r = \frac{n!}{(n-r)!}$, where *n* is 3 and *r* is 1.

$${}_nP_r = \frac{n!}{(n-r)!} \Rightarrow {}_3P_1 = \frac{3!}{(3-1)!} = \frac{3!}{2!} = \frac{6}{2} = 3$$

Find the sum of the three formulas: $6 + 6 + 3 = 15$ total possible permutations.

Alternatively, the general formula for total possible permutations can be written as follows:

$$P_T = \sum_{i=1}^{n} \frac{n!}{(i-1)!}$$

COMBINATIONS

Combinations are essentially defined as permutations where the order in which the elements appear does not matter. Going back to the earlier example of the set {1, 2, 3}, the possible combinations that can be made from that set are 1, 2, 3, 12, 13, 23, and 123.

In a set containing n elements, the number of combinations of r items from the set can be found using the formula ${}_nC_r = \frac{n!}{r!(n-r)!}$. Notice the similarity to the formula for permutations. In effect, you are dividing the number of permutations by $r!$ to get the number of combinations, and the formula may be written ${}_nC_r = \frac{{}_nP_r}{r!}$. When finding the number of combinations, it is important to remember that the elements in the set must be unique (i.e., there must not be any duplicate items), and that no item may be used more than once in any given sequence.

Review Video: Probability - Permutation and Combination
Visit mometrix.com/academy and enter code: 907664

Sequences

A sequence is a set of numbers that continues on in a define pattern. The function that defines a sequence has a domain composed of the set of positive integers. Each member of the sequence is an element, or individual term. Each element is identified by the notation a_n, where a is the term of the sequence, and n is the integer identifying which term in the sequence a is. There are two different ways to represent a sequence that contains the element a_n. The first is the simple notation $\{a_n\}$. The expanded notation of a sequence is $a_1, a_2, a_3, \dots a_n, \dots$. Notice that the expanded form does not end with the nth term. There is no indication that the nth term is the last term in the sequence, only that the nth term is an element of the sequence.

Limits

Some sequences will have a limit, or a value the sequence approaches or sometimes even reaches but never passes. A sequence that has a limit is known as a convergent sequence because all the values of the sequence seemingly converge at that point. Sequences that do not converge at a particular limit are divergent sequences. The easiest way to determine whether a sequence converges or diverges is to find the limit of the sequence. If the limit is a real number, the sequence is a convergent sequence. If the limit is infinity, the sequence is a divergent sequence.

Remember the following rules for finding limits:

$$\lim_{n\to\infty} k = k \text{ for all real numbers } k$$

$$\lim_{n\to\infty} \frac{1}{n} = 0$$

$$\lim_{n\to\infty} n = \infty$$

$$\lim_{n\to\infty} \frac{k}{n^p} = 0 \text{ for all real numbers } k \text{ and positive rational numbers } p.$$

The limit of the sums of two sequences is equal to the sum of the limits of the two sequences: $\lim_{n\to\infty}(a_n + b_n) = \lim_{n\to\infty} a_n + \lim_{n\to\infty} b_n$.

The limit of the difference between two sequences is equal to the difference between the limits of the two sequences:

$$\lim_{n\to\infty}(a_n - b_n) = \lim_{n\to\infty} a_n - \lim_{n\to\infty} b_n$$

The limit of the product of two sequences is equal to the product of the limits of the two sequences:

$$\lim_{n\to\infty}(a_n \cdot b_n) = \lim_{n\to\infty} a_n \cdot \lim_{n\to\infty} b_n$$

The limit of the quotient of two sequences is equal to the quotient of the limits of the two sequences, with some exceptions: $\lim_{n\to\infty}\left(\frac{a_n}{b_n}\right) = \frac{\lim_{n\to\infty} a_n}{\lim_{n\to\infty} b_n}$. In the quotient formula, it is important to consider that $b_n \neq 0$ and $\lim_{n\to\infty} b_n \neq 0$.

The limit of a sequence multiplied by a scalar is equal to the scalar multiplied by the limit of the sequence: $\lim_{n\to\infty} ka_n = k \lim_{n\to\infty} a_n$, where k is any real number.

Monotonic Sequences

A **monotonic sequence** is a sequence that is either nonincreasing or nondecreasing. The term *nonincreasing* is used to describe a sequence whose terms either get progressively smaller in value or remain the same. The term *nondecreasing* is used to describe a sequence whose terms either get progressively larger in value or remain the same. A nonincreasing sequence is bounded above. This means that all elements of the sequence must be less than a given real number. A nondecreasing sequence is bounded below. This means that all elements of the sequence must be greater than a given real number.

Recursive Sequences

When one element of a sequence is defined in terms of a previous element or elements of the sequence, the sequence is a **recursive sequence**. For example, given the recursive definition $a_1 = 0$; $a_2 = 1$; $a_n = a_{n-1} + a_{n-2}$ for all $n \geq 2$, you get the sequence 0, 1, 1, 2, 3, 5, 8, … . This particular sequence is known as the Fibonacci sequence, and is defined as the numbers zero and one, and a continuing sequence of numbers, with each number in the sequence equal to the sum of the two previous numbers. It is important to note that the Fibonacci sequence can also be defined as the first two terms being equal to one, with the remaining terms equal to the sum of the previous two terms. Both definitions are considered correct in mathematics. Make sure you know which definition you are working with when dealing with Fibonacci numbers.

Sometimes one term of a sequence with a recursive definition can be found without knowing the previous terms of the sequence. This case is known as a closed-form expression for a recursive definition. In this case, an alternate formula will apply to the sequence to generate the same sequence of numbers. However, not all sequences based on recursive definitions will have a closed-form expression. Some sequences will require the use of the recursive definition. For example, the Fibonacci sequence has a closed-form expression given by the formula $a_n = \frac{\phi^n - \left(\frac{-1}{\phi}\right)^n}{\sqrt{5}}$, where φ is the golden ratio, which is equal to $\frac{1+\sqrt{5}}{2}$. In this case, $a_0 = 0$ and $a_1 = 1$, so you know which definition of the Fibonacci sequence you have.

Arithmetic Sequences

An **arithmetic sequence**, or arithmetic progression, is a special kind of sequence in which each term has a specific quantity, called the common difference, that is added to the previous term. The common difference may be positive or negative. The general form of an arithmetic sequence containing n terms is $a_1, a_1 + d, a_1 + 2d, \dots, a_1 + (n-1)d$, where d is the common difference. The formula for the general term of an arithmetic sequence is $a_n = a_1 + (n-1)d$, where a_n is the term you are looking for and d is the common difference. To find the sum of the first n terms of an arithmetic sequence, use the formula $s_n = \frac{n}{2}(a_1 + a_n)$.

Review Video: Arithmetic Sequence
Visit mometrix.com/academy and enter code: 676885

Geometric Sequences

A **geometric sequence**, or geometric progression, is a special kind of sequence in which each term has a specific quantity, called the common ratio, multiplied by the previous term. The common ratio may be positive or negative. The general form of a geometric sequence containing n terms is $a_1, a_1r, a_1r^2, \dots, a_1r^{n-1}$, where r is the common ratio. The formula for the general term of a geometric sequence is $a_n = a_1r^{n-1}$, where a_n is the term you are looking for and r is the common ratio. To find the sum of the first n terms of a geometric sequence, use the formula $s_n = \frac{a_1(1-r^n)}{1-r}$.

Any function with the set of all natural numbers as the domain is also called a sequence. An element of a sequence is denoted by the symbol a_n, which represents the nth element of sequence a. Sequences may be arithmetic or geometric, and may be defined by a recursive definition, closed-form expression or both. Arithmetic and geometric sequences both have recursive definitions based on the first term of the sequence, as well as both having formulas to find the sum of the first n terms in the sequence, assuming you know what the first term is. The sum of all the terms in a sequence is called a **series**.

Series

An infinite series, also referred to as just a series, is a series of partial sums of a defined sequence. Each infinite sequence represents an infinite series according to the equation $\sum_{n=1}^{\infty} a_n = a_1 + a_2 + a_3 + \cdots + a_n + \cdots$. This notation can be shortened to $\sum_{n=1}^{\infty} a_n$ or $\sum a_n$. Every series is a sequence of partial sums, where the first partial sum is equal to the first element of the series, the second partial sum is equal to the sum of the first two elements of the series, and the nth partial sum is equal to the sum of the first n elements of the series.

Every infinite sequence of partial sums (infinite series) either converges or diverges. Like the test for convergence in a sequence, finding the limit of the sequence of partial sums will indicate whether it is a converging series or a diverging series. If there exists a real number S such that $\lim\limits_{n\to\infty} S_n = S$, where S_n is the sequence of partial sums, then the series converges. If the limit equals infinity, then the series diverges. If $\lim\limits_{n\to\infty} S_n = S$ and S is a real number, then S is also the convergence value of the series.

To find the sum as n approaches infinity for the sum of two convergent series, find the sum as n approaches infinity for each individual series and add the results.

$$\sum_{n=1}^{\infty}(a_n + b_n) = \sum_{n=1}^{\infty} a_n + \sum_{n=1}^{\infty} b_n$$

To find the sum as n approaches infinity for the difference between two convergent series, find the sum as n approaches infinity for each individual series and subtract the results.

$$\sum_{n=1}^{\infty}(a_n - b_n) = \sum_{n=1}^{\infty} a_n - \sum_{n=1}^{\infty} b_n$$

To find the sum as n approaches infinity for the product of a scalar and a convergent series, find the sum as n approaches infinity for the series and multiply the result by the scalar.

$$\sum_{n=1}^{\infty} ka_n = k\sum_{n=1}^{\infty} a_n$$

GEOMETRIC SERIES

A **geometric series** is an infinite series in which each term is multiplied by a constant real number r, called the ratio. This is represented by the equation

$$\sum_{n=1}^{\infty} ar^{n-1} = a_1 + a_2r + a_3r^2 + \cdots + a_nr^{n-1} + \cdots$$

If the absolute value of r is greater than or equal to one, then the geometric series is a diverging series. If the absolute value of r is less than one but greater than zero, the geometric series is a converging series. To find the sum of a converging geometric series, use the formula

$$\sum_{n=1}^{\infty} ar^{n-1} = \frac{a}{1-r}, \text{where } 0 < |r| < 1$$

The **n^{th} term test for divergence** involves taking the limit of the nth term of a sequence and determining whether or not the limit is equal to zero. If the limit of the nth term is not equal to zero, then the series is a diverging series. This test only works to prove divergence, however. If the nth term is equal to zero, the test is inconclusive.

CARTESIAN PRODUCTS/RELATIONS

A Cartesian product is the product of two sets of data, X and Y, such that all elements x are a member of set X, and all elements y are a member of set Y. The product of the two sets, $X \times Y$ is the set of all ordered pairs (x, y). For example, given a standard deck of 52 playing cards, there are four possible suits (hearts, diamonds, clubs, and spades) and thirteen possible card values (the numbers 2 through 10, ace, jack, queen, and king). If the card suits are set X and the card values are set Y, then there are $4 \times 13 = 52$ possible different (x, y) combinations, as seen in the 52 cards of a standard deck.

A binary relation, also referred to as a relation, dyadic relation, or 2-place relation, is a subset of a Cartesian product. It shows the relation between one set of objects and a second set of object, or between one set of objects and itself. The prefix *bi-* means *two*, so there are always two sets involved – either two different sets, or the same set used twice. The ordered pairs of the Cartesian product are used to indicate a binary relation. Relations are possible for situations involving more than two sets, but those are not called binary relations.

The five types of relations are reflexive, symmetric, transitive, antisymmetric, and equivalence. A reflexive relation has $x\Re x$ (x related to x) for all values of x in the set. A symmetric relation has $x\Re y \Rightarrow y\Re x$ for all values of x and y in the set. A transitive relation has $(x\Re y$ and $y\Re z) \Rightarrow x\Re z$ for all values of x, y, and z in the set. An antisymmetric relation has $(x\Re y$ and $y\Re x) \Rightarrow x = y$ for all values of x and y in the set. A relation that is reflexive, symmetric, and transitive is called an equivalence relation.

VERTEX-EDGE GRAPHS

A vertex-edge graph is a set of items or objects connected by pathways or links. Below is a picture of a very basic vertex-edge graph.

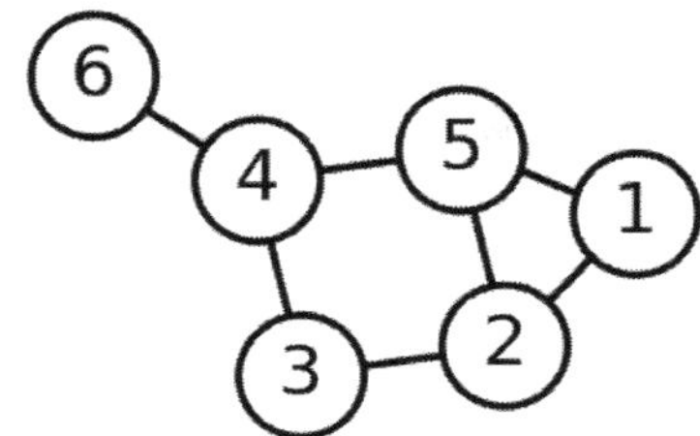

Vertex-edge graphs are useful for solving problems involving schedules, relationships, networks, or paths among a set number of objects. The number of objects may be large, but it will never be infinite. The vertices or points on the graph represent the objects and are referred to as *nodes*. The nodes are joined by line segments called *edges* or links that show the specific paths that connect the various elements represented by the nodes. The number of nodes does not have to equal the number of edges. There may be more or less, depending on the number of allowable paths.

An endpoint on a vertex-edge graph is a vertex on exactly one edge. In the case of a vertex that is an endpoint, the edge that the vertex is on is incident with the vertex. Two edges are considered to be adjacent if they share a vertex. Two vertices are considered to be adjacent if they share an edge.

In a vertex-edge graph, a loop is an edge that has the same vertex as both endpoints. To calculate the degree of a vertex in a vertex-edge graph, count the number of edges that are incident with the vertex, counting loops twice since they meet the vertex at both ends. The degree sum formula states that the sum of the degrees of all vertices on a vertex-edge graph is always equal to twice the number of edges on the graph. Thus, the sum of the degrees will never be odd, even if there are an odd number of vertices.

In a vertex-edge graph, a path is a given sequence of vertices that follows one or more edges to get from vertex to vertex. There is no jumping over spaces to get from one vertex to the next, although doubling back over an edge already traveled is allowed. A simple path is a path that does not repeat an edge in traveling from beginning to end. Think of the vertex-edge graph as a map, with the vertices as cities on the map, and the edges as roads between the cities. To get from one city to another, you must drive on the roads. A simple path allows you to complete your trip without driving on the same road twice.

In a vertex-edge graph, a circuit is a path that has the same starting and stopping point. Picturing the vertex-edge graph as a map with cities and roads, a circuit is like leaving home on vacation and then returning home after you have visited your intended destinations. You may go in one direction and then turn around, or you may go in a circle. A simple circuit on the graph completes the circuit without repeating an edge. This is like going on vacation without driving on the same road twice.

On a vertex-edge graph, any path that uses each edge exactly one time is called an Euler path. One simple way to rule out the possibility of an Euler path is to calculate the degree of each vertex. If more than two vertices have an odd degree, an Euler path is impossible. A path that uses each vertex exactly one time is called a Hamiltonian path.

If every pair of vertices is joined by an edge, the vertex-edge graph is said to be connected. If the vertex-edge graph has no simple circuits in it, then the graph is said to be a tree.

Geometry and Measurement

Common Metric Measurements

Fluids

1 liter = 1000 milliliters
1 liter = 1000 cubic centimeters

Note: Do not confuse *cubic centimeters* with *centiliters*. 1 liter = 1000 cubic centi*meters*, but 1 liter = 100 centi*liters*.

Distance

1 meter = 1000 millimeters
1 meter = 100 centimeters

Weight

1 gram = 1000 milligrams
1 kilogram = 1000 grams

Measurement Prefixes

Kilo-: one thousand (1 *kilo*gram is one thousand grams.)
Centi-: one hundredth (1 *centi*meter is one hundredth of a meter.)
Milli-: one thousandth (1 *milli*liter is one thousandth of a liter.)

Common Imperial Measurements

Volume

1 cup = 8 fluid ounces

Note: This does NOT mean that one cup of something is the same as a half pound. Fluid ounces are measures of volume and have no correspondence with measures of weight.

1 pint = 2 cups
1 pint = 16 ounces

Again, the phrase, "A pint's a pound the world round," does not apply. A pint of something does not necessarily weigh one pound, since one fluid ounce is not the same as one ounce in weight. The expression is valid only for helping you remember the number 16, since most people can remember there are 16 ounces in a pound.

Distance

1 yard = 3 feet
1 yard = 36 inches
1 mile = 5280 feet
1 mile = 1760 yards
1 acre = 43,560 square feet

Volume

1 quart = 2 pints
1 quart = 4 cups
1 gallon = 4 quarts
1 gallon = 8 pints
1 gallon = 16 cups

Weight

1 pound = 16 ounces

Do not assume that because something weighs one pound that its volume is one pint. Ounces of weight are not equivalent to fluid ounces, which measure volume.

1 ton = 2000 pounds

In the United States, the word "ton" by itself refers to a short ton or a net ton. Do not confuse this with a long ton (also called a gross ton) or a metric ton (also spelled *tonne*), which have different measurement equivalents.

Precision, Accuracy, and Error

Precision: How reliable and repeatable a measurement is. The more consistent the data is with repeated testing, the more precise it is. For example, hitting a target consistently in the same spot, which may or may not be the center of the target, is precision.

Accuracy: How close the data is to the correct data. For example, hitting a target consistently in the center area of the target, whether or not the hits are all in the same spot, is accuracy.

Note: it is possible for data to be precise without being accurate. If a scale is off balance, the data will be precise, but will not be accurate. For data to have precision and accuracy, it must be repeatable and correct.

Approximate Error: The amount of error in a physical measurement. Approximate error is often reported as the measurement, followed by the ± symbol and the amount of the approximate error.

Maximum Possible Error: Half the magnitude of the smallest unit used in the measurement. For example, if the unit of measurement is 1 centimeter, the maximum possible error is $\frac{1}{2}$ cm, written as ± 0.5 cm following the measurement. It is important to apply significant figures in reporting maximum possible error. Do not make the answer appear more accurate than the least accurate of your measurements.

Lines and Planes

A **point** is a fixed location in space; has no size or dimensions; commonly represented by a dot.

A **line** is a set of points that extends infinitely in two opposite directions. It has length, but no width or depth. A line can be defined by any two distinct points that it contains. A line segment is a portion of a line that has definite endpoints. A ray is a portion of a line that extends from a single point on that line in one direction along the line. It has a definite beginning, but no ending.

A **plane** is a two-dimensional flat surface defined by three non-collinear points. A plane extends an infinite distance in all directions in those two dimensions. It contains an infinite number of points, parallel lines and segments, intersecting lines and segments, as well as parallel or intersecting rays.

A plane will never contain a three-dimensional figure or skew lines. Two given planes will either be parallel or they will intersect to form a line. A plane may intersect a circular conic surface, such as a cone, to form conic sections, such as the parabola, hyperbola, circle or ellipse.

Perpendicular lines are lines that intersect at right angles. They are represented by the symbol ⊥. The shortest distance from a line to a point not on the line is a perpendicular segment from the point to the line.

Parallel lines are lines in the same plane that have no points in common and never meet. It is possible for lines to be in different planes, have no points in common, and never meet, but they are not parallel because they are in different planes.

A **bisector** is a line or line segment that divides another line segment into two equal lengths. A perpendicular bisector of a line segment is composed of points that are equidistant from the endpoints of the segment it is dividing.

Intersecting lines are lines that have exactly one point in common. Concurrent lines are multiple lines that intersect at a single point.

A **transversal** is a line that intersects at least two other lines, which may or may not be parallel to one another. A transversal that intersects parallel lines is a common occurrence in geometry.

The **projection of a point on a line** is the point at which a perpendicular line drawn from the given point to the given line intersects the line. This is also the shortest distance from the given point to the line.

The **projection of a segment on a line** is a segment whose endpoints are the points formed when perpendicular lines are drawn from the endpoints of the given segment to the given line. This is similar to the length a diagonal line appears to be when viewed from above.

Angles

An **angle** is formed when two lines or line segments meet at a common point. It may be a common starting point for a pair of segments or rays, or it may be the intersection of lines. Angles are represented by the symbol ∠.

The **vertex** is the point at which two segments or rays meet to form an angle. If the angle is formed by intersecting rays, lines, and/or line segments, the vertex is the point at which four angles are formed. The pairs of angles opposite one another are called vertical angles, and their measures are equal.

- An *acute* angle is an angle with a degree measure less than 90°.
- A *right* angle is an angle with a degree measure of exactly 90°.
- An *obtuse* angle is an angle with a degree measure greater than 90° but less than 180°.
- A *straight angle* is an angle with a degree measure of exactly 180°. This is also a semicircle.
- A *reflex angle* is an angle with a degree measure greater than 180° but less than 360°.
- A *full angle* is an angle with a degree measure of exactly 360°.

Review Video: Geometric Symbols: Angles
Visit mometrix.com/academy and enter code: 452738

Two angles whose sum is exactly 90° are said to be **complementary**. The two angles may or may not be adjacent. In a right triangle, the two acute angles are complementary.

Two angles whose sum is exactly 180° are said to be **supplementary**. The two angles may or may not be adjacent. Two intersecting lines always form two pairs of supplementary angles. Adjacent supplementary angles will always form a straight line.

Two angles that have the same vertex and share a side are said to be **adjacent**. Vertical angles are not adjacent because they share a vertex but no common side.

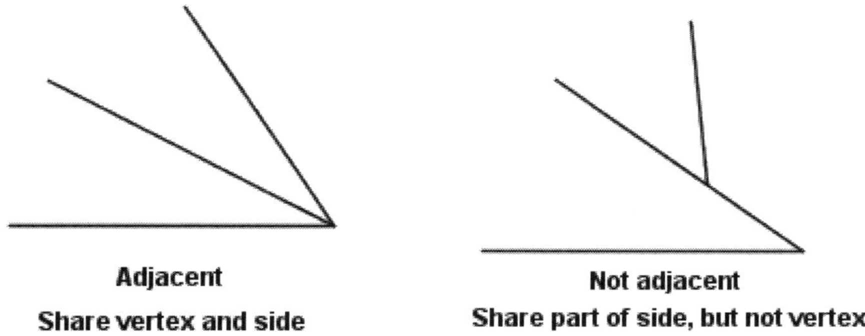

When two parallel lines are cut by a transversal, the angles that are between the two parallel lines are **interior angles**. In the diagram below, angles 3, 4, 5, and 6 are interior angles.

When two parallel lines are cut by a transversal, the angles that are outside the parallel lines are **exterior angles**. In the diagram below, angles 1, 2, 7, and 8 are exterior angles.

When two parallel lines are cut by a transversal, the angles that are in the same position relative to the transversal and a parallel line are *corresponding angles*. The diagram below has four pairs of corresponding angles: angles 1 and 5; angles 2 and 6; angles 3 and 7; and angles 4 and 8. Corresponding angles formed by parallel lines are congruent.

When two parallel lines are cut by a transversal, the two interior angles that are on opposite sides of the transversal are called *alternate interior angles*. In the diagram below, there are two pairs of alternate interior angles: angles 3 and 6, and angles 4 and 5. Alternate interior angles formed by parallel lines are congruent.

When two parallel lines are cut by a transversal, the two exterior angles that are on opposite sides of the transversal are called *alternate exterior angles*.

In the diagram below, there are two pairs of alternate exterior angles: angles 1 and 8, and angles 2 and 7. Alternate exterior angles formed by parallel lines are congruent.

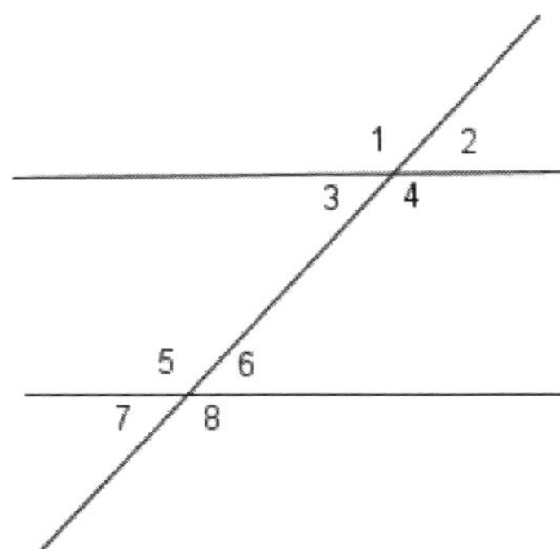

When two lines intersect, four angles are formed. The non-adjacent angles at this vertex are called vertical angles. Vertical angles are congruent. In the diagram, $\angle ABD \cong \angle CBE$ and $\angle ABC \cong \angle DBE$.

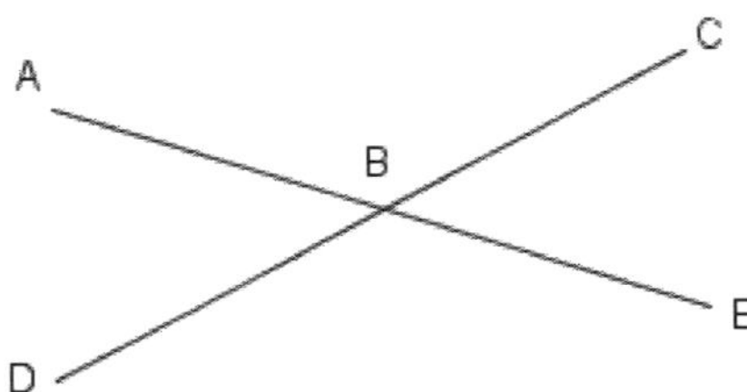

POLYGONS

Each straight line segment of a polygon is called a **side**.

The point at which two sides of a polygon intersect is called the **vertex**. In a polygon, the number of sides is always equal to the number of vertices.

A polygon with all sides congruent and all angles equal is called a **regular polygon**.

A line segment from the center of a polygon perpendicular to a side of the polygon is called the **apothem**. In a regular polygon, the apothem can be used to find the area of the polygon using the formula $A = \frac{1}{2}ap$, where a is the apothem and p is the perimeter.

A line segment from the center of a polygon to a vertex of the polygon is called a **radius**. The radius of a regular polygon is also the radius of a circle that can be circumscribed about the polygon.

- Triangle – 3 sides
- Quadrilateral – 4 sides
- Pentagon – 5 sides
- Hexagon – 6 sides
- Heptagon – 7 sides
- Octagon – 8 sides
- Nonagon – 9 sides
- Decagon – 10 sides
- Dodecagon – 12 sides

More generally, an n-gon is a polygon that has n angles and n sides.

The sum of the interior angles of an n-sided polygon is $(n - 2)180°$. For example, in a triangle $n = 3$, so the sum of the interior angles is $(3- 2)180° = 180°$. In a quadrilateral, $n = 4$, and the sum of the angles is $(4- 2)180° = 360°$. The sum of the interior angles of a polygon is equal to the sum of the interior angles of any other polygon with the same number of sides.

A **diagonal** is a line segment that joins two non-adjacent vertices of a polygon.

A **convex polygon** is a polygon whose diagonals all lie within the interior of the polygon.

A **concave polygon** is a polygon with a least one diagonal that lies outside the polygon. In the diagram below, quadrilateral $ABCD$ is concave because diagonal $\overline{AC}$ lies outside the polygon.

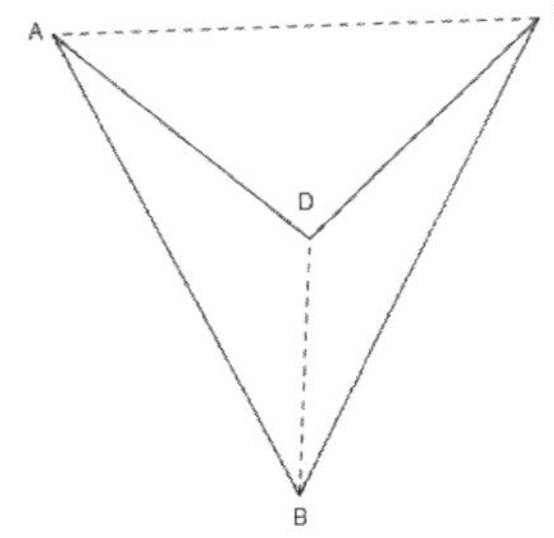

The number of diagonals a polygon has can be found by using the formula: number of diagonals = $\frac{n(n-3)}{2}$, where n is the number of sides in the polygon. This formula works for all polygons, not just regular polygons.

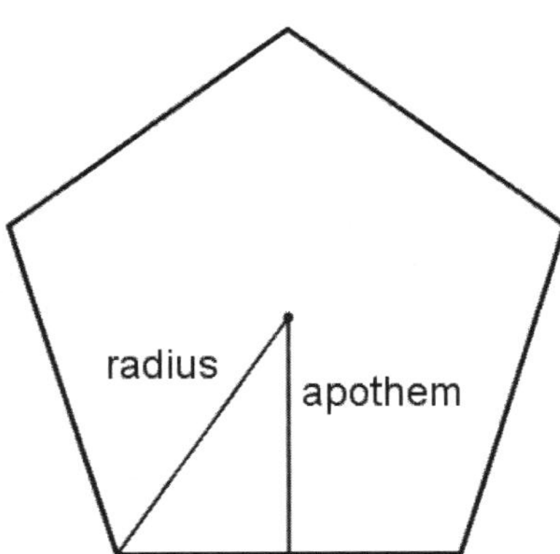

Congruent figures are geometric figures that have the same size and shape. All corresponding angles are equal, and all corresponding sides are equal. It is indicated by the symbol ≅.

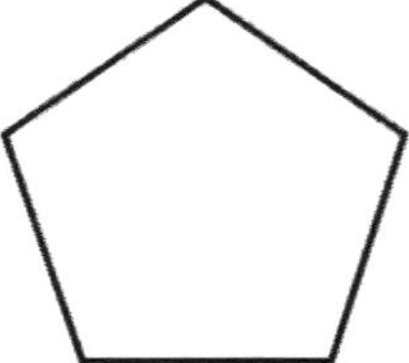
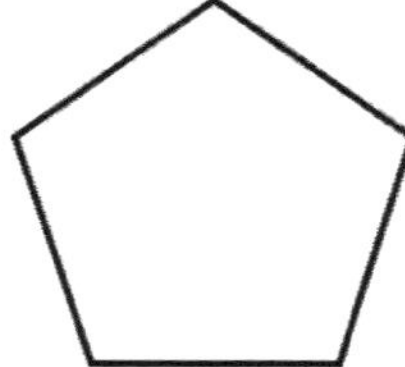

Congruent polygons

Similar figures are geometric figures that have the same shape, but do not necessarily have the same size. All corresponding angles are equal, and all corresponding sides are proportional, but they do not have to be equal. It is indicated by the symbol ~.

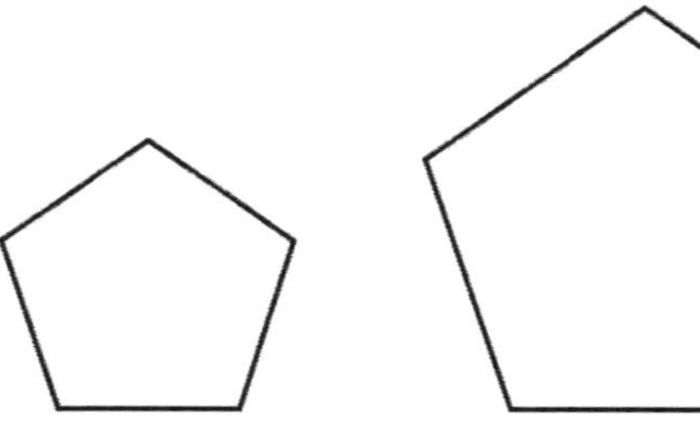

Similar polygons

Note that all congruent figures are also similar, but not all similar figures are congruent.

Review Video: Polygons, Similarity, and Congruence
Visit mometrix.com/academy and enter code: 686174

Line of Symmetry

A **line of symmetry** is a line that divides a figure or object into two symmetric parts. Each symmetric half is congruent to the other. An object may have no lines of symmetry, one line of symmetry, or more than one line of symmetry.

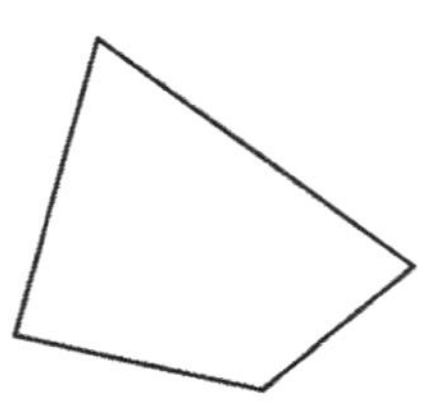

No lines of symmetry

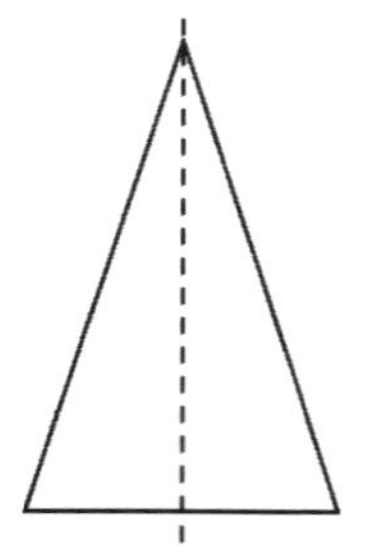

One line of symmetry

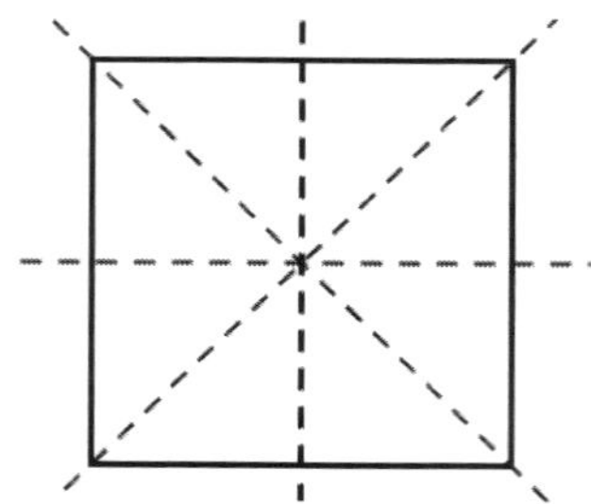

Multiple lines of symmetry

Quadrilateral: A closed two-dimensional geometric figure composed of exactly four straight sides. The sum of the interior angles of any quadrilateral is 360°.

Review Video: Symmetry
Visit mometrix.com/academy and enter code: 528106

PARALLELOGRAM

A **parallelogram** is a quadrilateral that has exactly two pairs of opposite parallel sides. The sides that are parallel are also congruent. The opposite interior angles are always congruent, and the consecutive interior angles are supplementary. The diagonals of a parallelogram bisect each other. Each diagonal divides the parallelogram into two congruent triangles.

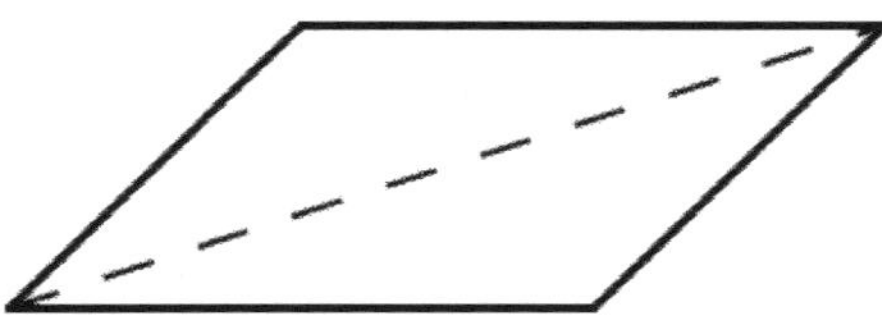

Review Video: Parallelogram
Visit mometrix.com/academy and enter code: 129981

TRAPEZOID

Traditionally, a **trapezoid** is a quadrilateral that has exactly one pair of parallel sides. Some math texts define trapezoid as a quadrilateral that has at least one pair of parallel sides. Because there are no rules governing the second pair of sides, there are no rules that apply to the properties of the diagonals of a trapezoid.

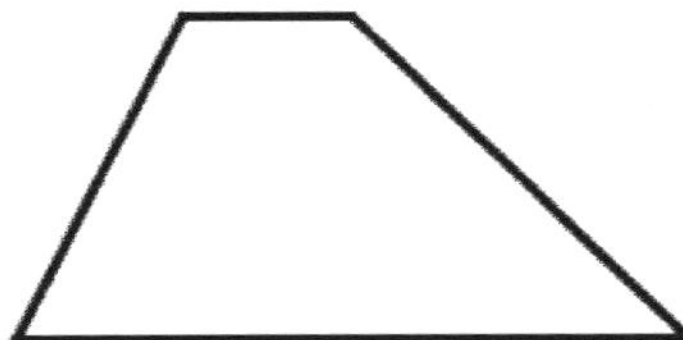

Rectangles, rhombuses, and squares are all special forms of parallelograms.

RECTANGLE

A **rectangle** is a parallelogram with four right angles. All rectangles are parallelograms, but not all parallelograms are rectangles. The diagonals of a rectangle are congruent.

Rhombus

A **rhombus** is a parallelogram with four congruent sides. All rhombuses are parallelograms, but not all parallelograms are rhombuses. The diagonals of a rhombus are perpendicular to each other.

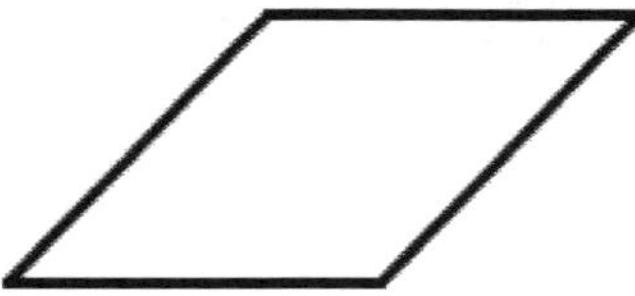

Review Video: Diagonals of Parallelograms, Rectangles, and Rhombi
Visit mometrix.com/academy and enter code: 320040

Square

A **square** is a parallelogram with four right angles and four congruent sides. All squares are also parallelograms, rhombuses, and rectangles. The diagonals of a square are congruent and perpendicular to each other.

A quadrilateral whose diagonals bisect each other is a **parallelogram**. A quadrilateral whose opposite sides are parallel (2 pairs of parallel sides) is a parallelogram.

A quadrilateral whose diagonals are perpendicular bisectors of each other is a **rhombus**. A quadrilateral whose opposite sides (both pairs) are parallel and congruent is a rhombus.

A parallelogram that has a right angle is a **rectangle**. (Consecutive angles of a parallelogram are supplementary. Therefore if there is one right angle in a parallelogram, there are four right angles in that parallelogram.)

A rhombus with one right angle is a **square**. Because the rhombus is a special form of a parallelogram, the rules about the angles of a parallelogram also apply to the rhombus.

Area and Perimeter Formulas

Triangle

The *perimeter of any triangle* is found by summing the three side lengths; $P = a + b + c$. For an equilateral triangle, this is the same as $P = 3s$, where s is any side length, since all three sides are the same length.

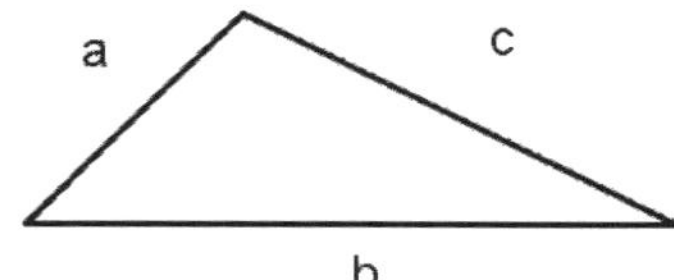

Square

The *area of a square* is found by using the formula $A = s^2$, where and s is the length of one side.

The *perimeter of a square* is found by using the formula $P = 4s$, where s is the length of one side. Because all four sides are equal in a square, it is faster to multiply the length of one side by 4 than to add the same number four times. You could use the formulas for rectangles and get the same answer.

Review Video: Area and Perimeter of a Square
Visit mometrix.com/academy and enter code: 620902

Rectangle

The *area of a rectangle* is found by the formula $A = lw$, where A is the area of the rectangle, l is the length (usually considered to be the longer side) and w is the width (usually considered to be the shorter side). The numbers for l and w are interchangeable.

The *perimeter of a rectangle* is found by the formula $P = 2l + 2w$ or $P = 2(l + w)$, where l is the length, and w is the width. It may be easier to add the length and width first and then double the result, as in the second formula.

Review Video: Area and Perimeter of a Rectangle
Visit mometrix.com/academy and enter code: 933707

Parallelogram

The *area of a parallelogram* is found by the formula $A = bh$, where b is the length of the base, and h is the height. Note that the base and height correspond to the length and width in a rectangle, so this formula would apply to rectangles as well. Do not confuse the height of a parallelogram with the length of the second side. The two are only the same measure in the case of a rectangle.

The *perimeter of a parallelogram* is found by the formula $P = 2a + 2b$ or $P = 2(a + b)$, where a and b are the lengths of the two sides.

Review Video: Area and Perimeter of a Parallelogram
Visit mometrix.com/academy and enter code: 718313

TRAPEZOID

The *area of a trapezoid* is found by the formula $A = \frac{1}{2}h(b_1 + b_2)$, where h is the height (segment joining and perpendicular to the parallel bases), and b_1 and b_2 are the two parallel sides (bases). Do not use one of the other two sides as the height unless that side is also perpendicular to the parallel bases.

The *perimeter of a trapezoid* is found by the formula $P = a + b_1 + c + b_2$, where a, b_1, c, and b_2 are the four sides of the trapezoid.

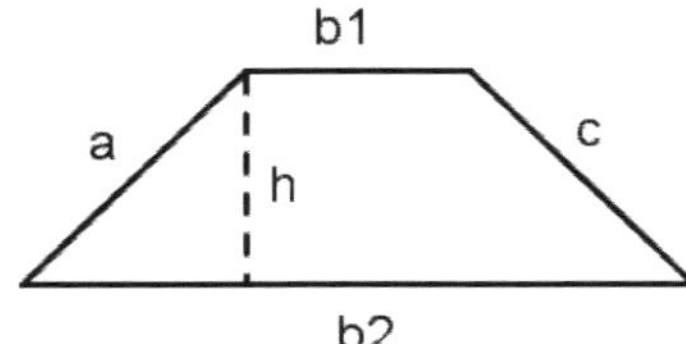

Review Video: Area and Perimeter of a Trapezoid
Visit mometrix.com/academy and enter code: 587523

TRIANGLES

An **equilateral triangle** is a triangle with three congruent sides. An equilateral triangle will also have three congruent angles, each 60°. All equilateral triangles are also acute triangles.

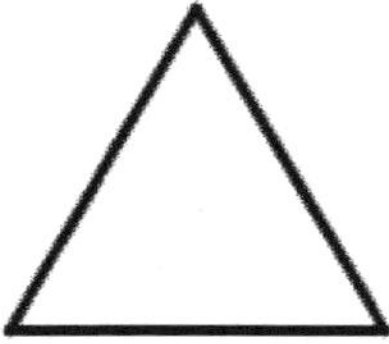

An **isosceles triangle** is a triangle with two congruent sides. An isosceles triangle will also have two congruent angles opposite the two congruent sides.

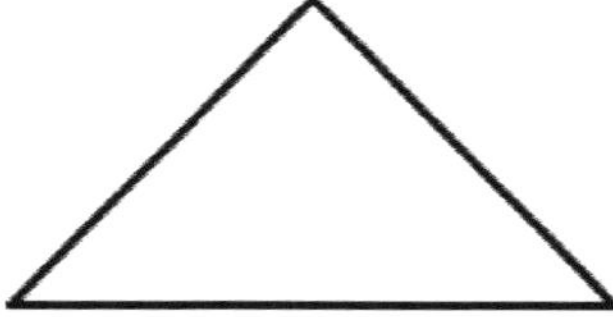

A **scalene triangle** is a triangle with no congruent sides. A scalene triangle will also have three angles of different measures. The angle with the largest measure is opposite the longest side, and the angle with the smallest measure is opposite the shortest side.

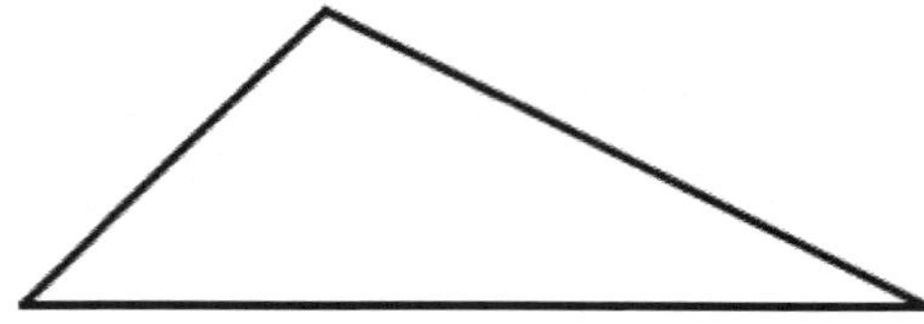

An **acute triangle** is a triangle whose three angles are all less than 90°. If two of the angles are equal, the acute triangle is also an isosceles triangle. If the three angles are all equal, the acute triangle is also an equilateral triangle.

A **right triangle** is a triangle with exactly one angle equal to 90°. All right triangles follow the Pythagorean theorem. A right triangle can never be acute or obtuse.

An **obtuse triangle** is a triangle with exactly one angle greater than 90°. The other two angles may or may not be equal. If the two remaining angles are equal, the obtuse triangle is also an isosceles triangle.

Review Video: Introduction to Types of Triangles
Visit mometrix.com/academy and enter code: 511711

TERMINOLOGY

ALTITUDE OF A TRIANGLE

A line segment drawn from one vertex perpendicular to the opposite side. In the diagram below, $\overline{BE}$, $\overline{AD}$, and $\overline{CF}$ are altitudes. The three altitudes in a triangle are always concurrent.

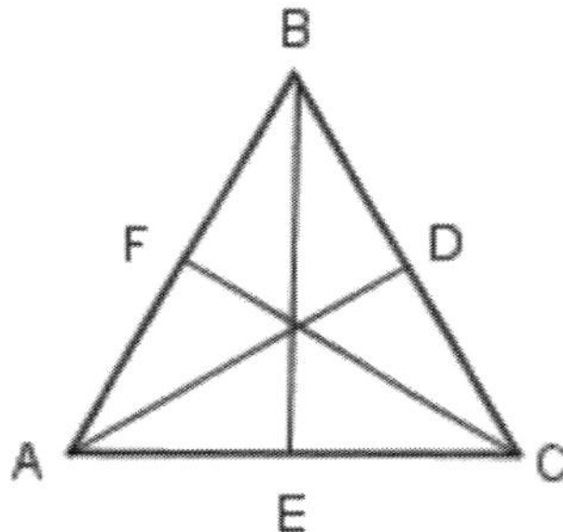

Height of a triangle

The length of the altitude, although the two terms are often used interchangeably.

Orthocenter of a triangle

The point of concurrency of the altitudes of a triangle. Note that in an obtuse triangle, the orthocenter will be outside the triangle, and in a right triangle, the orthocenter is the vertex of the right angle.

Median of a triangle

A line segment drawn from one vertex to the midpoint of the opposite side. This is not the same as the altitude, except the altitude to the base of an isosceles triangle and all three altitudes of an equilateral triangle.

Centroid of a triangle

The point of concurrency of the medians of a triangle. This is the same point as the orthocenter only in an equilateral triangle. Unlike the orthocenter, the centroid is always inside the triangle. The centroid can also be considered the exact center of the triangle. Any shape triangle can be perfectly balanced on a tip placed at the centroid. The centroid is also the point that is two-thirds the distance from the vertex to the opposite side.

Pythagorean Theorem

The side of a triangle opposite the right angle is called the **hypotenuse**. The other two sides are called the legs. The Pythagorean theorem states a relationship among the legs and hypotenuse of a right triangle: $a^2 + b^2 = c^2$, where a and b are the lengths of the legs of a right triangle, and c is the length of the hypotenuse. Note that this formula will only work with right triangles.

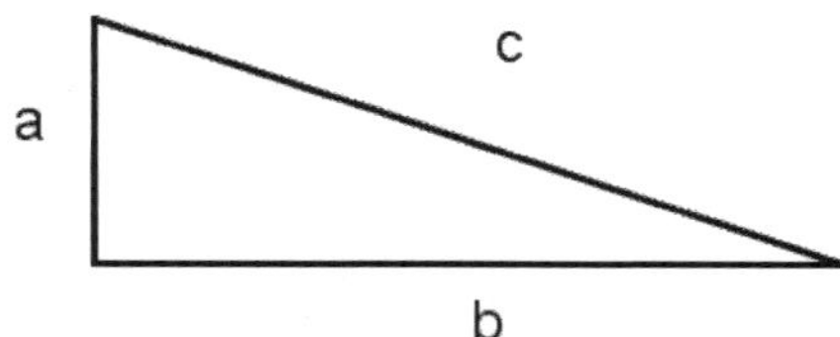

Review Video: Pythagorean Theorem
Visit mometrix.com/academy and enter code: 906576

General Rules

The *triangle inequality theorem* states that the sum of the measures of any two sides of a triangle is always greater than the measure of the third side. If the sum of the measures of two sides were equal to the third side, a triangle would be impossible because the two sides would lie flat across the third side and there would be no vertex. If the sum of the measures of two of the sides was less than the third side, a closed figure would be impossible because the two shortest sides would never meet.

The sum of the measures of the interior angles of a triangle is always 180°. Therefore, a triangle can never have more than one angle greater than or equal to 90°.

In any triangle, the angles opposite congruent sides are congruent, and the sides opposite congruent angles are congruent. The largest angle is always opposite the longest side, and the smallest angle is always opposite the shortest side.

The line segment that joins the midpoints of any two sides of a triangle is always parallel to the third side and exactly half the length of the third side.

Similarity and Congruence Rules

Similar triangles are triangles whose corresponding angles are equal and whose corresponding sides are proportional. Represented by AA. Similar triangles whose corresponding sides are congruent are also congruent triangles.

Review Video: Similar Triangles
Visit mometrix.com/academy and enter code: 398538

Three sides of one triangle are congruent to the three corresponding sides of the second triangle. Represented as SSS.

Two sides and the included angle (the angle formed by those two sides) of one triangle are congruent to the corresponding two sides and included angle of the second triangle. Represented by SAS.

Two angles and the included side (the side that joins the two angles) of one triangle are congruent to the corresponding two angles and included side of the second triangle. Represented by ASA.

Two angles and a non-included side of one triangle are congruent to the corresponding two angles and non-included side of the second triangle. Represented by AAS.

Note that AAA is not a form for congruent triangles. This would say that the three angles are congruent, but says nothing about the sides. This meets the requirements for similar triangles, but not congruent triangles.

Area and Perimeter Formulas

The *perimeter of any triangle* is found by summing the three side lengths; $P = a + b + c$. For an equilateral triangle, this is the same as $P = 3s$, where s is any side length, since all three sides are the same length.

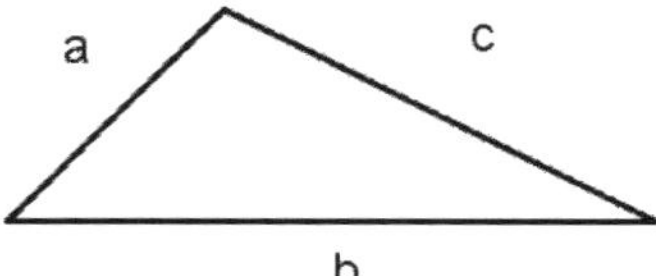

The area of any triangle can be found by taking half the product of one side length (base or b) and the perpendicular distance from that side to the opposite vertex (height or h). In equation form, $A = \frac{1}{2}bh$. For many triangles, it may be difficult to calculate h, so using one of the other formulas given here may be easier.

Another formula that works for any triangle is $A = \sqrt{s(s-a)(s-b)(s-c)}$, where A is the area, s is the semiperimeter $s = \frac{a+b+c}{2}$, and a, b, and c are the lengths of the three sides.

The area of an equilateral triangle can be found by the formula $A = \frac{\sqrt{3}}{4}s^2$, where A is the area and s is the length of a side. You could use the $30° - 60° - 90°$ ratios to find the height of the triangle and then use the standard triangle area formula, but this is faster.

The area of an isosceles triangle can be found by the formula, $A = \frac{1}{2}b\sqrt{a^2 - \frac{b^2}{4}}$, where A is the area, b is the base (the unique side), and a is the length of one of the two congruent sides. If you do not remember this formula, you can use the Pythagorean theorem to find the height so you can use the standard formula for the area of a triangle.

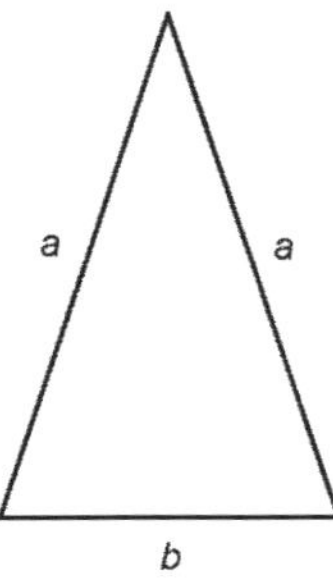

Review Video: Area and Perimeter of a Triangle
Visit mometrix.com/academy and enter code: 853779

Rotation, Center of Rotation, and Angle of Rotation

A *rotation* is a transformation that turns a figure around a point called the **center of rotation**, which can lie anywhere in the plane. If a line is drawn from a point on a figure to the center of rotation, and another line is drawn from the center to the rotated image of that point, the angle between the two lines is the **angle of rotation**. The vertex of the angle of rotation is the center of rotation.

Review Video: Rotation
Visit mometrix.com/academy and enter code: 602600

Reflection Over a Line and Reflection in a Point

A reflection of a figure over a *line* (a "flip") creates a congruent image that is the same distance from the line as the original figure but on the opposite side. The **line of reflection** is the perpendicular bisector of any line segment drawn from a point on the original figure to its reflected image (unless the point and its reflected image happen to be the same point, which happens when a figure is reflected over one of its own sides).

A reflection of a figure in a *point* is the same as the rotation of the figure 180° about that point. The image of the figure is congruent to the original figure. The **point of reflection** is the midpoint of a line segment which connects a point in the figure to its image (unless the point and its reflected image happen to be the same point, which happens when a figure is reflected in one of its own points).

Review Video: Reflection
Visit mometrix.com/academy and enter code: 955068

Example

Use the coordinate plane of the given image below to reflect the image across the y-axis.

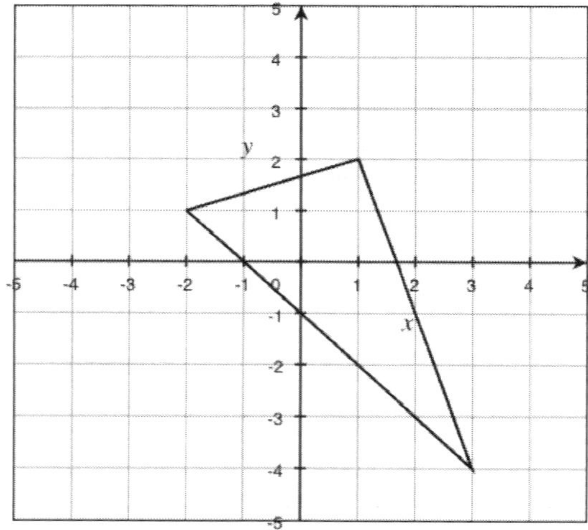

To reflect the image across the y-axis, replace each x-coordinate of the points that are the vertex of the triangle, x, with its negative, $-x$.

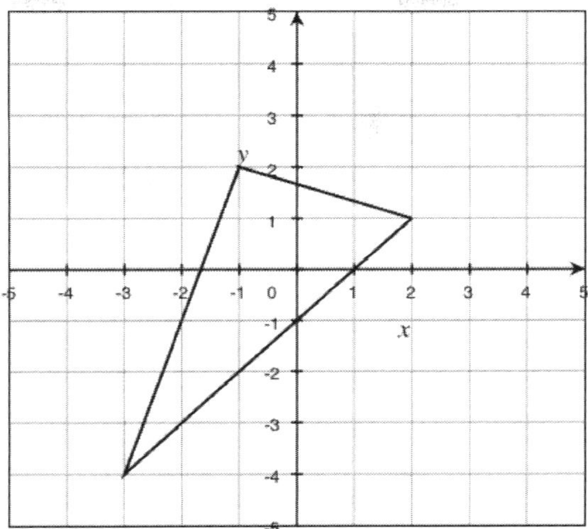

Translation

A *translation* is a transformation which slides a figure from one position in the plane to another position in the plane. The original figure and the translated figure have the same size, shape, and orientation.

Review Video: Translation
Visit mometrix.com/academy and enter code: 718628

Transforming a Given Figure Using Rotation, Reflection, and Translation

To **rotate** a given figure: 1. Identify the point of rotation. 2. Using tracing paper, geometry software, or by approximation, recreate the figure at a new location around the point of rotation.

To **reflect** a given figure: 1. Identify the line of reflection. 2. By folding the paper, using geometry software, or by approximation, recreate the image at a new location on the other side of the line of reflection.

To **translate** a given figure: 1. Identify the new location. 2. Using graph paper, geometry software, or by approximation, recreate the figure in the new location. If using graph paper, make a chart of the x- and y-values to keep track of the coordinates of all critical points.

Evidence of Transformation

To identify that a figure has been *rotated*, look for evidence that the figure is still face-up, but has changed its orientation.

To identify that a figure has been *reflected* across a line, look for evidence that the figure is now face-down.

To identify that a figure has been *translated*, look for evidence that a figure is still face-up and has not changed orientation; the only change is location.

To identify that a figure has been *dilated*, look for evidence that the figure has changed its size but not its orientation.

DILATION

A **dilation** is a transformation which proportionally stretches or shrinks a figure by a **scale factor**. The dilated image is the same shape and orientation as the original image but a different size. A polygon and its dilated image are similar.

EXAMPLE 1

Use the coordinate plane to create a dilation of the given image below, where the dilation is the enlargement of the original image.

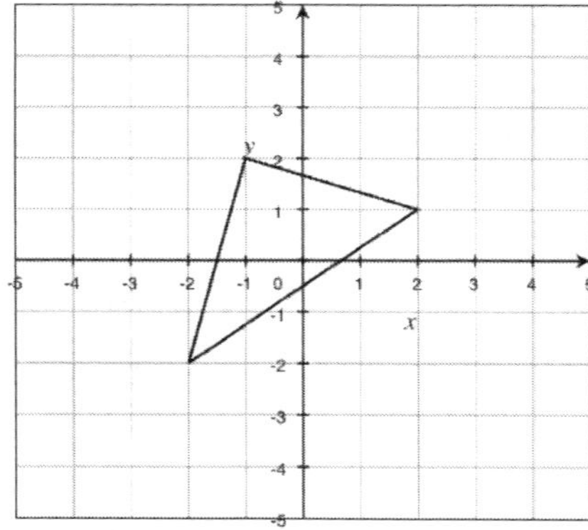

An enlargement can be found by multiplying each coordinate of the coordinate pairs located at the triangles vertices by a constant. If the figure is enlarged by a factor of 2, the new image would be:

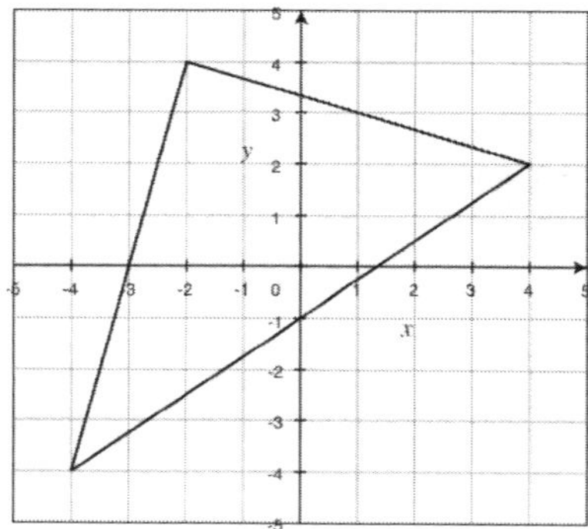

Review Video: Dilation
Visit mometrix.com/academy and enter code: 471630

TRIGONOMETRIC FORMULAS

In the diagram below, angle C is the **right angle**, and side c is the **hypotenuse**. Side a is the side adjacent to angle B and side b is the side adjacent to angle A. These formulas will work for any acute angle in a right triangle. They will *not* work for any triangle that is not a right triangle. Also, they will not work for the right angle in a right triangle, since there are not distinct adjacent and opposite sides to differentiate from the hypotenuse.

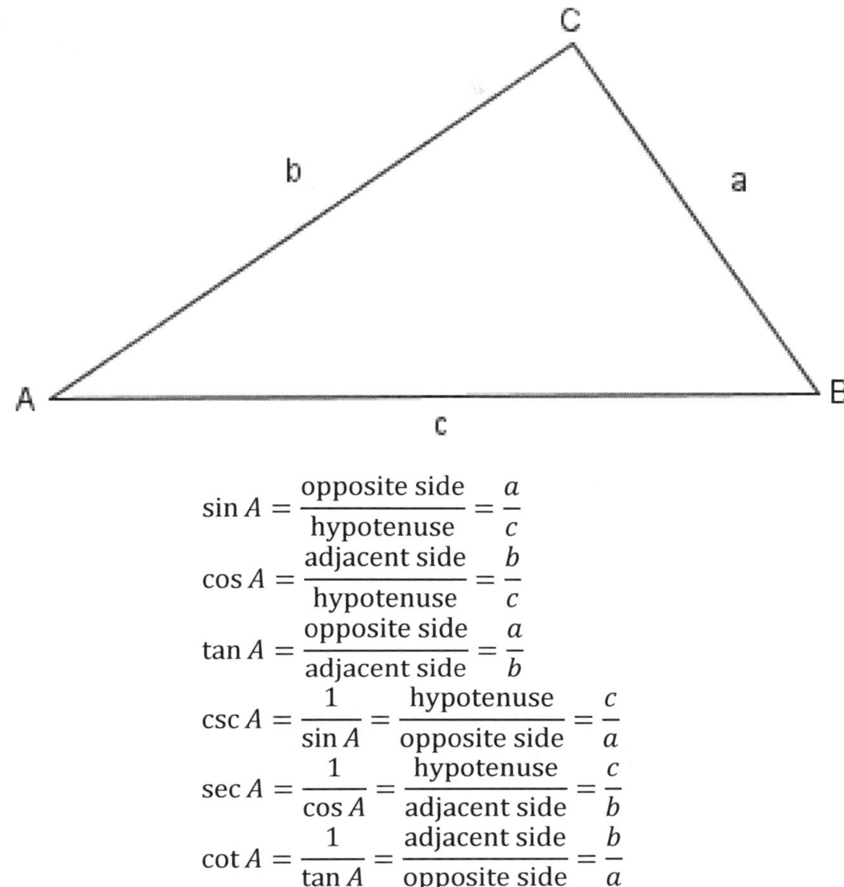

$$\sin A = \frac{\text{opposite side}}{\text{hypotenuse}} = \frac{a}{c}$$
$$\cos A = \frac{\text{adjacent side}}{\text{hypotenuse}} = \frac{b}{c}$$
$$\tan A = \frac{\text{opposite side}}{\text{adjacent side}} = \frac{a}{b}$$
$$\csc A = \frac{1}{\sin A} = \frac{\text{hypotenuse}}{\text{opposite side}} = \frac{c}{a}$$
$$\sec A = \frac{1}{\cos A} = \frac{\text{hypotenuse}}{\text{adjacent side}} = \frac{c}{b}$$
$$\cot A = \frac{1}{\tan A} = \frac{\text{adjacent side}}{\text{opposite side}} = \frac{b}{a}$$

Laws of Sines and Cosines

The **law of sines** states that $\frac{\sin A}{a} = \frac{\sin B}{b} = \frac{\sin C}{c}$, where A, B, and C are the angles of a triangle, and a, b, and c are the sides opposite their respective angles. This formula will work with all triangles, not just right triangles.

The **law of cosines** is given by the formula $c^2 = a^2 + b^2 - 2ab(\cos C)$, where a, b, and c are the sides of a triangle, and C is the angle opposite side c. This formula is similar to the p*ythagorean theorem*, but unlike the pythagorean theorem, it can be used on any triangle.

Review Video: Cosine
Visit mometrix.com/academy and enter code: 361120

Circles

The **center** is the single point inside the circle that is **equidistant** from every point on the circle. (Point O in the diagram below.)

Review Video: Points of a Circle
Visit mometrix.com/academy and enter code: 420746

The **radius** is a line segment that joins the center of the circle and any one point on the circle. All radii of a circle are equal. (Segments OX, OY, and OZ in the diagram below.)

The **diameter** is a line segment that passes through the center of the circle and has both endpoints on the circle. The length of the diameter is exactly twice the length of the radius. (Segment XZ in the diagram below.)

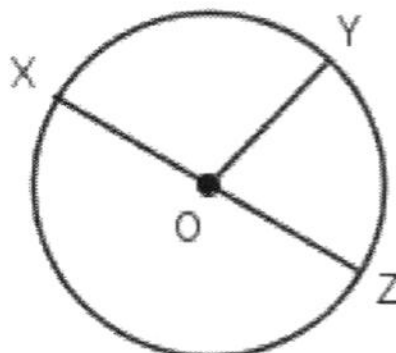

The **area of a circle** is found by the formula $A = \pi r^2$, where r is the length of the radius. If the diameter of the circle is given, remember to divide it in half to get the length of the radius before proceeding.

Review Video: The Diameter, Radius, and Circumference of Circles
Visit mometrix.com/academy and enter code: 448988

The **circumference** of a circle is found by the formula $C = 2\pi r$, where r is the radius. Again, remember to convert the diameter if you are given that measure rather than the radius.

Review Video: Area and Circumference of a Circle
Visit mometrix.com/academy and enter code: 243015

Concentric circles are circles that have the same center, but not the same length of radii. A bulls-eye target is an example of concentric circles.

An **arc** is a portion of a circle. Specifically, an arc is the set of points between and including two points on a circle. An arc does not contain any points inside the circle. When a segment is drawn from the endpoints of an arc to the center of the circle, a sector is formed.

A **central angle** is an angle whose vertex is the center of a circle and whose legs intercept an arc of the circle. Angle XOY in the diagram above is a central angle. A minor arc is an arc that has a measure less than 180°. The measure of a central angle is equal to the measure of the minor arc it intercepts. A major arc is an arc having a measure of at least 180°. The measure of the major arc can be found by subtracting the measure of the central angle from 360°.

A **semicircle** is an arc whose endpoints are the endpoints of the diameter of a circle. A semicircle is exactly half of a circle.

An **inscribed angle** is an angle whose vertex lies on a circle and whose legs contain chords of that circle. The portion of the circle intercepted by the legs of the angle is called the intercepted arc. The measure of the intercepted arc is exactly twice the measure of the inscribed angle. In the following diagram, angle ABC is an inscribed angle. $\widehat{AC} = 2(\text{m}\angle ABC)$

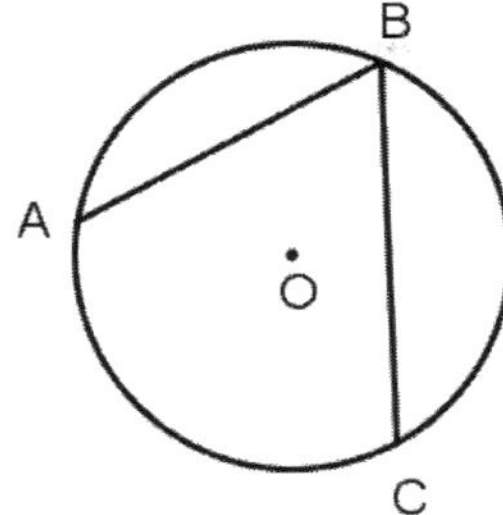

Any angle inscribed in a semicircle is a right angle. The intercepted arc is 180°, making the inscribed angle half that, or 90°. In the diagram below, angle ABC is inscribed in semicircle ABC, making angle ABC equal to 90°.

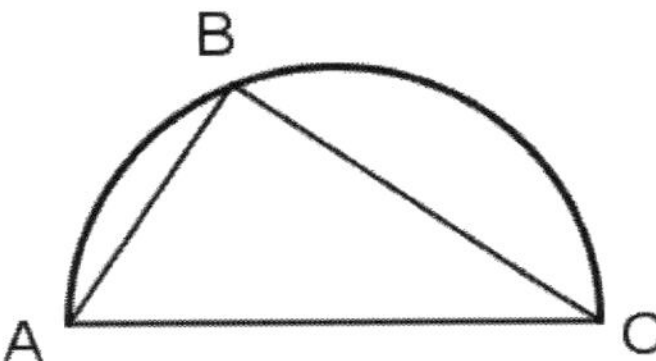

A **chord** is a line segment that has both endpoints on a circle. In the diagram below, $\overline{EB}$ is a chord.

Secant: A line that passes through a circle and contains a chord of that circle. In the diagram below, $\overleftrightarrow{EB}$ is a secant and contains chord $\overline{EB}$.

A **tangent** is a line in the same plane as a circle that touches the circle in exactly one point. While a line segment can be tangent to a circle as part of a line that is tangent, it is improper to say a tangent can be simply a line segment that touches the circle in exactly one point. In the diagram below, $\overleftrightarrow{CD}$ is tangent to circle A. Notice that $\overline{FB}$ is not tangent to the circle. $\overline{FB}$ is a line segment that touches the circle in exactly one point, but if the segment were extended, it would touch the circle in a second point. The point at which a tangent touches a circle is called the point of tangency. In the diagram below, point B is the point of tangency.

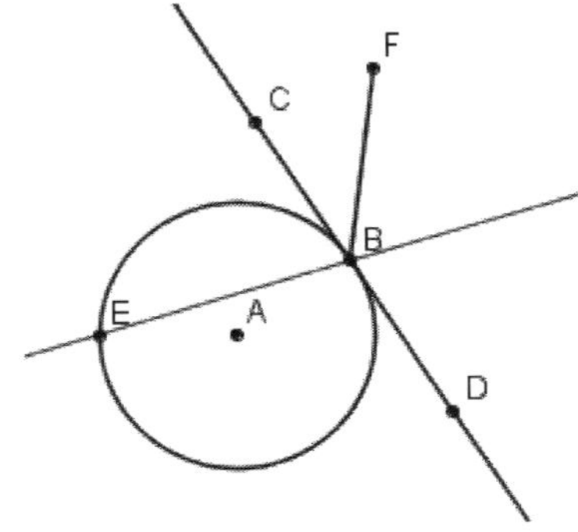

A **secant** is a line that intersects a circle in two points. Two secants may intersect inside the circle, on the circle, or outside the circle. When the two secants intersect on the circle, an inscribed angle is formed.

When two secants intersect inside a circle, the measure of each of two vertical angles is equal to half the sum of the two intercepted arcs. In the diagram below, $m\angle AEB = \frac{1}{2}(\widehat{AB} + \widehat{CD})$ and $m\angle BEC = \frac{1}{2}(\widehat{BC} + \widehat{AD})$.

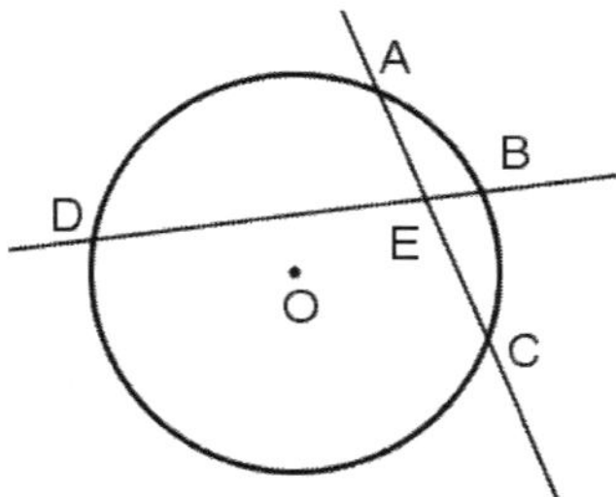

When two secants intersect outside a circle, the measure of the angle formed is equal to half the difference of the two arcs that lie between the two secants. In the diagram below, $m\angle AEB = \frac{1}{2}(\widehat{AB} - \widehat{CD})$.

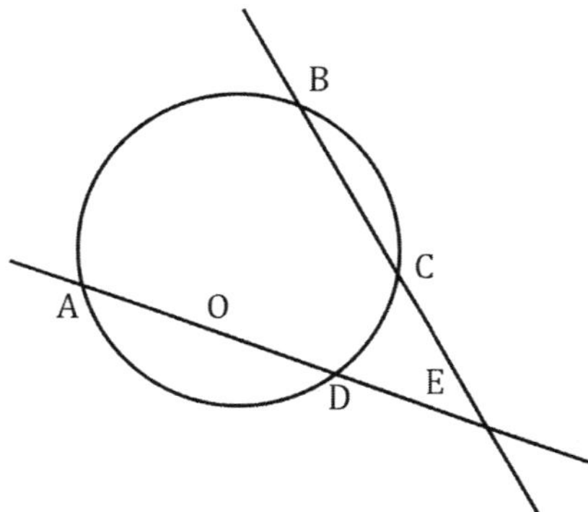

The **arc length** is the length of that portion of the circumference between two points on the circle. The formula for arc length is $s = \frac{\pi r\theta}{180°}$ where s is the arc length, r is the length of the radius, and θ is the angular measure of the arc in degrees, or $s = r\theta$, where θ is the angular measure of the arc in radians (2π radians $= 360$ degrees).

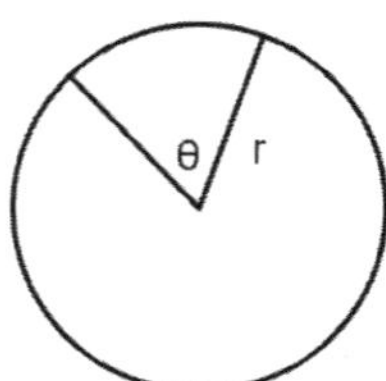

A **sector** is the portion of a circle formed by two radii and their intercepted arc. While the arc length is exclusively the points that are also on the circumference of the circle, the sector is the entire area bounded by the arc and the two radii.

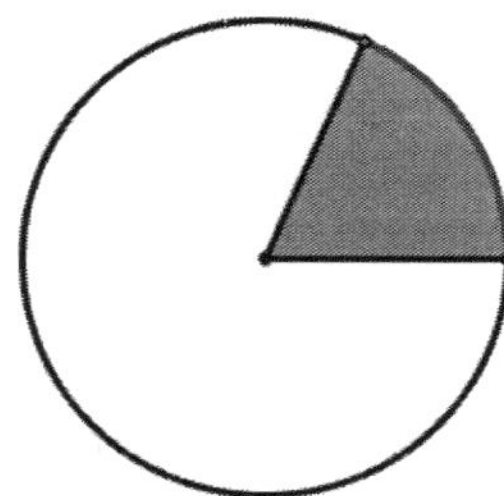

The **area of a sector** of a circle is found by the formula, $A = \frac{\theta r^2}{2}$, where A is the area, θ is the measure of the central angle in radians, and r is the radius. To find the area when the central angle is in degrees, use the formula, $A = \frac{\theta \pi r^2}{360}$, where θ is the measure of the central angle in degrees and r is the radius.

A circle is inscribed in a polygon if each of the sides of the polygon is tangent to the circle. A polygon is inscribed in a circle if each of the vertices of the polygon lies on the circle.

A circle is circumscribed about a polygon if each of the vertices of the polygon lies on the circle. A polygon is circumscribed about the circle if each of the sides of the polygon is tangent to the circle.

If one figure is inscribed in another, then the other figure is circumscribed about the first figure.

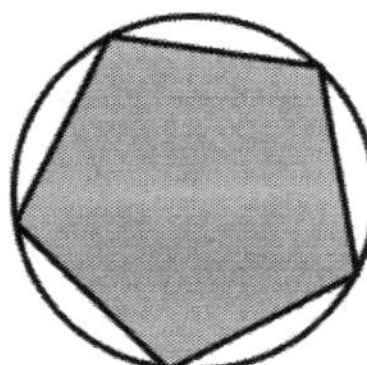

Circle circumscribed about a pentagon
Pentagon inscribed in a circle

OTHER CONIC SECTIONS

ELLIPSE

An **ellipse** is the set of all points in a plane, whose total distance from two fixed points called the foci (singular: focus) is constant, and whose center is the midpoint between the foci.

The standard equation of an ellipse that is taller than it is wide is $\frac{(y-k)^2}{a^2} + \frac{(x-h)^2}{b^2} = 1$, where a and b are coefficients. The center is the point (h, k) and the foci are the points $(h, k + c)$ and $(h, k - c)$, where $c^2 = a^2 - b^2$ and $a^2 > b^2$.

The major axis has length $2a$, and the minor axis has length $2b$.

Eccentricity (e) is a measure of how elongated an ellipse is, and is the ratio of the distance between the foci to the length of the major axis. Eccentricity will have a value between 0 and 1. The closer to 1 the eccentricity is, the closer the ellipse is to being a circle. The formula for eccentricity is $= \frac{c}{a}$.

PARABOLA

Parabola: The set of all points in a plane that are equidistant from a fixed line, called the **directrix**, and a fixed point not on the line, called the **focus**.

Axis: The line perpendicular to the directrix that passes through the focus.

For parabolas that open up or down, the standard equation is $(x - h)^2 = 4c(y - k)$, where h, c, and k are coefficients. If c is positive, the parabola opens up. If c is negative, the parabola opens down. The vertex is the point (h, k). The directrix is the line having the equation $y = -c + k$, and the focus is the point $(h, c + k)$.

For parabolas that open left or right, the standard equation is $(y - k)^2 = 4c(x - h)$, where k, c, and h are coefficients. If c is positive, the parabola opens to the right. If c is negative, the parabola opens to the left. The vertex is the point (h, k). The directrix is the line having the equation $x = -c + h$, and the focus is the point $(c + h, k)$.

HYPERBOLA

A **hyperbola** is the set of all points in a plane, whose distance from two fixed points, called foci, has a constant difference.

The standard equation of a horizontal hyperbola is $\frac{(x-h)^2}{a^2} - \frac{(y-k)^2}{b^2} = 1$, where a, b, h, and k are real numbers. The center is the point (h, k), the vertices are the points $(h + a, k)$ and $(h - a, k)$, and the foci are the points that every point on one of the parabolic curves is equidistant from and are found using the formulas $(h + c, k)$ and $(h - c, k)$, where $c^2 = a^2 + b^2$. The asymptotes are two lines the graph of the hyperbola approaches but never reaches, and are given by the equations $y = \left(\frac{b}{a}\right)(x - h) + k$ and $y = -\left(\frac{b}{a}\right)(x - h) + k$.

A **vertical hyperbola** is formed when a plane makes a vertical cut through two cones that are stacked vertex-to-vertex.

The standard equation of a vertical hyperbola is $\frac{(y-k)^2}{a^2} - \frac{(x-h)^2}{b^2} = 1$, where a, b, k, and h are real numbers. The center is the point (h, k), the vertices are the points $(h, k + a)$ and $(h, k - a)$, and the foci are the points that every point on one of the parabolic curves is equidistant from and are found using the formulas $(h, k + c)$ and $(h, k - c)$, where $c^2 = a^2 + b^2$. The asymptotes are two lines the graph of the hyperbola approaches but never reach, and are given by the equations $y = \left(\frac{a}{b}\right)(x - h) + k$ and $y = -\left(\frac{a}{b}\right)(x - h) + k$.

SOLIDS

The **surface area of a solid object** is the area of all sides or exterior surfaces. For objects such as prisms and pyramids, a further distinction is made between base surface area (B) and lateral surface area (LA). For a prism, the total surface area (SA) is $SA = LA + 2B$. For a pyramid or cone, the total surface area is $SA = LA + B$.

Review Video: How to Calculate the Volume of 3D Objects
Visit mometrix.com/academy and enter code: 163343

The **surface area of a sphere** can be found by the formula $A = 4\pi r^2$, where r is the radius. The volume is given by the formula $V = \frac{4}{3}\pi r^3$, where r is the radius. Both quantities are generally given in terms of π.

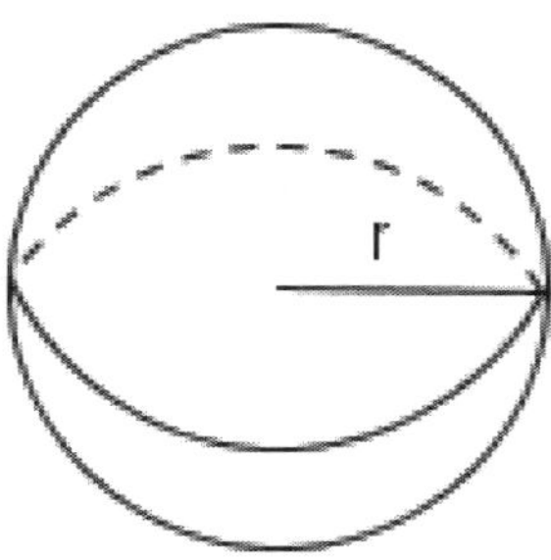

Review Video: Volume and Surface Area of a Sphere
Visit mometrix.com/academy and enter code: 786928

The **volume of any prism** is found by the formula $V = Bh$, where B is the area of the base, and h is the height (perpendicular distance between the bases). The surface area of any prism is the sum of the areas of both bases and all sides. It can be calculated as $SA = 2B + Ph$, where P is the perimeter of the base.

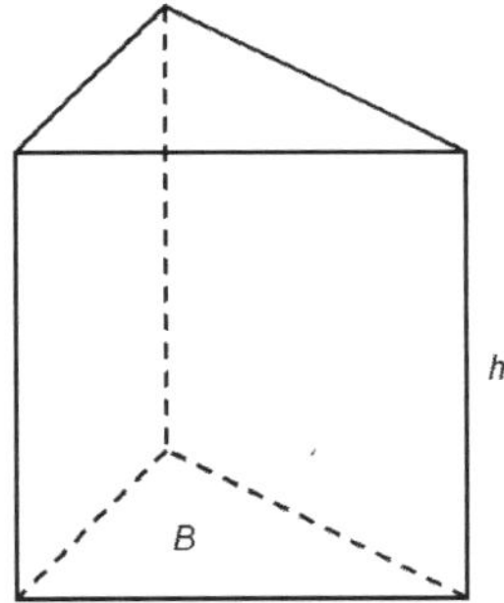

For a *rectangular prism*, the **volume** can be found by the formula $V = lwh$, where V is the volume, l is the length, w is the width, and h is the height. The surface area can be calculated as $SA = 2lw + 2hl + 2wh$ or $SA = 2(lw + hl + wh)$.

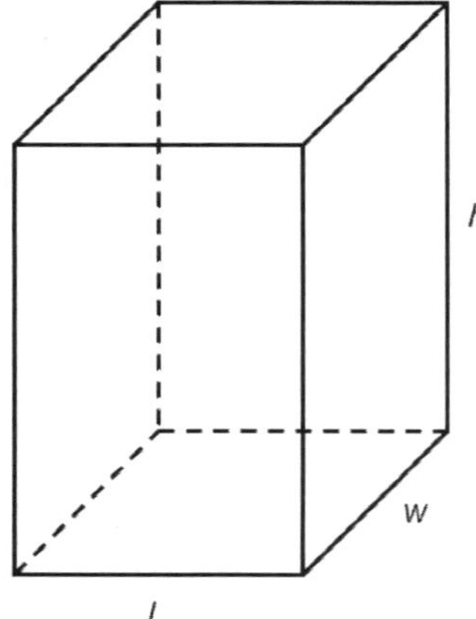

The **volume of a cube** can be found by the formula $V = s^3$, where s is the length of a side. The surface area of a cube is calculated as $SA = 6s^2$, where SA is the total surface area and s is the length of a side. These formulas are the same as the ones used for the volume and surface area of a rectangular prism, but simplified since all three quantities (length, width, and height) are the same.

Review Video: Volume and Surface Area of a Cube
Visit mometrix.com/academy and enter code: 664455

The **volume of a cylinder** can be calculated by the formula $V = \pi r^2 h$, where r is the radius, and h is the height. The surface area of a cylinder can be found by the formula $SA = 2\pi r^2 + 2\pi rh$. The first term is the base area multiplied by two, and the second term is the perimeter of the base multiplied by the height.

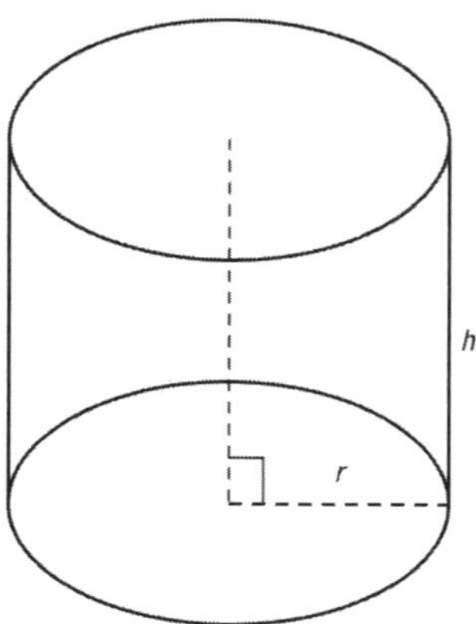

Review Video: Volume and Surface Area of a Right Circular Cylinder
Visit mometrix.com/academy and enter code: 226463

The **volume of a pyramid** is found by the formula $V = \frac{1}{3}Bh$, where B is the area of the base, and h is the height (perpendicular distance from the vertex to the base). Notice this formula is the same as $\frac{1}{3}$ times the volume of a prism. Like a prism, the base of a pyramid can be any shape.

Review Video: Volume and Surface Area of a Pyramid
Visit mometrix.com/academy and enter code: 621932

Finding the **surface area of a pyramid** is not as simple as the other shapes we've looked at thus far. If the pyramid is a right pyramid, meaning the base is a regular polygon and the vertex is directly over the center of that polygon, the surface area can be calculated as $SA = B + \frac{1}{2}Ph_s$, where P is the perimeter of the base, and h_s is the slant height (distance from the vertex to the midpoint of one side of the base). If the pyramid is irregular, the area of each triangle side must be calculated individually and then summed, along with the base.

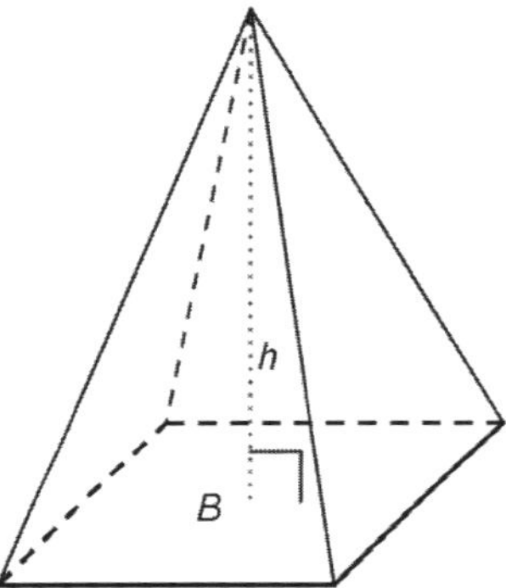

The **volume of a cone** is found by the formula $V = \frac{1}{3}\pi r^2 h$, where r is the radius, and h is the height. Notice this is the same as $\frac{1}{3}$ times the volume of a cylinder. The surface area can be calculated as $SA = \pi r^2 + \pi rs$, where s is the slant height. The slant height can be calculated using the Pythagorean Thereom to be $\sqrt{r^2 + h^2}$, so the surface area formula can also be written as $SA = \pi r^2 + \pi r\sqrt{r^2 + h^2}$.

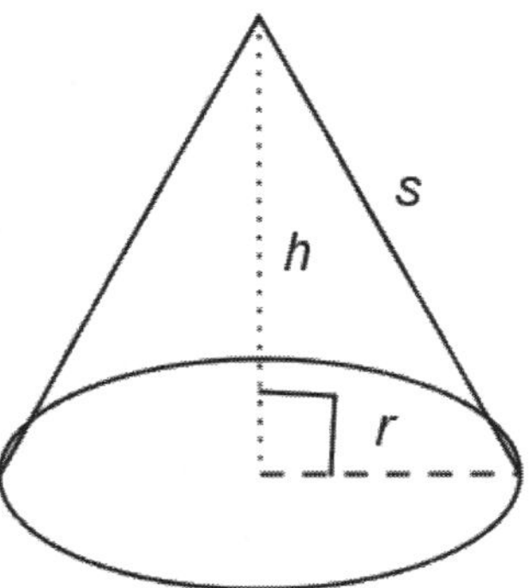

Review Video: Volume and Surface Area of a Right Circular Cone
Visit mometrix.com/academy and enter code: 573574

Probability and Statistics

Probability Terminology

Probability is a branch of statistics that deals with the likelihood of something taking place. One classic example is a coin toss. There are only two possible results: heads or tails. The likelihood, or probability, that the coin will land as heads is 1 out of 2 ($\frac{1}{2}$, 0.5, 50%). Tails has the same probability. Another common example is a 6-sided die roll. There are six possible results from rolling a single die, each with an equal chance of happening, so the probability of any given number coming up is 1 out of 6.

Terms Frequently Used in Probability

- **Event** – a situation that produces results of some sort (a coin toss)
- **Compound event** – event that involves two or more independent events (rolling a pair of dice; taking the sum)
- **Outcome** – a possible result in an experiment or event (heads, tails)
- **Desired outcome** (or success) – an outcome that meets a particular set of criteria (a roll of 1 or 2 if we are looking for numbers less than 3)
- **Independent events** – two or more events whose outcomes do not affect one another (two coins tossed at the same time)
- **Dependent events** – two or more events whose outcomes affect one another (two cards drawn consecutively from the same deck)
- **Certain outcome** – probability of outcome is 100% or 1
- **Impossible outcome** – probability of outcome is 0% or 0
- **Mutually exclusive outcomes** – two or more outcomes whose criteria cannot all be satisfied in a single event (a coin coming up heads and tails on the same toss)
- **Random variable** – refers to all possible outcomes of a single event which may be discrete or continuous.

Review Video: Intro to Probability
Visit mometrix.com/academy and enter code: 212374

Calculating Probability

Probability is the likelihood of a certain outcome occurring for a given event. The **theoretical probability** can usually be determined without actually performing the event. The likelihood of a outcome occurring, or the probability of an outcome occurring, is given by the formula

$$P(A) = \frac{\text{Number of acceptable outcomes}}{\text{Number of possible outcomes}}$$

where $P(A)$ is the probability of an outcome A occurring, and each outcome is just as likely to occur as any other outcome. If each outcome has the same probability of occurring as every other possible outcome, the outcomes are said to be equally likely to occur. The total number of acceptable outcomes must be less than or equal to the total number of possible outcomes. If the two are equal, then the outcome is certain to occur and the probability is 1. If the number of acceptable outcomes is zero, then the outcome is impossible and the probability is 0.

Review Video: Theoretical and Experimental Probability
Visit mometrix.com/academy and enter code: 444349

Example:

There are 20 marbles in a bag and 5 are red. The theoretical probability of randomly selecting a red marble is 5 out of 20, ($\frac{5}{20} = \frac{1}{4}$, 0.25, or 25%).

Permutations and Combinations

When trying to calculate the probability of an event using the $\frac{\text{desired outcomes}}{\text{total outcomes}}$ formula, you may frequently find that there are too many outcomes to individually count them. **Permutation** and **combination formulas** offer a shortcut to counting outcomes. A permutation is an arrangement of a specific number of a set of objects in a specific order. The number of **permutations** of *r* items given a set of *n* items can be calculated as ${}_nP_r = \frac{n!}{(n-r)!}$. Combinations are similar to permutations, except there are no restrictions regarding the order of the elements. While ABC is considered a different permutation than BCA, ABC and BCA are considered the same combination. The number of **combinations** of *r* items given a set of *n* items can be calculated as ${}_nC_r = \frac{n!}{r!(n-r)!}$ or ${}_nC_r = \frac{{}_nP_r}{r!}$.

Example:

Suppose you want to calculate how many different 5-card hands can be drawn from a deck of 52 cards. This is a combination since the order of the cards in a hand does not matter. There are 52 cards available, and 5 to be selected. Thus, the number of different hands is ${}_{52}C_5 = \frac{52!}{5! \times 47!} =$ 2,598,960.

Complement of an Event

Sometimes it may be easier to calculate the possibility of something not happening, or the **complement of an event**. Represented by the symbol $\bar{A}$, the complement of *A* is the probability that event *A* does not happen. When you know the probability of event *A* occurring, you can use the formula $P(\bar{A}) = 1 - P(A)$, where $P(\bar{A})$ is the probability of event *A* not occurring, and $P(A)$ is the probability of event *A* occurring.

Addition Rule

The **addition rule** for probability is used for finding the probability of a compound event. Use the formula $P(A \text{ or } B) = P(A) + P(B) - P(A \text{ and } B)$, where $P(A \text{ and } B)$ is the probability of both events occurring to find the probability of a compound event. The probability of both events occurring at the same time must be subtracted to eliminate any overlap in the first two probabilities.

Conditional Probability

Conditional probability is the probability of an event occurring once another event has already occurred. Given event *A* and dependent event *B*, the probability of event *B* occurring when event *A* has already occurred is represented by the notation $P(A|B)$. To find the probability of event *B* occurring, take into account the fact that event *A* has already occurred and adjust the total number of possible outcomes. For example, suppose you have ten balls numbered 1–10 and you want ball number 7 to be pulled in two pulls. On the first pull, the probability of getting the 7 is $\frac{1}{10}$ because there is one ball with a 7 on it and 10 balls to choose from. Assuming the first pull did not yield a 7, the probability of pulling a 7 on the second pull is now $\frac{1}{9}$ because there are only 9 balls remaining for the second pull.

MULTIPLICATION RULE

The **multiplication rule** can be used to find the probability of two independent events occurring using the formula $P(A \text{ and } B) = P(A) \times P(B)$, where $P(A \text{ and } B)$ is the probability of two independent events occurring, $P(A)$ is the probability of the first event occurring, and $P(B)$ is the probability of the second event occurring.

The multiplication rule can also be used to find the probability of two dependent events occurring using the formula $P(A \text{ and } B) = P(A) \times P(B|A)$, where $P(A \text{ and } B)$ is the probability of two dependent events occurring and $P(B|A)$ is the probability of the second event occurring after the first event has already occurred.

Before using the multiplication rule, you MUST first determine whether the two events are *dependent* or *independent*.

Use a **combination of the multiplication** rule and the rule of complements to find the probability that at least one outcome of the element will occur. This given by the general formula $P(\text{at least one event occurring}) = 1 - P(\text{no outcomes occurring})$. For example, to find the probability that at least one even number will show when a pair of dice is rolled, find the probability that two odd numbers will be rolled (no even numbers) and subtract from one. You can always use a tree diagram or make a chart to list the possible outcomes when the sample space is small, such as in the dice-rolling example, but in most cases it will be much faster to use the multiplication and complement formulas.

EXPECTED VALUE

Expected value is a method of determining expected outcome in a random situation. It is really a sum of the weighted probabilities of the possible outcomes. Multiply the probability of an event occurring by the weight assigned to that probability (such as the amount of money won or lost). A practical application of the expected value is to determine whether a game of chance is really fair. If the sum of the weighted probabilities is equal to zero, the game is generally considered fair because the player has a fair chance to at least to break even. If the expected value is less than zero, then players lose more than they win. For example, a lottery drawing might allow the player to choose any three-digit number, 000–999. The probability of choosing the winning number is 1:1000. If it costs \$1 to play, and a winning number receives \$500, the expected value is $\left(-\$1 \cdot \frac{999}{1{,}000}\right) + \left(\$500 \cdot \frac{1}{1{,}000}\right) = -0.499 \text{ or } -\$0.50$. You can expect to lose on average 50 cents for every dollar you spend.

EMPIRICAL PROBABILITY

Most of the time, when we talk about probability, we mean theoretical probability. **Empirical probability**, or experimental probability or relative frequency, is the number of times an outcome occurs in a particular experiment or a certain number of observed events. While theoretical probability is based on what *should* happen, experimental probability is based on what *has* happened. Experimental probability is calculated in the same way as theoretical, except that actual outcomes are used instead of possible outcomes.

Theoretical and experimental probability do not always line up with one another. Theoretical probability says that out of 20 coin-tosses, 10 should be heads. However, if we were actually to toss

20 coins, we might record just 5 heads. This doesn't mean that our theoretical probability is incorrect; it just means that this particular experiment had results that were different from what was predicted. A practical application of empirical probability is the insurance industry. There are no set functions that define lifespan, health, or safety. Insurance companies look at factors from hundreds of thousands of individuals to find patterns that they then use to set the formulas for insurance premiums.

Objective Probability

Objective probability is based on mathematical formulas and documented evidence. Examples of objective probability include raffles or lottery drawings where there is a pre-determined number of possible outcomes and a predetermined number of outcomes that correspond to an event. Other cases of objective probability include probabilities of rolling dice, flipping coins, or drawing cards. Most gambling games are based on objective probability.

Subjective Probability

Subjective probability is based on personal or professional feelings and judgments. Often, there is a lot of guesswork following extensive research. Areas where subjective probability is applicable include sales trends and business expenses. Attractions set admission prices based on subjective probabilities of attendance based on varying admission rates in an effort to maximize their profit.

Sample Space

The total set of all possible results of a test or experiment is called a **sample space**, or sometimes a universal sample space. The sample space, represented by one of the variables S, Ω, or U (for universal sample space) has individual elements called outcomes. Other terms for outcome that may be used interchangeably include elementary outcome, simple event, or sample point. The number of outcomes in a given sample space could be infinite or finite, and some tests may yield multiple unique sample sets. For example, tests conducted by drawing playing cards from a standard deck would have one sample space of the card values, another sample space of the card suits, and a third sample space of suit-denomination combinations. For most tests, the sample spaces considered will be finite.

An **event**, represented by the variable E, is a portion of a sample space. It may be one outcome or a group of outcomes from the same sample space. If an event occurs, then the test or experiment will generate an outcome that satisfies the requirement of that event. For example, given a standard deck of 52 playing cards as the sample space, and defining the event as the collection of face cards, then the event will occur if the card drawn is a J, Q, or K. If any other card is drawn, the event is said to have not occurred.

For every sample space, each possible outcome has a specific likelihood, or probability, that it will occur. The probability measure, also called the **distribution**, is a function that assigns a real number probability, from zero to one, to each outcome. For a probability measure to be accurate, every outcome must have a real number probability measure that is greater than or equal to zero and less than or equal to one. Also, the probability measure of the sample space must equal one, and the probability measure of the union of multiple outcomes must equal the sum of the individual probability measures.

Probabilities of events are expressed as real numbers from zero to one. They give a numerical value to the chance that a particular event will occur. The probability of an event occurring is the sum of the probabilities of the individual elements of that event. For example, in a standard deck of 52 playing cards as the sample space and the collection of face cards as the event, the probability of drawing a specific face card is $\frac{1}{52} = 0.019$, but the probability of drawing any one of the twelve face cards is $12(0.019) = 0.228$. Note that rounding of numbers can generate different results. If you multiplied 12 by the fraction $\frac{1}{52}$ before converting to a decimal, you would get the answer $\frac{12}{52} = 0.231$.

TREE DIAGRAM

For a simple sample space, possible outcomes may be determined by using a **tree diagram** or an organized chart. In either case, you can easily draw or list out the possible outcomes. For example, to determine all the possible ways three objects can be ordered, you can draw a tree diagram:

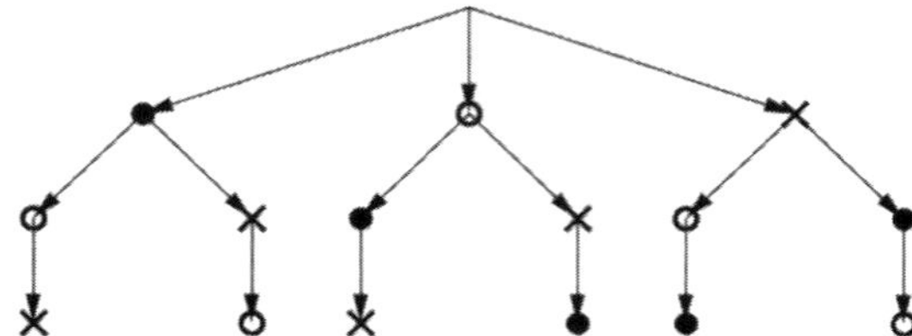

You can also make a chart to list all the possibilities:

First object	Second object	Third object
•	x	o
•	o	x
o	•	x
o	x	•
x	•	o
x	o	•

Either way, you can easily see there are six possible ways the three objects can be ordered.

If two events have no outcomes in common, they are said to be **mutually exclusive**. For example, in a standard deck of 52 playing cards, the event of all card suits is mutually exclusive to the event of all card values. If two events have no bearing on each other so that one event occurring has no influence on the probability of another event occurring, the two events are said to be independent. For example, rolling a standard six-sided die multiple times does not change that probability that a particular number will be rolled from one roll to the next. If the outcome of one event does affect the probability of the second event, the two events are said to be dependent. For example, if cards are drawn from a deck, the probability of drawing an ace after an ace has been drawn is different than the probability of drawing an ace if no ace (or no other card, for that matter) has been drawn.

In probability, the **odds in favor of an event** are the number of times the event will occur compared to the number of times the event will not occur. To calculate the odds in favor of an event, use the formula $\frac{P(A)}{1-P(A)}$, where $P(A)$ is the probability that the event will occur. Many times, odds in favor is given as a ratio in the form $\frac{a}{b}$ or $a{:}b$, where a is the probability of the event occurring and b is the complement of the event, the probability of the event not occurring. If the odds in favor are given as 2:5, that means that you can expect the event to occur two times for every 5 times that it does not occur. In other words, the probability that the event will occur is $\frac{2}{2+5} = \frac{2}{7}$.

In probability, the **odds against an event** are the number of times the event will not occur compared to the number of times the event will occur. To calculate the odds against an event, use the formula $\frac{1-P(A)}{P(A)}$, where $P(A)$ is the probability that the event will occur. Many times, odds against is given as a ratio in the form $\frac{b}{a}$ or $b{:}a$, where b is the probability the event will not occur (the complement of the event) and a is the probability the event will occur. If the odds against an event are given as 3:1, that means that you can expect the event to not occur 3 times for every one time it does occur. In other words, 3 out of every 4 trials will fail.

Experimental and Theoretical Probability

Probability, P(A), is the likelihood that event A will occur. Probability is often expressed as the ratio of ways an event can occur to the total number of **outcomes**, also called the **sample space**. For example, the probability of flipping heads on a two-sided coin can be written as $\frac{1}{2}$ since there is one side with heads and a total of two sides, which means that there are two possible outcomes. Probabilities can also be expressed as decimals or percentages.

Tree diagrams are used to list all possible outcomes. Suppose you are packing for vacation and have set aside 4 shirts, 3 pairs of pants, and 2 hats. How many possible outfits are there? To construct a tree diagram, start with the first group of events, the shirts. You can use letters to label each of the articles (SA refers to the first shirt, SB refers to the second shirt, and so on). Then, from each shirt draw branches to each pair of pants that it could be paired with. Next, from each pair of pants, draw a branch to each hat that it could be paired to and finally, repeat the process with the shoes. This method allows you to list all of the possible outcomes.

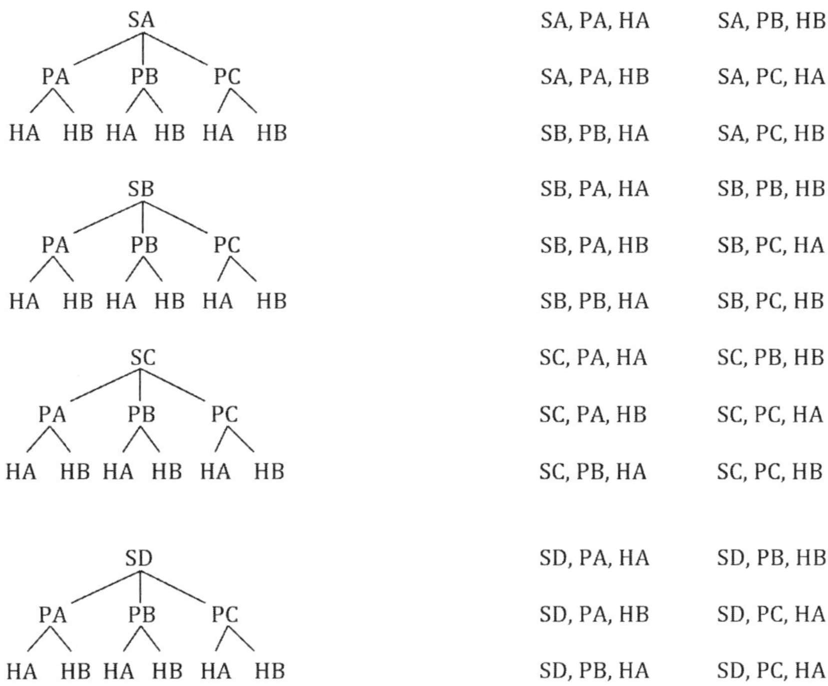

Altogether, there are 24 different combinations of shirts, pants, and hats.

Addition Principle

The **addition principle** is used to determine the sample space of 2 or more events. The addition principle states that if two events, x and y, with a number of possible outcomes, n_x and n_y, have no shared outcomes, then the events are called **mutually exclusive** and the union of the events, or the total number of outcomes of the sample space, is: $x \cap y = n_x + n_y$.

For example: In a regular deck of 52 playing cards with events defined as $x =$ [drawing a jack] and $y =$ [drawing a king], there is no way for both of these to occur at the same time. Since there are 4 ways to get a jack and 4 ways to get a king the union of those events is: $x \cap y = 4 + 4 = 8$. There are 8 ways that one or the other event can occur.

If the two events share any outcomes then they are not mutually exclusive and the total number of possible outcomes for the two events is $x \cap y = n_x + n_y - (x \cup y)$. Where $(x \cup y)$ is the number of outcomes common to both events. An example of this with a regular deck of cards would be if event $x =$ [drawing a jack] and event $y =$ [drawing a spade]. Now, since there are 4 ways to draw a jack, 13 ways to draw a spade, and 1 way to draw the jack of spades, the union of the events would be $x \cap y = 4 + 13 - 1 = 16$. There are 16 ways that one or the other event can occur.

Fundamental Counting Principle

The **fundamental counting principle** deals specifically with situations in which the order that something happens affects the outcome. Specifically, the fundamental counting principle states that if one event can have x possible different outcomes, and after the first outcome has been established the event can then have y possible outcomes, then there are $x \times y$ possible different ways the outcomes can happen in that order. For example, if two dice are rolled, one at a time, there are 6 possible outcomes for the first die, and 6 possible outcomes for the second die, for a total of $6 \times 6 = 36$ total possible outcomes. Suppose you have a bag containing a penny, a nickel, a dime, a quarter, and a half dollar. There are 5 different possible outcomes the first time you pull a coin. Without replacing the first coin, there are 4 different possible outcomes for the second coin. This makes $5 \times 4 = 20$ different possible outcomes for the first two coins drawn when the order the coins are drawn makes a difference.

Multiplication Counting Principle

A faster way to find the sample space without listing each individual outcome employs the **multiplication counting principle**. If one event can occur in a ways and a second event in b ways, then the two events can occur in $a \times b$ ways. In the previous example, there are 4 possible shirts, 3 possible pairs of pants, and 2 possible hats, so the possible number of combinations is $4 \times 3 \times 2$, or 24.

A similar principle is employed to determine the probability of two **independent events**. $P(A \text{ and } B) = P(A) \times P(B)$, where A is the first event and B is the second such that the outcome of B does not depend on the outcome of A. For instance, suppose you choose a marble from a bag of 2 red marbles, 7 blue marbles, and 4 green marbles. The probability that you would choose a red marble, replace it, and then choose a green marble is found by multiplying the probabilities of each independent event:

$$\frac{2}{13} \times \frac{4}{13} = \frac{8}{169}, \text{or } 0.047, \text{or } 4.7\%$$

This method can also be used when finding the probability of more than 2 independent events.

When two events are dependent on one another, the likelihood of the second event is affected by the outcome of the first event. This formula for finding the probability of **dependent events** is

$P(A \text{ then } B) = P(A) \times P(B \text{ after } A)$. The probability that you choose a 2 and then choose a 5 from a deck of 52 cards without replacement is

$$\frac{4}{52} \times \frac{4}{51} = \frac{1}{13} \times \frac{4}{51} = \frac{4}{663} \text{ or } 0.0060, \text{ or } 0.60\%$$

Note that there are four of each number in a deck of cards, so the probability of choosing a 2 is $\frac{4}{52}$. Since you keep this card out of the deck, there are only 51 cards to choose from when selecting a 5.

Thus far, the discussion of probability has been limited to **theoretical probability, which is used to predict the likelihood of an event. Experimental probability** expresses the ratio of the number of times an event actually occurs to the number of **trials** performed in an experiment. Theoretically, the probability of rolling a one on an unloaded, six-sided die is $\frac{1}{6}$. Suppose you conduct an experiment to determine whether a dice is a fair one and obtain these results.

Trial #	1	2	3	4	5	6	7	8	9	10	11	12	13	14	15	16	17	18	19	20
Outcome	6	1	2	6	4	2	1	3	4	5	4	1	6	6	4	5	6	4	1	6

Out of the 20 trials, you rolled a 1 six times. $\frac{6}{20} = \frac{3}{10} = 0.30$, or 30%. This probability is different than the theoretical probability of $\frac{1}{6}$ or 16.6%. You might conclude that the die is loaded, but it would be advisable to conduct more trials to verify your conclusion: the larger the number of trials, the more accurate the experimental probability.

Statistics Terminology

Statistics is the branch of mathematics that deals with collecting, recording, interpreting, illustrating, and analyzing large amounts of **data**. The following terms are often used in the discussion of data and **statistics**:

- **Data** – the collective name for pieces of *information* (singular is datum).
- **Quantitative data** – measurements (such as length, mass, and speed) that provide information about *quantities* in numbers
- **Qualitative data** – information (such as colors, scents, tastes, and shapes) that *cannot be measured* using numbers
- **Discrete data** – information that can be expressed only by a *specific value*, such as whole or half numbers. For example, since people can be counted only in whole numbers, a population count would be discrete data.
- **Continuous data** – information (such as time and temperature) that can be expressed by *any value within a given range*
- **Primary data** – information that has been *collected* directly from a survey, investigation, or experiment, such as a questionnaire or the recording of daily temperatures. Primary data that has not yet been organized or analyzed is called raw data.
- **Secondary data** – information that has been collected, sorted, and *processed* by the researcher
- **Ordinal data** – information that *can be placed in numerical order*, such as age or weight
- **Nominal data** – information that *cannot be placed in numerical order*, such as names or places.

STATISTICS

POPULATION

In statistics, the **population** is the entire collection of people, plants, etc., that data can be collected from. For example, a study to determine how well students in the area schools perform on a standardized test would have a population of all the students enrolled in those schools, although a study may include just a small sample of students from each school. A **parameter** is a numerical value that gives information about the population, such as the mean, median, mode, or standard deviation. Remember that the symbol for the mean of a population is μ and the symbol for the standard deviation of a population is σ.

SAMPLE

A **sample** is a portion of the entire population. Whereas a parameter helped describe the population, a **statistic** is a numerical value that gives information about the sample, such as mean, median, mode, or standard deviation. Keep in mind that the symbols for mean and standard deviation are different when they are referring to a sample rather than the entire population. For a sample, the symbol for mean is $\bar{x}$ and the symbol for standard deviation is s. The mean and standard deviation of a sample may or may not be identical to that of the entire population due to a sample only being a subset of the population. However, if the sample is random and large enough, statistically significant values can be attained. Samples are generally used when the population is too large to justify including every element or when acquiring data for the entire population is impossible.

INFERENTIAL STATISTICS

Inferential statistics is the branch of statistics that uses samples to make predictions about an entire population. This type of statistics is often seen in political polls, where a sample of the population is questioned about a particular topic or politician to gain an understanding about the attitudes of the entire population of the country. Often, exit polls are conducted on election days using this method. Inferential statistics can have a large margin of error if you do not have a valid sample.

SAMPLING DISTRIBUTION

Statistical values calculated from various samples of the same size make up the **sampling distribution**. For example, if several samples of identical size are randomly selected from a large population and then the mean of each sample is calculated, the distribution of values of the means would be a sampling distribution.

The **sampling distribution of the mean** is the distribution of the sample mean, $\bar{x}$, derived from random samples of a given size. It has three important characteristics. First, the mean of the sampling distribution of the mean is equal to the mean of the population that was sampled. Second, assuming the standard deviation is non-zero, the standard deviation of the sampling distribution of the mean equals the standard deviation of the sampled population divided by the square root of the sample size. This is sometimes called the standard error. Finally, as the sample size gets larger, the sampling distribution of the mean gets closer to a normal distribution via the Central Limit Theorem.

SURVEY STUDY

A **survey study** is a method of gathering information from a small group in an attempt to gain enough information to make accurate general assumptions about the population. Once a survey study is completed, the results are then put into a summary report.

Survey studies are generally in the format of surveys, interviews, or questionnaires as part of an effort to find opinions of a particular group or to find facts about a group.

It is important to note that the findings from a survey study are only as accurate as the sample chosen from the population.

Correlational Studies

Correlational studies seek to determine how much one variable is affected by changes in a second variable. For example, correlational studies may look for a relationship between the amount of time a student spends studying for a test and the grade that student earned on the test or between student scores on college admissions tests and student grades in college.

It is important to note that correlational studies cannot show a cause and effect, but rather can show only that two variables are or are not potentially correlated.

Experimental Studies

Experimental studies take correlational studies one step farther, in that they attempt to prove or disprove a cause-and-effect relationship. These studies are performed by conducting a series of experiments to test the hypothesis. For a study to be scientifically accurate, it must have both an experimental group that receives the specified treatment and a control group that does not get the treatment. This is the type of study pharmaceutical companies do as part of drug trials for new medications. Experimental studies are only valid when proper scientific method has been followed. In other words, the experiment must be well-planned and executed without bias in the testing process, all subjects must be selected at random, and the process of determining which subject is in which of the two groups must also be completely random.

Observational Studies

Observational studies are the opposite of experimental studies. In observational studies, the tester cannot change or in any way control all of the variables in the test. For example, a study to determine which gender does better in math classes in school is strictly observational. You cannot change a person's gender, and you cannot change the subject being studied. The big downfall of observational studies is that you have no way of proving a cause-and-effect relationship because you cannot control outside influences. Events outside of school can influence a student's performance in school, and observational studies cannot take that into consideration.

Random Samples

For most studies, a **random sample** is necessary to produce valid results. Random samples should not have any particular influence to cause sampled subjects to behave one way or another. The goal is for the random sample to be a **representative sample**, or a sample whose characteristics give an accurate picture of the characteristics of the entire population. To accomplish this, you must make sure you have a proper **sample size**, or an appropriate number of elements in the sample.

Biases

In statistical studies, biases must be avoided. **Bias** is an error that causes the study to favor one set of results over another. For example, if a survey to determine how the country views the president's job performance only speaks to registered voters in the president's party, the results will be skewed because a disproportionately large number of responders would tend to show approval, while a disproportionately large number of people in the opposite party would tend to express disapproval.

Extraneous Variables

Extraneous variables are, as the name implies, outside influences that can affect the outcome of a study. They are not always avoidable, but could trigger bias in the result.

Data Organization

Example

A nurse found the heart rates of ten different patients to be 76, 80, 90, 86, 70, 76, 72, 88, 88, and 68 beats per minute. Organize this information in a table.

There are several ways to organize data in a table. The table below is an example.

Patient Number	1	2	3	4	5	6	7	8	9	10
Heart Rate (bpm)	76	80	90	86	70	76	72	88	88	68

When making a table, be sure to label the columns and rows appropriately.

Data Analysis

Measures of Central Tendency

The **measure of central tendency** is a statistical value that gives a general tendency for the center of a group of data. There are several different ways of describing the measure of central tendency. Each one has a unique way it is calculated, and each one gives a slightly different perspective on the data set. Whenever you give a measure of central tendency, always make sure the units are the same. If the data has different units, such as hours, minutes, and seconds, convert all the data to the same unit, and use the same unit in the measure of central tendency. If no units are given in the data, do not give units for the measure of central tendency.

Mean

The **statistical mean** of a group of data is the same as the arithmetic average of that group. To find the mean of a set of data, first convert each value to the same units, if necessary. Then find the sum of all the values, and count the total number of data values, making sure you take into consideration each individual value. If a value appears more than once, count it more than once. Divide the sum of the values by the total number of values and apply the units, if any. Note that the mean does not have to be one of the data values in the set, and may not divide evenly.

$$\text{mean} = \frac{\text{sum of the data values}}{\text{quantity of data values}}$$

The mean of the data set {88, 72, 61, 90, 97, 68, 88, 79, 86, 93, 97, 71, 80, 84, 89, 72, 91, 95, 89, 83, 94, 90, 63, 69, 89} would be the sum of the twenty-five numbers divided by 25:

$$\frac{88 + 72 + 61 + 90 + 97 + \cdots + 94 + 90 + 63 + 69 + 89}{25} = \frac{2078}{25} = 83.12$$

While the mean is relatively easy to calculate and averages are understood by most people, the mean can be very misleading if used as the sole measure of central tendency. If the data set has outliers (data values that are unusually high or unusually low compared to the rest of the data values), the mean can be very distorted, especially if the data set has a small number of values. If unusually high values are countered with unusually low values, the mean is not affected as much. For example, if five of twenty students in a class get a 100 on a test, but the other 15 students have an average of 60 on the same test, the class average would appear as 70. Whenever the mean is skewed by outliers, it is always a good idea to include the median as an alternate measure of central tendency.

Review Video: Mean, Median, and Mode
Visit mometrix.com/academy and enter code: 286207

MEDIAN

The **statistical median** is the value in the middle of the set of data. To find the median, list all data values in order from smallest to largest or from largest to smallest. Any value that is repeated in the set must be listed the number of times it appears. If there are an odd number of data values, the median is the value in the middle of the list. If there is an even number of data values, the median is the arithmetic mean of the two middle values.

MODE

The **statistical mode** is the data value that occurs the most number of times in the data set. It is possible to have exactly one mode, more than one mode, or no mode. To find the mode of a set of data, arrange the data like you do to find the median (all values in order, listing all multiples of data values). Count the number of times each value appears in the data set. If all values appear an equal number of times, there is no mode. If one value appears more than any other value, that value is the mode. If two or more values appear the same number of times, but there are other values that appear fewer times and no values that appear more times, all of those values are the modes.

The big disadvantage of using the median as a measure of central tendency is that is relies solely on a value's relative size as compared to the other values in the set. When the individual values in a set of data are evenly dispersed, the median can be an accurate tool. However, if there is a group of rather large values or a group of rather small values that are not offset by a different group of values, the information that can be inferred from the median may not be accurate because the distribution of values is skewed.

The main disadvantage of the mode is that the values of the other data in the set have no bearing on the mode. The mode may be the largest value, the smallest value, or a value anywhere in between in the set. The mode only tells which value or values, if any, occurred the most number of times. It does not give any suggestions about the remaining values in the set.

DISPERSION

The **measure of dispersion** is a single value that helps to "interpret" the measure of central tendency by providing more information about how the data values in the set are distributed about the measure of central tendency. The measure of dispersion helps to eliminate or reduce the disadvantages of using the mean, median, or mode as a single measure of central tendency, and give a more accurate picture of the dataset as a whole. To have a measure of dispersion, you must know or calculate the range, standard deviation, or variance of the data set.

RANGE

The **range** of a set of data is the difference between the greatest and lowest values of the data in the set. To calculate the range, you must first make sure the units for all data values are the same, and then identify the greatest and lowest values. Use the formula $range = highest\ value -$

lowest value. If there are multiple data values that are equal for the highest or lowest, just use one of the values in the formula. Write the answer with the same units as the data values you used to do the calculations.

STANDARD DEVIATION

Standard deviation is a measure of dispersion that compares all the data values in the set to the mean of the set to give a more accurate picture. To find the standard deviation of a population, use the formula

$$\sigma = \sqrt{\frac{\sum_{i=1}^{n}(x_i - \bar{x})^2}{n}}$$

where σ is the standard deviation of a population, x represents the individual values in the data set, $\bar{x}$ is the mean of the data values in the set, and n is the number of data values in the set. The higher the value of the standard deviation is, the greater the variance of the data values from the mean. The units associated with the standard deviation are the same as the units of the data values.

VARIANCE

The **variance** of a population, or just variance, is the square of the standard deviation of that population. While the mean of a set of data gives the average of the set and gives information about where a specific data value lies in relation to the average, the variance of the population gives information about the degree to which the data values are spread out and tell you how close an individual value is to the average compared to the other values. The units associated with variance are the same as the units of the data values squared.

PERCENTILE

Percentiles and **quartiles** are other methods of describing data within a set. *Percentiles* tell what percentage of the data in the set fall below a specific point. For example, achievement test scores are often given in percentiles. A score at the 80th percentile is one which is equal to or higher than 80 percent of the scores in the set. In other words, 80 percent of the scores were lower than that score.

QUARTILE

Quartiles are percentile groups that make up quarter sections of the data set. The first quartile is the 25th percentile. The second quartile is the 50th percentile; this is also the median of the dataset. The third quartile is the 75th percentile.

SKEWNESS

Skewness is a way to describe the symmetry or asymmetry of the distribution of values in a dataset. If the distribution of values is symmetrical, there is no skew. In general the closer the mean of a data set is to the median of the data set, the less skew there is. Generally, if the mean is to the right of the median, the data set is *positively skewed*, or right-skewed, and if the mean is to the left of the median, the data set is *negatively skewed*, or left-skewed. However, this rule of thumb is not infallible. When the data values are graphed on a curve, a set with no skew will be a perfect bell curve. To estimate skew, use the formula

$$\text{skew} = \frac{\sqrt{n(n-1)}}{n-2}\left(\frac{\frac{1}{n}\sum_{i=1}^{n}(x_i-\bar{x})^3}{\left(\frac{1}{n}\sum_{i=1}^{n}(x_i-\bar{x})^2\right)^{\frac{3}{2}}}\right)$$

where n is the number of values is the set, x_i is the ith value in the set, and $\bar{x}$ is the mean of the set.

Simple Regression

In statistics, **simple regression** is using an equation to represent a relation between an independent and dependent variables. The independent variable is also referred to as the explanatory variable or the predictor, and is generally represented by the variable x in the equation. The dependent variable, usually represented by the variable y, is also referred to as the response variable. The equation may be any type of function – linear, quadratic, exponential, etc. The best way to handle this task is to use the regression feature of your graphing calculator. This will easily give you the curve of best fit and provide you with the coefficients and other information you need to derive an equation.

Line of Best Fit

In a scatter plot, the **line of best fit** is the line that best shows the trends of the data. The line of best fit is given by the equation $\hat{y} = ax + b$, where a and b are the regression coefficients. The regression coefficient a is also the slope of the line of best fit, and b is also the y-coordinate of the point at which the line of best fit crosses the x-axis. Not every point on the scatter plot will be on the line of best fit. The differences between the y-values of the points in the scatter plot and the corresponding y-values according to the equation of the line of best fit are the residuals. The line of best fit is also called the least-squares regression line because it is also the line that has the lowest sum of the squares of the residuals.

Correlation Coefficient

The **correlation coefficient** is the numerical value that indicates how strong the relationship is between the two variables of a linear regression equation. A correlation coefficient of –1 is a perfect negative correlation. A correlation coefficient of +1 is a perfect positive correlation. Correlation coefficients close to –1 or +1 are very strong correlations. A correlation coefficient equal to zero indicates there is no correlation between the two variables. This test is a good indicator of whether or not the equation for the line of best fit is accurate. The formula for the correlation coefficient is

$$r = \frac{\sum_{i=1}^{n}(x_i-\bar{x})(y_i-\bar{y})}{\sqrt{\sum_{i=1}^{n}(x_i-\bar{x})^2}\sqrt{\sum_{i=1}^{n}(y_i-\bar{y})^2}}$$

where r is the correlation coefficient, n is the number of data values in the set, (x_i, y_i) is a point in the set, and $\bar{x}$ and $\bar{y}$ are the means.

Z-Score

A **z-score** is an indication of how many standard deviations a given value falls from the mean. To calculate a z-score, use the formula $= \frac{x-\mu}{\sigma}$, where x is the data value, μ is the mean of the data set, and σ is the standard deviation of the population. If the z-score is positive, the data value lies above the mean. If the z-score is negative, the data value falls below the mean. These scores are useful in interpreting data such as standardized test scores, where every piece of data in the set has been counted, rather than just a small random sample. In cases where standard deviations are calculated from a random sample of the set, the z-scores will not be as accurate.

Central Limit Theorem

According to the ***central limit theorem***, regardless of what the original distribution of a sample is, the distribution of the means tends to get closer and closer to a normal distribution as the sample size gets larger and larger (this is necessary because the sample is becoming more all-encompassing of the elements of the population). As the sample size gets larger, the distribution of the sample mean will approach a normal distribution with a mean of the population mean and a variance of the population variance divided by the sample size.

Shape of Data Distribution

Symmetry and Skewness

Symmetry is a characteristic of the shape of the plotted data. Specifically, it refers to how well the data on one side of the median *mirrors* the data on the other side.

A **skewed data** set is one that has a distinctly longer or fatter tail on one side of the peak or the other. A data set that is *skewed left* has more of its values to the left of the peak, while a set that is *skewed right* has more of its values to the right of the peak. When actually looking at the graph, these names may seem counterintuitive since, in a left-skewed data set, the bulk of the values seem to be on the right side of the graph, and vice versa. However, if the graph is viewed strictly in relation to the peak, the direction of skewness makes more sense.

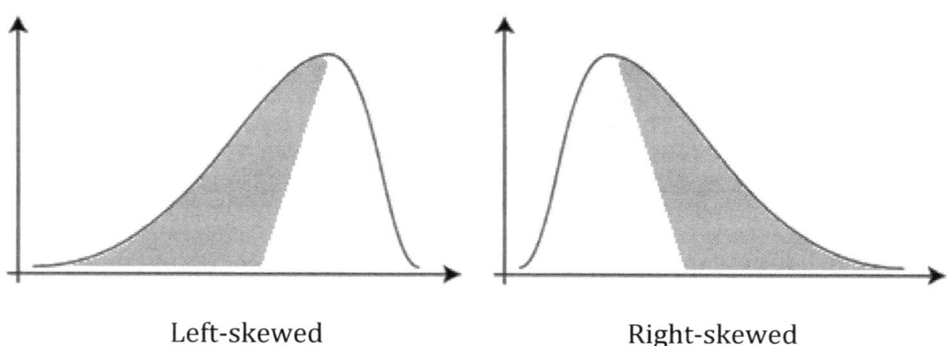

Left-skewed Right-skewed

Unimodal vs. Bimodal

If a distribution has a single peak, it would be considered **unimodal**. If it has two discernible peaks it would be considered **bimodal**. Bimodal distributions may be an indication that the set of data being considered is actually the combination of two sets of data with significant differences.

Uniformity

A uniform distribution is a distribution in which there is *no distinct peak or variation* in the data. No values or ranges are particularly more common than any other values or ranges.

Displaying Information

Charts and Tables

Charts and tables are ways of organizing information into separate rows and columns that are labeled to identify and explain the data contained in them. Some charts and tables are organized horizontally, with row lengths giving the details about the labeled information. Other charts and tables are organized vertically, with column heights giving the details about the labeled information.

Frequency Tables

Frequency tables show how frequently each unique value appears in the set. A r*elative frequency table* is one that shows the proportions of each unique value compared to the entire set. Relative frequencies are given as percents; however, the total percent for a relative frequency table will not necessarily equal 100 percent due to rounding. An example of a frequency table with relative frequencies is below.

Favorite Color	Frequency	Relative Frequency
Blue	4	13%
Red	7	22%
Purple	3	9%
Green	6	19%
Cyan	12	38%

Pictographs

A **pictograph** is a graph, generally in the horizontal orientation, that uses pictures or symbols to represent the data. Each pictograph must have a key that defines the picture or symbol and gives the quantity each picture or symbol represents. Pictures or symbols on a pictograph are not always shown as whole elements. In this case, the fraction of the picture or symbol shown represents the same fraction of the quantity a whole picture or symbol stands for. For example, a row with $3\frac{1}{2}$ ears of corn, where each ear of corn represents 100 stalks of corn in a field, would equal $3\frac{1}{2} \cdot 100 = 350$ stalks of corn in the field.

Circle Graphs

Circle graphs, also known as *pie charts*, provide a visual depiction of the relationship of each type of data compared to the whole set of data. The circle graph is divided into sections by drawing radii to create central angles whose percentage of the circle is equal to the individual data's percentage of the whole set. Each 1% of data is equal to 3.6° in the circle graph. Therefore, data represented by a 90° section of the circle graph makes up 25% of the whole. When complete, a circle graph often looks like a pie cut into uneven wedges. The pie chart below shows the data from the frequency table referenced earlier where people were asked their favorite color.

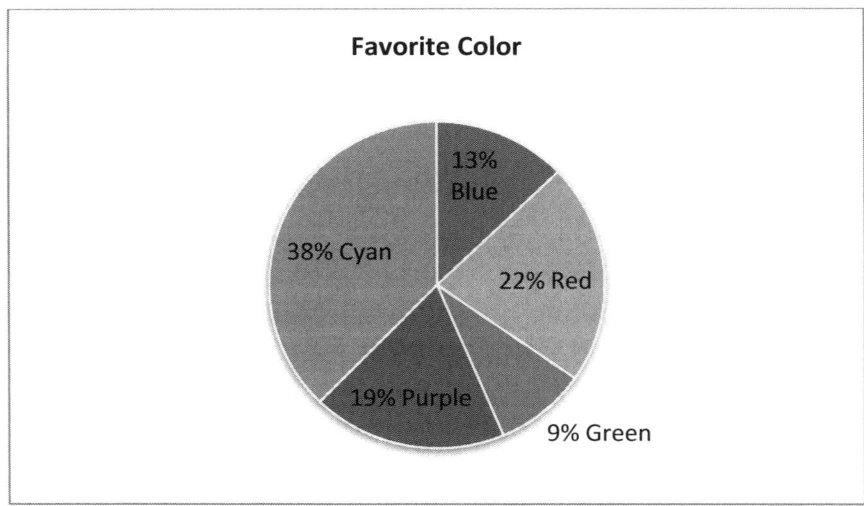

Review Video: Pie Chart
Visit mometrix.com/academy and enter code: 895285

LINE GRAPHS

Line graphs have one or more lines of varying styles (solid or broken) to show the different values for a set of data. The individual data are represented as ordered pairs, much like on a Cartesian plane. In this case, the *x*- and *y*-axes are defined in terms of their units, such as dollars or time. The individual plotted points are joined by line segments to show whether the value of the data is increasing (line sloping upward), decreasing (line sloping downward) or staying the same (horizontal line). Multiple sets of data can be graphed on the same line graph to give an easy visual comparison. An example of this would be graphing achievement test scores for different groups of students over the same time period to see which group had the greatest increase or decrease in performance from year-to-year (as shown below).

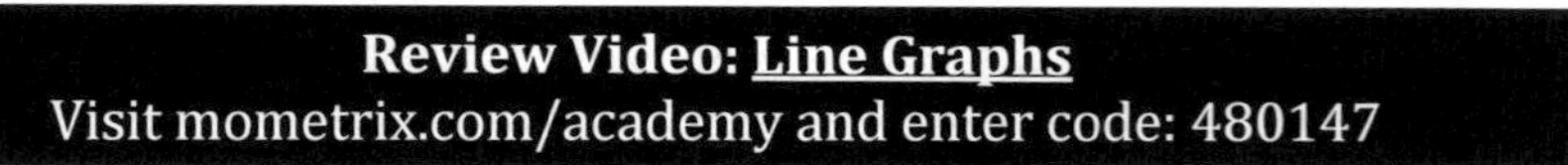

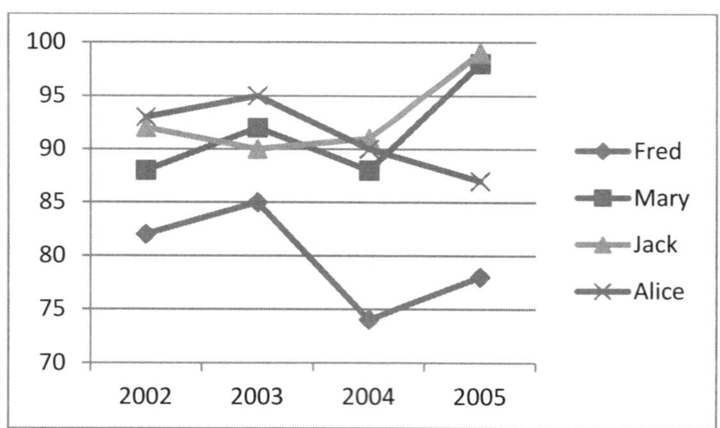

LINE PLOTS

A **line plot**, also known as a *dot plot*, has plotted points that are not connected by line segments. In this graph, the horizontal axis lists the different possible values for the data, and the vertical axis lists the number of times the individual value occurs. A single dot is graphed for each value to show the number of times it occurs. This graph is more closely related to a bar graph than a line graph. Do not connect the dots in a line plot or it will misrepresent the data.

Review Video: Line Plot
Visit mometrix.com/academy and enter code: 754610

STEM AND LEAF PLOTS

A **stem and leaf plot** is useful for depicting groups of data that fall into a range of values. Each piece of data is separated into two parts: the first, or left, part is called the stem; the second, or right, part is called the leaf. Each stem is listed in a column from smallest to largest. Each leaf that has the common stem is listed in that stem's row from smallest to largest. For example, in a set of two-digit numbers, the digit in the tens place is the stem, and the digit in the ones place is the leaf. With a stem and leaf plot, you can easily see which subset of numbers (10s, 20s, 30s, etc.) is the largest. This information is also readily available by looking at a histogram, but a stem and leaf plot also allows you to look closer and see exactly which values fall in that range. Using all of the test scores from above, we can assemble a stem and leaf plot like the one below.

Test Scores									
7	4	8							
8	2	5	7	8	8				
9	0	0	1	2	2	3	5	8	9

BAR GRAPHS

A **bar graph** is one of the few graphs that can be drawn correctly in two different configurations – both horizontally and vertically. A bar graph is similar to a line plot in the way the data is organized on the graph. Both axes must have their categories defined for the graph to be useful. Rather than placing a single dot to mark the point of the data's value, a bar, or thick line, is drawn from zero to the exact value of the data, whether it is a number, percentage, or other numerical value. Longer bar lengths correspond to greater data values. To read a bar graph, read the labels for the axes to find the units being reported. Then look where the bars end in relation to the scale given on the corresponding axis and determine the associated value.

The bar chart below represents the responses from our favorite color survey.

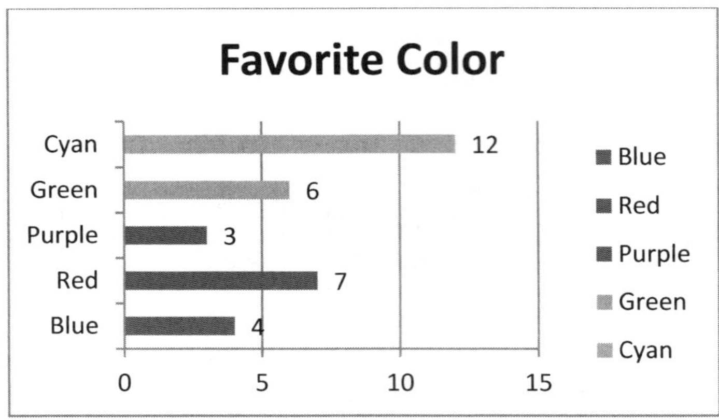

Review Video: Bar Graph
Visit mometrix.com/academy and enter code: 226729

Histograms

At first glance, a **histogram** looks like a vertical bar graph. The difference is that a bar graph has a separate bar for each piece of data and a histogram has one continuous bar for each *range* of data. For example, a histogram may have one bar for the range 0–9, one bar for 10–19, etc. While a bar graph has numerical values on one axis, a histogram has numerical values on both axes. Each range is of equal size, and they are ordered left to right from lowest to highest. The height of each column on a histogram represents the number of data values within that range. Like a stem and leaf plot, a histogram makes it easy to glance at the graph and quickly determine which range has the greatest quantity of values. A simple example of a histogram is below.

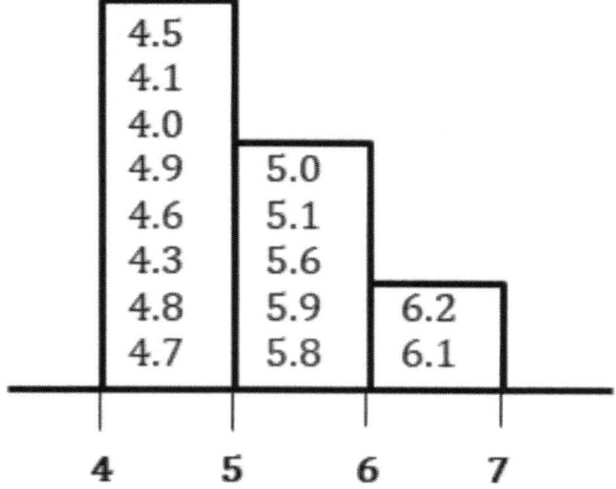

Review Video: Histogram
Visit mometrix.com/academy and enter code: 735897

Bivariate Data

Bivariate data is simply data from two different variables. (The prefix *bi-* means *two.*) In a *scatter plot,* each value in the set of data is plotted on a grid similar to a Cartesian plane, where each axis represents one of the two variables. By looking at the pattern formed by the points on the grid, you can often determine whether or not there is a relationship between the two variables, and what that relationship is, if it exists. The variables may be directly proportionate, inversely proportionate, or show no proportion at all. It may also be possible to determine if the data is linear, and if so, to find an equation to relate the two variables. The following scatter plot shows the relationship between preference for brand "A" and the age of the consumers surveyed.

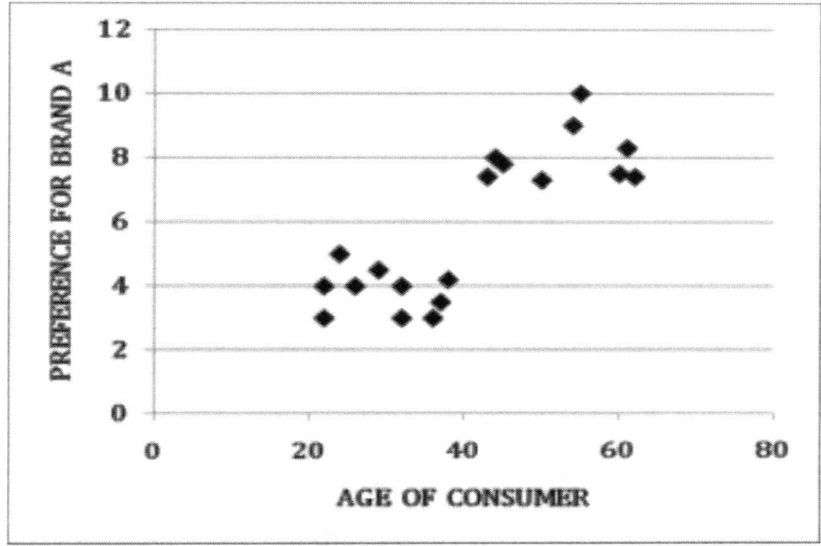

Scatter Plots

Scatter plots are also useful in determining the type of function represented by the data and finding the simple regression. Linear scatter plots may be positive or negative. Nonlinear scatter plots are generally exponential or quadratic. Below are some common types of scatter plots:

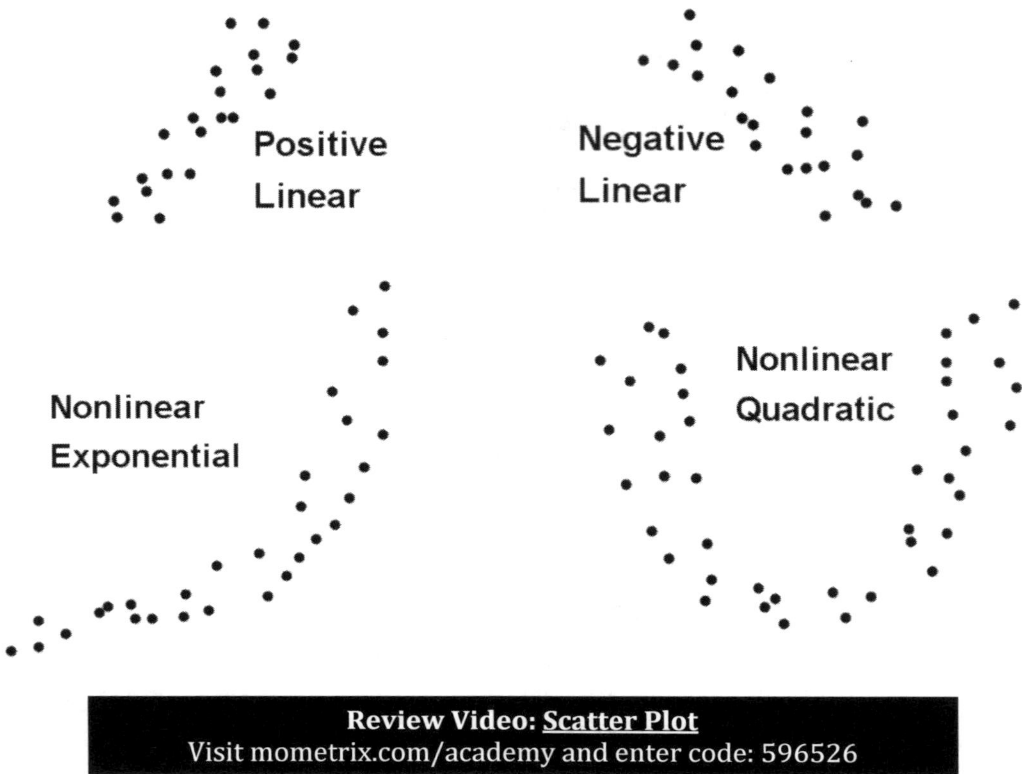

Review Video: Scatter Plot
Visit mometrix.com/academy and enter code: 596526

5-Number Summary

The **5-number summary** of a set of data gives a very informative picture of the set. The five numbers in the summary include the minimum value, maximum value, and the three quartiles. This information gives the reader the range and median of the set, as well as an indication of how the data is spread about the median.

Box and Whisker Plots

A **box-and-whisker plot** is a graphical representation of the 5-number summary. To draw a box-and-whiskers plot, plot the points of the 5-number summary on a number line. Draw a box whose ends are through the points for the first and third quartiles. Draw a vertical line in the box through the median to divide the box in half. Draw a line segment from the first quartile point to the minimum value, and from the third quartile point to the maximum value.

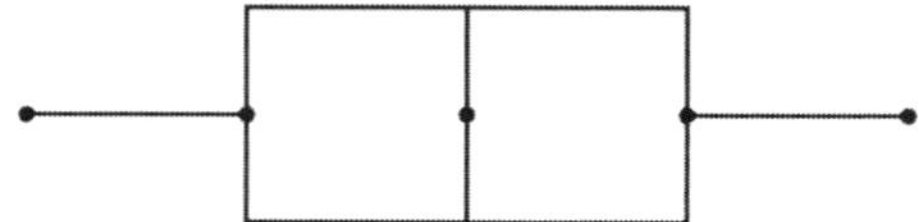

68-95-99.7 Rule

The **68–95–99.7 rule** describes how a normal distribution of data should appear when compared to the mean. This is also a description of a normal bell curve. According to this rule, 68 percent of the data values in a normally distributed set should fall within one standard deviation of the mean (34 percent above and 34 percent below the mean), 95 percent of the data values should fall within two standard deviations of the mean (47.5 percent above and 47.5 percent below the mean), and 99.7 percent of the data values should fall within three standard deviations of the mean, again, equally distributed on either side of the mean. This means that only 0.3 percent of all data values should fall more than three standard deviations from the mean. On the graph below, the normal curve is centered on the y-axis. The x-axis labels are how many standard deviations away from the center you are.

Therefore, it is easy to see how the 68-95-99.7 rule can apply.

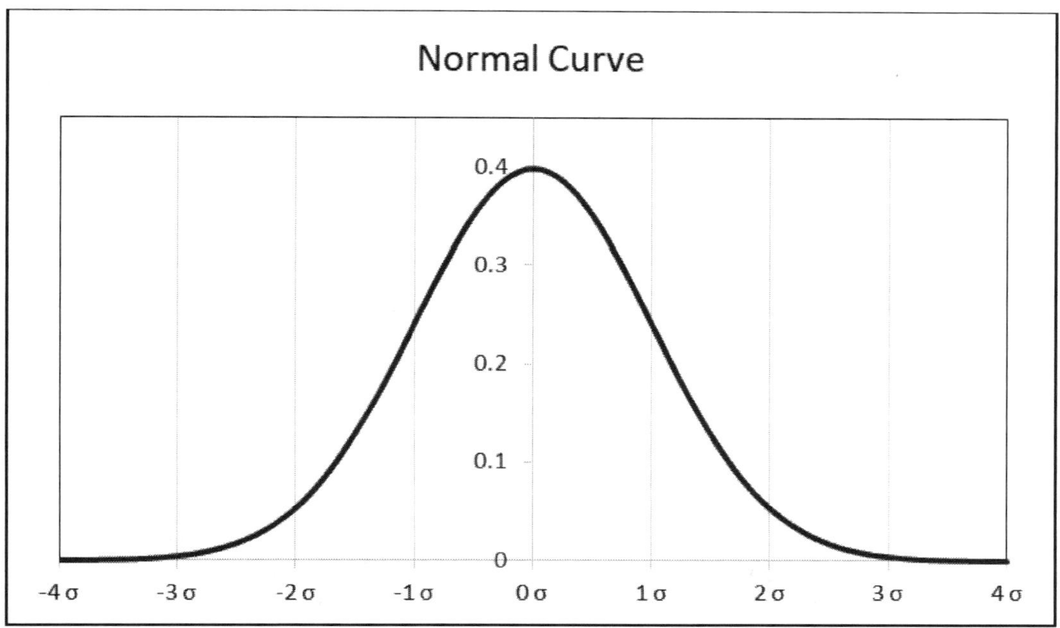

Shapes of Frequency Curves

The five general **shapes of frequency curves** are *symmetrical*, u-*shaped*, *skewed*, j-*shaped*, and *multimodal*. Symmetrical curves are also known as bell curves or normal curves. Values equidistant from the median have equal frequencies. U-shaped curves have two maxima – one at each end. Skewed curves have the maximum point off-center. Curves that are negative skewed, or left skewed, have the maximum on the right side of the graph so there is longer tail and lower slope on the left side. The opposite is true for curves that are positive-skewed, or right-skewed. J-shaped curves have a maximum at one end and a minimum at the other end. Multimodal curves have multiple maxima. For example, if the curve has exactly two maxima, it is called a bimodal curve.

Interpretation of Graphs

Example

The following graph shows the ages of five patients being cared for in a hospital:

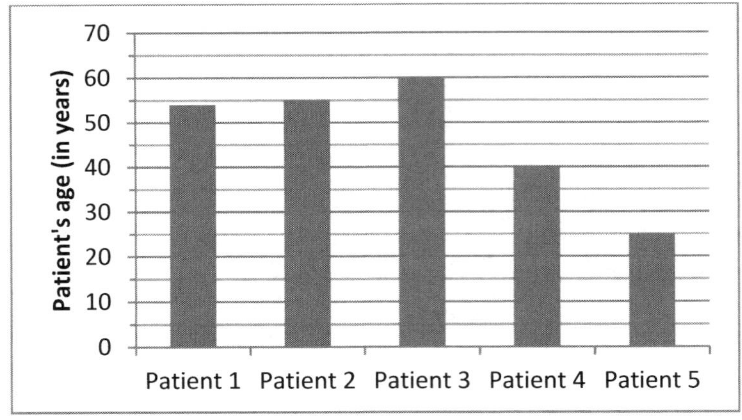

Determine the range of patient ages.

Patient 1 is 54 years old; Patient 2 is 55 years old; Patient 3 is 60 years old; Patient 4 is 40 years old; and Patient 5 is 25 years old. The range of patient ages is the age of the oldest patient minus the age of the youngest patient. In other words, $60 - 25 = 35$. The range of ages is 35 years.

Consistency between Studies

Example

In a drug study containing 100 patients, a new cholesterol drug was found to decrease low-density lipoprotein (LDL) levels in 25% of the patients. In a second study containing 50 patients, the same drug administered at the same dosage was found to decrease LDL levels in 50% of the patients. Are the results of these two studies **consistent** with one another?

Even though in both studies 25 people (25% of 100 is 25 and 50% of 50 is 25) showed improvements in their LDL levels, the results of the studies are inconsistent. The results of the second study indicate that the drug has a much higher efficacy (desired result) than the results of the first study. Because 50 out of 150 total patients showed improvement on the medication, one could argue that the drug is effective in one third (or approximately 33%) of patients. However, one should be wary of the reliability of results when they're not **reproducible** from one study to the next and when the **sample size** is fairly low.

Mathematical Processes and Perspectives

PROOFS

A proof serves to show the deductive or inductive process that relates the steps leading from a hypothesis to a conclusion. A proof may be direct $(p \rightarrow q)$, meaning that a conclusion is shown to be true, given a hypothesis. There are also proofs by contradiction $(p \land \neg q)$, whereby the hypothesis is assumed to be true, and the negation of the conclusion is assumed to be true. (In other words, the statement is assumed to be false.) Proofs by contraposition $(\neg q \rightarrow \neg p)$ show that the negation of the conclusion leads to the negation of the hypothesis. (In other words, the negation of the conclusion is assumed to be true, and it must be shown that the negation of the hypothesis is also true.) A mathematical induction proof seeks to show that $P(1)$ is true and that $P(k+1)$ is true, given that $P(k)$ is true. Direct proofs, proofs by contradiction, and proofs by contraposition use deductive methods, while a mathematical induction proof uses an inductive method.

Direct proofs are those that assume a statement to be true. The purpose of such a proof is to show that the conclusion is true, given that the hypothesis is true. A sample of a direct proof is shown below:

Prove "If m divides a and m divides b, then m divides a + b."

Proof:

- Assume m divides a and m divides b.
- Thus, a equals the product of m and some integer factor, p, by the definition of division, and b equals the product of m and some integer factor, q, by the definition of division. According to substitution, a + b may be rewritten as $(m \cdot p) + (m \cdot q)$. Factoring out the m gives $m(p + q)$. Since m divides p + q, and p + q is an integer, according to the closure property, we have shown that m divides a + b, by the definition of division.

Indirect proofs (or proofs by contradiction) are those that assume a statement to be false. The purpose of such a proof is to show that a hypothesis is false, given the negation of the conclusion, indicating that the conclusion must be true. A sample of an indirect proof is shown below:

Prove "If 3x + 7 is odd, then x is even."

Proof:

- Assume 3x + 7 is odd and x is odd.
- According to the definition of odd, x = 2a + 1, where a is an element of the integers.
- Thus, by substitution, 3x + 7 = 3(2a + 1) + 7, which simplifies as 6a + 3 + 7, or 6a + 10, which may be rewritten as 2(3a + 5). Any even integer may be written as the product of 2 and some integer, k. Thus, we have shown the hypothesis to be false, meaning that the conditional statement must be true.

A proof by contraposition is one written in the form, $\neg q \rightarrow \neg p$. In other words, a proof by contraposition seeks to show that the negation of q will yield the negation of p. A sample of a proof by contraposition is shown below:

Prove "If 5x + 7 is even, then x is odd."

Proof:

- Assume that if x is even, then 5x + 7 is odd.
- Assume x is even.
- Thus, by the definition of an even integer, x = 2a.

By substitution, 5x + 7 may be rewritten as 5(2a) + 7, which simplifies as 10a + 7. This expression cannot be written as the product of 2 and some factor, k. Thus, 5x + 7 is odd, by definition of an odd integer. So, when 5x + 7 is even, x is odd, according to contraposition.

A proof by contradiction is one written in the form, $p \wedge$ ▯q. In other words, a proof by contradiction seeks to show the negation of q will result in a false hypothesis, indicating that the conclusion of the statement, as written, must be true. In other words, the conditional statement of $p \rightarrow q$ is true.

A proof by mathematical induction must first show that $P(1)$ is true. Once that is shown, such a proof must show that $P(k+1)$ is true when $P(k)$ is true. A sample proof by induction is shown below:

Prove "If n is a natural number, then $2+4+6+8+\cdots+2n=n(n+1)$."

Show that $P(1)$ is true.

$2(1)=1(1+1)$.

Assume P(k) is true.

$$2+4+6+8+\cdots+2k=k(k+1)$$

We want to show that $2+4+6+8+\cdots+2(k+1)=(k+1)((k+1)+1)$.

$2+4+6+8+\cdots+2(k+1)=k(k+1)+2(k+1)$.

$2+4+6+8+\cdots+2(k+1)=(k+1)(k+2)$.

$P(k+1)$ is true. Thus, according to mathematical induction, $2+4+6+8+\cdots+2n=n(n+1)$.

Problem

Use any proof type to prove the following: "The sum of the natural numbers is equal to n^2."

Proof by induction:

Show that $P(1)$ is true.

$1=1^2$.

Assume $P(k)$ is true.

$1+3+5+7+\cdots+2k+1=k^2$.

We want to show that $1 + 3 + 5 + 7 + \cdots + 2(k+1) + 1 = (k+1)^2$.

$$2 + 4 + 6 + 8 + \cdots + 2(k+1) = k^2 + 2(k+1).$$

$$2 + 4 + 6 + 8 + \cdots + 2(k+1) = k^2 + 2k + 2.$$

P(k+1) is true. Thus, according to mathematical induction,

$$1 + 3 + 5 + 7 + \cdots + 2n + 1 = n^2.$$

PREMISE AND ARGUMENT

A premise is a statement that precedes a conclusion, in an argument. It is the proposition, or assumption, of an argument.

An argument will have two or more premises.

Example:

If it is hot, then I will go swimming. (Premise)
It is hot today. (Premise)

____

Therefore, I will go swimming today. (Conclusion)

TRUTH TABLE TO VALIDATE THE RULE OF DETACHMENT

The Rule of Detachment states that given the premises, $p \to q$ and p, the valid conclusion is q.

In other words, for every case where $(p \to q) \wedge p$ is true, q will also be true. The truth table below illustrates this fact:

p	q	$p \to q$	$(p \to q) \bigwedge p$
T	T	T	T
T	F	F	F
F	T	T	F
F	F	T	F

Notice the first cell under $(p \to q) \wedge p$ is true, while the first cell under q is also true. Thus, for every case where $(p \to q) \wedge p$ was true, q was also true.

TRUTH TABLE TO VALIDATE THE CHAIN RULE

The Chain Rule states that given the premises, $p \to q$ and $q \to r$, the valid conclusion is $p \to r$.

In other words, for every case where $(p \to q) \wedge (q \to r)$ is true, $p \to r$ will also be true. The truth table below illustrates this fact:

p	q	r	$p \to q$	$q \to r$	$(p \to q) \wedge (q \to r)$	$p \to r$
T	T	T	T	T	T	T
T	T	F	T	F	F	F
T	F	T	F	T	F	T
T	F	F	F	T	F	F
F	T	T	T	T	T	T
F	T	F	T	F	F	T
F	F	T	T	T	T	T
F	F	F	T	T	T	T

Notice that for every case where $(p \to q) \wedge (q \to r)$ was true, $p \to r$ was also true.

Consider the premises below:

- If I hike a mountain, I will not eat a sandwich.
- If I do not eat a sandwich, I will drink some water.
- I will not drink some water.

Write a valid conclusive statement. Explain how you arrived at your answer. Be specific in your explanation.

Valid conclusive statement: I will not hike a mountain.

Application of the chain rule and rule of contraposition give the valid conclusion of ⍰p. According to the chain rule, given $p \to$ ⍰q and ⍰$q \to r$, then $p \to r$. According to the rule of contraposition, $p \to r$ and ⍰r yields ⍰p. On a truth table, for every place where $(p \to r) \wedge$ ⍰r is true, ⍰p is also true. Thus, this is a valid conclusive statement.

Inductive Reasoning

Inductive reasoning is a method used to make a conjecture, based on patterns and observations. The conclusion of an inductive argument may be true or false.

Mathematical Example:

- A cube has 6 faces, 8 vertices, and 12 edges. A square pyramid has 5 faces, 5 vertices, and 8 edges. A triangular prism has 5 faces, 6 vertices, and 9 edges. Thus, the sum of the numbers of faces and vertices, minus the number of edges, will always equal 2, for any solid.

Non-Mathematical Example:

- Almost all summer days in Tucson are hot. It is a summer day in Tucson. Therefore, it will probably be hot.

Deductive Reasoning

Deductive reasoning is a method that proves a hypothesis or set of premises. The conclusion of a valid deductive argument will be true, given that the premises are true. Deductive reasoning utilizes logic to determine a conclusion.

Example:

If a ding is a dong, then a ping is a pong.

If a ping is a pong, then a ring is a ting.

A ding is a dong.

Therefore, a ring is a ting.

This example is a deductive argument. A set of premises is used to determine a valid conclusion. In this example, the chain rule is illustrated. Specifically,

$$\begin{array}{c} p \to q \\ q \to r \\ p \\ \hline \therefore q \end{array}$$

Rules of Logic

The rules of logic are related to deductive reasoning because one conclusion must be made, given a set of premises (or statements). A truth table may be used to determine the validity of an argument. In all cases, the determination of the conclusion is based on a top-down approach, whereby a set of premises yields a certain conclusion, albeit true or false, depending on the truth values of all premises.

Mathematical Induction Proof Utilizing Inductive Reasoning

A mathematical induction proof utilizes inductive reasoning in its assumption that if $P(k)$ is true, then $P(k+1)$ is also true. The induction hypothesis is $P(k)$. This step utilizes inductive reasoning because an observation is used to make the conjecture that $P(k+1)$ is also true.

Example:

For all natural numbers, n, the sum is equal to $(n+1)\left(\frac{n}{2}\right)$.

Show that $P(1)$ is true.

$1 = (1+1)\left(\frac{1}{2}\right)$.

Assume P(k) is true.

$1 + 2 + 3 + 4 + \cdots + k = (k+1)\left(\frac{k}{2}\right)$.

This previous step is the inductive hypothesis. Using this hypothesis, it may be used to write the conjecture that $P(k+1)$ is also true.

Formal Reasoning

Formal reasoning, in mathematics, involves justification using formal steps and processes to arrive at a conclusion. Formal reasoning is utilized when writing proofs and using logic. For example, when applying logic, validity of a conclusion is determined by truth tables. A set of premises will yield a given conclusion. This type of thinking is formal reasoning. Writing a geometric proof also employs formal reasoning.

Example:

> If a quadrilateral has four congruent sides, it is a rhombus.
>
> If a shape is a rhombus, then the diagonals are perpendicular.
>
> A shape is a quadrilateral.
>
> Therefore, the diagonals are perpendicular.
>
> This example employs the chain rule, shown below:

$$\begin{gathered} p \rightarrow q \\ q \rightarrow r \\ p \\ \therefore r \end{gathered}$$

Informal Reasoning

Informal reasoning, in mathematics, uses patterns and observations to make conjectures. The conjecture may be true or false. Several, or even many, examples may show a certain pattern, shedding light on a possible conclusion. However, informal reasoning does not provide a justifiable conclusion. A conjecture may certainly be deemed as likely or probable. However, informal reasoning will not reveal a certain conclusion.

Example:

- Mathematical Idea – Given a sequence that starts with 1 and increases by a factor of $\frac{1}{2}$, the limit of the sum will be 2.
- Informal Reasoning – The sum of 1 and $\frac{1}{2}$ is $1\frac{1}{2}$. The sum of 1, $\frac{1}{2}$, and $\frac{1}{4}$ is $1\frac{3}{4}$. The sum of 1, $\frac{1}{2}$, $\frac{1}{4}$, and $\frac{1}{8}$ is $1\frac{7}{8}$, Thus, it appears that as the sequence approaches infinity, the sum of the sequence approaches 2.

Problems

Use informal reasoning to justify the statement,

"If n is a whole number, then $n^2 + n + 1$ is odd."

Explain the reasoning steps used.

> Given the sequence, 0, 1, 2, 3, 4, 5, 6, ..., evaluation of the expression, $n^2 + n + 1$, gives $0^2 + 0 + 1$, $1^2 + 1 + 1$, $2^2 + 2 + 1$, $3^2 + 3 + 1$, $4^2 + 4 + 1$, $5^2 + 5 + 1$, and $6^2 + 6 + 1$, or 1, 3, 7, 13, 21, 31, and 43, all of which are odd numbers. Thus, it appears that given any whole number, n, evaluation of the expression $n^2 + n + 1$ will yield an odd number.

Use formal reasoning to justify the statement,

"If a divides b, a divides c, and a divides d, then a divides the sum of b, c, and d."

Show the formal proof.

Direct Proof:

- Assume a divides b, a divides c, a divides d.

  Given the definition of divides, a divides b indicates that there exists some integer, r, such that $b = a \cdot r$. Also, a divides c indicates that there exists some integer, s, such that $c = a \cdot s$. Finally, a divides d indicates that there exists some integer, t, such that $d = a \cdot t$. By substitution, the sum of b, c, and d may be written as $(a \cdot r) + (a \cdot s) + (a \cdot t)$. Factoring out an a gives $a(r + s + t)$. The factor $(r + s + t)$ is an integer, according to the closure property under addition. Thus, a divides the sum of b, c, and d.

Describe two different strategies for solving the problem,

"Kevin can mow the yard in 4 hours. Mandy can mow the same yard in 5 hours. If they work together, how long will it take them to mow the yard?"

Two possible strategies both involve the use of rational equations to solve. The first strategy involves representing the fractional part of the yard mowed by each person in one hour and setting this sum equal to the ratio of 1 to the total time needed. The appropriate equation is $1/4 + 1/5 = 1/t$, which simplifies as $9/20 = 1/t$, and finally as $t = 20/9$. So, the time it will take them to mow the yard, when working together, is a little more than 2.2 hours. A second strategy involves representing the time needed for each person as two fractions and setting the sum equal to 1 (representing 1 yard). The appropriate equation is $t/4 + t/5 = 1$, which simplifies as $9t/20 = 1$, and finally as $t = 20/9$. This strategy also shows the total time to be a little more than 2.2 hours.

Describe two different strategies for solving the problem, "A car, traveling at 65 miles per hour, leaves Flagstaff and heads east on I-40. Another car, traveling at 75 miles per hour, leaves Flagstaff 2 hours later, from the same starting point and also heads east on I-40. After how many hours will the second car catch the first car?"

One strategy might involve creating a table of values for the number of hours and distances for each car. The table may be examined to find the same distance traveled and the corresponding number of hours taken. Such a table is shown below:

Car A		**Car B**	
x (hours)	**y (distance)**	**x (hours)**	**y (distance)**
0	0	0	–150
1	65	1	–75
2	130	2	0
3	195	3	75
4	260	4	150
5	325	5	225
6	390	6	300
7	455	7	375
8	520	8	450
9	585	9	525
10	650	10	600
11	715	11	675
12	780	12	750
13	845	13	825
14	910	14	900
15	975	15	975

The table shows that after 15 hours, the distance traveled is the same. Thus, the second car catches up with the first car after a distance of 975 miles and 15 hours.

A second strategy might involve setting up and solving an algebraic equation. This situation may be modeled as $65x = 75(x - 2)$. This equation sets the distances traveled by each car equal to one another. Solving for x gives $x = 15$. Thus, once again, the second car will catch up with the first car after 15 hours.

The path of a ball, tossed into the air, from a given height, may be modeled with the function, $(x) = -2x^2 + 4x + 9$. Erica states that the ball will reach the ground after 4 seconds. Describe two different approaches for determining if her solution is, or is not, reasonable.

The ball will reach the ground when the x-value is 0. Thus, one approach involves finding a possible root for the function, by setting the equation equal to 0 and applying the quadratic formula. Doing so gives $0 = -2x^2 + 4x + 9$, where $a = -2$, $b = 4$, and $c = 9$. The positive x-value is approximately 3.3. Thus, her solution is not reasonable, since the ball would have reached ground level prior to 4 seconds. Another approach involves graphing the function and looking for the positive root. Since the root is less than 4, it can be determined that her solution is not reasonable.

Write a mixture word problem. Select and illustrate a strategy that may be used to solve the problem. State the solution.

Martin needs a 20% medicine solution. The pharmacy has a 5% solution and a 30% solution. He needs 50 mL of the solution. If the pharmacist must mix the two solutions, how many milliliters of 5% solution and 30% solution should be used?

To solve this problem, a table may be created to represent the variables, percentages, and total amount of solution. Such a table is shown below:

	mL solution	% medicine	Total mL medicine
5% solution	x	0.05	$0.05x$
30% solution	y	0.30	$0.30y$
Mixture	$x + y = 50$	0.20	$(0.20)(50) = 10$

The variable, x, may be rewritten as $50 - y$, so the equation, $0.05(50 - y) + 0.30y = 10$, may be written and solved for y. Doing so gives $y = 30$. So, 30 mL of 5% solution are needed. Evaluating the expression, $50 - y$ for a y-value of 30, shows that 20 mL of 30% solution are needed.

The relationship between Statistics Final Exam scores and Calculus Final Exam scores, for a random sample of students, is represented by the table below.

Statistics Final Exam Scores	Calculus Final Exam Scores
74	82
78	72
84	88
89	86
93	97

A teacher models this relationship with the function, $f(x) = 0.9x + 8.4$. *Describe how well this model fits the situation. Explain the process used to evaluate the model.*

The linear function is a good model for the relationship between the two sets of scores, as evidenced by a correlation coefficient of approximately 0.78. Any r-value that is 0.70 or higher indicates a strong correlation. The r^2-value is approximately 0.61. A residual plot of the data would show no clear pattern, indicating that a linear model would be appropriate. The residual plot is shown below:

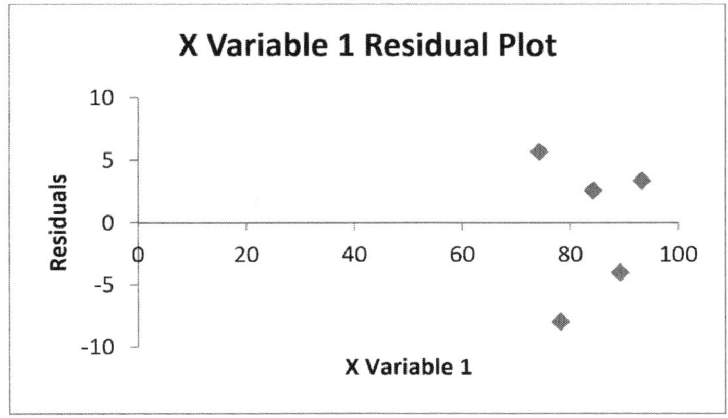

A residual plot does not show a clear pattern. Based on this information alone, explain how it may be determined whether or not the data may be represented by a linear model. Identify the appropriate model as linear or non-linear.

When a residual plot does not show a clear pattern (meaning the placement of the points are sporadic), it may be determined that the data represent a linear relationship. In other words, a linear model would be a good fit for the data. In order for the residual plot to indicate a non-linear model, the points would need to indicate some clear pattern. Examples of residual plots indicating a linear model and non-linear model are shown below:

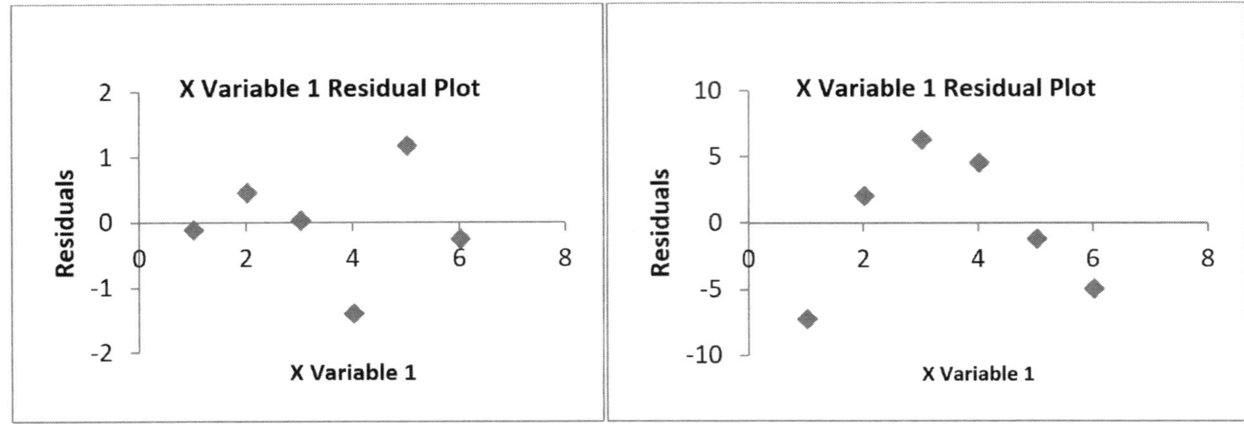

Carla wants to determine if the amount of her savings may best be modeled with a linear, cubic, other polynomial, or exponential function. Given some data points, describe at least two different strategies that she may employ to find the best fit function.

She may create a residual plot of the data to determine whether a linear model is appropriate. She may also use Excel or a graphing calculator to calculate and compare the r-values for different types of functions. This will show the best fit model. Note that some r-values may be quite similar, so the highest one will indicate the best fit model. There may be more than one appropriate model. She may also graph the data and visually compare the trendlines, deciding on the most appropriate fit.

The correlation between instructional strategy used and student achievement scores shows a correlation coefficient of approximately 0.84. Discuss whether a linear model is an appropriate function for this data.

The correlation coefficient is very high, thus a linear model would be very appropriate for modeling this data. Any correlation coefficient over 0.70 indicates a strong correlation, with one over 0.80 indicating a very strong correlation. The residual plot would not show any clear pattern. In other words, the points on the residual plot would be sporadic, for example, not showing a clear U-shaped or curved pattern. Shown below is a residual plot that represents data with an r-value of approximately 0.84:

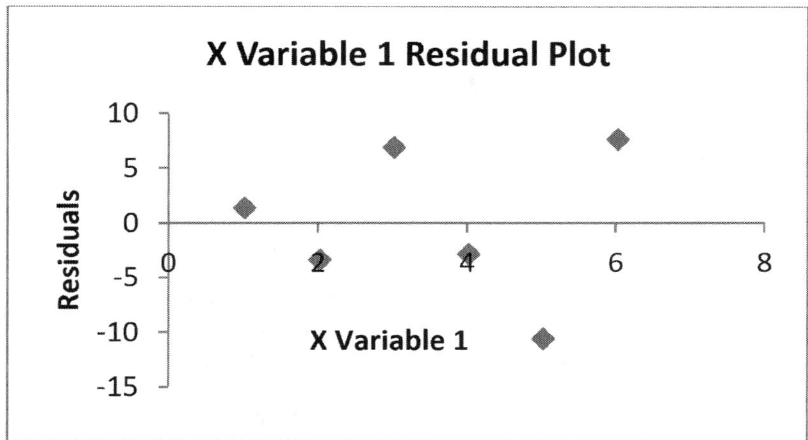

Notice that there is no clear pattern, and no curve or U-shape. Thus, this residual plot represents a linear relationship and may be modeled with a linear function.

Mathematical Learning, Instruction, and Assessment

Cognitive Theorists and Constructivists

Constructivists believe that students may construct knowledge by themselves. In other words, students are actively engaged in the construction of their own knowledge. Students will assimilate and accommodate in order to build new knowledge, based on previous knowledge. Thus, in planning instruction based on constructivism, a teacher would focus on grouping designs, environment, problem-solving tasks, and inclusion of multiple representations. The goal in such a classroom would be for students to construct knowledge on their own. There are different levels of constructivism, including weak constructivism and radical constructivism.

Cognitivists differ from constructivists in that they believe that active exploration is important in helping students make sense of observations and experiences. However, the students are not expected to invent or construct knowledge by themselves. They are only expected to make sense of the mathematics. In planning instruction based on cognitivism, a teacher would employ similar methods to those discussed above, with the focus on active exploration. Students would do a lot of comparisons of mathematical methods in making sense of ideas.

Constructivism

Three types of constructivism are weak constructivism, social constructivism, and radical constructivism. Weak constructivists believe that students construct their own knowledge, but also accept certain preconceived notions or facts. Social constructivists believe that students construct knowledge by interacting with one another and holding discussions and conversations. Radical constructivists believe that all interpretations of knowledge are subjective, based on the individual learner. In other words, there is no real truth; it is all subjective. Classroom instructional planning based on a weak constructivist viewpoint might involve incorporation of some accepted theorems and definitions, while continuing to plan active explorations and discussions. Planning based on a social constructivist viewpoint might involve group activities, debates, discussion forums, etc. Planning based on a radical constructivist viewpoint would involve activities that are open-ended, where there is more than one correct answer. The problems would invite more than one correct answer.

Project-Based Learning

Project-based learning is learning that centers on the solving of a problem. Students learn many different ideas by solving one "big" problem. For example, for a unit on sine and cosine functions, a teacher may design a problem whereby the students are asked to model a real-world phenomenon using both types of functions. Students must investigate the effects of changes in amplitude, period, shifts, etc., on the graphs of the functions. Students will also be able to make connections between the types of functions when modeling the same phenomenon. Such a problem will induce high-level thinking.

Project-based learning is derived from constructivist theory, which contends that students learn by doing and constructing their own knowledge.

Cooperative Learning

Cooperative learning simply means that students will learn by cooperating with one another. Students will be placed into groups of a size determined by the teacher. With such an approach, students work together to succeed in learning. Students may work together to learn a topic, complete an assignment, or compete with other groups.

Examples of cooperative learning include Think-Pair-Share and Jigsaw. Think-Pair-Share is a cooperative learning strategy that involves thinking about some given topic, sharing ideas, thoughts, or questions with a partner, and then sharing the partner discussion with the whole group. For example, in the mathematics classroom, a teacher may ask the class to think about the meaning of a proportional relationship. Each student would think for a set period of time, share ideas with a partner, and then each partner group would share their ideas regarding the meaning of proportionality. Jigsaw is another cooperative learning strategy that involves dividing among each group member reading material or ideas to be learned. Each student will then read his or her information, summarize it, and share the findings or ideas with the group. In mathematics, students might be given information on modeling with cosine and sine functions. Students could then share what they learned about real-world phenomena modeled by each. Different students may also be assigned to read in-depth material on amplitude, period, shifts, etc.

Control Strategies

"Control strategies" is another name for "metacognitive learning strategies," which indicate any strategy that promotes a learner's awareness of his or her level of learning. With such strategies, the student will work to determine what he or she knows and does not know regarding a subject. Possible control strategies are thinking, self-regulation, and discussing ideas with peers.

Example:

> A student may discover his or her level of "knowing" about functions by keeping a journal of any questions he or she might have regarding the topic. The student may list everything that he or she understands, as well as aspects not understood. As the student progresses through the course, he or she may go back and reconfirm any correct knowledge and monitor progress on any previous misconceptions.

Memorization and Elaboration Strategies

Memorization is simply a technique whereby rote repetition is used to learn information. Elaboration strategies involve the connection of new information to some previously learned information. In mathematics, for example, students may use elaboration strategies when learning how to calculate the volume of a cone, based on their understood approach for calculating the volume of a cylinder. The student would be making connections in his or her mind between this new skill and other previously acquired skills. A memorization technique would simply involve memorization of the volume of a cone formula, as well as ways to evaluate the formula.

Prior Knowledge

Three ways of activating students' prior knowledge are concept mapping, visual imagery, and comparing and contrasting. With concept mapping, a student would detail and connect all known aspects of a mathematics topic. Ideas would be grouped into subgroups. Such an approach would allow a student to see what he or she does not know, prompting the activation of any prior knowledge on the subject. Visual imagery is simply the use of any pictures or diagrams to promote activation of prior knowledge. For example, giving a picture of Pascal's triangle would likely activate students' prior knowledge regarding the Binomial Theorem. Comparing and contrasting means that the student will compare and contrast ideas or approaches. For example, a student might be given a mapping of an inverse function. He or she could then compare and contrast this mapping to a known mapping of a function, in order to decide how they are the same and different. This would activate a student's prior understanding of functions and the definition thereof.

Three methods for ascertaining, or assessing, students' prior knowledge are portfolios, pre-tests, and self-inventories. Portfolios are simply a compilation of prior student activity related to mathematics topics. For example, a portfolio might show a student's work with transforming functions. Pre-tests are designed to measure a student's understanding of mathematics topics that will be taught in the course during the year. Self-inventories are just what the name implies: inventories that ask the students to name, list, describe, and explain information understood about various mathematics topics.

Once a teacher has assessed students' level of prior knowledge regarding some mathematics topic, he or she may use that information to scaffold the instruction. In other words, the teacher may decide to further break down the mathematics material into more integral parts. Exact processes or steps may be shown, including justification for using certain properties or theorems. More examples may be shown, while including examples of many different variations of problems, in order to ensure that students are not simply memorizing one approach that will be incorrectly applied to any problem of that sort. The teacher may also decide that more group work, peer cooperation, and discussion are needed.

For example, suppose a teacher determines that students have very little understanding of logic and valid arguments. The teacher may decide to re-teach the creation of truth tables, including truth values for intersections and "if p, then q" statements. The teacher may also decide to re-teach how a truth table may be used to show if an argument is valid. Students may be placed into groups and asked to determine the validity of several simple arguments. Once students understand the concept, they may move on to more rigorous arguments, including equivalence relations.

Concept Whereby Usage of Manipulatives Would Increase Conceptual Understanding

Understanding of how to solve one-variable equations would certainly be enhanced by using rods and counters. With this manipulative, the rod would represent the variable, or x, while the counters would represent the constants on each side of the equation. A sample diagram of the equation, $x + 4 = 8$, is shown below. Note that the vertical line represents the equals sign.

In order to solve the equation (and isolate x), four counters may be removed from each side of the mat. This process is shown below:

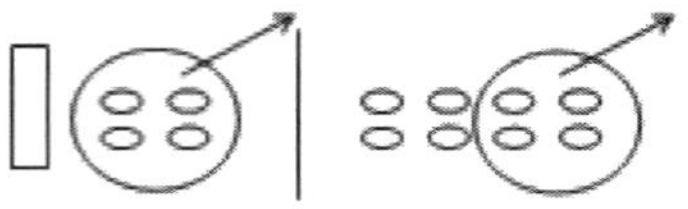

Now, the final illustration is:

Thus, the solution is $x = 4$. The manipulative helps students understand the meaning of the subtraction property of equality in action, without simply memorizing its meaning.

Problems

Problem #1

EXPLAIN HOW AN UNDERSTANDING OF THE AREA UNDER THE NORMAL CURVE MAY BE SUPPORTED BY USING A GRAPHING CALCULATOR. PROVIDE A SAMPLE PROBLEM AND DESCRIBE THE STEPS INVOLVED IN SOLVING, USING BOTH A MANUAL APPROACH AND A TECHNOLOGICAL APPROACH.

The area under the normal curve may be found by calculating z-scores for certain endpoint values. The mean to z areas for these z-scores may be used to find the area. A graphing calculator may use the normalpdf function and ShadeNorm function in order to show the same area under the normal curve, between two values. Consider the following problem: The class average on a statistics exam is 90, with a standard deviation of 4 points. Find the percentage of students who scored above 87 on the exam.

This problem may be solved manually by first calculating the z-score.

$$z = \frac{87 - 90}{4} = \frac{-3}{4}$$

Since the score falls below the mean, the area above the score will equal the sum of 0.5 (or the area of one-half of the normal curve) and the mean to z area, which is 0.2734. Thus, the area above the z-score of −0.75 is 0.7734. The percentage of students who scored above 87 was 77.34%.

This problem may also be solved by using the graphing calculator:

- Enter normalpdf(x, 0, 1) into the y = screen. (This represents the normal curve having a mean of 0 and standard deviation of 1.)
- Choose 2nd Vars, ShadeNorm(.
- Enter ShadeNorm(87,100,90,4). (This represents the lower bound, upper bound, mean, and standard deviation.)
- Record the area of approximately 0.77.
- Thus, the calculator also shows that approximately 77% of the students scored above an 87.

Problem #2

DESCRIBE HOW THE UNDERSTANDING OF DERIVATIVE AND ANTI-DERIVATIVE MAY BE ENHANCED/SUPPORTED USING A GRAPHING CALCULATOR. PROVIDE AN EXAMPLE AND SHOW HOW TO SOLVE, USING A MANUAL APPROACH AND TECHNOLOGICAL APPROACH.

The derivative of an expression is the slope of a tangent line to the curve, at a specific point. The anti-derivative of an expression is the inverse operation of the derivative. Taking the derivative of the anti-derivative will give the original expression. The derivative and anti-derivative can be calculated manually as shown below:

Given $f(x) = 3x^2 + 8x + 4$, the derivative is $f(x) = 6x + 8$. The anti-derivative is $f(x) = x^3 + 4x^2 + 4x$. Thus, evaluation of the derivative and anti-derivative for an x-value of 2 gives $f(x) = 20$ and $f(x) = 32$, respectively. The student can confirm his or her derivative and anti-derivative expressions by evaluating the graphed functions for the same x-value. If the expressions were correctly determined, then evaluation of the derivative and anti-derivative for the x-value should give the same y-value, for each.

Using the graphing calculator, the derivative and anti-derivative for a given point may be evaluated by entering the expression into the y = screen, graphing the function, selecting 2nd Trace, and then choosing dy/dx and $\int f(x)dx$. After selecting the derivative or anti-derivative, the x-value may be typed. Evaluation of the derivative or anti-derivative for that x-value will appear on the screen.

Piaget's Cognitive Development Theory

Piaget's cognitive development theory is aligned with constructivism. In fact, constructivism is built on his ideas. Piaget's cognitive development theory indicates that students actively participate in the construction of their own knowledge via assimilation and accommodation. Current cognitive theorists do not believe that students have to construct their own knowledge, but instead that they only have to make sense of what they are observing.

The four stages of learning, as developed by Piaget, are sensorimotor, preoperational, concrete operational, and formal operational. The defined stages show the progression from concrete thinking to abstract thinking. In other words, a child would need an object to understand properties, in the first stage. By the fourth stage, the child would be able to think abstractly, without some concrete form. In mathematics, this idea might be illustrated by first working with diagrams and manipulatives of numbers and then later writing symbolic forms of the numbers, including the numerals. This would illustrate the progression from 0 to 7 years. In the years of 11 to adulthood, much deeper abstraction is utilized. For example, people would be able to discuss functions and general properties, without looking at any concrete graphs or representations.

Progression That a Student Undergoes as He or She Learns Mathematics

When learning mathematics, students begin with concrete representations and ideas. Later, students are able to abstract meaning and make generalizations. Students will also be asked to apply abstract ideas from one topic to another mathematics topic. In other words, students would move from concrete representations, ideas, and facts to symbolic representations and generalizations. Piaget outlined such a progression in his general four stages of cognitive learning. For example, a student may first learn about solving equations by using a balance scale. After the student understands the process, he or she can solve alone, using the symbolic equations. He or she would also be able to describe the process for solving any equation.

Direct Instruction Versus Student-Centered Instruction

Direct instruction is instruction whereby the teacher delivers all content knowledge to be learned, and students, more or less, passively listen. The teacher employs a step-by-step instruction method for learning content. Student-centered instruction is learning whereby the teacher serves as a facilitator of learning and students actively participate in their own learning. Research has shown that students show a higher level of procedural and conceptual understanding when learning in a student-centered approach. Direct instruction might be more appropriate when teaching basic or fundamental theorems. Student-centered learning might be more appropriate when helping students make connections or develop higher-level thinking regarding a topic.

Cooperative Learning Task Versus Traditional Task

Think-Pair-Share is an activity whereby a topic is first given for consideration on an individual basis. Next, the students are arranged in pairs and asked to discuss the topic (e.g., any questions, comments, generalizations, etc.). Finally, each pair will contribute to a whole-class discussion on the topic.

In mathematics, students would likely develop a higher level of understanding by using such an activity as Think-Pair-Share when learning about trigonometric functions. For example, students might be asked to consider different real-world situations that may be modeled with sine and cosine functions. Students could individually make a list and then share with a partner. Each partner group could then contribute to a whole class list. This list could be used as a reference sheet.

Implementing Technology in Classroom Instruction

Technology may be implemented in the mathematics classroom in many ways. For example, Excel may be used to perform regressions, calculate lines of best fit, calculate correlation coefficients, plot residuals, show convergence or divergence of a sequence, etc. Calculators may be used to evaluate and graph functions, find area under the normal curve, calculate combinations and permutations, perform statistical tests, etc. Graphing software, such as GeoGebra, may be used to graph and explore many shapes and functions. Students may also use it to graph reflections, rotations, translations, and dilations.

Modifying Instruction to Accommodate English-Language Learners

In mathematics specifically, instruction may be modified to include illustrations of ideas, in addition to given words. Audio may also be included for problem tasks. English-language learners may also be grouped with other fluent English-speaking students in order to assist with learning of the mathematics topic. Students will be able to hear the conversation, in addition to seeing the topic in print. In addition, problems may be broken down into smaller pieces, which can help the student focus on one step at a time. Further, additional one-on-one time with the teacher may be needed, whereby the teacher reads aloud and illustrates examples to be learned.

Effective Learning Environment for ELL Students

Characteristics of an effective learning environment for ELL students include creation of a low threshold for anxiety, use of pictures to teach vocabulary and mathematics ideas, implementation of graphic organizers, explicit teaching of vocabulary words, and use of active learning strategies. The latter two are extremely important, since ELL students need to learn exact terms and exact definitions while also engaging with fellow students, as opposed to sitting alone at a desk. Research completed by professors at the University of Houston and University of California list collaborative learning, use of multiple representations, and technology integration as important facets of an effective learning environment for ELL students (Waxman & Tellez, 2002).

Mathematics Question That is Closed-Ended and Then Rewritten in an Open-Ended Manner

Closed-Ended:

- Look at the graph of $y = x^2 + 2$. Decide if the graph represents a function.

Open-Ended:

- Provide an example of an equation that represents a function. Provide an example of an equation that does not represent a function. Explain how the graphs of the two equations compare to one another.

The first question will elicit a simple, straightforward response, or "Yes, it is a function."

The second question prompts the student to come up with two equations and then describe how the graphs of the two equations would compare. There is more than one possible answer, and the student has to make a comparison as well.

Good Questioning Response Techniques

A few good questioning response techniques are:

- Make sure the wait time is sufficient;
- Do not include leading prompts within questions;
- Ask more questions based on student answers;
- Confirm or restate correct student comments.

The key to good questioning response techniques is to show the student that his or her comments are important and to connect those comments to other student comments. The student should feel that he or she has made a contribution to the community of learners. A teacher should always ask a meaningful, thought-provoking question and provide sufficient time for the student to provide a meaningful and well-thought-out response. Student answers should lead to more questions and ideas and not serve as an endpoint.

NCTM Categories of Questions That Teachers Should Ask

The Professional Standards describe five categories of questions that teachers should ask. These categories are: 1) working together to make sense of problems; 2) individually making sense of problems; 3) reasoning about mathematics; 4) providing conjectures about mathematics; and 5) making connections within and outside of mathematics. Sample questions include "What does this mean?," "How can you prove that?," and "What does this relate to?". Categories 4 and 5 are high level and include questions that prompt students to invent ideas and make meaningful connections.

Accountants and Mathematical Modeling

Accountants use mathematical modeling in a variety of ways. For example, an accountant models the future value of a certificate of deposit (CD) using the compound interest formula. An accountant also may fit a regression line to a client's overall savings over x years. An accountant may model tax payments with residual plots. Accountants may use past income tax returns to predict future tax expenses. Accountants may compare rates of return when investing in different mutual funds, by fitting and comparing regression lines.

Scientists and Functions

Scientists use functions to model real-world phenomena. For example, scientists use quadratic functions to model the height of an object tossed into the air or dropped from a certain height. Scientists use sine and cosine functions to model real-world occurrences such as the depth of water at various times of the day, the movement of a pendulum, etc. Scientists use exponential functions to analyze and predict the number of bacteria present after x amount of time. Scientists also use functions when analyzing the time it takes a rocket to reach a destination.

Making Mathematics Relevant to Students' Lives

Teachers can make mathematics relevant to students, using a variety of strategies. Teachers may include items relevant and pertinent to students within question stems, such as including "iPad," "apps," and video game names. Teachers should pose questions that are similar to what students may have asked themselves, such as, "If I invest this much money in an account and save for x years, after how many years will I have y dollars?" Teachers should include real-world problems to solve, and not simply include rote solving of equations. Students should know what sorts of scenarios may be modeled with rational expressions. Many researchers believe that curricula should be centered on the "real world," with all facets of mathematics learning spawning from that center. In other words, students often know how to convert a decimal to a percentage, but when reading *The Wall Street Journal*, they may not be able to interpret a percentage yield.

Assessment Tool

A mathematics assessment tool is used to assess a student's prior knowledge, current knowledge, skill set, procedural knowledge, conceptual understanding, depth of understanding, and ability to make abstractions and generalizations. Perhaps the most important purpose of such a tool is to help the student develop and modify instruction. A teacher may determine that students are ready to surpass the current lesson or need it to be much more scaffolded. A teacher may also use the assessment to track students' progress. For example, a portfolio might show students' initial understanding of functions and end with their work with function modeling.

When a teacher needs to decide on an appropriate assessment tool, he or she needs to consider the purpose of the assessment. For example, if the purpose of an assessment is to direct the instruction, a pre-test may be a good assessment to use. If the purpose of the assessment is to determine the level of student understanding, then a whole-class discussion may be desired. If the purpose of an assessment is to assess student understanding of a unit of material, then an exam would be appropriate. If a teacher wishes to analyze student understanding and ability to abstract knowledge, then a performance assessment may be used. If a teacher wishes to check off skills mastered by students, then a checklist would be appropriate.

Valid Test

A test is valid if it tests what it is supposed to test. In other words, a test is valid if it appropriately covers the material it is supposed to cover. For example, a topic not taught in class should not be included on a valid test. In order to construct a valid test, a teacher should make a list of all standards covered during that time period. The teacher should also closely mirror the design of problems examined in class, for homework, and in group discussions. Finally, the teacher should make sure that there is an even balance of questions to cover all of the material.

Valid Exam

In order to select a valid exam, a teacher should make sure that the test aligns with the objectives and standards covered in the unit. The teacher should also make sure that the test problems are similar to those covered during class time. The teacher should make sure the percentages of questions devoted to each objective are balanced. In order for a test to be valid, it must be reliable, meaning that it produces similar results with different groups. A teacher may wish to check the validity and reliability results of an exam.

In general, an exam is considered invalid if it does not measure what it is supposed to measure. The exam may include questions from another unit. It may include questions with different wording techniques, making it much more difficult. The exam may include representations different from those covered in class. An invalid exam would not be reliable, meaning the results would not be consistent with different administrations of the exam. Biased questions and wording may also make an exam invalid.

Assessing Students' Understanding of What Has Been Taught

In order to assess thought processes, open-ended questions are needed. The teacher may wish to have students write an essay, write entries in a mathematics journal, undergo a performance task, or participate in a debate or discussion. The teacher may also design a pre-test that includes all constructed response questions. In particular, a performance task requires students to justify solutions, which provide the teacher with insight into students' understanding and reasoning. In general, the assessment should include questions that ask students to make abstractions and justify their thinking.

Testing Issue

Example: A student claims that an exam is more difficult and includes more content than what was presented in class. How might a teacher determine if the student's claim is true?

The teacher would need to make a list of all objectives and standards covered during the time period. The teacher would also need to compile all problems and examples covered in class and as homework. Finally, the teacher would need to do a careful analysis of the wording of the problems covered in class and as homework. If any of these items are not aligned to the exam, the teacher would need to go back and re-teach the material, using the created test as a guide for instruction.

Performance Task

A performance task allows the teacher to assess process as well as product, meaning that a teacher can assess students' thought processes as well as their final answer. The level of student learning will be much clearer when reviewing a performance task. A performance task goes beyond a multiple-choice format, allowing for oral and tactile-kinesthetic performances. Furthermore, a performance task may combine several mathematics concepts into one assessment instrument. This type of assessment often includes real-world problems, which helps the student connect mathematics to the outside world.

Formative and Summative Assessments

Formative assessments are those given during the learning process. Formative assessments provide the teacher with information related to a student's progress at various stages throughout a time period. Formative assessments are used to modify instruction as needed. In other words, formative assessments inform instruction. Summative assessments are those given at the end of a learning period. Summative assessments serve to measure the cumulative knowledge gained. Examples of formative assessments include quizzes, checklists, observations, and discussion. Examples of summative assessments include exams, portfolios, performance tasks, and standardized tests.

Four formative assessments include quizzes, checklists, observations, and discussion. Quizzes are often short assessments that may include multiple-choice items, short response items, or essay items. Quizzes are often administered following presentation of a portion of a mathematics unit. Checklists include a list of skills or concepts that should be mastered or understood. A teacher will check off all items mastered by a student. Observations are informal means of assessing students' understanding of a topic. A teacher may observe students' questions, engagement, and performance on projects. Discussion is another informal formative assessment. Discussions, both in groups and whole-class formats, allow the teacher to analyze students' thinking.

Four summative assessments include exams, portfolios, performance tasks, and standardized tests. Exams may include closed-ended or open-ended questions. Exams may be administered after each unit, semester, or at the end of the year. Portfolios include tasks created by a student and may include writing pieces and other large projects. Although the portfolio contains formative work, the tool itself may be used as a summative assessment piece. Performance tasks are large-scale problems that include many different components that relate to some big idea. For example, a student may be asked to formulate a plan for modeling a real-world phenomenon with a sine function. The student may be asked to explain how the function would change, given changes to the amplitude, period, shifts, etc. The student may then explain how these components would need to change to fit a new function. Standardized tests are tests that compare a student's performance to that of other students. They are often given at the end of the school year.

Scoring Rubric

A strong rubric will include unique performance criteria for each bullet. In other words, a portion of one criteria statement should not be included in a portion of another criteria statement. Each criteria statement should be clearly delineated, describing exactly what the student must be able to do. Furthermore, a strong rubric will often have scoring options, ranging from 0 to 4. When designing the rubric, it is helpful to create a model student response that will warrant each rubric score. It is also helpful to provide a space to provide feedback to students.

Enhancing Student Understanding

In order for an assessment to enhance student understanding, it should provide an opportunity for the student to learn something. The assessment should be a learning opportunity for the student. It should prompt the student to think deeper about a mathematics topic. In other words, the student should think, "Okay. I understand this. I wonder how the process/solution would change if I did this." The assessment might prompt the student to ask deeper questions in the next class session or complete research on a certain topic. In order to create such an assessment, open-ended and challenging questions should be included on the exam. The exam should not consist of simple, lower-level, one-answer questions.

Testing Mathematical Misconceptions

In order to design such an assessment, the teacher should include mathematical error-type problems, whereby the student must look at a solution process or conjecture and determine if he or she agrees, of if and where an error occurred. The student would need to identify the error, correct it, and explain why it was erroneous. The assessment should include a variety of mathematical misconceptions. One solution process may include more than one error. A teacher may also simply ask students to participate in a collaborative learning activity, whereby the students must share ideas and thoughts regarding a new mathematical topic.

Assessing Prior Knowledge

Such a pre-test must not include any leading prompts. It should include open-ended and constructed-response items as well. A pre-test with solely multiple-choice items will not be sufficient, since a student has the option of guessing. The test should include higher-level questions that require connections within the field of mathematics. In other words, the questions should not all be mutually exclusive. They should build on one another. Finally, the test might include student error problems as well.

Assessing Both Procedural Knowledge and Conceptual Understanding

The assessment should include rote, algorithmic-type problems, as well as those that ask the student to utilize higher-level thinking, abstractions, and generalizations. The test should include open-ended, constructed-response-type problems. A performance task is an excellent assessment for assessing a student's ability to solve a problem, while also examining the student's thought processes, rationales, etc. In order to assess both types of understanding, the assessment will need to ask students to justify and explain solutions. In other words, the assessments should include questions at both ends of Bloom's Taxonomy.

Pre-Test and Post-Test

A post-test should be exactly the same as an administered pre-test. If the teacher is to compare the results of a post-test to a pre-test, then the test and testing conditions should be identical. The pre-test assesses students' prior knowledge, while a post-test assesses students post knowledge. Comparing the results, side by side, allows the teacher to track student progress. The teacher may wish to add additional questions to the post-test, but the original questions should remain.

Assessment That Will Show What Students Do and Do Not Know

The teacher should include questions that are straightforward, involve errors, require justification, and require shown work. A student self-assessment is one such tool that would show misconceptions, understood material, and advanced knowledge. The assessment should include more than multiple-choice questions. Designing a performance assessment with scaffolded questions, whereby only one solution may be found based on a previous answer, will also show students' exact level of understanding. A debate format is one type of assessment whereby the teacher will be able to see a student's level of understanding, as he or she seeks to respond with a rebuttal.

Assessment to Hone in on Any Error Patterns Evident in Students' Work

A portfolio would be an excellent assessment for monitoring any student error patterns. The teacher would be able to track student errors as the course progressed. The teacher would be given insight into how, and if, errors improved, or if some knowledge was acquired but other knowledge was still incorrect. The portfolio might include a series of similar questions related to a certain topic. For example, a portfolio may include function transformation questions. A student's ability to transform functions may be tracked, starting with simple linear functions and ending with complex sine functions.

Components That Must Be Present in an Assessment That Supports Student Learning

The assessment must require students to think deeper than what they have covered in class. It should prompt them to make connections between topics. It should invite different ways of thinking about problem solving. In other words, the student may think, "Okay. I have seen a similar version in class. This problem is slightly different, in that the parabola is shifted left. This is the opposite of shifting right, so I will add the constant to the x-term." The assessment will thus solidify the student's understanding of how to shift any function.

Using Assessment Results of Assessments Given to ELL Learners in Order to Modify Instruction

The teacher would be able to see if language itself is a barrier in learning. In other words, if the group of ELL students, as a whole, show difficulty with a mathematics topic, the teacher may deduce that the content was not clear due to minimal supporting pictures, diagrams, and auditory support. The teacher may decide to reteach the lesson, using more visual cues, verbal pronunciations, explicit vocabulary usage, and peer-group placement. Collaborative learning may be employed.

Questions That a Teacher May Ask After Reviewing the Results of an Administered Exam

The teacher may ask the following:

- Did I cover the content in an explicit manner?
- Did I show plenty of examples?
- Did I use multiple representations when teaching the concepts?
- Did I design instruction such as to accommodate all modes of learning?
- Was the test valid?
- Did students have an adequate amount of time to complete the test?
- Why did some groups of students score lower or higher?
- Did any biased questions affect the results?

How Focus on Career and College Readiness Affects Assessment and Instructional Design

The focus on college and career-readiness standards prompts publishers and teachers to utilize more real-world problems in instruction and assessments. The focus in mathematics classrooms is shifting to more real-world, cumulative problems that require understanding of many different mathematics concepts in order to solve. Problems are related to science, finance, medicine, etc. The focus includes the ability to apply the algorithms to many different career situations. In summary, the recent focus shifts the instructional design to an application-based status.

Role of Assessment in a Classroom Focused on Cognitive Instruction

A cognitively guided classroom would be similar to a constructivist classroom, in that active participation would be present. However, in a cognitive classroom (as advocated by current cognitive theorists), students are not required to invent their own knowledge. Instead, they must simply make sense of what they are observing and experiencing. They may be assisted by the teacher. Thus, the role of an assessment in such a classroom is to ascertain student thought processes. Such an assessment would ask students to describe thinking and perhaps make connections to other mathematics topics. The assessment must ascertain students' reasoning abilities.

Instructional Cycle Described by a Learning Theorist

The 5E Learning Model is based on the thinking of Jean Piaget. It is a constructivist learning model. Piaget believed that students construct their own knowledge via active participation and experiences. Problem solving is integral to student learning. The cycle is listed as engagement, exploration, explanation, elaboration, and evaluation. Thus, with active engagement and exploration, the student is able to develop his or her own explanation, use assimilation and accommodation to make sense of the information, and then evaluate the material and make conjectures, etc.

TExES Practice Test

1. Determine the number of diagonals of a dodecagon.

a. 12
b. 24
c. 54
d. 108

2. A circular bracelet contains 5 charms, A, B, C, D, and E, attached at specific points around the bracelet, with the clasp located between charms A and B. The bracelet is unclasped and stretched out into a straight line. On the resulting linear bracelet, charm C is between charms A and B, charm D is between charms A and C, and charm E is between charms C and D. Which of these statements is (are) necessarily true?

I. The distance between charms B and E is greater than the distance between charms A and D.
II. Charm E is between charms B and D.
III. The distance between charms D and E is less than the distance of bracelet between charms A and C.

a. I, II, and III
b. II and III
c. II only
d. None of these is necessarily true.

3. In a town of 35,638 people, about a quarter of the population is under the age of 35. Of those, just over a third attend local K-12 schools. If the number of students in each grade is about the same, how many fourth graders likely reside in the town?

a. Fewer than 100
b. Between 200 and 300
c. Between 300 and 400
d. More than 400

4. Identical rugs are offered for sale at two local shops and one online retailer, designated Stores A, B, and C, respectively. The rug's regular sales price is \$296 at Store A, \$220 at Store B, and \$198.00 at Store C. Stores A and B collect 8% in sales tax on any after-discount price, while Store C collects no tax but charges a \$35 shipping fee. A buyer has a 30% off coupon for Store A and a \$10 off coupon for Store B. Which of these lists the stores in order of lowest to highest final sales price after all discounts, taxes, and fees are applied?

a. Store A, Store B, Store C
b. Store B, Store C, Store A
c. Store C, Store A, Store C
d. Store C, Store B, Store A

5. Two companies offer monthly cell phone plans, both of which include free text messaging. Company A charges a $25 monthly fee plus five cents per minute of phone conversation, while Company B charges a $50 monthly fee and offers unlimited calling. Both companies charge the same amount when the total duration of monthly calls is

a. 500 hours.
b. 8 hours and 33 minutes.
c. 8 hours and 20 minutes.
d. 5 hours.

6. A dress is marked down by 20% and placed on a clearance rack, on which is posted a sign reading, "Take an extra 25% off already reduced merchandise." What fraction of the original price is the final sales price of the dress?

a. $\frac{9}{20}$
b. $\frac{11}{20}$
c. $\frac{2}{5}$
d. $\frac{3}{5}$

7. On a floor plan drawn at a scale of 1:100, the area of a rectangular room is 30 cm^2. What is the actual area of the room?

a. 30,000 cm^2
b. 3,000 cm^2
c. 3,000 m^2
d. 30 m^2

8. The ratio of employee wages and benefits to all other operational costs of a business is 2:3. If a business's operating expenses are $130,000 per month, how much money does the company spend on employee wages and benefits?

a. $43,333.33
b. $86,666.67
c. $52,000.00
d. $78,000.00

9. The path of ball thrown into the air is modeled by the first quadrant graph of the equation $h = -16t^2 + 64t + 5$, where h is the height of the ball in feet and t is time in seconds after the ball is thrown. What is the average rate of change in the ball's height with respect to time over the interval [1, 3]?

a. 0 feet/second
b. 48 feet/second
c. 53 feet/second
d. 96 feet/second

10. Zeke drove from his house to a furniture store in Atlanta and then back home along the same route. It took Zeke three hours to drive to the store. By driving an average of 20 mph faster on his return trip, Zeke was able to save an hour of diving time. What was Zeke's average driving speed on his round trip?

a. 24 mph
b. 48 mph
c. 50 mph
d. 60 mph

11. The graph below shows Aaron's distance from home at times throughout his morning run. Which of the following statements is (are) true?

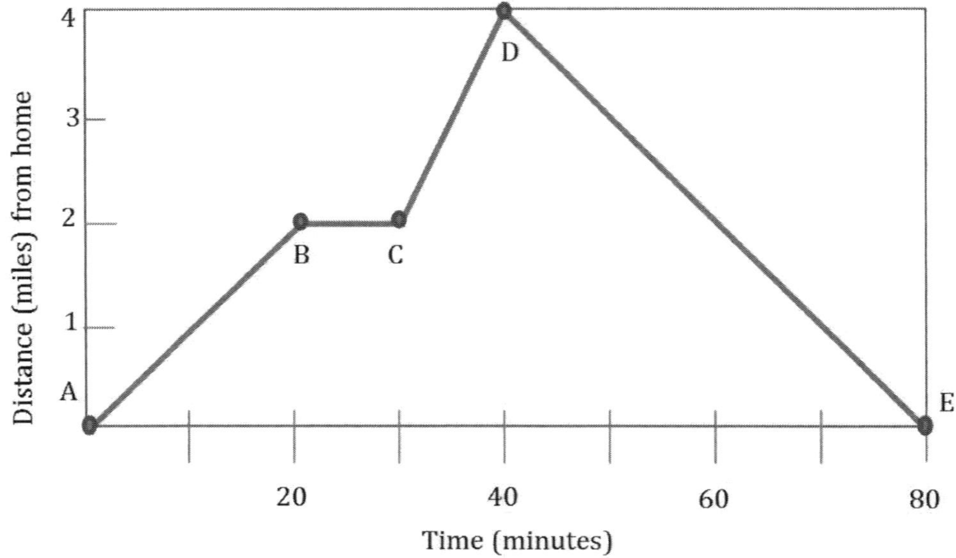

I. Aaron's average running speed was 6 mph.
II. Aaron's running speed from point A to point B was the same as his running speed from point D to E.
III. Aaron ran a total distance of four miles.

a. I only
b. II only
c. I and II
d. I, II, and III

12. Use the operation table to determine $(a * b) * (c * d)$.

$*$	a	b	c	d
a	d	a	b	c
b	a	b	c	d
c	b	c	d	a
d	c	d	a	b

a. a
b. b
c. c
d. d

13. Complete the analogy.

$$x^3 \text{ is to } \sqrt[3]{y} \text{ as } \ldots$$

a. $x + a$ is to $x - y$.
b. e^x is to $\ln y, y > 0$.
c. $\frac{1}{x}$ is to $y, x, y \neq 0$.
d. $\sin x$ is to $\cos y$.

14. Which of these statements is (are) true for deductive reasoning?

I. A general conclusion is drawn from specific instances.

II. If the premises are true and proper reasoning is applied, the conclusion must be true.

a. Statement I is true
b. Statement II is true
c. Both statements are true
d. Neither statement is true

15. Given that premises "all *a* are *b*," "all *b* are *d*," and "no *b* are *c*" are true and that premise "all *b* are *e*" is false, determine the validity and soundness of the following arguments:

Argument I: All a are b. No b are c. Therefore, no a are c.
Argument II: All a are b. All d are b. Therefore, all d are a.
Argument III: All a are b. All b are e. Therefore, all a are e.

a.

	Invalid	Valid	Sound
Argument I		X	X
Argument II	X		
Argument III		X	

b.

	Invalid	Valid	Sound
Argument I	X		
Argument II		X	X
Argument III	X		

c.

	Invalid	Valid	Sound
Argument I		X	X
Argument II		X	X
Argument III	X		

d.

	Invalid	Valid	Sound
Argument I		X	X
Argument II	X		
Argument III	X		

16. If $p \rightarrow q$ is true, which of these is also necessarily true?

a. $q \rightarrow p$
b. ▯$p \rightarrow$ ▯q
c. ▯$q \rightarrow$ ▯p
d. None of these

17. Given statements p and q, which of the following is the truth table for the statement $q \leftrightarrow$ ▯$(p \wedge q)$?

a.

p	q	$q \leftrightarrow \sim(p \wedge q)$
T	T	F
T	F	T
F	T	T
F	F	T

b.

p	q	$q \leftrightarrow \sim(p \wedge q)$
T	T	T
T	F	T
F	T	T
F	F	F

c.

p	q	$q \leftrightarrow \sim(p \wedge q)$
T	T	F
T	F	F
F	T	F
F	F	T

d.

p	q	$q \leftrightarrow \sim(p \wedge q)$
T	T	F
T	F	F
F	T	T
F	F	F

18. Which of the following is the truth table for logic circuit shown below?

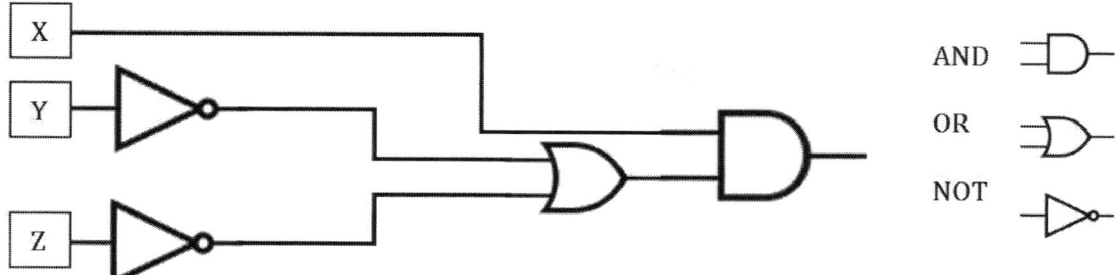

a.

X	Y	Z	Output
0	0	0	1
0	0	1	0
0	1	0	0
0	1	1	0
1	0	0	0
1	0	1	0
1	1	0	0
1	1	1	1

b.

X	Y	Z	Output
0	0	0	0
0	0	1	1
0	1	0	1
0	1	1	1
1	0	0	1
1	0	1	1
1	1	0	1
1	1	1	1

c.

X	Y	Z	Output
0	0	0	0
0	0	1	0
0	1	0	0
0	1	1	1
1	0	0	1
1	0	1	1
1	1	0	1
1	1	1	0

d.

X	Y	Z	Output
0	0	0	0
0	0	1	0
0	1	0	0
0	1	1	0
1	0	0	1
1	0	1	1
1	1	0	1
1	1	1	0

19. Which of these is a major contribution of the Babylonian civilization to the historical development of mathematics?

a. The division of an hour into 60 minutes, and a minute into 60 seconds, and a circle into 360 degrees
b. The development of algebra as a discipline separate from geometry
c. The use of deductive reasoning in geometric proofs
d. The introduction of Boolean logic and algebra

20. Which mathematician is responsible for what is often called the most remarkable and beautiful mathematical formula, $e^{i\pi} + 1 = 0$?

a. Pythagoras
b. Euclid
c. Euler
d. Fermat

21. Which of these demonstrates the relationship between the sets of prime numbers, real numbers, natural numbers, complex numbers, rational numbers, and integers?

$\mathbb{P}$ – Prime; $\mathbb{R}$ – Real; $\mathbb{N}$ – Natural; $\mathbb{C}$ – Complex; $\mathbb{Q}$ – Rational; $\mathbb{Z}$ – Integer

a. $\mathbb{P} \subseteq \mathbb{Q} \subseteq \mathbb{R} \subseteq \mathbb{Z} \subseteq \mathbb{C} \subseteq \mathbb{N}$
b. $\mathbb{P} \subseteq \mathbb{N} \subseteq \mathbb{Z} \subseteq \mathbb{Q} \subseteq \mathbb{R} \subseteq \mathbb{C}$
c. $\mathbb{C} \subseteq \mathbb{R} \subseteq \mathbb{Q} \subseteq \mathbb{Z} \subseteq \mathbb{N} \subseteq \mathbb{P}$
d. None of these

22. To which of the following sets of numbers does -4 NOT belong?

a. The set of whole numbers
b. The set of rational numbers
c. The set of integers
d. The set of real numbers

23. Which of these forms a group?

a. The set of prime numbers under addition
b. The set of negative integers under multiplication
c. The set of negative integers under addition
d. The set of non-zero rational numbers under multiplication

24. Simplify $\frac{2+3i}{4-2i}$.

a. $\frac{1}{10} + \frac{4}{5}i$
b. $\frac{1}{10}$
c. $\frac{7}{6} + \frac{2}{3}i$
d. $\frac{1}{10} + \frac{3}{10}i$

25. Simplify $|(2 - 3i)^2 - (1 - 4i)|$.

a. $\sqrt{61}$
b. $-6 - 8i$
c. $6 + 8i$
d. 10

26. Which of these sets forms a group under multiplication?

a. $\{-i, 0, i\}$
b. $\{-1, 1, i, -i\}$
c. $\{i, 1\}$
d. $\{ i, -i, 1\}$

27. The set $\{a, b, c, d\}$ forms a group under operation #. Which of these statements is (are) true about the group?

#	*a*	*b*	*c*	*d*
a	*c*	*d*	*b*	*a*
b	*d*	*c*	*a*	*b*
c	*b*	*a*	*d*	*c*
d	*a*	*b*	*c*	*d*

I. The identity element of the group is *d*.
II. The inverse of *c* is *c*.
III. The operation # is commutative.

a. I
b. III
c. I, III
d. I, II, III

28. If the square of twice the sum of *x* and three is equal to the product of twenty-four and *x*, which of these is a possible value of *x*?

a. $6 + 3\sqrt{2}$
b. $\frac{3}{2}$
c. $-3i$
d. -3

29. Given that x is a prime number and that the greatest common factor of x and y is greater than 1, compare the two quantities.

Quantity A	Quantity B
y	the least common multiple of x and y

a. Quantity A is greater.
b. Quantity B is greater.
c. The two quantities are the same.
d. The relationship cannot be determined from the given information.

30. If *a*, *b*, and *c* are even integers and $3a^2 + 9b^3 = c$, which of these is the largest number which must be factor of *c*?

a. 2
b. 3
c. 6
d. 12

31. Which of these relationships represents *y* as a function of *x*?

a. $x = y^2$

b.

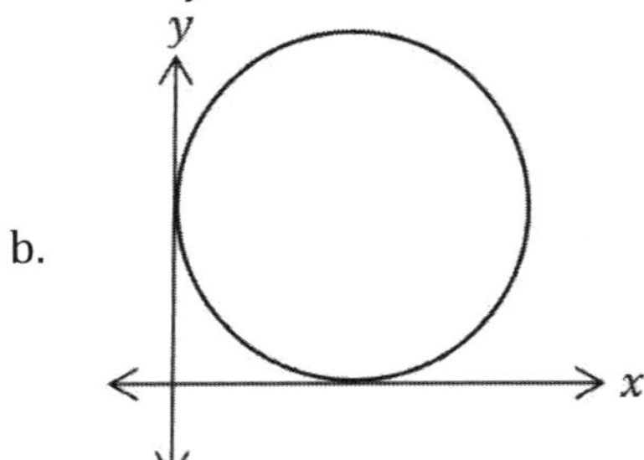

c. $y = [\![x]\!]$s

d.

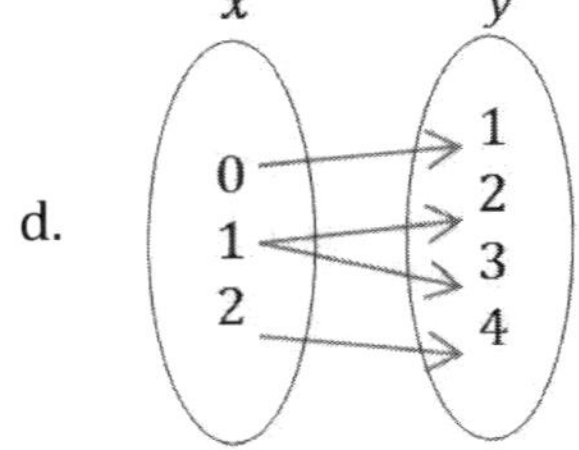

32. Express the area of the given triangle as a function of *x*.

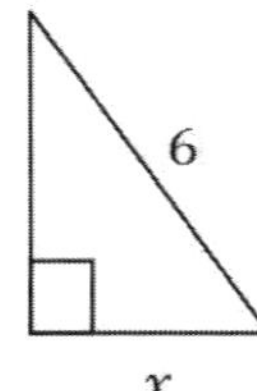

a. $A(x) = 3x$
b. $A(x) = \frac{x\sqrt{36-x^2}}{2}$
c. $A(x) = \frac{x^2}{2}$
d. $A(x) = 18 - \frac{x^2}{2}$

33. Find $[g \circ f\,]x$ when $f(x) = 2x + 4$ and $g(x) = x^2 - 3x + 2$.

a. $4x^2 + 10x + 6$
b. $2x^2 - 6x + 8$
c$4x^2 + 13x + 18$.
d. $2x^2 - 3x + 6$

34. Given the partial table of values for $f(x)$ and $g(x)$, find $f(g(-4))$. (Assume that $f(x)$ and $g(x)$ are the simplest polynomials that fit the data.)

x	f(x)	g(x)
-2	8	1
-1	2	3
0	0	5
1	2	7
2	8	9

a. 69
b. 31
c. 18
d. -3

35. If $f(x)$ and $g(x)$ are inverse functions, which of these is the value of x when $f(g(x)) = 4$?

a. -4
b. $\frac{1}{4}$
c. 2
d. 4

36. Determine which pair of equations are NOT inverses.

a. $y = x + 6; y = x - 6$
b. $y = 2x + 3; y = 2x - 3$
c. $y = \frac{2x+3}{x-1}; y = \frac{x+3}{x-2}$
d. $y = \frac{x-1}{2}; \ y = 2x + 1$

37. Which of these statements is (are) true for function $g(x)$?

$$g(x) = \begin{cases} 2x - 1 & x \geq 2 \\ -x + 3 & x < 2 \end{cases}$$

I. $g(3) = 0$
II. The graph of $g(x)$ is discontinuous at $x = 2$.
III. The range of $g(x)$ is all real numbers.

a. II
b. III
c. I, II
d. II, III

38. Which of the following piecewise functions can describe the graph below?

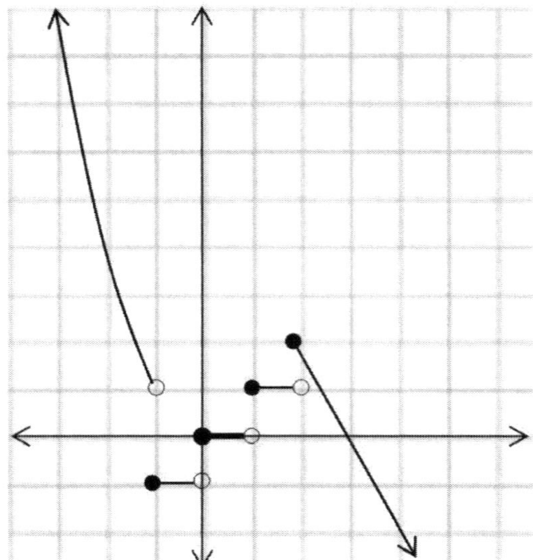

a. $f(x) = \begin{cases} x^2 & x < -1 \\ [\![x]\!] & -1 \leq x < 2 \\ -2x + 6 & x \geq 2 \end{cases}$

b. $f(x) = \begin{cases} x^2 & x \leq -1 \\ [\![x]\!] & -1 \leq x \leq 2 \\ -2x + 6 & x > 2 \end{cases}$

c. $f(x) = \begin{cases} (x+1)^2 & x < -1 \\ [\![x]\!] + 1 & -1 \leq x < 2 \\ -2x + 6 & x \geq 2 \end{cases}$

d. $f(x) = \begin{cases} (x+1)^2 & x < -1 \\ [\![x - 1]\!] & -1 \leq x < 2 \\ -2x + 6 & x \geq 2 \end{cases}$

39. Which of the following could be the graph of $y = a(x + b)(x + c)^2$ if $a > 0$?

a.

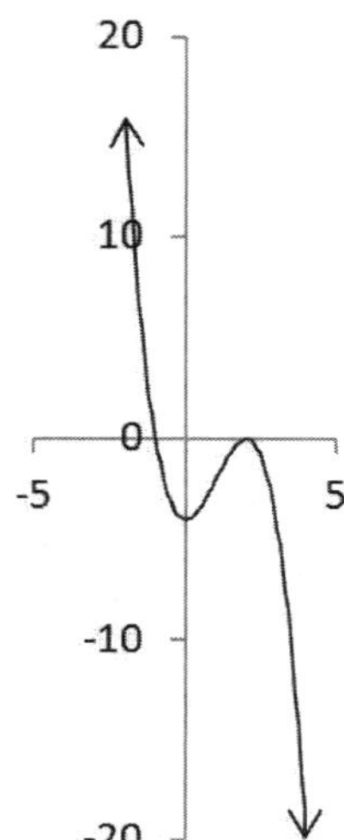

c.

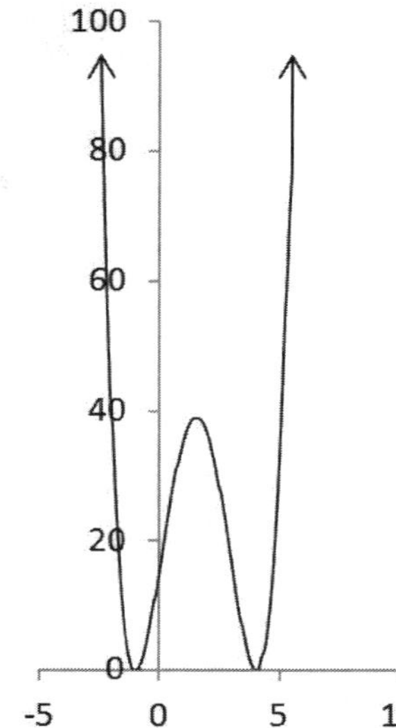

b.

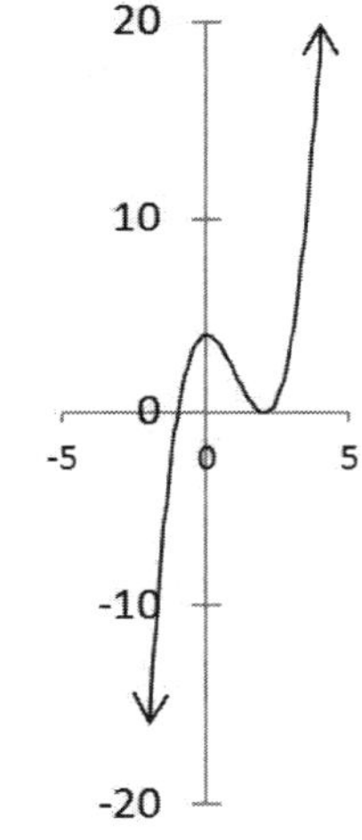

d.

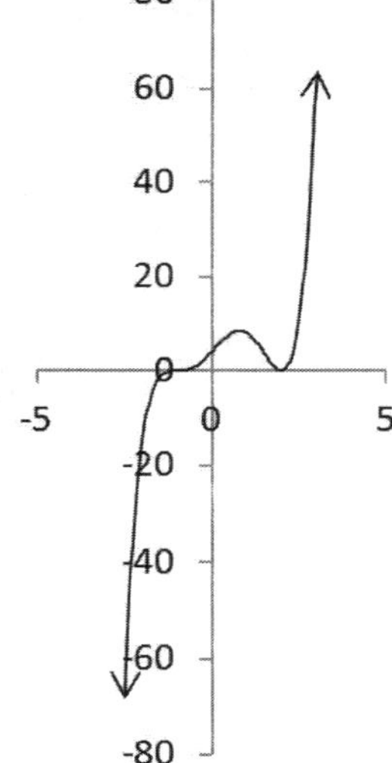

40. A school is selling tickets to its production of *Annie Get Your Gun*. Student tickets cost $3 each, and non-student tickets are $5 each. In order to offset the costs of the production, the school must earn at least $300 in ticket sales. Which graph shows the number of tickets the school must sell to offset production costs?

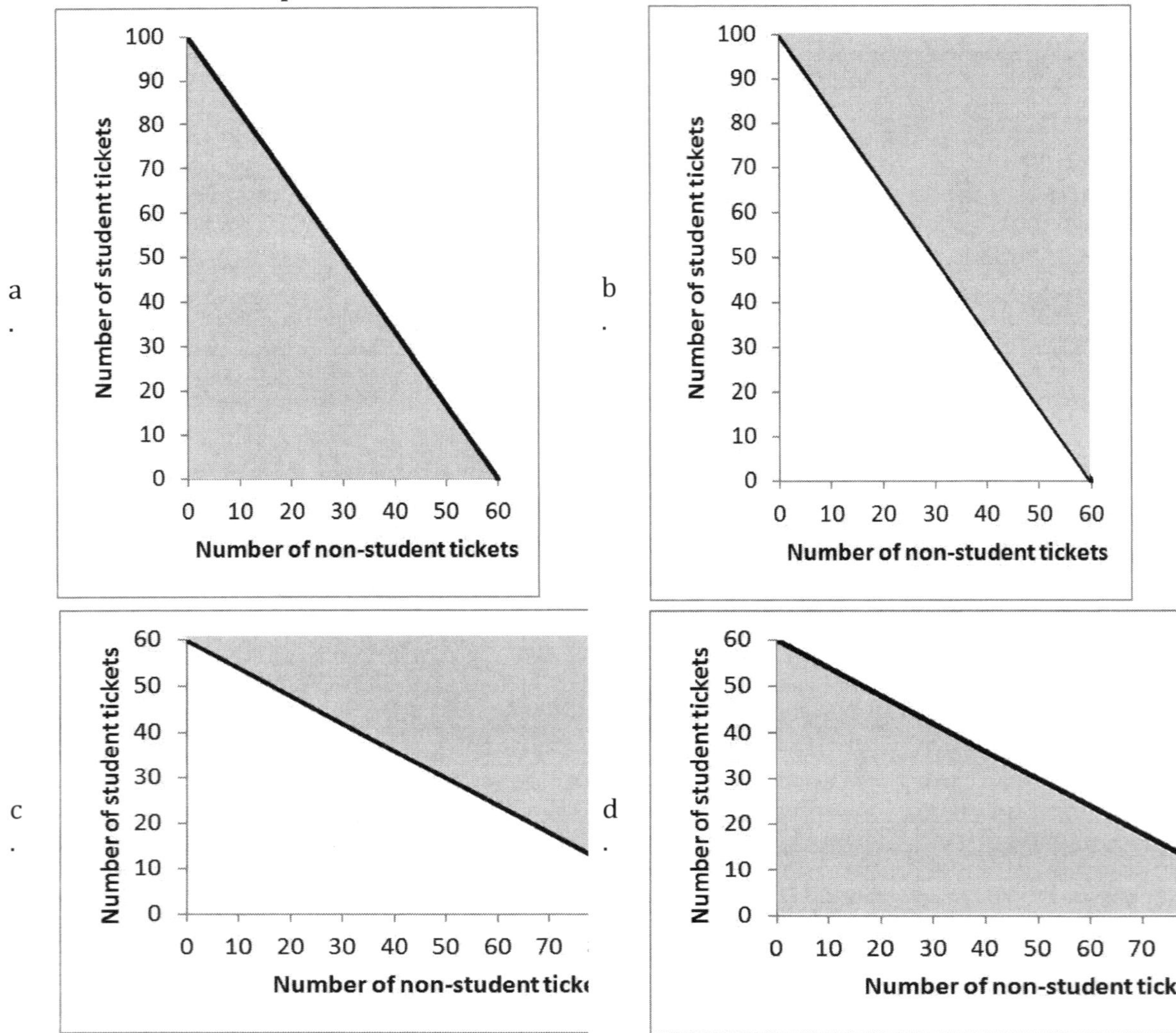

41. Which of these is the equation graphed below?

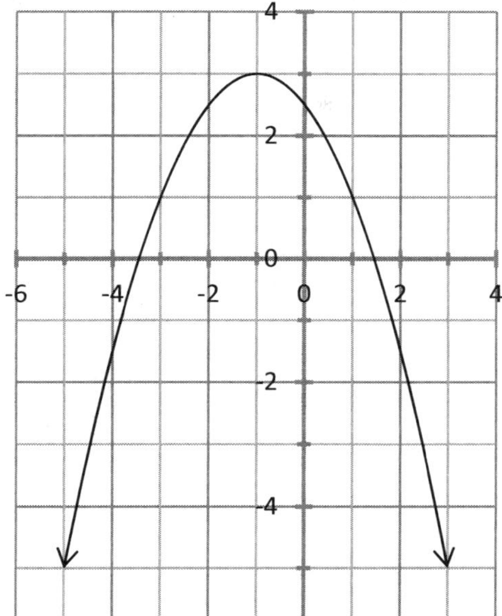

a. $y = -2x^2 - 4x + 1$
b. $y = -x^2 - 2x + 5$
c. $y = -x^2 - 2x + 2$
d. $y = -\frac{1}{2}x^2 - x + \frac{5}{2}$

42. Solve $7x^2 + 6x = -2$.

a. $x = \frac{-3 \pm \sqrt{23}}{7}$
b. $x = \pm i\sqrt{5}$
c. $x = \pm \frac{2i\sqrt{2}}{7}$
d. $x = \frac{-3 \pm i\sqrt{5}}{7}$

43. Solve the system of equations.

$$3x + 4y = 2$$

$$2x + 6y = -2$$

a. $\left(0, \frac{1}{2}\right)$
b. $\left(\frac{2}{5}, \frac{1}{5}\right)$
c. $(2, -1)$
d. $\left(-1, \frac{5}{4}\right)$

44. Which system of linear inequalities has no solution?

a. $x - y < 3$

$x - y \geq -3$

b. $y \leq 6 - 2x$

$\frac{1}{3}y + \frac{2}{3}x \geq 2$

c. $6x + 2y \leq 12$

$3x \geq 8 - y$

d. $x + 4y \leq -8$

$y + 4x > -8$

45. The cost of admission to a theme park is shown below.

Under age 10	Ages 10-55	Over age 65
\$15	\$25	\$20

Yesterday, the theme park sold 810 tickets and earned \$14,500. There were twice as many children under 10 at the park as there were other visitors. If x, y, and z represent the number of \$15, \$25, and \$20 tickets sold, respectively, which of the following matrix equations can be used to find the number of each type of ticket sold?

a. $\begin{bmatrix} 1 & 1 & 1 \\ 15 & 25 & 20 \\ 1 & -2 & -2 \end{bmatrix}\begin{bmatrix} x \\ y \\ z \end{bmatrix} = \begin{bmatrix} 810 \\ 14500 \\ 0 \end{bmatrix}$

b. $\begin{bmatrix} 1 & 1 & 1 \\ 15 & 25 & 20 \\ 1 & -2 & -2 \end{bmatrix}\begin{bmatrix} 810 \\ 14500 \\ 0 \end{bmatrix} = \begin{bmatrix} x \\ y \\ z \end{bmatrix}$

c. $\begin{bmatrix} 1 & 15 & 1 \\ 1 & 25 & -2 \\ 1 & 20 & -2 \end{bmatrix}\begin{bmatrix} x \\ y \\ z \end{bmatrix} = \begin{bmatrix} 810 \\ 14500 \\ 0 \end{bmatrix}$

d. $\begin{bmatrix} 1 & 15 & 1 \\ 1 & 25 & -2 \\ 1 & 20 & -2 \end{bmatrix}\begin{bmatrix} 810 \\ 14500 \\ 0 \end{bmatrix} = \begin{bmatrix} x \\ y \\ z \end{bmatrix}$

46. Solve the system of equations.

$$2x - 4y + z = 10$$
$$-3x + 2y - 4z = -7$$
$$x + y - 3z = -1$$

a. $(-1, -3, 0)$
b. $(1, -2, 0)$
c. $(-\frac{3}{4}, -\frac{21}{8}, -1)$
d. No solution

47. Solve $x^4 + 64 = 20x^2$.

a. $x = \{2, 4\}$
b. $x = \{-2, 2, -4, 4\}$
c. $x = \{2i, 4i\}$
d. $x = \{-2i, 2i, -4i, 4i\}$

48. Solve $3x^3y^2 - 45x^2y = 15x^3y - 9x^2y^2$ for x and y.

a. $x = \{0, -3\},\ y = \{0, 5\}$
b. $x = \{0\},\ y = \{0\}$
c. $x = \{0, -3\},\ y = \{0\}$
d. $x = \{0\},\ y = \{0, 5\}$

49. Which of these statements is true for functions $f(x)$, $g(x)$, and $h(x)$?

$$f(x) = 2x - 2$$
$$g(x) = 2x^2 - 2$$
$$h(x) = 2x^3 - 2$$

a. The degree of each polynomial function is 2.
b. The leading coefficient of each function is -2.
c. Each function has exactly one real zero at $x = 1$.
d. None of these is true for functions $f(x)$, $g(x)$, and $h(x)$.

50. Which of these can be modeled by a quadratic function?

a. The path of a sound wave
b. The path of a bullet
c. The distance an object travels over time when the rate is constant
d. Radioactive decay

51. Which of these is equivalent to $\log_y 256$ if $2\log_4 y + \log_4 16 = 3$?

a. 16
b. 8
c. 4
d. 2

52. Simplify $\frac{(x^2y)(2xy^{-2})^3}{16x^5y^2} + \frac{3}{xy}$

a. $\frac{3x+24y^6}{8xy^7}$
b. $\frac{x+6y^6}{2xy^7}$
c. $\frac{x+24y^5}{8xy^6}$
d. $\frac{x+6y^5}{2xy^6}$

53. Given: $f(x) = 10^x$. If $f(x) = 5$, which of these approximates x?

a. 100,000
b. 0.00001
c. 0.7
d. 1.6

54. Which of these could be the equation of the function graphed below?

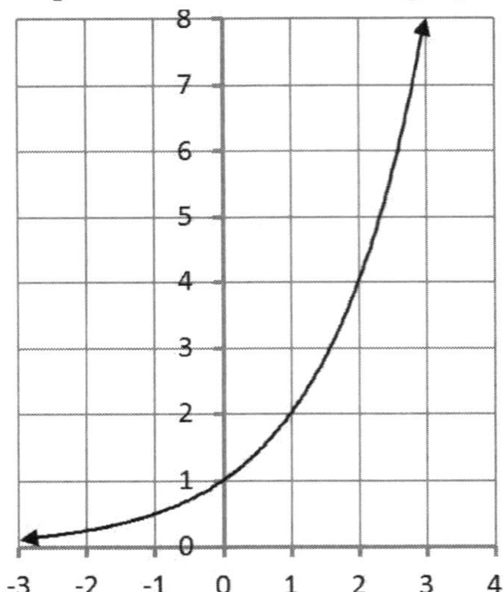

a. $f(x) = x^2$
b. $f(x) = \sqrt{x}$
c. $f(x) = 2^x$
d. $f(x) = log_2 x$

55. Which of these statements is NOT necessarily true when $f(x) = \log_b x$ and $b > 1$?

a. The x-intercept of the graph of $f(x)$ is 1.
b. The graph of $f(x)$ passes through $(b, 1)$
c. $f(x) < 0$ when $x < 1$
d. If $g(x) = b^x$, the graph of $f(x)$ is symmetric to the graph of $g(x)$ with respect to $y = x$.

56. A colony of *Escherichia coli* is inoculated from a Petri dish into a test tube containing 50 mL of nutrient broth. The test tube is placed in a 37°C incubator/shaker; after one hour, the number of bacteria in the test tube is determined to be 8×10^6. Given that the doubling time of *E. coli* is 20 minutes with agitation at 37°C, approximately how many bacteria should the test tube contain after eight hours of growth?

a. 2.56×10^8
b. 2.05×10^9
c. 1.7×10^{10}
d. 1.7×10^{13}

57. The strength of an aqueous acid solution is measured by pH. $\text{pH} = -\log[\text{H}^+]$, where $[\text{H}^+]$ is the molar concentration of hydronium ions in the solution. A solution is acidic if its pH is less than 7. The lower the pH, the stronger the acid; for example, gastric acid, which has a pH of about 1, is a much stronger acid than urine, which has a pH of about 6. How many times stronger is an acid with a pH of 3 than an acid with pH of 5?

a. 2
b. 20
c. 100
d. 1000

58. Simplify $\sqrt{\frac{-28x^6}{27y^5}}$.

a. $\frac{2x^3 i\sqrt{21y}}{9y^3}$
b. $\frac{2x^3 i\sqrt{21y}}{27y^4}$
c. $\frac{-2x^3\sqrt{21y}}{9y^3}$
d. $\frac{12x^3 y i\sqrt{7}}{27y^2}$

59. Which of these does NOT have a solution set of $\{x: -1 \leq x \leq 1\}$?

a. $-4 \leq 2 + 3(x-1) \leq 2$
b. $-2x^2 + 2 \geq x^2 - 1$
c. $\frac{11-|3x|}{7} \geq 2$
d. $3|2x| + 4 \leq 10$

60. Solve $2 - \sqrt{x} = \sqrt{x - 20}$.

a. $x = 6$
b. $x = 36$
c. $x = 144$
d. No solution

61. Solve $\frac{x-2}{x-1} = \frac{x-1}{x+1} + \frac{2}{x-1}$.

a. $x = 2$
b. $x = -5$
c. $x = 1$
d. No solution

62. Which of these equations is represented by the graph below?

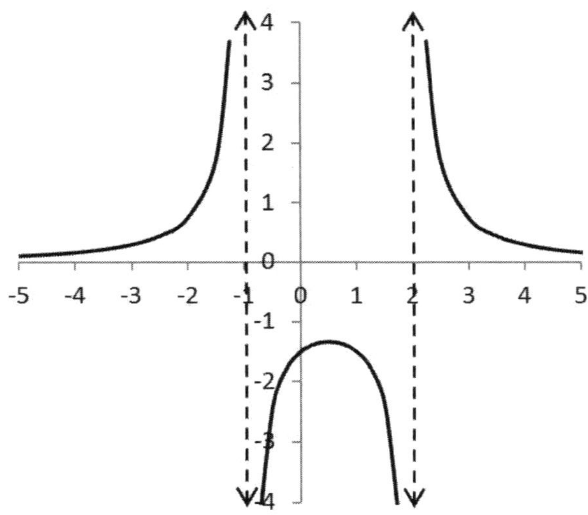

a. $y = \frac{3}{x^2-x-2}$
b. $y = \frac{3x+3}{x^2-x-2}$
c. $y = \frac{1}{x+1} + \frac{1}{x-2}$
d. None of these

63. Which of the graphs shown represents $f(x) = -2|-x+4| - 1$?

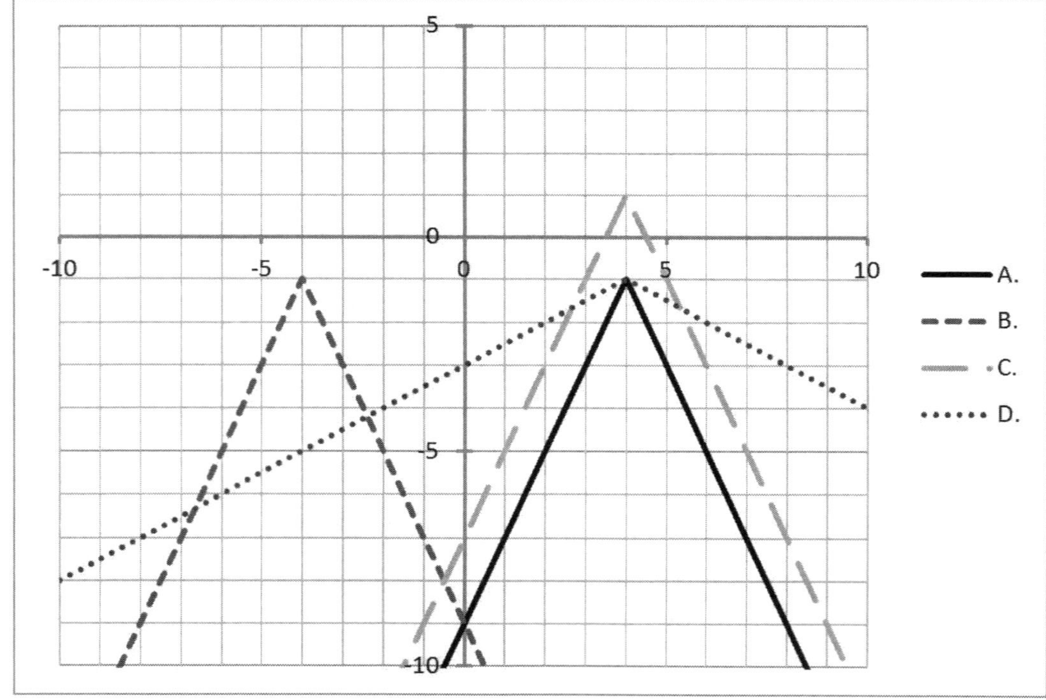

64. Which of these functions includes 1 as an element of the domain and 2 as an element of the range?

a. $y = \frac{1}{x-1} + 1$
b. $y = -\sqrt{x+2} - 1$
c. $y = |x+2| - 3$
d. $y = \begin{cases} x & x < -1 \\ -x-3 & x \geq -1 \end{cases}$

65. Which of the following statements is (are) true when $f(x) = \frac{x^2-x-6}{x^3+2x^2-x-2}$?

I. The graph $f(x)$ has vertical asymptotes at $x = -2$, $x = -1$, and $x = 1$.
II. The x- and y-intercepts of the graph of $f(x)$ are both 3.

a. I
b. II
c. I and II
d. Neither statement is true.

66. In the 1600s, Galileo Galilei studied the motion of pendulums and discovered that the period of a pendulum, the time it takes to complete one full swing, is a function of the square root of the length of its string: $2\pi\sqrt{\frac{L}{g}}$, where L is the length of the string and g is the acceleration due to gravity.

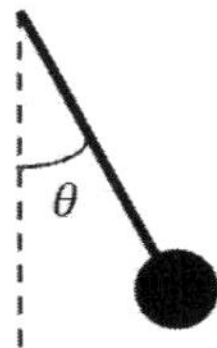

Consider two pendulums released from the same pivot point and at the same angle, $\theta = 30°$. Pendulum 1 has a mass of 100 g, while Pendulum 2 has a mass of 200 g. If Pendulum 1 has a period four times the period of Pendulum 2, what is true of the lengths of the pendulums' strings?

a. The length of Pendulum 1's string is four times the length of Pendulum 2's string.
b. The length of Pendulum 1's string is eight times the length of Pendulum 2's string.
c. The length of Pendulum 1's string is sixteen times the length of Pendulum 2's string.
d. The length of Pendulum 1's string is less than the length of Pendulum 2's string.

67. At today's visit to her doctor, Josephine was prescribed a liquid medication with instructions to take 25 cc's every four hours. She filled the prescription on her way to work, but when it came time to take the medicine, she realized that the pharmacist did not include a measuring cup. Josephine estimated that the plastic spoon in her desk drawer was about the same size as a teaspoon and decided to use it to measure the approximate dosage. She recalled that one cubic centimeter (cc) is equal to one milliliter (mL) but was not sure how many milliliters were in a teaspoon. So, she noted that a two-liter bottle of soda contains about the same amount as a half-gallon container of milk and applied her knowledge of the customary system of measurement to determine how many teaspoons of medicine to take. Which of these calculations might she have used to approximate her dosage?

a. $25 \cdot \frac{1}{1000} \cdot \frac{2}{0.5} \cdot 16 \cdot 48$
b. $25 \cdot \frac{1}{100} \cdot \frac{0.5}{2} \cdot 16 \cdot 4 \cdot 12$
c. $\frac{1000}{25} \cdot \frac{0.5}{2} \cdot 16 \cdot 4 \cdot 12$
d. $\frac{25}{1000} \cdot \frac{1}{4} \cdot 16 \cdot 48$

68. If 1" on a map represents 60 ft, how many yards apart are two points if the distance between the points on the map is 10"?

a. 1800
b. 600
c. 200
d. 2

69. Roxana walks x meters west and $x + 20$ meters south to get to her friend's house. On a neighborhood map which has a scale of 1cm:10 m, the distance between Roxana's house and her friend's house is 10 cm. How far did Roxana walk to her friend's house?

a. 60 m
b. 80 m
c. 100 m
d. 140 m

70. For ΔABC, what is AB?

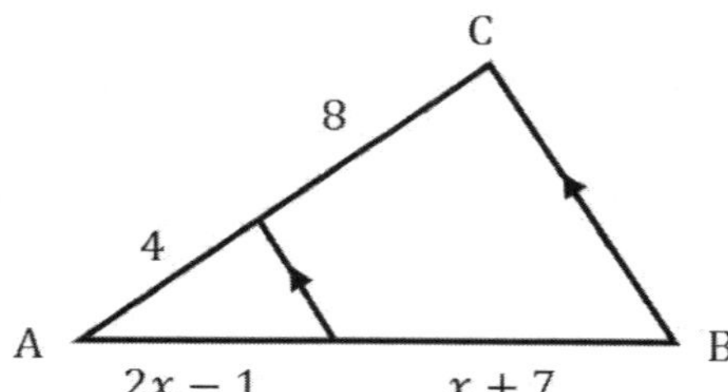

a. 3
b. 10
c. 12
d. 15

71. To test the accuracy and precision of two scales, a student repeatedly measured the mass of a 10 g standard and recorded these results.

	Trial 1	Trial 2	Trial 3	Trial 4
Scale 1	9.99 g	9.98 g	10.02g	10.01g
Scale 2	10.206 g	10.209 g	10.210 g	10.208 g

Which of these conclusions about the scales is true?

a. Scale 1 has an average percent error of 0.15%, and Scale 2 has an average percent error of 2.08%. Scale 1 is more accurate and precise than Scale 2.
b. Scale 1 has an average percent error of 0.15%, and Scale 2 has an average percent error of 2.08%. Scale 1 is more accurate than Scale 2; however, Scale 2 is more precise.
c. Scale 1 has an average percent error of 0%, and Scale 2 has an average percent error of 2.08%. Scale 1 is more accurate and precise than Scale 2.
d. Scale 1 has an average percent error of 0%, and Scale 2 has an average percent error of 2.08%. Scale 1 is more accurate than Scale 2; however, Scale 2 is more precise.

72. A developer decides to build a fence around a neighborhood park, which is positioned on a rectangular lot. Rather than fencing along the lot line, he fences *x* feet from each of the lot's boundaries. By fencing a rectangular space 141 yd^2 smaller than the lot, the developer saves $432 in fencing materials, which cost $12 per linear foot. How much does he spend?

a. $160
b. $456
c. $3,168
d. The answer cannot be determined from the given information.

73. Natasha designs a square pyramidal tent for her children. Each of the sides of the square base measures *x* ft, and the tent's height is *h* feet. If Natasha were to increase by 1 ft the length of each side of the base, how much more interior space would the tent have?

a. $\frac{h(x^2+2x+1)}{3}$ ft^3
b. $\frac{h(2x+1)}{3}$ ft^3
c. $\frac{x^2h+3}{3}$ ft^3
d. 1 ft^3

74. A rainbow pattern is designed from semi-circles as shown below.

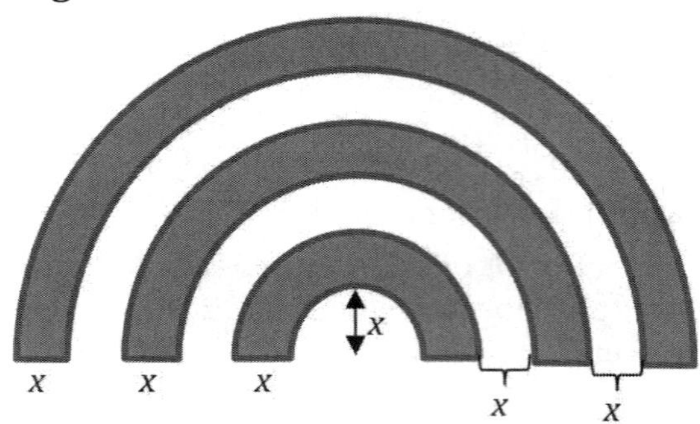

Which of the following gives the area A of the shaded region as a function of x?

a. $A = \frac{21x^2\pi}{2}$
b. $A = 21x^2\pi$
c. $A = 42x^2\pi$
d. $A = 82x^2\pi$

75. Categorize the following statements as axioms of Euclidean, hyperbolic, or elliptical geometry.

I. In a plane, for any line l and point A not on l, at least two lines which pass through A do not intersect l.
II. In a plane, for any line l and point A not on l, exactly one line which passes through A does not intersect l.
III. In a plane, for any line l and point A not on l, all lines which pass through A intersect l.

a.

Statement I	Elliptical geometry
Statement II	Euclidean geometry
Statement III	Hyperbolic geometry

b.

Statement I	Hyperbolic geometry
Statement II	Euclidean geometry
Statement III	Elliptical geometry

c.

Statement I	Hyperbolic geometry
Statement II	Elliptical geometry
Statement III	Euclidean geometry

d.

Statement I	Elliptical geometry
Statement II	Hyperbolic geometry
Statement III	Euclidean geometry

76. As shown below, four congruent isosceles trapezoids are positioned such that they form an arch. Find x for the indicated angle.

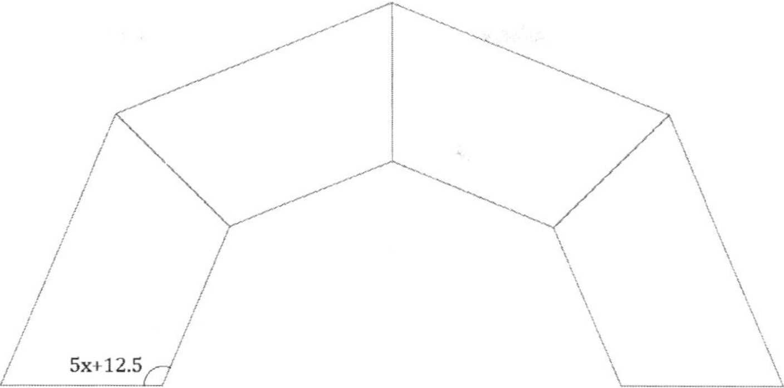

a. $x = 11$
b. $x = 20$
c. $x = 24.5$
d. The value of x cannot be determined from the information given.

77. A circle is inscribed inside quadrilateral $ABCD$. $\overline{CD}$ is bisected by the point at which it is tangent to the circle. If $AB = 14$, $BC = 10$, $DC = 8$, then

a. $AD = 11$
b. $AD = 2\sqrt{34}$
c. $AD = 12$
d. $AD = 17.5$

78. Which of the following equations gives the area A of the triangle below as a function of a and b?

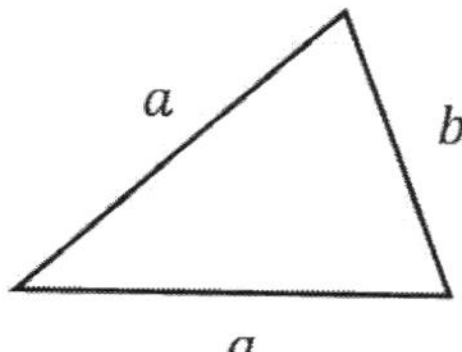

a. $\frac{2a^2-b^2}{4}$
b. $\frac{ab-a^2}{2}$
c. $\frac{b\sqrt{a^2-b^2}}{2}$
d. $\frac{b\sqrt{4a^2-b^2}}{4}$

79. Given the figure and the following information, find DE to the nearest tenth.

$\overline{AD}$ is an altitude of ΔABC

$\overline{DE}$ is an altitude of triangle ΔADC

$BD \cong DC$

$BC = 24; AD = 5$

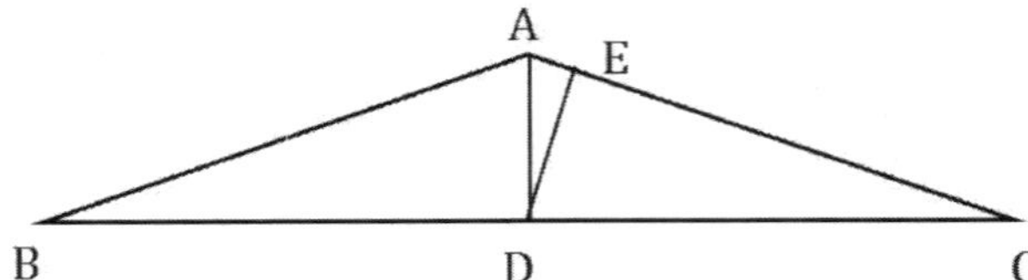

a. 4.2
b. 4.6
c. 4.9
d. 5.4

80. A cube inscribed in a sphere has a volume of 64 cubic units. What is the volume of the sphere in cubic units?

a. $4\pi\sqrt{3}$
b. $8\pi\sqrt{3}$
c. $32\pi\sqrt{3}$
d. $256\pi\sqrt{3}$

Questions 81 and 82 are based on the following proof:

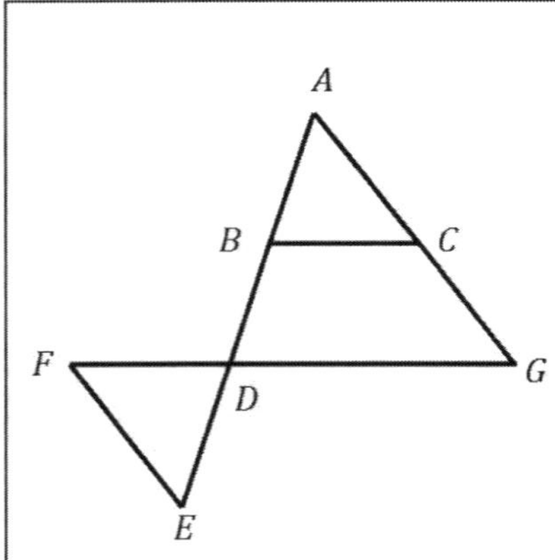

Statement	Reason
1. $\overline{BC} \parallel \overline{FG}$	Given
2.	
3. $\overline{FD} \cong \overline{BC}$	Given
4. $\overline{AB} \cong \overline{DE}$	Given
5. $\Delta ABC \cong \Delta EDF$	81.
6. 82.	
7. $\overline{FE} \parallel \overline{AG}$	

Given: $\overline{BC} \parallel \overline{FG}$; $\overline{FD} \cong \overline{BC}$; $\overline{AB} \cong \overline{DE}$
Prove: $\overline{FE} \parallel \overline{AG}$

81. Which of the following justifies step 5 in the proof?

a. AAS
b. SSS
c. ASA
d. SAS

82. Step 6 in the proof should contain which of the following statements?

a. $\angle BAC \cong \angle DEF$
b. $\angle ABC \cong \angle EDF$
c. $\angle ACB \cong \angle EFD$
d. $\angle GDA \cong \angle EDF$

83. Which of these is NOT a net of a cube?

a.
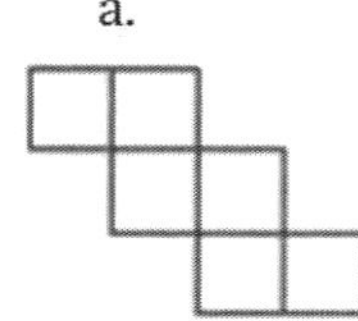

b.
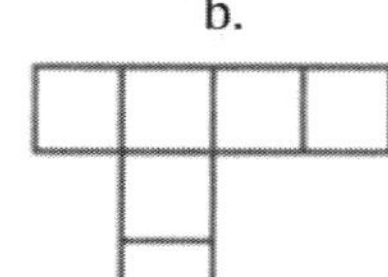

c.
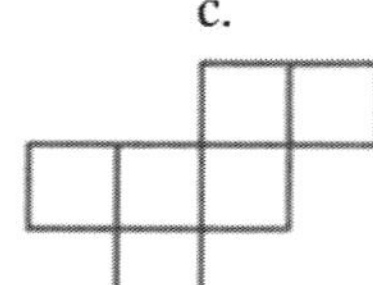

d.
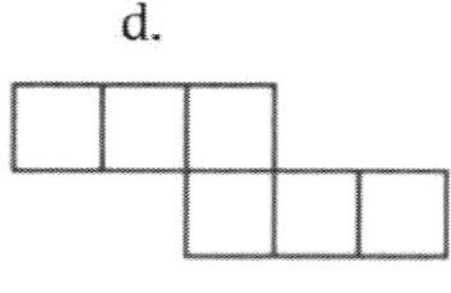

84. Identify the cross-section polygon formed by a plane containing the given points on the cube.

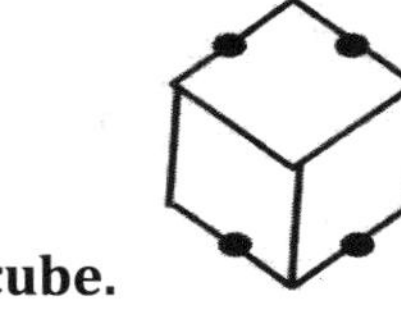

a. Rectangle
b. Trapezoid
c. Pentagon
d. Hexagon

85. Which of these represents the equation of a sphere which is centered in the xyz-space at the point (1, 0, -2) and which has a volume of 36π cubic units?

a. $x^2 + y^2 + z^2 - 2x + 4z = 4$
b. $x^2 + y^2 + z^2 + 2x - 4z = 4$
c. $x^2 + y^2 + z^2 - 2x + 4z = -2$
d. $x^2 + y^2 + z^2 + 2x - 4z = 2$

86. A triangle has vertices $(0, 0, 0)$, $(0, 0, 4)$, and $(0, 3, 0)$ in the xyz-space. In cubic units, what is the difference in the volume of the solid formed by rotating the triangle about the z-axis and the solid formed by rotating the triangle about the y-axis?

a. 0
b. 4π
c. 5π
d. 25

87. If the midpoint of a line segment graphed on the xy-coordinate plane is $(3, -1)$ and the slope of the line segment is -2, which of these is a possible endpoint of the line segment?

a. $(-1,1)$
b. $(0,-5)$
c. $(7,1)$
d. $(5,-5)$

88. The vertices of a polygon are $(2, 3)$, $(8, 1)$, $(6, -5)$, and $(0, -3)$. Which of the following describes the polygon most specifically?

a. Parallelogram
b. Rhombus
c. Rectangle
d. Square

89. What is the radius of the circle defined by the equation $x^2 + y^2 - 10x + 8y + 29 = 0$?

a. $2\sqrt{3}$
b. $2\sqrt{5}$
c. $\sqrt{29}$
d. 12

90. Which of these describes the graph of the equation $2x^2 - 3y^2 - 12x + 6y - 15 = 0$?

a. Circular
b. Elliptical
c. Parabolic
d. Hyperbolic

91. The graph of $f(x)$ is a parabola with a focus of (a, b) and a directrix of $y = -b$, and $g(x)$ represents a transformation of $f(x)$. If the vertex of the graph of $g(x)$ is $(a, 0)$, which of these is a possible equation for $g(x)$ for nonzero integers a and b?

a. $g(x) = f(x) + b$
b. $g(x) = -f(x)$
c. $g(x) = f(x + a)$
d. $g(x) = f(x - a) + b$

92. A triangle with vertices $A(-4, 2)$, $B(-1, 3)$, and $C(-5, 7)$ is reflected across $y = x + 2$ to give $\Delta A'B'C'$, which is subsequently reflected across the y-axis to give $\Delta A''B''C''$. Which of these statements is true?

a. A 90° rotation of ΔABC about $(-2,0)$ gives ΔA″B″C″.
b. A reflection of ΔABC about the x-axis gives ΔA″B″C″.
c. A 270° rotation of ΔABC about $(0,2)$ gives ΔA″B″C″.
d. A translation of ΔABC two units down gives ΔA″B″C″.

93. For which of these does a rotation of 120° about the center of the polygon map the polygon onto itself?

a. Square
b. Regular hexagon
c. Regular octagon
d. Regular decagon

94. Line segment $\overline{PQ}$ has endpoints (a, b) and (c, b). If $\overline{P'Q'}$ is the translation of $\overline{PQ}$ along a diagonal line such that P' is located at point (c, d), what is the area of quadrilateral $PP'Q'Q$?

a. $|a - c| \cdot |b - d|$
b. $|a - b| \cdot |c - d|$
c. $|a - d| \cdot |b - c|$
d. $(a - c)^2$

95. For the right triangle below, which of the following is a true statement of equality?

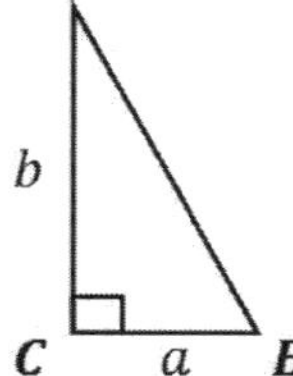

a. $tan\ B = \frac{a}{b}$
b. $cos\ B = \frac{a\sqrt{a^2+b^2}}{a^2+b^2}$
c. $sec\ B = \frac{\sqrt{a^2+b^2}}{b}$
d. $csc\ B = \frac{a^2+b^2}{b}$

96. A man looks out of a window of a tall building at a 45° angle of depression and sees his car in the parking lot. When he turns his gaze downward to a 60° angle of depression, he sees his wife's car. If his car is parked 60 feet from his wife's car, about how far from the building did his wife park her car?

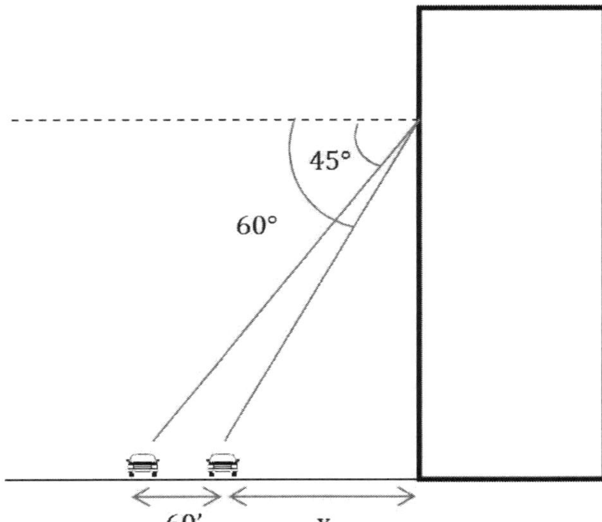

a. 163 feet
b. 122 feet
c. 82 feet
d. 60 feet

97. What is the exact value of $\tan(-\frac{2\pi}{3})$?

a. $\sqrt{3}$
b. $-\sqrt{3}$
c. $\frac{\sqrt{3}}{3}$
d. 1

98. If $\sin\theta = \frac{1}{2}$ when $\frac{\pi}{2} < \theta < \pi$, what is the value of θ?

a. $\frac{\pi}{6}$
b. $\frac{\pi}{3}$
c. $\frac{2\pi}{3}$
d. $\frac{5\pi}{6}$

99. Which of the following expressions is equal to $\cos\theta \cot\theta$?

a. $sin\,\theta$
b. $sec\,\theta\ tan\,\theta$
c. $csc\,\theta - sin\,\theta$
d. $sec\,\theta - sin\,\theta$

100. Solve $\sec^2\theta = 2\tan\theta$ for $0 < \theta \leq 2\pi$.

a. $\theta = \frac{\pi}{6}$ or $\frac{7\pi}{6}$
b. $\theta = \frac{\pi}{4}$ or $\frac{5\pi}{4}$
c. $\theta = \frac{3\pi}{4}$ or $\frac{7\pi}{4}$
d. There is no solution to the equation.

101. A car is driving along the highway at a constant speed when it runs over a pebble, which becomes lodged in one of the tire's treads. If this graph represents the height *h* of the pebble above the road in inches as a function of time *t* in seconds, which of these statements is true?

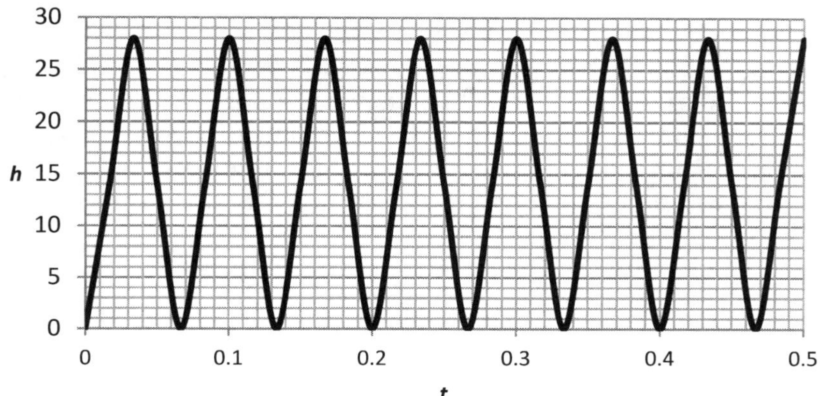

a. The outer radius of the tire is 14 inches, and the tire rotates 900 times per minute.
b. The outer radius of the tire is 28 inches, and the tire rotates 900 times per minute.
c. The outer radius of the tire is 14 inches, and the tire rotates 120 times per minute.
d. The outer radius of the tire is 28 inches, and the tire rotates 120 times per minute.

Below are graphed functions $f(x) = a_1 \sin(b_1 x)$ and $g(x) = a_2 \cos(b_2 x)$; a_1 and a_2 are integers, and b_1 and b_2 are positive rational numbers. Use this information to answer questions 102-103:

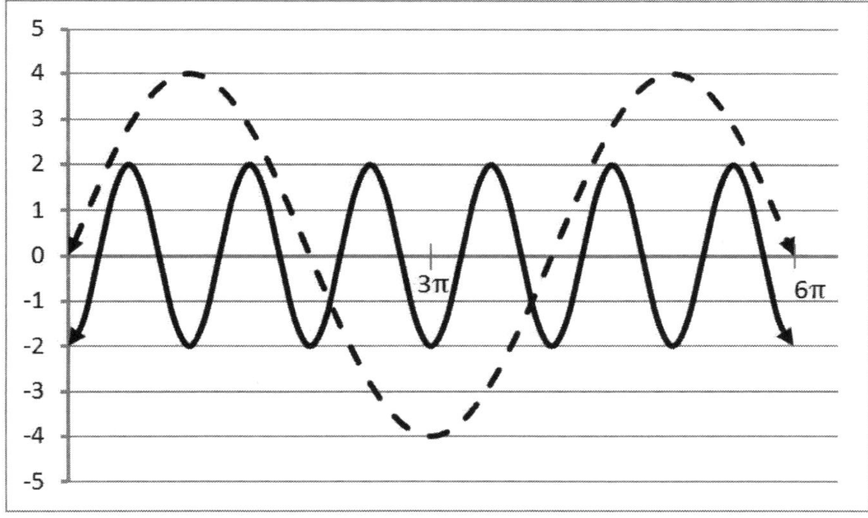

102. Which of the following statements is true?

a. The graph of $f(x)$ is represented by a solid line.
b. The amplitude of the graph of $g(x)$ is 4.
c. $0 < b_1 < 1$.
d. $b_2 = \pi$.

103. Which of the following statements is true?

a. $0 < a_2 < a_1$
b. $a_2 < 0 < a_1$
c. $0 < a_1 < a_2$
d. $a_2 < a_1 < 0$

104. A weight suspended on a spring is at its equilibrium point five inches above the top of a table. When the weight is pulled down two inches, it bounces above the equilibrium point and returns to the point from which it was released in one second. Which of these can be used to model the weight's height h above the table as a function of time t in seconds?

a. $h = -2\,cos(2\pi t) + 5$
b. $h = 5\,sin(t) - 2$
c. $h = -2\,sin(2\pi t) + 5$
d. $h = -2cos(0.5\pi t) + 3$

105. Evaluate $\lim\limits_{x \to -3} \frac{x^3+3x^2-x-3}{x^2-9}$.

a. 0
b. $\frac{1}{3}$
c. $-\frac{4}{3}$
d. ∞

106. Evaluate $\lim\limits_{x \to \infty} \frac{x^2+2x-3}{2x^2+1}$.

a. 0
b. $\frac{1}{2}$
c. -3
d. ∞

107. Evaluate $\lim\limits_{x \to 3^+} \frac{|x-3|}{3-x}$.

a. 0
b. -1
c. 1
d. ∞

108. If $f(x) = \frac{1}{4}x^2 - 3$, find the slope of the line tangent to graph of $f(x)$ at $x = 2$.

a. -2
b. 0
c. 1
d. 4

109. If $f(x) = 2x^3 - 3x^2 + 4$, what is $\lim\limits_{h \to 0} \frac{f(2+h)-f(2)}{h}$?

a. -4
b. 4
c. 8
d. 12

110. Find the derivative of $f(x) = e^{3x^2-1}$.

a. $6xe^{6x}$
b. e^{3x^2-1}
c. $(3x^2-1)e^{3x^2-2}$
d. $6xe^{3x^2-1}$

111. Find the derivative of $f(x) = \ln(2x+1)$.

a. $\frac{1}{2x+1}$
b. $2e^{2x+1}$
c. $\frac{2}{2x+1}$
d. $\frac{1}{2}$

112. For functions $f(x)$, $g(x)$, and $h(x)$, determine the limit of the function as x approaches 2 and the continuity of the function at $x = 2$.

a.

$\lim_{x\to2+} f(x) = 4$ $\lim_{x\to2-} f(x) = 2$ $f(2) = 2$	$\lim_{x\to2} f(x)$ DNE	The function $f(x)$ is discontinuous at 2.
$\lim_{x\to2+} g(x) = 2$ $\lim_{x\to2-} g(x) = 2$ $g(2) = 4$	$\lim_{x\to2} g(x) = 2$	The function $g(x)$ is discontinuous at 2.
$\lim_{x\to2+} h(x) = 2$ $\lim_{x\to2-} h(x) = 2$ $h(2) = 2$	$\lim_{x\to2} h(x) = 2$	The function $h(x)$ is continuous at 2.

b.

$\lim_{x\to2+} f(x) = 4$ $\lim_{x\to2-} f(x) = 2$ $f(2) = 2$	$\lim_{x\to2} f(x)$ DNE	The function $f(x)$ is continuous at 2.
$\lim_{x\to2+} g(x) = 2$ $\lim_{x\to2-} g(x) = 2$ $g(2) = 4$	$\lim_{x\to2} g(x)$ DNE	The function $g(x)$ is continuous at 2.
$\lim_{x\to2+} h(x) = 2$ $\lim_{x\to2-} h(x) = 2$ $h(2) = 2$	$\lim_{x\to2} h(x) = 2$	The function $h(x)$ is continuous at 2.

c.

$\lim_{x\to2+} f(x) = 4$ $\lim_{x\to2-} f(x) = 2$ $f(2) = 2$	$\lim_{x\to2} f(x) = 2$	The function $f(x)$ is continuous at 2.
$\lim_{x\to2+} g(x) = 2$ $\lim_{x\to2-} g(x) = 2$ $g(2) = 4$	$\lim_{x\to2} g(x) = 2$	The function $g(x)$ is discontinuous at 2.
$\lim_{x\to2+} h(x) = 2$ $\lim_{x\to2-} h(x) = 2$ $h(2) = 2$	$\lim_{x\to2} h(x) = 2$	The function $h(x)$ is continuous at 2.

d.

$\lim_{x\to2+} f(x) = 4$ $\lim_{x\to2-} f(x) = 2$ $f(2) = 2$	$\lim_{x\to2} f(x) = 2$	The function $f(x)$ is discontinuous at 2.
$\lim_{x\to2+} g(x) = 2$ $\lim_{x\to2-} g(x) = 2$ $g(2) = 4$	$\lim_{x\to2} g(x) = 2$	The function $g(x)$ is discontinuous at 2.
$\lim_{x\to2+} h(x) = 2$ $\lim_{x\to2-} h(x) = 2$ $h(2) = 2$	$\lim_{x\to2} h(x) = 2$	The function $h(x)$ is continuous at 2.

113. Find $f''(x)$ if $f(x) = 2x^4 - 4x^3 + 2x^2 - x + 1$.

a. $24x^2 - 24x + 4$
b. $8x^3 - 12x^2 + 4x - 1$
c. $32x^2 - 36x^2 + 8$
d. $\frac{2}{5}x^5 - x^4 + \frac{2}{3}x^3 - \frac{1}{2}x^2 + x + c$

114. If $f(x) = 4x^3 - x^2 - 4x + 2$, which of the following statements is(are) true of its graph?

I. The point $\left(-\frac{1}{2}, 3\frac{1}{4}\right)$ is a relative maximum.

II. The graph of f is concave upward on the interval $(-\infty, \frac{1}{2})$.

a. I
b. II
c. I and II
d. Neither I nor II

115. Suppose the path of a baseball hit straight up from three feet above the ground is modeled by the first quadrant graph of the function $h = -16t^2 + 50t + 3$, where t is the flight time of the ball in seconds and h is the height of the ball in feet. What is the velocity of the ball two seconds after it is hit?

a. 39 ft/s upward
b. 19.5 ft/s upward
c. 19.5 ft/s downward
d. 14 ft/s downward

116. A manufacturer wishes to produce a cylindrical can which can hold up to 0.5 L of liquid. To the nearest tenth, what is the radius of the can which requires the least amount of material to make?

a. 2.8 cm
b. 4.3 cm
c. 5.0 cm
d. 9.2 cm

117. Approximate the area A under the curve by using a Riemann sum with $\Delta x = 1$.

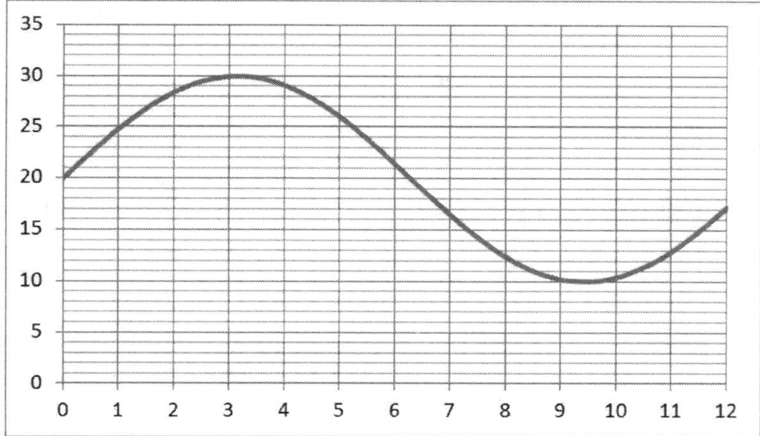

a. $209 < A < 211$
b. $230 < A < 235$
c. $238 < A < 241$
d. $246 < A < 250$

118. To the nearest hundredth, what is the area in square units under the curve of $f(x) = \frac{1}{x}$ on [1,2]?

a. 0.50
b. 0.69
c. 1.30
d. 1.50

119. Calculate $\int 3x^2 + 2x - 1\ dx$.

a. $x^3 + x^2 - x + c$
b. $6x^2 + 2$
c. $\frac{3}{2}x^3 + 2x^2 - x + c$
d. $6x^2 + 2 + c$

120. Calculate $\int 3x^2 e^{x^3}\ dx$

a. $x^3 e^{x^3} + c$
b. $e^{x^3} + c$
c. $x^3 e^{\frac{x^4}{4}} + c$
d. $ln\, x^3 + c$

121. Find the area A of the finite region between the graphs of $y = -x + 2$ and $y = x^2 - 4$.

a. 18
b. $\frac{125}{6}$
c. $\frac{45}{2}$
d. 25

122. The velocity of a car which starts at position 0 at time 0 is given by the equation $v(t) = 12t - t^2$ for $0 \leq t \leq 12$. Find the position of the car when its acceleration is 0.

a. 18
b. 36
c. 144
d. 288

123. Which of these graphs is NOT representative of the data set shown below?

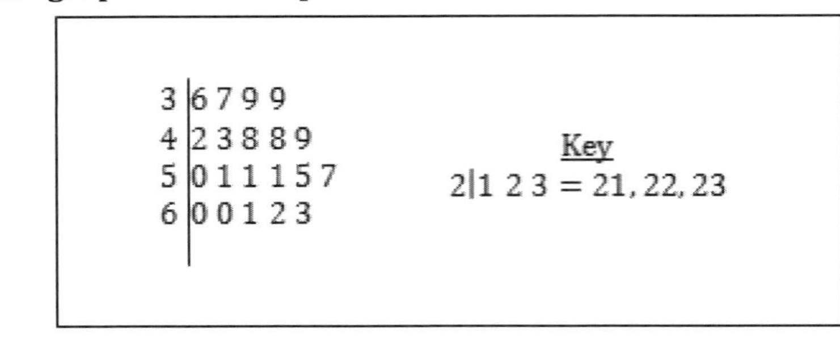

a.

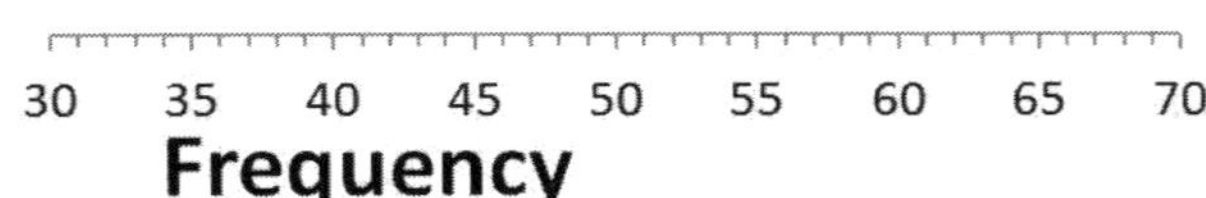

b.

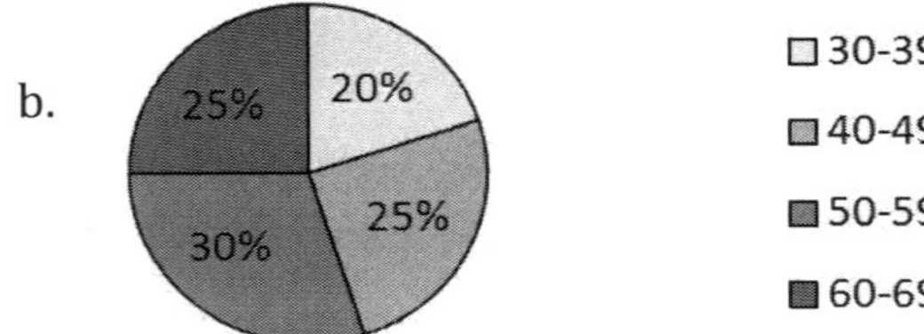

c.

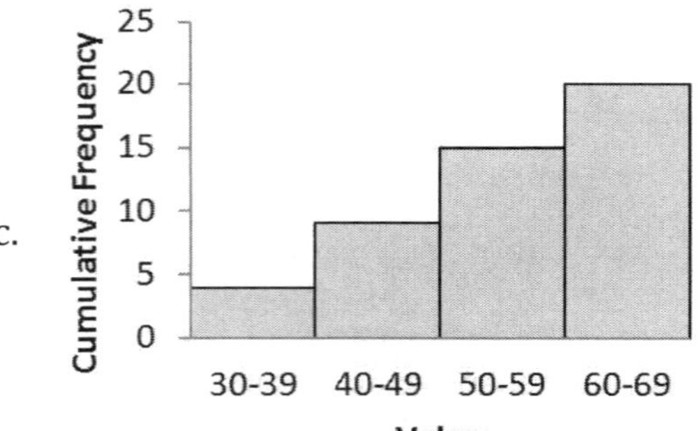

d. All of these graphs represent the data set.

124. Which of these would best illustrate change over time?

a. Pie chart
b. Line graph
c. Box-and-whisker plot
d. Venn diagram

125. Which of these is the least biased sampling technique?

a. To assess his effectiveness in the classroom, a teacher distributes a teacher evaluation to all of his students. Responses are anonymous and voluntary.
b. To determine the average intelligence quotient (IQ) of students in her school of 2,000 students, a principal uses a random number generator to select 300 students by student identification number and has them participate in a standardized IQ test.
c. To determine which video game is most popular among his fellow eleventh graders at school, a student surveys all of the students in his English class.
d. Sixty percent of students at the school have a parent who is a member of the Parent-Teacher Association (PTA). To determine parent opinions regarding school improvement programs, the Parent-Teacher Association (PTA) requires submission of a survey response with membership dues.

126. Which of these tables properly displays the measures of central tendency which can be used for nominal, interval, and ordinal data?

a.

	Mean	**Median**	**Mode**
Nominal			x
Interval	x	x	x
Ordinal		x	x

b.

	Mean	**Median**	**Mode**
Nominal			x
Interval	x	x	x
Ordinal	x	x	x

c.

	Mean	**Median**	**Mode**
Nominal	x	x	x
Interval	x	x	x
Ordinal	x	x	x

d.

	Mean	**Median**	**Mode**
Nominal			x
Interval	x	x	
Ordinal	x	x	x

Use the following data to answer questions 127-129:

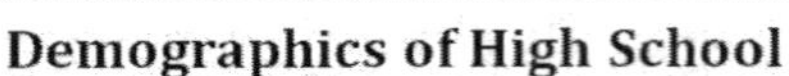

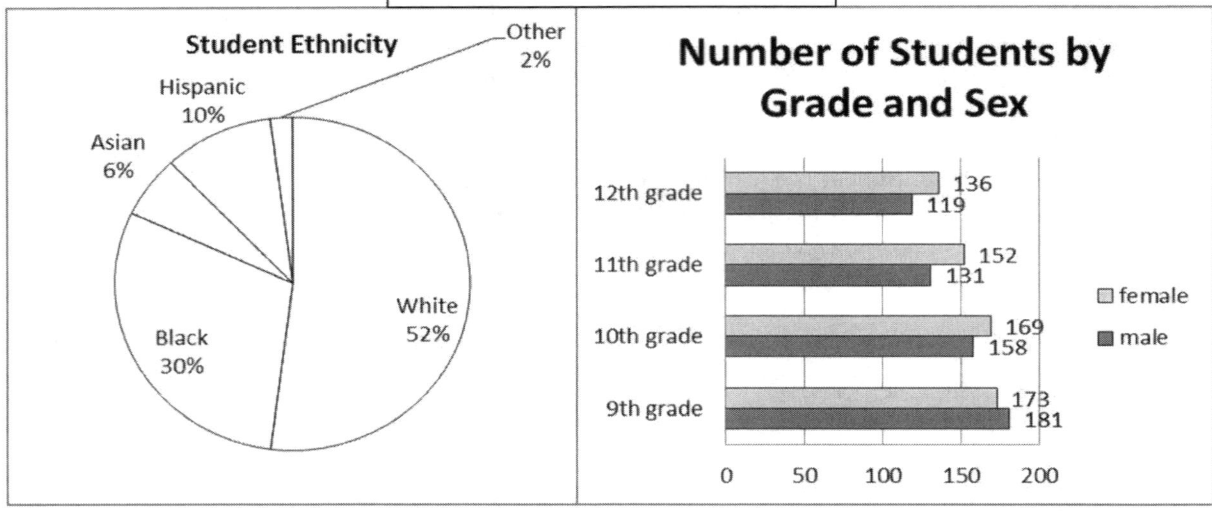

127. Which of these is the greatest quantity?

a. The average number of male students in the 11th and 12th grades
b. The number of Hispanic students at the school
c. The difference in the number of male and female students at the school
d. The difference in the number of 9th and 12th grader students at the school

128. Compare the two quantities.

Quantity A	**Quantity B**
The percentage of white students at the school, rounded to the nearest whole number	The percentage of female students at the school, rounded to the nearest whole number

a. Quantity A is greater.
b. Quantity B is greater.
c. The two quantities are the same.
d. The relationship cannot be determined from the given information.

129. An eleventh grader is chosen at random to represent the school at a conference. What is the approximate probability that the student is male?

a. 0.03
b. 0.11
c. 0.22
d. 0.46

The box-and-whisker plot displays student test scores by class period. Use the data to answer questions 130 through 132:

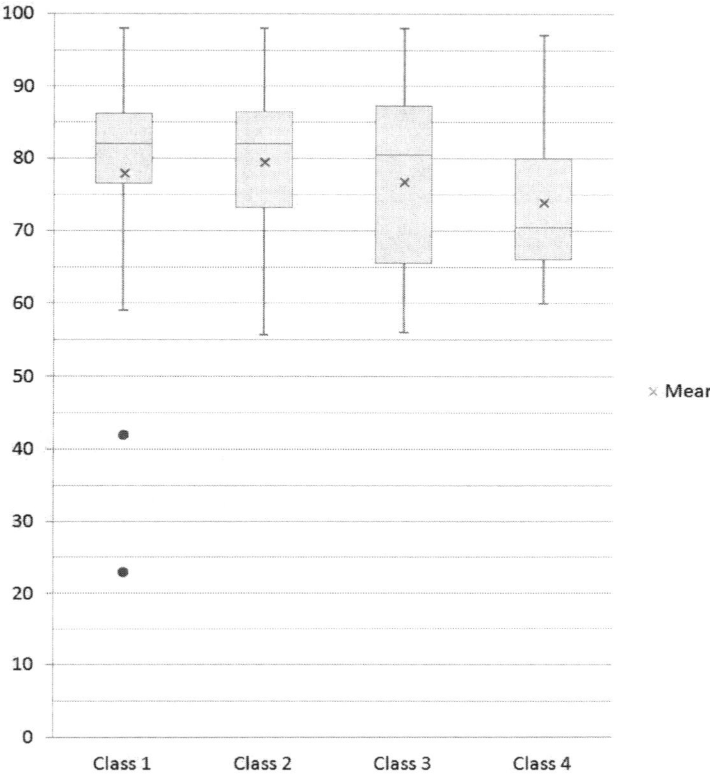

30. Which class has the greatest range of test scores?

a. Class 1
b. Class 2
c. Class 3
d. Class 4

131. What is the probability that a student chosen at random from class 2 made above a 73 on this test?

a. 0.25
b. 0.5
c. 0.6
d. 0.75

132. Which of the following statements is true of the data?

a. The mean better reflects student performance in class 1 than the median.
b. The mean test score for class 1 and 2 is the same.
c. The median test score for class 1 and 2 is the same.
d. The median test score is above the mean for class 4.

133. In order to analyze the real estate market for two different zip codes within the city, a realtor examines the most recent 100 home sales in each zip code. She considered a house which sold within the first month of its listing to have a market time of one month; likewise, she considered a house to have a market time of two months if it sold after having been on the market for one month but by the end of the second month. Using this definition of market time, she determined the frequency of sales by number of months on the market. The results are displayed below.

Which of the following is a true statement for these data?

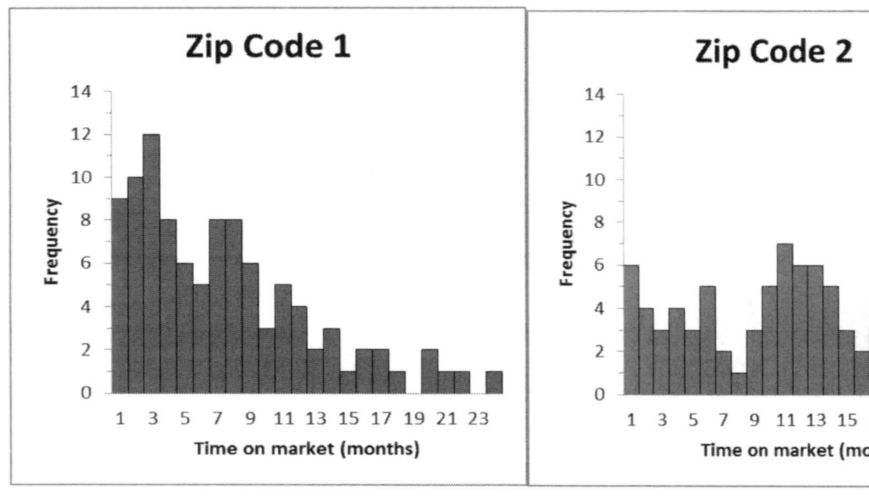

a. The median time a house spends on the market in Zip Code 1 is five months less than Zip Code 2

b. On average, a house spent seven months longer on the market in Zip Code 2 than in Zip Code 1.

c. The mode time on the market is higher for Zip Code 1 than for Zip Code 2.

d. The median time on the market is less than the mean time on the market for Zip Code 1.

134. Attending a summer camp are 12 six-year-olds, 15 seven-year-olds, 14 eight-year-olds, 12 nine-year-olds, and 10 ten-year-olds. If a camper is randomly selected to participate in a special event, what is the probability that he or she is at least eight years old?

a. $\frac{2}{9}$

b. $\frac{22}{63}$

c. $\frac{4}{7}$

d. $\frac{3}{7}$

135. A small company is divided into three departments as shown. Two individuals are chosen at random to attend a conference. What is the approximate probability that two women from the same department will be chosen?

	Department 1	Department 2	Department 3
Women	12	28	16
Men	18	14	15

a. 8.6%
b. 10.7%
c. 11.2%
d. 13.8%

136. A random sample of 90 students at an elementary school were asked these three questions:

Do you like carrots?
Do you like broccoli?
Do you like cauliflower?

The results of the survey are shown below. If these data are representative of the population of students at the school, which of these is most probable?

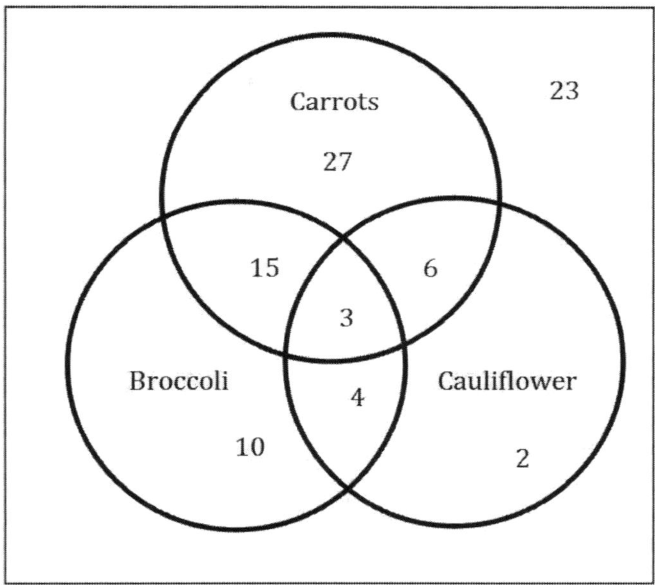

a. A student chosen at random likes broccoli.
b. If a student chosen at random likes carrots, he also likes at least one other vegetable.
c. If a student chosen at random likes cauliflower and broccoli, he also likes carrots.
d. A student chosen at random does not like carrots, broccoli, or cauliflower.

Use the information below to answer questions 137 and 138:

Each day for 100 days, a student tossed a single misshapen coin three times in succession and recorded the number of times the coin landed on heads. The results of his experiment are shown below.

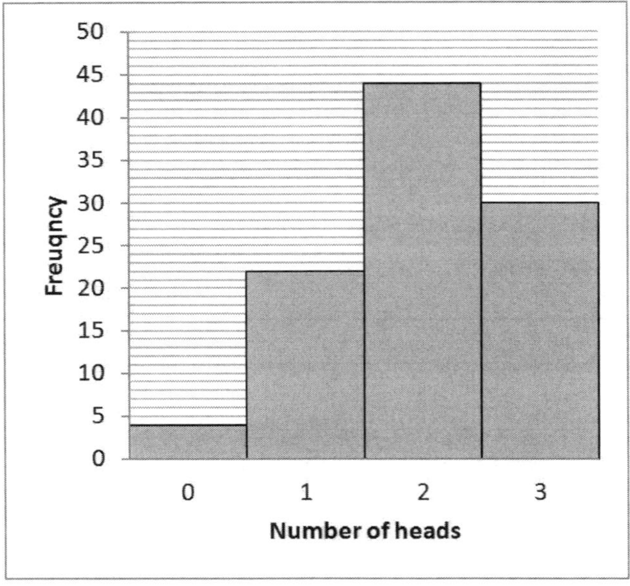

137. Given these experimental data, which of these approximates P(heads) for a single flip of this coin.

a. 0.22
b. 0.5
c. 0.67
d. 0.74

138. Which of these shows the graphs of the probability distributions from ten flips of this misshapen coin and ten flips of a fair coin?

a.

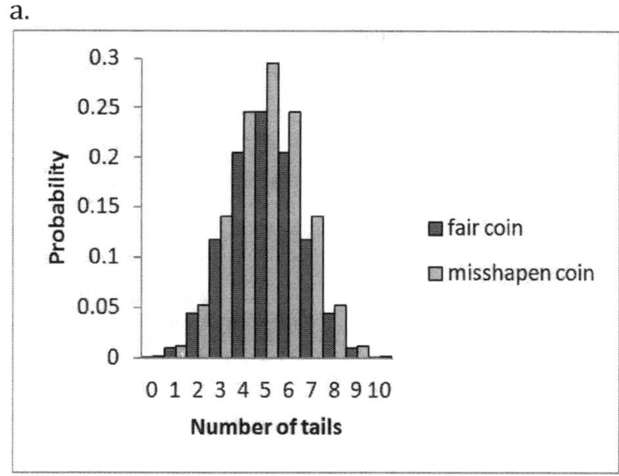

b.

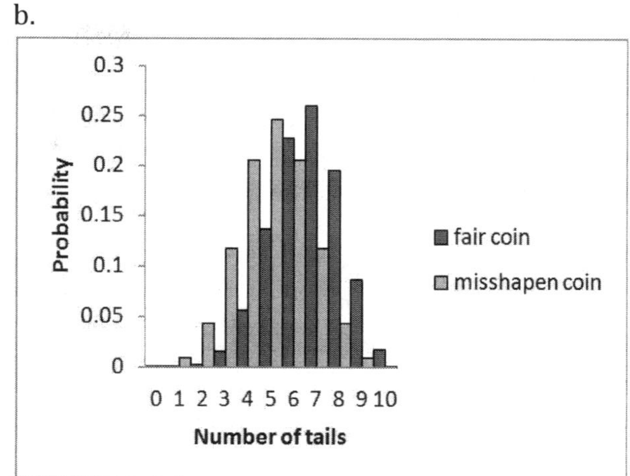

c.

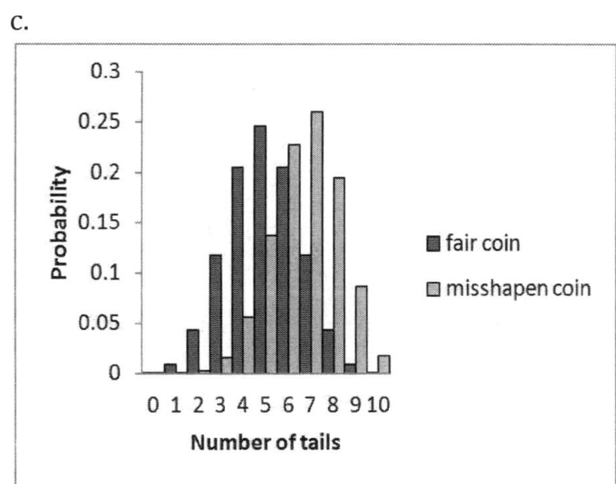

d.

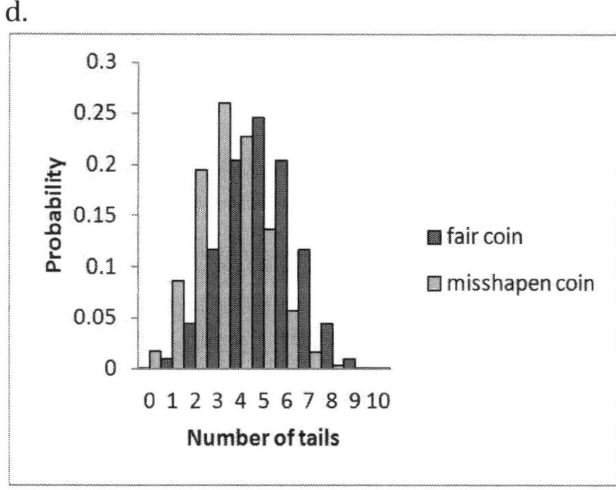

139. Which of these does NOT simulate randomly selecting a student from a group of 11 students?

a. Assigning each student a unique card value of A, 1, 2, 3, 4, 5, 6, 7, 8, 9, or J, removing queens and kings from a standard deck of 52 cards, shuffling the remaining cards, and drawing a single card from the deck
b. Assigning each student a unique number 0-10 and using a computer to randomly generate a number within that range
c. Assigning each student a unique number from 2 to 12 ; rolling two dice and finding the sum of the numbers on the dice
d. All of these can be used as a simulation of the event.

140. Gene P has three possible alleles, or gene forms, called a, b and c. Each individual carries two copies of Gene P, one of which is inherited from his or her mother and the other of which is inherited from his or her father. If the two copies of Gene P are of the same form, the individual is homozygous for that allele; otherwise, the individual is heterozygous. A simulation is performed to determine the genotypes, or genetic make-ups, of 500 individuals selected at random from the population. 500 two-digit numbers are generator using a random number generator. Based on the relative frequencies of each allele, the digit 0 is assigned to represent allele a, the digits 1 and 2 to represent allele b, and the digits 3-9 to represent allele c.

28 93 97 37 92 00 27 21 87 13 62 62 15 31 55 09 47 07 54 88 38 88 10 98 34 01 45 14 34 46 38 61
93 22 37 39 57 03 93 50 53 16 28 65 81 60 21 12 13 10 19 91 04 18 49 01 99 30 11 16 00 48 04 63
59 24 02 42 23 06 32 52 19 18 94 94 46 63 87 41 79 39 85 20 43 20 15 03 39 33 77 45 66 77 70 92
25 27 68 71 89 35 98 55 85 47 60 97 12 92 53 44 45 41 51 22 09 23 81 33 04 35 43 48 32 80 36 95
64 56 34 74 55 37 64 84 51 50 25 99 51 94 19 46 10 44 17 25 75 52 47 35 70 65 08 50 98 09 02 24
30 59 00 03 21 40 30 86 16 53 91 28 17 97 58 75 76 73 83 54 40 54 13 38 36 67 74 80 63 12 41 27
96 61 66 05 60 69 96 15 56 82 57 31 83 26 24 78 42 76 49 56 06 57 78 67 02 96 40 82 29 14 07 29
62 90 31 08 26 71 61 18 22 84 23 33 49 29 90 07 08 05 14 59 72 86 44 69 68 99 06 11 95 43 72 58
28 93 97 37 92 00 27 21 87 13 62 62 15 31 55 09 47 07 54 88 38 88 10 98 34 01 45 14 34 46 38 61
93 22 37 39 57 03 93 50 53 16 28 65 81 60 21 12 13 10 19 91 04 18 49 01 99 30 11 16 00 48 04 63
59 24 02 42 23 06 32 52 19 18 94 94 46 63 87 41 79 39 85 20 43 20 15 03 39 33 77 45 66 77 70 92
25 27 68 71 89 35 98 55 85 47 60 97 12 92 53 44 45 41 51 22 09 23 81 33 04 35 43 48 32 80 36 95
64 56 34 74 55 37 64 84 51 50 25 99 51 94 19 46 10 44 17 25 75 52 47 35 70 65 08 50 98 09 02 24
30 59 00 03 21 40 30 86 16 53 91 28 17 97 58 75 76 73 83 54 40 54 13 38 36 67 74 80 63 12 41 27
96 61 66 05 60 69 96 15 56 82 57 31 83 26 24 78 42 76 49 56 06 57 78 67 02 96 40 82 29 14 07 29
62 90 31 08 26 71 61 18 22 84 23 33 49 29 90 07 08 05 14 59

Using the experimental probability that an individual will be homozygous for allele a (light grey) or for allele b (dark grey), predict the number of individuals in a population of 100,000 who will be homozygous for either allele.

a. 2,800
b. 5,000
c. 5,400
d. 9,000

141. The intelligence quotients (IQs) of a randomly selected group of 300 people are normally distributed with a mean IQ of 100 and a standard deviation of 15. In a normal distribution, approximately 68% of values are within one standard deviation of the mean. About how many individuals from the selected group have IQs of at least 85?

a. 96
b. 200
c. 216
d. 252

142. How many different seven-digit telephone numbers can be created in which no digit repeats and in which zero cannot be the first digit?

a. 5,040
b. 35,280
c. 544,320
d. 3, 265,920

143. A teacher wishes to divide her class of twenty students into four groups, each of which will have three boys and two girls. How many possible groups can she form?

a. 248
b. 6,160
c. 73,920
d. 95,040

144. In how many distinguishable ways can a family of five be seated at a circular table with five chairs if Tasha and Mac must be kept separated?

a. 6
b. 12
c. 24
d. 60

145. Which of these defines the recursive sequence $a_1 = -1, a_{n+1} = a_n + 2$ explicitly?

a. $a_n = 2n - 3$
b. $a_n = -n + 2$
c. $a_n = n - 2$
d. $a_n = -2n + 3$

146. What is the sum of the series 200 + 100 + 50 + 25 + ...?

a. 300
b. 400
c. 600
d. The sum is infinite.

147. For vector $v = (4, 3)$ and vector $w = (-3, 4)$, find $2(v + w)$.

a. $(2, 14)$
b. $(14, -2)$
c. $(1,7)$
d. $(7, -1)$

148. Simplify:

$$\begin{bmatrix} 2 & 0 & -5 \end{bmatrix} \left(\begin{bmatrix} 4 \\ 2 \\ -1 \end{bmatrix} - \begin{bmatrix} 3 \\ 5 \\ -5 \end{bmatrix} \right).$$

a. [-18]
b. $\begin{bmatrix} 2 \\ 0 \\ -20 \end{bmatrix}$
c. $\begin{bmatrix} 2 & 0 & -20 \end{bmatrix}$
d. $\begin{bmatrix} 2 & 0 & -5 \\ -6 & 0 & 15 \\ 8 & 0 & -20 \end{bmatrix}$

149. Consider three sets, of which one contains the set of even integers, one contains the factors of twelve, and one contains elements 1, 2, 4, and 9. If each set is assigned the name A, B, or C, and $A \cap B \subseteq B \cap C$, which of these must be set C?

a. The set of even integers
b. The set of factors of 12
c. The set $\{1, 2, 4, 9\}$
d. The answer cannot be determined from the given information.

150. Last year, Jenny tutored students in math, in chemistry, and for the ACT. She tutored ten students in math, eight students in chemistry, and seven students for the ACT. She tutored five students in both math and chemistry, and she tutored four students both in chemistry and for the ACT, and five students both in math and for the ACT. She tutored three students in all three subjects. How many students did Jenny tutor last year?

a. 34
b. 25
c. 23
d. 14

Answers and Explanations

1. C: Because drawing a dodecagon and counting its diagonals is an arduous task, it is useful to employ a different problem-solving strategy. One such strategy is to draw polygons with fewer sides and look for a pattern in the number of the polygons' diagonals.

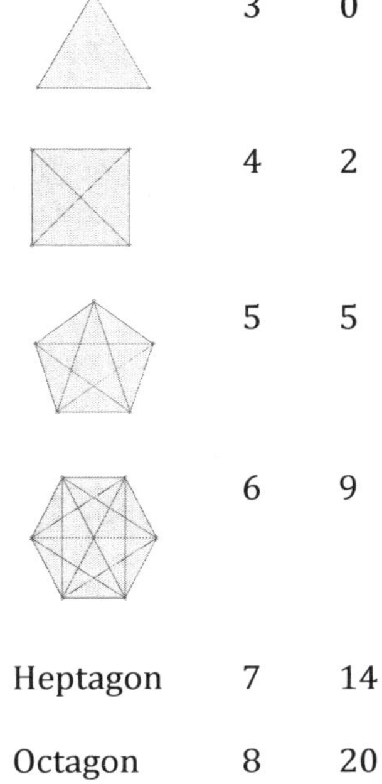

A quadrilateral has two more diagonals than a triangle, a pentagon has three more diagonals than a quadrilateral, and a hexagon has four more diagonals than a pentagon. Continue this pattern to find that a dodecagon has 54 diagonals.

2. B: The problem does not give any information about the size of the bracelet or the spacing between any of the charms. Nevertheless, creating a simple illustration which shows the order of the charms will help when approaching this problem. For example, the circle below represents the bracelet, and the dotted line between A and B represents the clasp. On the right, the line shows the stretched-out bracelet and possible positions of charms C, D, and E based on the parameters.

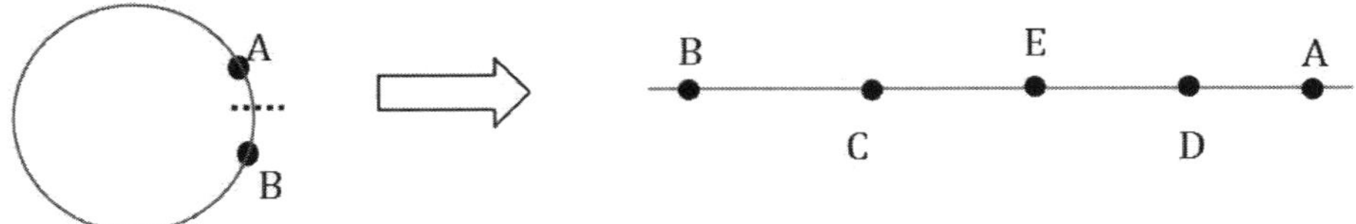

From the drawing above, it appears that statement I is true, but it is not necessarily so. The alternative drawing below also shows the charms ordered correctly, but the distance between B and E is now less than that between D and A.

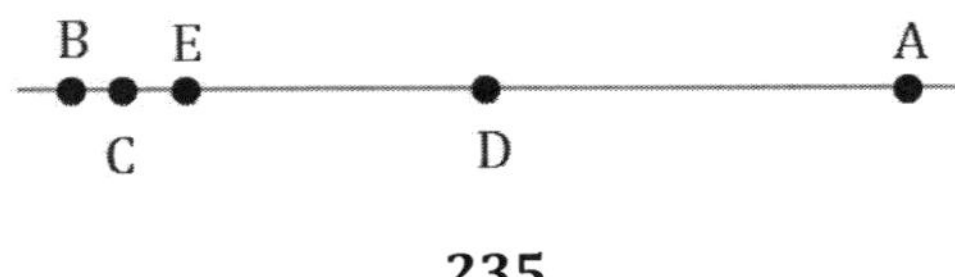

Statement II must be true: charm E must lie between B and D. Statement III must also be true: the distance between charms E and D must be less than that between C and A, which includes charms E and D in the space between them.

3. B: The population is approximately 36,000, so one quarter of the population consists of about 9,000 individuals under age 35. A third of 9,000 is 3,000, the approximate number of students in grades K-12. Since there are thirteen grades, there are about 230 students in each grade. So, the number of fourth graders is between 200 and 300.

4. A: The final sales price of the rug is $1.08(0.7 \cdot \$296) = \$223.78$ at Store A, $1.08(\$220 - \$10) = \$226.80$ at Store B, and $\$198 + \$35 = \$233$ at Store C.

5. C: The expression representing the monthly charge for Company A is $\$25 + \$0.05m$, where m is the time in minutes spent talking on the phone. Set this expression equal to the monthly charge for Company B, which is $50. Solve for m to find the number of minutes for which the two companies charge the same amount:

$$\$25 + \$0.05m = \$50$$

$$\$0.05m = \$25$$

$$m = 500$$

Notice that the answer choices are given in hours, not in minutes. Since there are 60 minutes in an hour, $m = \frac{500}{60}$ hours = $8\frac{1}{3}$ hours. One-third of an hour is twenty minutes, so m = 8 hours, 20 minutes.

6. D: When the dress is marked down by 20%, the cost of the dress is 80% of its original price; thus, the reduced price of the dress can be written as $\frac{80}{100}x$, or $\frac{4}{5}x$, where x is the original price. When discounted an extra 25%, the dress costs 75% of the reduced price, or $\frac{75}{100}\left(\frac{4}{5}x\right)$, or $\frac{3}{4}\left(\frac{4}{5}x\right)$, which simplifies to $\frac{3}{5}x$. So the final price of the dress is three-fifths of the original price.

7. D: Since there are 100 cm in a meter, on a 1:100 scale drawing, each centimeter represents one meter. Therefore, an area of one square centimeter on the drawing represents one square meter in actuality. Since the area of the room in the scale drawing is 30 cm^2, the room's actual area is 30 m^2.

Another way to determine the area of the room is to write and solve an equation, such as this one:

$\frac{l}{100} \cdot \frac{w}{100} = 30 \text{ cm}^2$, where l and w are the dimensions of the actual room

$$\frac{lw}{1000} = 30 \text{ m}^2$$

$$lw = 300{,}000 \text{ cm}^2$$

$$\text{Area} = 300{,}000 \text{ cm}^2$$

Since this is not one of the answer choices, convert cm^2 to m^2: $300{,}000 \text{ cm}^2 \cdot \frac{1 \text{ m}}{100 \text{ cm}} \cdot \frac{1 \text{ m}}{100 \text{ cm}} = 30 \text{ m}^2$.

8. C: Since the ratio of wages and benefits to other costs is 2:3, the amount of money spent on wages and benefits is $\frac{2}{5}$ of the business's total expenditure. $\frac{2}{5} \cdot \$130{,}000 = \$52{,}000$.

9\. A: The height of the ball is a function of time, so the equation can be expressed as $f(t) = -16t^2 + 64t + 5$, and the average rate of change can be found by calculating $\frac{f(3)-f(1)}{3-1}$.

$$\frac{-16(3)^2 + 64(3) + 5 - [-16(1)^2 + 64(1) + 5]}{2} = \frac{-144 + 192 + 5 - (-16 + 64 + 5)}{2} = \frac{0}{2} = 0$$

Alternatively, the rate of change can be determined by finding the slope of the secant line through points $(1, f(1))$ and $(3, f(3))$. Notice that this is a horizontal line, which has a slope of 0.

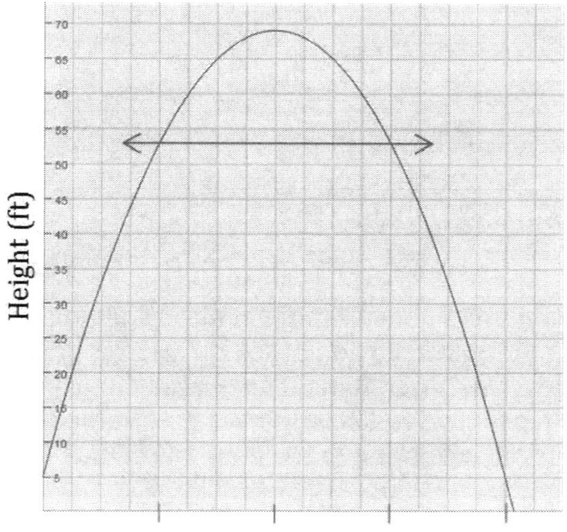

Time (sec)

10\. B: Since rate in mph $= \frac{\text{distance in miles}}{\text{time in hours}}$, Zeke's driving speed on the way to Atlanta and home from Atlanta in mph can be expressed as d/3 and d/2, respectively, when d=distance between Zeke's house and his destination. Since Zeke drove 20 mph faster on his way home, $\frac{d}{2} - \frac{d}{3} = 20$.

$$6\left(\frac{d}{2} - \frac{d}{3} = 20\right)$$

$$3d - 2d = 120$$

$$d = 120$$

Since the distance between Zeke's house and the store in Atlanta is 120 miles, Zeke drove a total distance of 240 miles in five hours. Therefore, his average speed was $\frac{240 \text{ miles}}{5 \text{ hours}} = 48$ mph.

11\. C: Aaron ran four miles from home and then back again, so he ran a total of eight miles. Therefore, statement III is false. Statements I and II, however, are both true. Since Aaron ran eight miles in eighty minutes, he ran an average of one mile every ten minutes, or six miles per hour; he ran two miles from point A to B in 20 minutes and four miles from D to E in 40 minutes, so his running speed between both sets of points was the same.

12. D: First, use the table to determine the values of $(a * b)$ and $(c * d)$.

*	*a*	*b*	*c*	*d*
a	*d*	*a*	*b*	*c*
b	*a*	*b*	*c*	*d*
c	*b*	*c*	*d*	*a*
d	*c*	*d*	*a*	*b*

$(a * b) = a$ and $(c * d) = a$, so $(a * b) * (c * d) = a * a$, which is equal to d.

13. B: When $y = x^3, x = \sqrt[3]{y}$. Similarly, when $y = e^x, x = \ln y$ for $y > 0$. On the other hand, when $y = x + a, x = y - a$; when $y = 1/x, x = 1/y$ for $x, y \neq 0$; and when $y = \sin x\,, x = \sin^{-1} y$.

14. B: Deductive reasoning moves from one or more general statements to a specific, while inductive reasoning makes a general conclusion based on a series of specific instances or observations. Whenever the premises used in deductive reasoning are true, the conclusion drawn is necessarily true. In inductive reasoning, it is possible for the premises to be true and the conclusion to be false since there may exist an exception to the general conclusion drawn from the observations made.

15. A: The first argument's reasoning is valid, and since its premises are true, the argument is also sound. The second argument's reasoning is invalid; that the premises are true is irrelevant. (For example, consider the true premises "all cats are mammals" and "all dogs are mammals;" it cannot be logically concluded that all dogs are cats.) The third argument's reasoning is valid, but since one of its premises is false, the argument is not sound.

16. C: The logical representation $p \rightarrow q$ means that p implies q. In other words, if p, then q. Unlike the contrapositive (Choice C), neither the converse (choice A) nor the inverse (choice B) is necessarily true. For example, consider this statement: all cats are mammals. This can be written as an if/then statement: if an animal is a cat, then the animal is a mammal. The converse would read, "If an animal is a mammal, then the animal is a cat;" of course, this is not necessarily true since there are many mammals other than cats. The inverse statement, "If an animal is not a cat, then the animal is not a mammal," is false. The contrapositive, "If an animal is not a mammal, then the animal is not a cat" is true since there are no cats which are not mammals.

17. D: The symbol $\wedge$ is the logical conjunction symbol. In order for statement $(p \wedge q)$ to be true, both statements p and q must be true. The ~ symbol means "not," so if $(p \wedge q)$ is true, then $\sim(p \wedge q)$ is false,

and if $(p \wedge q)$ is false, then $\sim(p \wedge q)$ is true. The statement $q \leftrightarrow \sim(p \wedge q)$ is true when the value of q is the same as the value of $\sim(p \wedge q)$.

p	q	$(p \wedge q)$	$\sim(p \wedge q)$	$q \leftrightarrow \sim(p \wedge q)$
T	T	T	F	F
T	F	F	T	F
F	T	F	T	T
F	F	F	T	F

18. D: The value "0" means "false," and the value "1" means "true." For the logical disjunction "or," the output value is true if either or both input values are true, else it is false. For the logical conjunction "and," the output value is true only if both input values are true. "Not *A*" is true when *A* is false and is false when *A* is true.

X	Y	Z	not Y	not Z	not Y or not Z	X and (not Y or not Z)
0	0	0	1	1	1	0
0	0	1	1	0	1	0
0	1	0	0	1	1	0
0	1	1	0	0	0	0
1	0	0	1	1	1	1
1	0	1	1	0	1	1
1	1	0	0	1	1	1
1	1	1	0	0	0	0

19. A: The Babylonians used a base-60 numeral system, which is still used in the division of an hour into 60 minutes, a minute into 60 seconds, and a circle into 360 degrees. (The word "algebra" and its development as a discipline separate from geometry are attributed to the Arabic/Islamic civilization. The Greek philosopher Thales is credited with using deductive reasoning to prove geometric concepts. Boolean logic and algebra were introduced by British mathematician George Boole.)

20. C: Leonhard Euler made many important contributions to the field of mathematics. One such contribution, Euler's formula $e^{i\varphi} = \cos\varphi + i\sin\varphi = 0$, can be written as $e^{i\pi} + 1 = 0$ when $\varphi = \pi$. This identity is considered both mathematically remarkable and beautiful, as it links together five important mathematical constants, e, i, π, 0 and 1.

21. B: The notation $\mathbb{P} \subseteq \mathbb{N} \subseteq \mathbb{Z} \subseteq \mathbb{Q} \subseteq \mathbb{R} \subseteq \mathbb{C}$ means that the set of prime numbers is a subset of the set natural numbers, which is a subset of the set of integers, which is a subset of the set of rational numbers, which is a subset of the set real numbers, which is a subset of the set of complex numbers.

22. A: The set of whole numbers, $\{0, 1, 2, 3, \dots\}$, does not contain the number -4. Since -4 is an integer, it is also a rational number and a real number.

23. D: In order for a set to be a group under operation $*$, the following conditions must be met:

The set must be closed under that operation. In other words, when the operation is performed on any two members of the set, the result must also be a member of that set.

The set must demonstrate associativity under the operation: $a * (b * c) = (a * b) * c$

There must exist an identity element e in the group: $a * e = e * a = a$

For every element in the group, there must exist an inverse element in the group: $a * b = b * a = e$

Note: the group need not be commutative for every pair of elements in the group. If the group demonstrates commutativity, it is called an abelian group.

The set of prime numbers under addition is not closed. For example, 3+5=8, and 8 is not a member of the set of prime numbers. Similarly, the set of negative integers under multiplication is not closed since the product of two negative integers is a positive integer. Though the set of negative integers under addition is closed and is associative, there exists no identity element (the number zero in this case) in the group. The set of positive rational numbers under multiplication is closed and associative; the multiplicative identity 1 is a member of the group, and for each element in the group, there is a multiplicative inverse (reciprocal).

24. A: First, multiply the numerator and denominator by the denominator's conjugate, $4 + 2i$. Then, simplify the result and write the answer in the form $a + bi$.

$$\frac{2+3i}{4-2i} \cdot \frac{4+2i}{4+2i} = \frac{8+4i+12i+6i^2}{16-4i^2} = \frac{8+16i-6}{16+4} = \frac{2+16i}{20} = \frac{1}{10} + \frac{4}{5}i$$

25. D: First, simplify the expression within the absolute value symbol.

$$|(2-3i)^2 - (1-4i)|$$

$$|4 - 12i + 9i^2 - 1 + 4i|$$

$$|4 - 12i - 9 - 1 + 4i|$$

$$|-6 - 8i|$$

The absolute value of a complex number is its distance from 0 on the complex plane. Use the Pythagorean Theorem (or the 3-4-5 Pythagorean triple and similarity) to find the distance of $-6 - 8i$ from the origin.

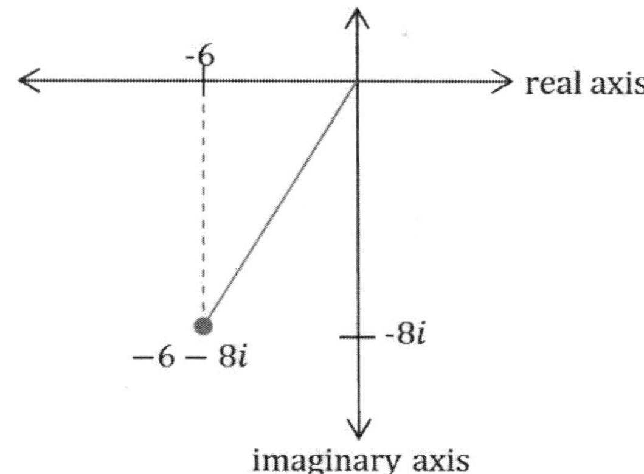

Since the distance from the origin to the point $-6 - 8i$ is 10, $|-6 - 8i|=10$.

26. B: In order for a set to be a group under operation $*$,

The set must be closed under that operation. In other words, when the operation is performed on any two members of the set, the result must also be a member of that set.

The set must demonstrate associativity under the operation: $a * (b * c) = (a * b) * c$

There must exist an identity element e in the group: $a * e = e * a = a$

For every element in the group, there must exist an inverse element in the group: $a * b = b * a = e$

Choice A can easily be eliminated as the correct answer because the set $\{-i, 0, i\}$ does not contain the multiplicative identity 1. Though choices C and D contain the element 1, neither is closed: for example, since $i \cdot i = -1$, -1 must be an element of the group. Choice B is closed, contains the multiplicative identity 1, and the inverse of each element is included in the set as well. Of course, multiplication is an associative operation, so the set $\{-1, 1, i, -i\}$ forms a group under multiplication

×	**-1**	**1**	***i***	***-i***
-1	1	-1	$-i$	i
1	-1	1	i	$-i$
i	$-i$	i	-1	1
-i	i	$-i$	1	-1

27. D: The identity element is d since $d\#a = a\#d = a, d\#b = b\#d = b, d\#c = c\#d = c$, and $d\#d = d$. The inverse of element c is c since $c\#c = d$, the identity element. The operation # is commutative because $a\#b = b\#a$, $a\#c = c\#a$, etc. Rather than check that the operation is commutative for each

pair of elements, note that elements in the table display symmetry about the diagonal elements; this indicates that the operation is indeed commutative.

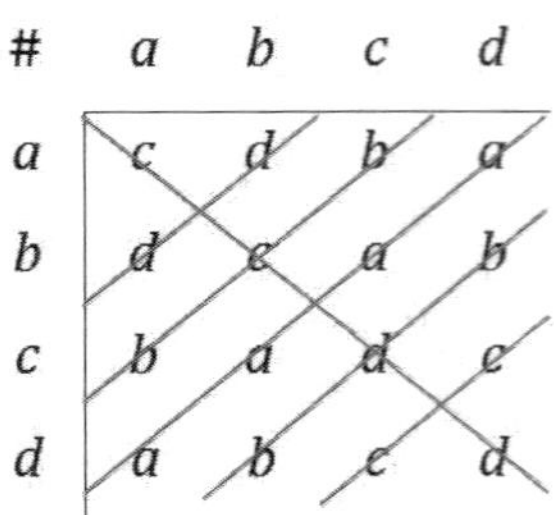

28. C: "The square of twice the sum of *x* and three is equal to the product of twenty-four and *x*" is represented by the equation $[2(x+3)]^2 = 24x$. Solve for *x*.

$$[2(x+3)]^2 = 24x$$

$$[2x+6]^2 = 24x$$

$$4x^2 + 24x + 36 = 24x$$

$$4x^2 = -36$$

$$x^2 = -9$$

$$x = \pm\sqrt{-9}$$

$$x = \pm 3i$$

So, $-3i$ is a possible value of *x*.

29. C: If x is a prime number and that the greatest common factor of x and y is greater than 1, the greatest common factor of x and y must be x. The least common multiple of two numbers is equal to the product of those numbers divided by their greatest common factor. So, the least common multiple of x and y is $\frac{xy}{x} = y$. Therefore, the values in the two columns are the same.

30. D: Since a and b are even integers, each can be expressed as the product of 2 and an integer. So, if we write $a = 2x$ and $b = 2y$, $3(2x)^2 + 9(2y)^3 = c$.

$$3(4x^2) + 9(8y^3) = c$$

$$12x^2 + 72y^3 = c$$

$$12(x^2 + 6y^3) = c$$

Since c is the product of 12 and some other integer, 12 must be a factor of c. Incidentally, the numbers 2, 3, and 6 must also be factors of c since each is also a factor of 12.

31. C: Choice C is the equation for the greatest integer function. A function is a relationship in which for every element of the domain (x), there is exactly one element of the range (y). Graphically, a relationship between x and y can be identified as a function if the graph passes the vertical line test.

The first relation is a parabola on its side, which fails the vertical line test for functions. A circle (Choice B) also fails the vertical line test and is therefore not a function. The relation in Choice D pairs two elements of the range with one of the elements of the domain, so it is also not a function.

32. B: The area of a triangle is $A = \frac{1}{2}bh$, where b and h are the lengths of the triangle's base and height, respectively. The base of the given triangle is x, but the height is not given. Since the triangle is a right triangle and the hypotenuse is given, the triangle's height can be found using the Pythagorean Theorem.

$$x^2 + h^2 = 6^2$$

$$h = \sqrt{36 - x^2}$$

To find the area of the triangle in terms of x, substitute $\sqrt{36 - x^2}$ for the height and x for the base of the triangle into the area formula.

$$A = \frac{1}{2}bh$$

$$A(x) = \frac{1}{2}(x)(\sqrt{36 - x^2})$$

$$A(x) = \frac{x\sqrt{36 - x^2}}{2}$$

33. A: $[g \circ f\,]x = g\big(f(x)\big) = g(2x + 4) = (2x + 4)^2 - 3(2x + 4) + 2 = 4x^2 + 16x + 16 - 6x - 12 + 2 = 4x^2 + 10x + 6$.

34. C: One way to approach the problem is to use the table of values to first write equations for $f(x)$ and $g(x)$: $f(x) = 2x^2$ and $g(x) = 2x + 5$. Then, use those equations to find $f(g(-4))$.

$$g(-4) = 2(-4) + 5 = -3$$

$$f(-3) = 2(-3)^2 = 18$$

So, $f(g(-4)) = 18$.

35. D: By definition, when $f(x)$ and $g(x)$ are inverse functions, $f(g(x)) = g(f(x)) = x$. So, $f(g(4)) = 4$.

36. B: To find the inverse of an equation, solve for x in terms of y; then, exchange the variables x and y. Or, to determine if two functions $f(x)$ and $g(x)$ are inverses, find $f(g(x))$ and $g(f(x))$; if both results are x, then $f(x)$ and $g(x)$ are inverse functions.

For example, to find the inverse of $y = x + 6$, rewrite the equation $x = y + 6$ and solve for y. Since $y = x - 6$, the two given equations given in Choice A are inverses. Likewise, to find the inverse of $y = \frac{2x+3}{x-1}$, rewrite the equation as $x = \frac{2y+3}{y-1}$ and solve for y:

$$xy - x = 2y + 3$$

$$xy - 2y = x + 3$$

$$y(x-2) = x+3$$

$$y = \frac{x+3}{x-2}$$

The two equations given in Choice C are inverses.

Here, the second method is used to determine if the two equations given in Choices B and D are inverses:

Choice B: $y = 2(2x+3) - 3 = 4x + 6$. The two given equations are **NOT** inverses. Choice D: $y = \frac{(2x+1)-1}{2} = \frac{2x}{2} = x$ and $y = 2\left(\frac{x-1}{2}\right) + 1 = x - 1 + 1 = x$, so the two given equations are inverses.

37. A: Below is the graph of $g(x)$.

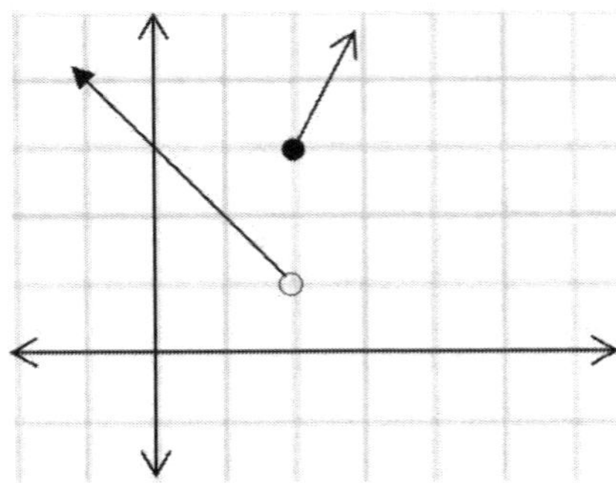

Statement II is true: the graph is indeed discontinuous at $x = 2$. Since $g(3) = 2(3) - 1 = 5$, Statement I is false, and since the range is $y > 1$, Statement III is also false.

38. A: In the range $(-\infty, -1)$, the graph represented is $y = x^2$. In the range $[-1,2)$, the graph is the greatest integer function, $y = [\![x]\!]$. In the range $[-2, \infty)$, the graph is $y = -2x + 6$.

39. B: If $y = a(x+b)(x+c)^2$, the degree of the polynomial is 3. Since the degree of the polynomial is odd and the leading coefficient is positive $(a > 0)$, the end behavior of the graph is below.

↙ ↗

Therefore, neither Choice A nor Choice C can be a graph of $y = a(x+b)(x+c)^2$. The maximum number of "bumps" (or critical points) in the graph is at most one less than the degree of the polynomial, so Choice D, which has three bumps, cannot be the graph of the function. Choice B displays the correct end behavior and has two bumps, so it is a possible graph of $y = a(x+b)(x+c)^2$.

40. B: $5n + 3s \geq 300$ when $n =$ number of non-student tickets which must be sold and $s =$ number of student tickets which must be sold. The intercepts of this linear inequality are $n = 60$ and $s = 100$. The solid line through the two intercepts represents the minimum number of each type of ticket which must be sold in order to offset production costs. All points above the line represent sales which result in a profit for the school.

41. D: The vertex form of a quadratic equation is $y = a(x-h)^2 + k$, where $x = h$ is the parabola's axis of symmetry and (h, k) is the parabola's vertex. The vertex of the graph is (-1,3), so the equation can be written as $y = a(x+1)^2 + 3$. The parabola passes through point (1,1), so $1 = a(1+1)^2 + 3$. Solve for a:

$$1 = a(1+1)^2 + 3$$

$$1 = a(2)^2 + 3$$

$$1 = 4a + 3$$

$$-2 = 4a$$

$$-\frac{1}{2} = a$$

So, the vertex form of the parabola is $y = -\frac{1}{2}(x+1)^2 + 3$. Write the equation in the form $y = ax^2 + bx + c$.

$$y = -\frac{1}{2}(x+1)^2 + 3$$

$$y = -\frac{1}{2}(x^2 + 2x + 1) + 3$$

$$y = -\frac{1}{2}x^2 - x - \frac{1}{2} + 3$$

$$y = -\frac{1}{2}x^2 - x + \frac{5}{2}$$

42. D: There are many ways to solve quadratic equations in the form $ax^2 + bx + c = 0$; however, some methods, such as graphing and factoring, may not be useful for some equations, such as those with irrational or complex roots. Solve this equation by completing the square or by using the Quadratic Formula, $x = \frac{-b \pm \sqrt{b^2 - 4ac}}{2a}$.

$$7x^2 + 6x + 2 = 0; a = 7, b = 6, c = 2$$

$$x = \frac{-b \pm \sqrt{b^2 - 4ac}}{2a}$$

$$x = \frac{-6 \pm \sqrt{6^2 - 4(7)(2)}}{2(7)}$$

$$x = \frac{-6 \pm \sqrt{36 - 56}}{14}$$

$$x = \frac{-6 \pm \sqrt{-20}}{14}$$

$$x = \frac{-6 \pm 2i\sqrt{5}}{14}$$

$$x = \frac{-3 \pm i\sqrt{5}}{7}$$

43. C: A system of linear equations can be solved by using matrices or by using the graphing, substitution, or elimination (also called linear combination) method. The elimination method is shown here:

$$3x + 4y = 2$$

$$2x + 6y = -2$$

In order to eliminate x by linear combination, multiply the top equation by 2 and the bottom equation by –3 so that the coefficients of the x-terms will be additive inverses.

$$2(3x + 4y = 2)$$

$$-3(2x + 6y = -2)$$

Then, add the two equations and solve for y.

$$6x + 8y = 4$$

$$\underline{-6x - 18y = 6}$$

$$-10y = 10$$

$$y = -1$$

Substitute -1 for y in either of the given equations and solve for x.

$$3x + 4(-1) = 2$$

$$3x - 4 = 2$$

$$3x = 6$$

$$x = 2$$

The solution to the system of equations is $(2, -1)$.

44. C: The graph below shows that the lines are parallel and that the shaded regions do not overlap. There is no solution to the set of inequalities given in Choice C.

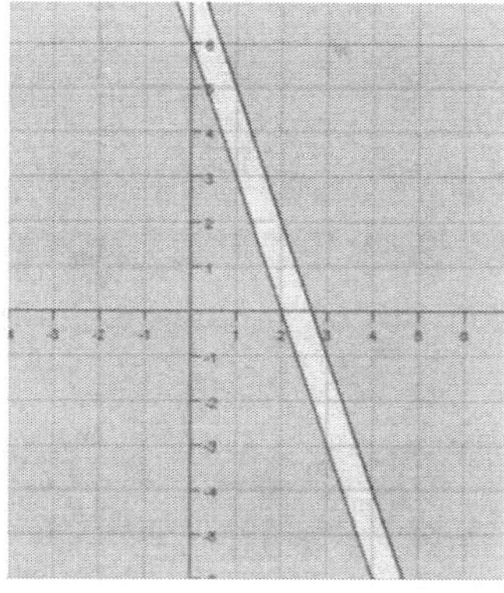

$$6x + 2y \leq 12$$

$$2y \leq -6x + 12$$

$$y \leq -3x + 6$$

$$3x \geq 8 - y$$

$$y \geq -3x + 8$$

As in Choice C, the two lines given in Choice A are parallel; however, the shading overlaps between the lines, so that region represents the solution to the system of inequalities.

The shaded regions for the two lines in Choice B do not overlap except at the boundary, but since the boundary is same, the solution to the system of inequalities is the line $y = -2x + 6$.

Choice D contains a set of inequalities which have intersecting shaded regions; the intersection represents the solution to the system of inequalities.

45. A: First, write three equations from the information given in the problem. Since the total number of tickets sold was 810, $\boldsymbol{x + y + z = 810}$. The ticket sales generated $14,500, so $\boldsymbol{15x + 25y + 20z = 14,500}$. The number of children under ten was the same as twice the number of adults and seniors, so $x = 2(y + z)$, which can be rewritten as $\boldsymbol{x - 2y - 2z = 0}$.

The coefficients of each equation are arranged in the rows of a 3x3 matrix, which, when multiplied by the 3x1 matrix arranging the variables x, y, and z, will give the 3x1 matrix which arranges the constants of the equations.

46. B: There are many ways to solve this system of equations. One is shown below.

Multiply the second equation by 2 and combine it with the first equation to eliminate the variable y.

$$\begin{array}{r} 2x - 4y + z = 10 \\ \underline{-6x + 4y - 8z = -14} \\ -4x \qquad - 7z = -4 \end{array}$$

Multiply the third equation by –2 and combine it with the original second equation to eliminate y.

$$\begin{array}{l} -3x + 2y - 4z = -7 \\ \underline{-2x - 2y + 6z = 2} \\ -5x \qquad + 2z = -5 \end{array}$$

Multiply the equation from step one by 5 and the equation from step two by -4 and combine to eliminate x.

$$\begin{array}{r} -20x - 35z = -20 \\ \underline{20x - 8z = 20} \\ -43z = 0 \\ z = 0 \end{array}$$

4. Substitute 0 for z in the equation from step 2 to find x.

$$\begin{gathered} -5x + 2(0) = -5 \\ -5x = -5 \\ x = 1 \end{gathered}$$

5. Substitute 0 for z and 1 for x into the first original equation to find y.

$$\begin{gathered} 2(1) - 4y + (0) = 10 \\ 2 - 4y = 10 \\ -4y = 8 \\ y = -2 \end{gathered}$$

47. B: One way to solve the equation is to write $x^4 + 64 = 20x^2$ in the quadratic form $(x^2)^2 - 20(x^2) + 64 = 0$. This trinomial can be factored as $(x^2 - 4)(x^2 - 16) = 0$. In each set of parentheses is a difference of squares, which can be factored further: $(x + 2)(x - 2)(x + 4)(x - 4) = 0$. Use the zero product property to find the solutions to the equation.

$$\begin{array}{cccc} x + 2 = 0 & x - 2 = 0 & x + 4 = 0 & x - 4 = 0 \\ x = -2 & x = 2 & x = -4 & x = 4 \end{array}$$

48. A: First, set the equation equal to zero.

$$3x^3y^2 - 45x^2y = 15x^3y - 9x^2y^2$$

$$3x^3y^2 - 15x^3y + 9x^2y^2 - 45x^2y = 0$$

Then, factor the equation.

$$3x^2y(xy - 5x + 3y - 15) = 0$$

$$3x^2y[x(y - 5) + 3(y - 5)] = 0$$

$$3x^2y[(y - 5)(x + 3)] = 0$$

Use the zero product property to find the solutions.

$$3x^2y = 0 \qquad y - 5 = 0 \qquad x + 3 = 0$$

$$x = 0 \qquad y = 5 \qquad x = -3$$

$$y = 0$$

So, the solutions are $x = \{0, -3\}$ and $y = \{0,5\}$.

49. D: The degree of $f(x)$ is 1, the degree of $g(x)$ is 2, and the degree of $h(x)$ is 3. The leading coefficient for each function is 2. Functions $f(x)$ and $h(x)$ have exactly one real zero ($x = 1$), while $g(x)$ has two real zeros ($x = \pm 1$):

$\boldsymbol{f(x)}$	$\boldsymbol{g(x)}$	$\boldsymbol{h(x)}$
$0 = 2x - 2$	$0 = 2x^2 - 2$	$0 = 2x^3 - 2$
$-2x = -2$	$-2x^2 = -2$	$-2x^3 = -2$
$x = 1$	$x^2 = 1$	$x^3 = 1$
	$x = 1;\ x = -1$	$x = 1$

50. B: The path of a bullet is a parabola, which is the graph of a quadratic function. The path of a sound wave can be modeled by a sine or cosine function. The distance an object travels over time given a constant rate is a linear relationship, while radioactive decay is modeled by an exponential function.

51. B: First, use the properties of logarithms to rewrite $2\log_4 y + \log_4 16 = 3$.

Since $N\log_a M = \log_a M^N$, $2\log_4 y = \log_4 y^2$. Replacing $2\log_4 y$ by its equivalent in the given equation gives $\log_4 y^2 + \log_4 16 = 3$.

Since $\log_a M + \log_a N = \log_a MN$, $\log_4 y^2 + \log_4 16 = \log_4 16y^2$. Thus, $\log_4 16y^2 = 3$.

Since $\log_a M = N$ is equivalent to $a^N = M$, $\log_4 16y^2 = 3$ is equivalent to $4^3 = 16y^2$.

Then, solve for y. (Note that y must be greater than zero.)

$$4^3 = 16y^2$$

$$64 = 16y^2$$

$$4 = y^2$$

$$2 = y$$

Finally, substitute 2 for y in the expression $\log_y 256$ and simplify: $\log_2 256 = 8$ since $2^8 = 256$.

52. B: First, apply the laws of exponents to simplify the expression on the left.

$$\frac{(x^2y)(2xy^{-2})^3}{16x^5y^2} + \frac{3}{xy}$$

$$\frac{(x^2y)(8x^3y^{-6})}{16x^5y^2} + \frac{3}{xy}$$

$$\frac{8x^5y^{-5}}{16x^5y^2} + \frac{3}{xy}$$

$$\frac{1}{2y^7} + \frac{3}{xy}$$

Then, add the two fractions.

$$\frac{1}{2y^7} \cdot \frac{x}{x} + \frac{3}{xy} \cdot \frac{2y^6}{2y^6}$$

$$\frac{x}{2xy^7} + \frac{6y^6}{2xy^7}$$

$$\frac{x + 6y^6}{2xy^7}$$

53. C: If $f(x) = 10^x$ and $f(x) = 5$, then $5 = 10^x$. Since $\log_{10}x$ is the inverse of 10^x, $\log_{10}5 = \log_{10}(10^x) = x$. Therefore, $0.7 \approx x$.

54. C: The graph shown is the exponential function $y = 2^x$. Notice that the graph passes through (-2, 0.25), (0,1), (2,4).

	Choice A	Choice B	Choice C	Choice D
x	x^2	$\sqrt{x}$	2^x	$\log_2 x$
-2	4	undefined in $\mathbb{R}$	0.25	undefined
0	0	0	1	undefined
2	4	$\sqrt{2}$	4	1

55. C: The x-intercept is the point at which $f(x) = 0$. When $0 = \log_b x$, $b^0 = x$; since $b^0 = 1$, the x-intercept of $f(x) = \log_b x$ is always 1. If $f(x) = \log_b x$ and $x = b$, then $f(x) = \log_b b$, which is, by definition, 1. ($b^1 = b$.) If $g(x) = b^x$, then $f(x)$ and g(x) are inverse functions and are therefore symmetric with respect to $y = x$. The statement choice C is not necessarily true since $x < 1$ includes numbers less than or equal to zero, the values for which the function is undefined. The statement $f(x) < 0$ is true only for x values between 0 and 1 ($0 < x < 1$).

56. D: Bacterial growth is exponential. Let x be the number of doubling times and a be the number of bacteria in the colony originally transferred into the broth and y be the number of bacteria in the broth after a doubling times.

Time	Number of doubling times (x)	$a(2^x)$	Number of bacteria (y)
0	0	$a(2^0) = a$	1×10^6
20 minutes	1	$a(2^1)$	2×10^6
40 minutes	2	$a(2^2)$	4×10^6
60 minutes	3	$\boldsymbol{a(2^3)}$	$\mathbf{8 \times 10^6}$

Determine how many bacteria were present in the original colony. Either work backwards by halving the number of bacteria (see gray arrows above) or calculate a:

$$a(2^3) = 8 \times 10^6$$

$$8a = 8 \times 10^6$$

$$a = 10^6$$

The equation for determining the number of bacteria is $y = (2^x) \cdot 10^6$. Since the bacteria double every twenty minutes, they go through three doubling times every hour. So, when the bacteria are allowed to grow for eight hours, they will have gone through 24 doubling times. When $x = 24$, $y = (2^{24}) \cdot 10^6 = 16777216 \times 10^6$, which is approximately 1.7×10^{13}.

57. C: Since the pH scale is a base–10 logarithmic scale, a difference in pH of 1 indicates a ratio between strengths of 10. So, an acid with a pH of 3 is 100 times stronger than an acid with a pH of 5.

58. A:

$$\sqrt{\frac{-28x^6}{27y^5}} = \frac{2x^3i\sqrt{7}}{3y^2\sqrt{3y}} \cdot \frac{\sqrt{3y}}{\sqrt{3y}} = \frac{2x^3i\sqrt{21y}}{9y^2}$$

59. C:

$-4 \le 2 + 3(x-1) \le 2$	$-2x^2 + 2 \ge x^2 - 1$	$\frac{11 - \lvert 3x \rvert}{7} \ge 2$	$3\lvert 2x \rvert + 4 \le 10$
$-6 \le 3(x-1) \le 0$	$-3x^2 \ge -3$	$11 - \lvert 3x \rvert \ge 14$	$3\lvert 2x \rvert \le 6$
$-2 \le x - 1 \le 0$	$x^2 \le 1$	$-\lvert 3x \rvert \ge 3$	$\lvert 2x \rvert \le 2$
$-1 \le x \le 1$	$-1 \le x \le 1$	$\lvert 3x \rvert \le -1$	$-2 \le 2x \le 2$
		No solution	$-1 \le x \le 1$

60. D: When solving radical equations, check for extraneous solutions.

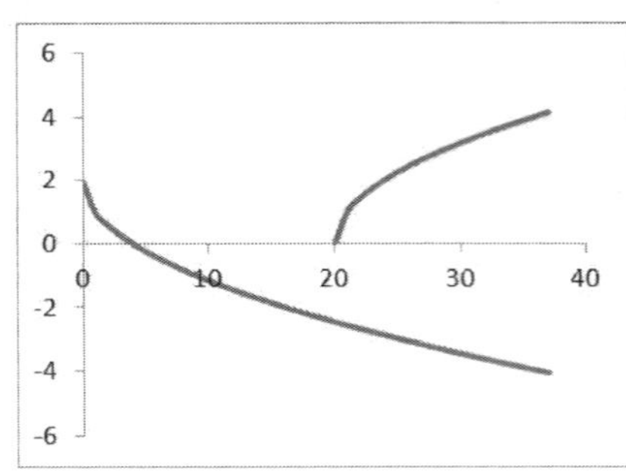

$$2-\sqrt{x}=\sqrt{x-20}$$
$$\left(2-\sqrt{x}\right)^2=\left(\sqrt{x-20}\right)^2$$
$$4-4\sqrt{x}+x=x-20$$
$$-4\sqrt{x}=-24$$
$$\sqrt{x}=6$$
$$\sqrt{x}^2=6^2$$
$$x=36$$
$$2-\sqrt{36}=\sqrt{36-20}$$
$$2-6=\sqrt{16}$$
$$-4\neq 4$$

Since the solution does not check, there is no solution. Notice that the graphs $y=2-\sqrt{x}$ and $y=\sqrt{x-20}$ do not intersect, which confirms there is no solution.

61. B: Notice that choice C cannot be correct since $x\neq 1$. ($x=1$ results in a zero in the denominator.)

$$\frac{x-2}{x-1}=\frac{x-1}{x+1}+\frac{2}{x-1}$$
$$(x-1)(x+1)\left(\frac{x-2}{x-1}\right)=(x-1)(x+1)\left(\frac{x-1}{x+1}+\frac{2}{x-1}\right)$$
$$(x+1)(x-2)=(x-1)^2+2(x+1)$$
$$x^2-x-2=x^2-2x+1+2x+2$$
$$x^2-x-2=x^2+3$$
$$-x=5$$
$$x=-5$$

62. A: The denominator of a fraction cannot equal zero. Therefore, for choices A and B,

$$x^2-x-2\neq 0$$

$$(x+1)(x-2)\neq 0$$

$$x+1\neq 0 \quad x-2\neq 0$$

$$x\neq -1 \quad x\neq 2.$$

Since choice A is in its simplest form, there are vertical asymptotes at $x = -1$ and $x = 2$. However, for choice B,

$$\frac{3x+3}{x^2-x-2} = \frac{3(x+1)}{(x+1)(x-2)} = \frac{3}{x-2}.$$

So, at $x = -2$ there is an asymptote, while at $x = -1$, there is simply a hole in the graph. So, choice B does not match the given graph. For choice C, there are asymptotes at $x = -1$ and $x = 2$; however, notice that it is possible for the graph of choice C to intersect the x-axis since it is possible that $y = 0$ (when $x = 0.5$). Since the given graph does not have an x-intercept, choice C is incorrect. For choice A, it is not possible that y=0, so it is a possible answer. Check a few points on the graph to make sure they satisfy the equation.

x	y
-2	$\frac{3}{4}$
0	$-\frac{3}{2}$
$\frac{1}{2}$	$-\frac{4}{3}$
1	$-\frac{3}{2}$
3	$\frac{3}{4}$

The points $\left(-2, \frac{3}{4}\right), \left(0, -\frac{3}{2}\right), \left(\frac{1}{2}, -\frac{4}{3}\right), \left(1, -\frac{3}{2}\right)$, and $(3, \frac{3}{4})$ are indeed points on the graph.

63. A: An easy way to determine which is the graph of $f(x) = -2|-x+4| - 1$ is to find $f(x)$ for a few values of x. For example, $f(x) = -2|0+4| - 1 = -9$. Graphs A and B pass through (0, –9), but graphs C and D do not. $f(4) = -2|-4+4| - 1 = -1$. Graphs A and D pass through (4, –1), but graphs B and C do not. Graph A is the correct graph. $f(x) = -2|-x+4| - 1$ shifts the graph of $y = |x|$ to the left four units, reflects it across the y-axis, inverts it, makes it narrower, and shifts it down one unit.

64. C: The first function shifts the graph of $y = \frac{1}{x}$ to the right one unit and up one unit. The domain and range of $y = \frac{1}{x}$ are $\{x: x \neq 0\}$ and $\{y: y \neq 0\}$, so the domain and range of $y = \frac{1}{x-1} + 1$ are $\{x: x \neq 1\}$ and $\{y: y \neq 1\}$. The element 1 is not in its domain.

The second function inverts the graph of $y = \sqrt{x}$ and shifts it to the left two units and down one unit. The domain and range of $y = \sqrt{x}$ are $\{x: x \geq 0\}$ and $\{y: y \geq 0\}$, so the domain and range of $y = -\sqrt{x+2} - 1$ are $\{x: x \geq -2\}$ and $\{y: y \leq -1\}$. The range does not contain the element 2.

The third function shifts the graph of $y = |x|$ to the left two units and down three units. The domain of $y = |x|$ the set of all real numbers and range is $\{y: y \geq 0\}$, so the domain of $y = |x+2| - 3$ is the set of all real numbers and the range is $\{y: y \geq -3\}$. The domain contains the element 1 and the range contains the element 2.

This is the graph of the fourth function. The domain of this piece-wise function is the set of all real numbers, and the range is $\{y: y < -1\}$. The range does not contain the element 2.

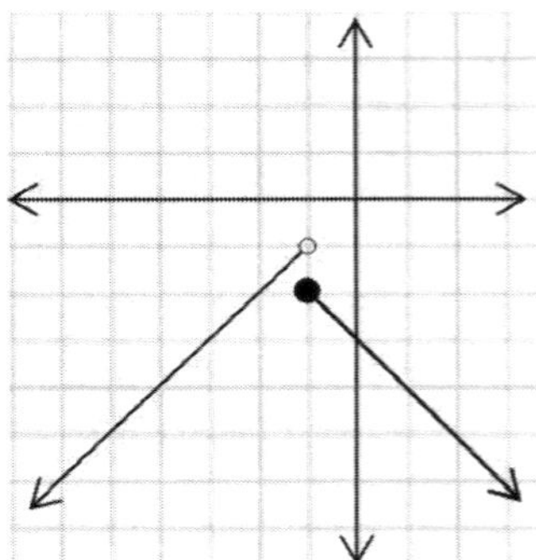

65. B: First, state the exclusions of the domain.

$$x^3 + 2x^2 - x - 2 \neq 0$$

$$(x + 2)(x - 1)(x + 1) \neq 0$$

$$x + 2 \neq 0 \quad x - 1 \neq 0 \quad x + 1 \neq 0$$

$$x \neq -2 \quad x \neq 1 \quad x \neq -1$$

To determine whether there are asymptotes or holes at these values of x, simplify the expression $\frac{x^2-x-6}{x^3+2x^2-x-2}$.

$$\frac{(x - 3)(x + 2)}{(x + 2)(x - 1)(x + 1)} = \frac{x - 3}{(x - 1)(x + 1)}$$

There are asymptotes at $x = 1$ and at $x = -1$ and a hole at $x = 2$. Statement I is false.

To find the x-intercept of $f(x)$, solve $f(x) = 0$. $f(x) = 0$ when the numerator is equal to zero. The numerator equals zero when $x = 2$ and $x = 3$; however, 2 is excluded from the domain of $f(x)$, so the x-intercept is 3. To find the y-intercept of $f(x)$, find $f(0)$. $\frac{0^2-0-6}{0^3+2(0)^2-0-2} = \frac{-6}{-2} = 3$. The y-intercept is 3. Statement II is true.

66. C: The period of the pendulum is a function of the square root of the length of its string, and is independent of the mass of the pendulum or the angle from which it is released. If the period of Pendulum 1's swing is four times the period of Pendulum 2's swing, then the length of Pendulum 1's string must be 16 times the length of Pendulum 2's swing since all other values besides L in the expression $2\pi\sqrt{\frac{L}{g}}$ remain the same.

67. D: There are many ways Josephine may have applied her knowledge to determine how to approximately measure her medicine using her plastic spoon. The only choice which correctly uses dimensional analysis is choice D: the dosage ≈ 25 cc $\cdot \frac{1 \text{ ml}}{1 \text{ cc}} \cdot \frac{1\text{L}}{1000\text{ml}} \cdot \frac{0.5 \text{ gal}}{2\text{L}} \cdot \frac{16\text{c}}{1 \text{ gal}} \cdot \frac{48\text{t}}{1\text{c}} \cdot \frac{1 \text{ spoonful}}{1\text{t}}$ $\rightarrow \frac{25}{1000} \cdot \frac{1}{4} \cdot 16 \cdot 48 \approx 5$.

68. C: If 1" represents 60 feet, 10" represents 600 ft, which is the same as 200 yards.

69. D: If the distance between the two houses is 10 cm on the map, then the actual distance between the houses is 100 m.

To find x, use the Pythagorean Theorem:

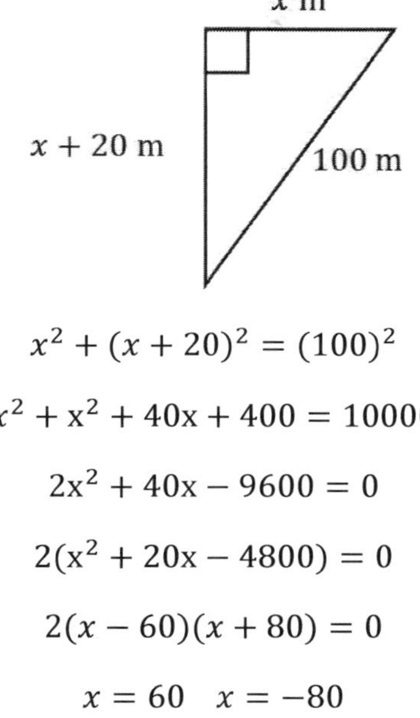

$$x^2 + (x + 20)^2 = (100)^2$$

$$x^2 + x^2 + 40x + 400 = 10000$$

$$2x^2 + 40x - 9600 = 0$$

$$2(x^2 + 20x - 4800) = 0$$

$$2(x - 60)(x + 80) = 0$$

$$x = 60 \quad x = -80$$

Since x represents a distance, it cannot equal −80. Since $x = 60$, $x + 20 = 80$. Roxana walks a total of 140 m to get to her friend's house.

70. D: ΔABC is similar to the smaller triangle with which it shares vertex A. $AB = (2x - 1) + (x + 7) = 3x + 6$. $AC = 4 + 8 = 12$. Set up a proportion and solve for x:

$$\frac{3x + 6}{12} = \frac{2x - 1}{4}$$

$$12x + 24 = 24x - 12$$

$$36 = 12x$$

$$3 = x$$

So, $AB = 3x + 6 = 3(3) + 6 = 15$.

71. B: Percent error $= \frac{|\text{actual value} - \text{measured value}|}{\text{actual value}} \times 100\%$, and the average percent error is the sum of the percent errors for each trial divided by the number of trials.

	% error Trial 1	**% error Trial 2**	**% error Trial 3**	**% error Trial 4**	**Average percent error**
Scale 1	0.1%	0.2%	0.2%	0.1%	0.15%
Scale 2	2.06%	2.09%	2.10%	2.08%	2.08%

The percent error for Scale 1 is less than the percent error for Scale 2, so it is more accurate. The more precise scale is Scale 2 because its range of values, $10.210 \text{ g} - 10.206 \text{ g} = 0.004 \text{ g}$, is smaller than the Scale 2's range of values, $10.02 \text{ g} - 9.98 \text{ g} = 0.04 \text{ g}$.

72. C: If l and w represent the length and width of the enclosed area, its perimeter is equal to $2l + 2w$; since the fence is positioned x feet from the lot's edges on each side, the perimeter of the lot is $2(l + 2x) + 2(w + 2x)$. Since the amount of money saved by fencing the smaller are is \$432, and since the fencing material costs \$12 per linear foot, 36 fewer feet of material are used to fence around the playground than would have been used to fence around the lot. This can be expressed as the equation $2(l + 2x) + 2(w + 2x) - (2l + 2w) = 36$.

$$2(l + 2x) + 2(w + 2x) - (2l + 2w) = 36$$

$$2l + 4x + 2w + 4x - 2l - 2w = 36$$

$$8x = 36$$

$$x = 4.5 \text{ ft}$$

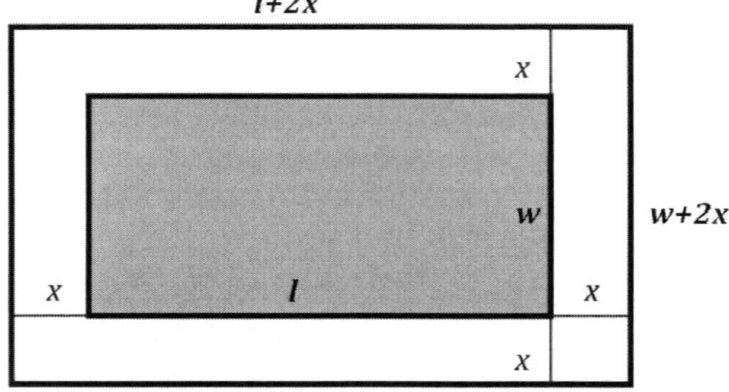

The difference in the area of the lot and the enclosed space is 141 yd^2, which is the same as 1269 ft^2. So, $(l + 2x)(w + 2x) - lw = 1269$. Substituting 4.5 for x,

$$\begin{aligned} (l + 9)(w + 9) - lw &= 1269 \\ lw + 9l + 9w + 81 - lw &= 1269 \\ 9l + 9w &= 1188 \\ 9(l + w) &= 1188 \\ l + w &= 132 \text{ ft} \end{aligned}$$

Therefore, the perimeter of the enclosed space, $2(l + w)$, is $2(132) = 264$ ft. The cost of 264 ft of fencing is $264 \cdot \$12 = \$3{,}168$.

73. B: The volume of Natasha's tent is $\frac{x^2h}{3}$. If she were to increase by 1 ft the length of each side of the square base, the tent's volume would be $\frac{(x+1)^2h}{3} = \frac{(x^2+2x+1)(h)}{3} = \frac{x^2h+2xh+h}{3} = \frac{x^2h}{3} + \frac{2xh+h}{3}$. Notice this is the volume of Natasha's tent, $\frac{x^2h}{3}$, increased by $\frac{2xh+h}{3}$, or $\frac{h(2x+1)}{3}$.

74. A: The area of a circle is πr^2, so the area of a semicircle is $\frac{\pi r^2}{2}$. Illustrated below is a method which can be used to find the area of the shaded region.

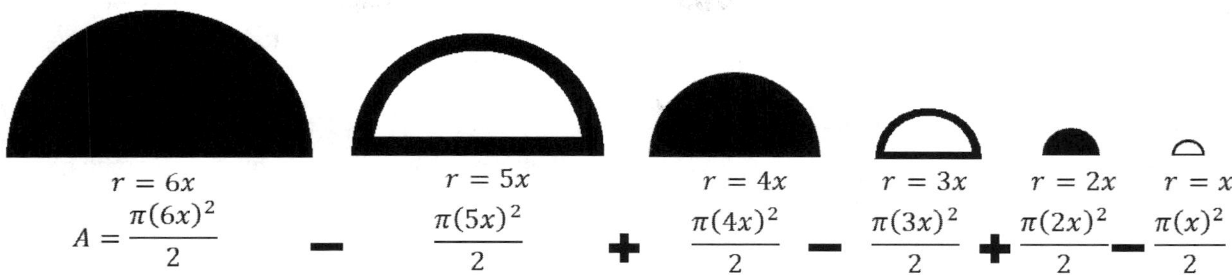

The area of the shaded region is $\frac{\pi(36x^2-25x^2+16x^2-9x^2+4x^3-x^2)}{2} = \frac{(21x^2)\pi}{2}$.

75. B. Euclidean geometry is based on the flat plane. One of Euclid's five axioms, from which all Euclidean geometric theorems are derived, is the parallel postulate, which states that in a plane, for any line l and point A not on l, exactly one line which passes through A does not intersect l.

Non-Euclidean geometry considers lines on surfaces which are not flat. For instance, on the Earth's surface, if point A represents the North Pole and line l represents the equator (which does not pass through A), all lines of longitude pass through point A and intersect line l. In elliptical geometry, there are infinitely many lines which pass though A and intersect l, and there is no line which passes through A which does not also intersect l. In hyperbolic geometry when A is not on l, many lines which pass through A diverge from l, or put more succinctly, at least two lines that go through A do not intersect l.

76. B: When four congruent isosceles trapezoids are arranged in an arch, the bases of the trapezoid come together to form regular octagons, the smaller of which is shown to the right. The measure of each angle of a regular octagon is 135° $\left(\frac{(8-2)(180°)}{8} = 135°\right)$. From the relationship of two of the trapezoid's base angles with one of the octagon's interior angles, write and solve an equation:

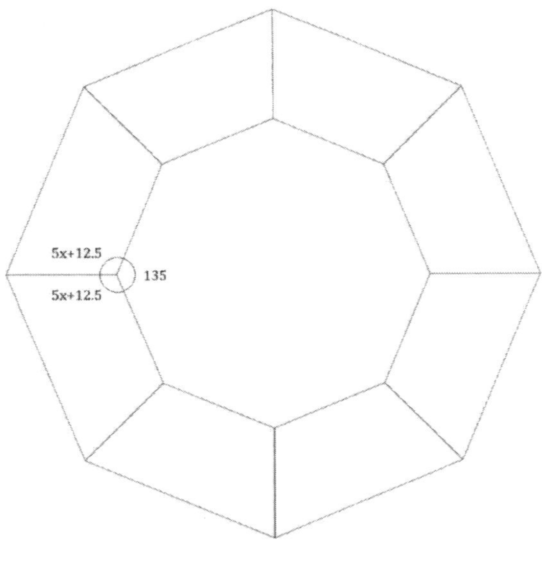

$$(5x + 12.5) + (5x + 12.5) + 135 = 360$$
$$10x + 160 = 360$$
$$10x = 200$$
$$x = 20$$

77. C: Sketch a diagram (this one is not to scale) and label the known segments. Use the property that two segments are congruent when they originate from the same point outside of a circle and are tangent to the circle.

The point of tangency of $\overline{CB}$ divides the segment into two pieces measuring 4 and 6; the point of tangency of $\overline{BA}$ divides the segment into two pieces measuring 6 and 8; the point of tangency of $\overline{AD}$ divides the segment into two pieces measuring 8 and 4. Therefore $AD = 8 + 4 = 12$.

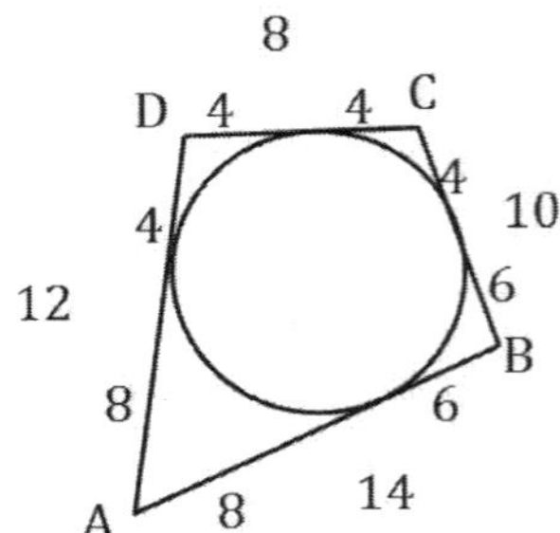

78. D: Let b represent the base of the triangle. The height h of the triangle is the altitude drawn from the vertex opposite of b to side b.

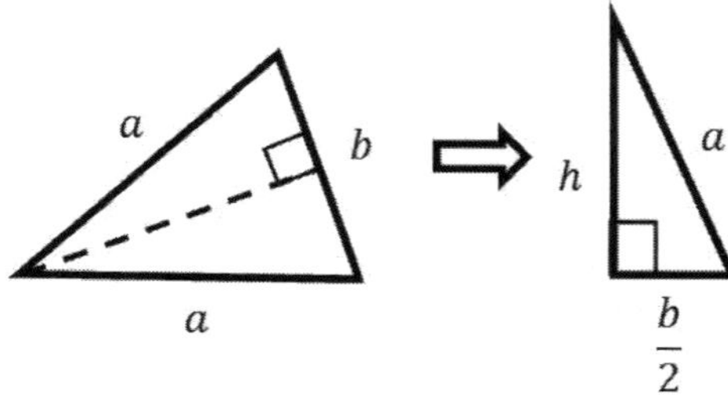

The height of the triangle can be found in terms of a and b by using the Pythagorean theorem:

$$h^2 + \left(\frac{b}{2}\right)^2 = a^2$$

$$h = \sqrt{a^2 - \frac{b^2}{4}} = \sqrt{\frac{4a^2 - b^2}{4}} = \frac{\sqrt{4a^2 - b^2}}{2}$$

The area of a triangle is $A = \frac{1}{2}bh, so\ A = \frac{1}{2}b\left(\frac{\sqrt{4a^2-b^2}}{2}\right) = \frac{b\sqrt{4a^2-b^2}}{4}$.

79. B: Since $\angle ADC$ is a right triangle with legs measuring 5 and 12, its hypotenuse measures 13. (5-12-13 is a Pythagorean triple.)

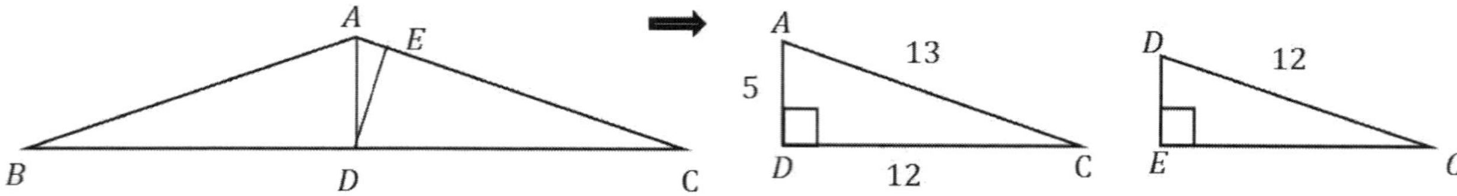

$\angle ADC$ and $\angle DEC$ are both right triangles which share vertex C. By the AA similarity theorem $\angle ADC \sim \angle DEC$. Therefore, a proportion can be written and solved to find DE.

$$\frac{5}{DE} = \frac{13}{12}$$

$$DE = 4.6$$

80. C: The center of the sphere is shared by the center of the cube, and each of the corners of the cube touches the surface of the sphere. Therefore, the diameter of the sphere is the line which passes through the center of the cube and connects one corner of the cube to the opposite corner on the opposite face. Notice in the illustration below that the diameter d of the sphere can be represented as the hypotenuse of a right triangle with a short leg measuring 4 units. (Since the volume of the cube is 64 cubic units, each of its sides measures $\sqrt[3]{64}$ =4 units.) The long leg of the triangle is the diagonal of the base of the cube. Its length can be found using the Pythagorean theorem: $4^2 + 4^2 = x^2; x = \sqrt{32} = 4\sqrt{2}$.

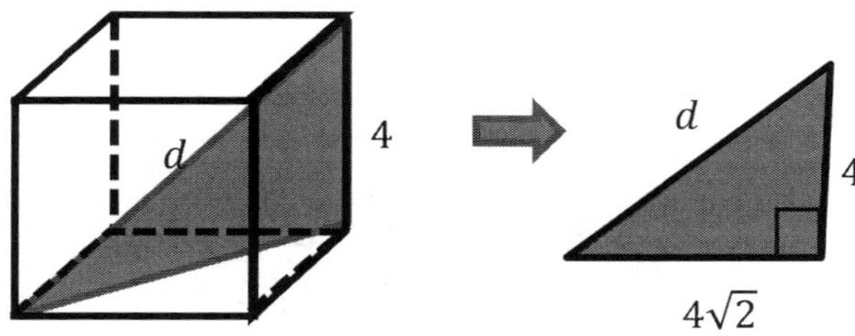

Use the Pythagorean theorem again to find d, the diameter of the sphere: $d^2 = \left(4\sqrt{2}\right)^2 + 4^2; d = \sqrt{48} = 4\sqrt{3}$. To find the volume of the sphere, use the formula $V = \frac{4}{3}\pi r^3$. Since the radius r of the sphere is half the diameter, $r = 2\sqrt{3}$, and $V = \frac{4}{3}\pi(2\sqrt{3})^3 = \frac{4}{3}\pi\left(24\sqrt{3}\right) = 32\pi\sqrt{3}$ cubic units.

81. D. Since it is given that $\overline{FD} \cong \overline{BC}$ and $\overline{AB} \cong \overline{DE}$, step 2 needs to establish either that $\overline{AC} \cong \overline{EF}$ or that $\Delta ABC \cong \Delta FDE$ in order for step 5 to show that $\Delta ABC \cong \Delta EDF$. The statement $\overline{AC} \cong \overline{EF}$ cannot be shown directly from the given information. On the other hand, $\Delta ABC \cong \Delta FDE$ can be determined: when two parallel lines ($\overline{BC} \| \overline{FG}$) are cut by a transversal ($\overline{AE}$), alternate exterior angles ($\Delta ABC, \Delta FDE$) are congruent. Therefore, $\Delta ABC \cong \Delta EDF$ by the side-angle-side (SAS) theorem.

82. A: Step 5 established that $\Delta ABC \cong \Delta EDF$. Because corresponding parts of congruent triangles are congruent (CPCTC), $\angle BAC \cong \angle DEF$. This is useful to establish when trying to prove $\overline{FE} \| \overline{AG}$: when two lines ($\overline{FE}$ and $\overline{AG}$) are cut by a transversal ($\overline{AE}$) and alternate interior angles ($\angle BAC, \angle DEF$) are congruent, then the lines are parallel. The completed proof is shown immediately following.

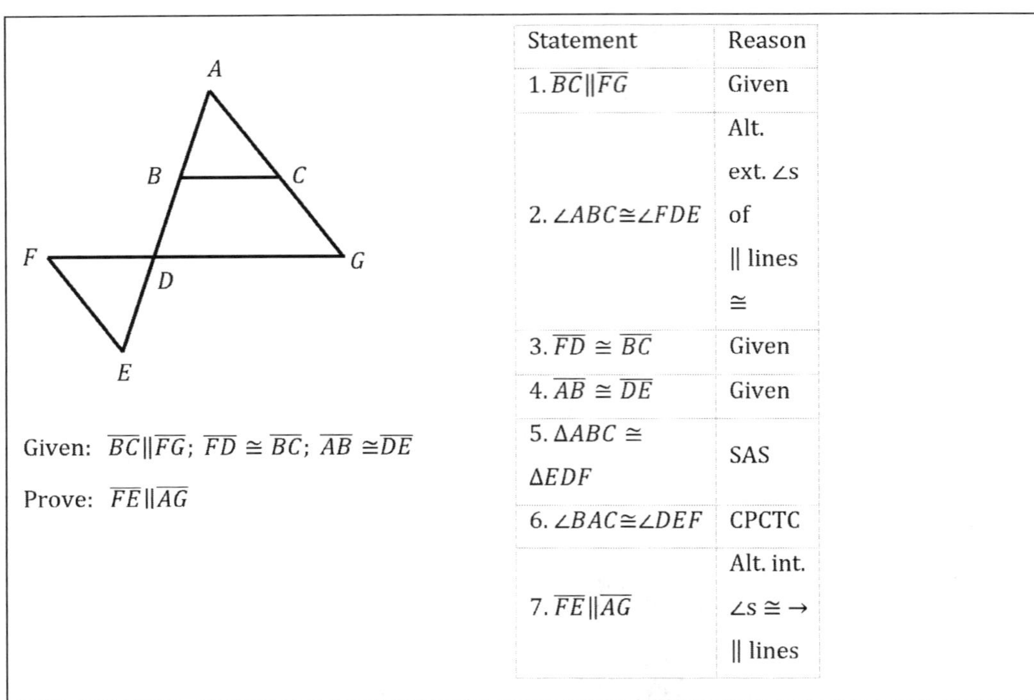

Given: $\overline{BC} \| \overline{FG}$; $\overline{FD} \cong \overline{BC}$; $\overline{AB} \cong \overline{DE}$

Prove: $\overline{FE} \| \overline{AG}$

Statement	Reason
1. $\overline{BC} \| \overline{FG}$	Given
2. $\angle ABC \cong \angle FDE$	Alt. ext. ∠s of ‖ lines ≅
3. $\overline{FD} \cong \overline{BC}$	Given
4. $\overline{AB} \cong \overline{DE}$	Given
5. $\Delta ABC \cong \Delta EDF$	SAS
6. $\angle BAC \cong \angle DEF$	CPCTC
7. $\overline{FE} \| \overline{AG}$	Alt. int. ∠s ≅ → ‖ lines

83. B: A cube has six square faces. The arrangement of these faces in a two-dimensional figure is a net of a cube if the figure can be folded to form a cube. Figures A, C, and D represent three of the eleven possible nets of a cube. If choice B is folded, however, the bottom square in the second column will overlap the fourth square in the top row, so the figure does not represent a net of a cube.

84. D: The cross-section is a hexagon.

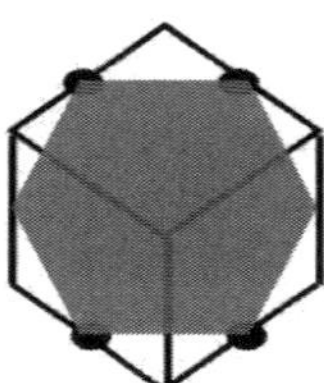

85. A: Use the formula for the volume of a sphere to find the radius of the sphere:

$$V = \frac{4}{3}\pi r^3$$
$$36\pi = \frac{4}{3}\pi r^3$$
$$36 = \frac{4}{3}r^3$$
$$36 = \frac{4}{3}r^3$$
$$27 = r^3$$
$$3 = r$$

Then, substitute the point $(h, k, l) = (1, 0, -2)$ and the radius $r = 3$ into the equation of a sphere:

$$(x-h)^2 + (y-k)^2 + (z-l)^2 = r^2$$
$$(x-1)^2 + y^2 + (z+2)^2 = 3^2$$
$$(x-1)^2 + y^2 + (z+2)^2 = 9$$
$$x^2 - 2x + 1 + y^2 + z^2 + 4z + 4 = 9$$
$$x^2 + y^2 + z^2 - 2x + 4z = 4$$

86. B: The triangle is a right triangle with legs 3 and 4 units long.

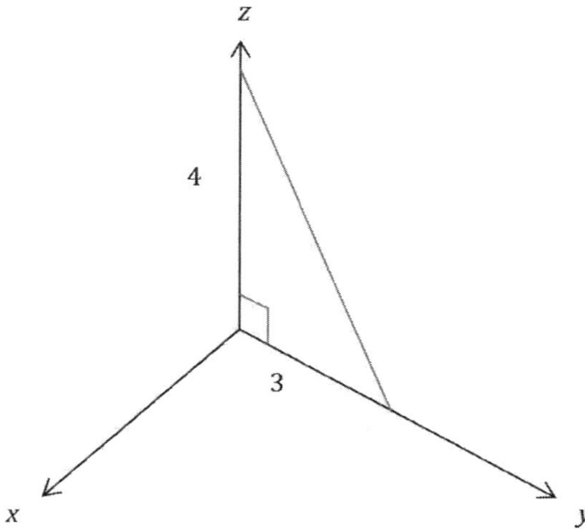

If the triangle is rotated about the z-axis, the solid formed is a cone with a height of 4 and a radius of 3; this cone has volume $V = \frac{1}{3}\pi r^2 h = \frac{1}{3}\pi 3^2 4 = 12\pi$ cubic units. If the triangle is rotated about the y-axis, the solid formed is a cone with a height of 3 and a radius of 4. This cone has volume $V = \frac{1}{3}\pi r^2 h = \frac{1}{3}\pi 4^2 3 = 16\pi$ cubic units. The difference in the volumes of the two cones is $16\pi - 12\pi = 4\pi$ cubic units.

87. D: The point $(5, -5)$ lies on the line which has a slope of -2 and which passes through $(3, -1)$. If $(5, -5)$ is one of the endpoints of the line, the other would be (1,3).

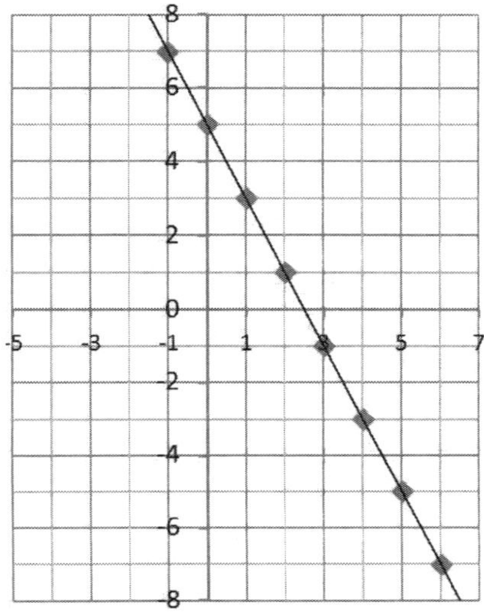

88. D: Since all of the answer choices are parallelograms, determine whether the parallelogram is also a rhombus or a rectangle or both. One way to do this is by examining the parallelogram's diagonals. If the parallelogram's diagonals are perpendicular, then the parallelogram is a rhombus. If the parallelogram's diagonals are congruent, then the parallelogram is a rectangle. If a parallelogram is both a rhombus and a rectangle, then it is a square.

To determine whether the diagonals are perpendicular, find the slopes of the diagonals of the quadrilateral:

Diagonal 1: $\frac{6-2}{-5-3} = \frac{4}{-8} = -\frac{1}{2}$

Diagonal 2: $\frac{0-8}{-3-1} = -\frac{8}{-4} = 2$

The diagonals have opposite inverse slopes and are therefore perpendicular. Thus, the parallelogram is a rhombus.

To determine whether the diagonals are congruent, find the lengths of the diagonals of the quadrilateral:

Diagonal 1: $\sqrt{(6-2)^2 + (-5-3)^2} = \sqrt{(4)^2 + (-8)^2} = \sqrt{16+64} = \sqrt{80} = 4\sqrt{5}$

Diagonal 2: $\sqrt{(0-8)^2 + (-3-1)\text{^}2} = \sqrt{(-8)^2 + (-4)\text{^}2} = \sqrt{64+16} = \sqrt{80} = 4\sqrt{5}$

The diagonals are congruent, so the parallelogram is a rectangle.

Since the polygon is a rhombus and a rectangle, it is also a square.

89. A: The equation of the circle is given in general form. When the equation is written in the standard form $(x-h)^2 + (y-k)^2 = r^2$, where (h, k) is the center of the circle and r is the radius of the circle, the radius is easy to determine. Putting the equation into standard form requires completing the square for x and y:

$$x^2 - 10x + y^2 + 8y = -29$$

$$(x^2 - 10x + 25) + (y^2 + 8y + 16) = -29 + 25 + 16$$

$$(x-5)^2 + (y+4)^2 = 12$$

Since $r^2 = 12,$ and since r must be a positive number, $r = \sqrt{12} = 2\sqrt{3}.$

90. D: One way to determine whether the equation represents an ellipse, a circle, a parabola, or a hyperbola is to find the determinant $b^2 - 4ac$ of the general equation form of a conic section, $ax^2 + bxy + cy^2 + dx + ey + f = 0$, where $a, b, c, d, e,$ and f are constants. Given that the conic section is non-degenerate, if the determinant is positive, then the equation is a hyperbola; if the determinant is negative, then the equation is a circle (when $a = c$ and $b = 0$) or an ellipse; and if the determinant is zero, then the equation is a parabola. For $2x^2 - 3y^2 - 12x + 6y - 15 = 0$, $a = 2$, $b = 0$, $c = -3$, $d = -12$, $e = 6$, and $f = -15$. The determinant $b^2 - 4ac$ is equal to $0^2 - 4(2)(-3) = 24$. Since the determinant is positive, the graph is hyperbolic.

Another way to determine the shape of the graph is to look at the coefficients for the x^2 and y^2 terms in the given equation. If one of the coefficients is zero (in other words, if there is either an x^2 or a y^2 term in the equation but not both), then the equation is a parabola; if the coefficients have the same sign, then the graph is an ellipse or circle; and if the coefficients have opposite signs, then the graph is a hyperbola. Since the coefficient of x^2 is 2 and the coefficient of y^2 is -3, the graph is a hyperbola. That the equation can be written in the standard form for a hyperbola, $\frac{(x-h)^2}{a^2} - \frac{(y-k)^2}{b^2} = 1$, confirms the conclusion.

$$2x^2 - 3y^2 - 12x + 6y - 15 = 0$$

$$2x^2 - 12x - 3y^2 + 6y = 15$$

$$2(x^2 - 6x) - 3(y^2 - 2y) = 15$$

$$2(x^2 - 6x + 9) - 3(y^2 - 2y + 1) = 15 + 2(9) - 3(1)$$

$$2(x - 3)^2 - 3(y - 1)^2 = 30$$

$$\frac{(x - 3)^2}{15} - \frac{(y - 1)^2}{10} = 1$$

91. B: The graph of $f(x)$ is a parabola with a focus of (a, b) and a directrix of $y = -b$. The axis of symmetry of a parabola passes through the focus and vertex and is perpendicular to the directrix. Since the directrix is a horizontal line, the axis of symmetry is $x = a$; therefore, the x-coordinate of the parabola's vertex must be a. The distance between a point on the parabola and the directrix is equal to the distance between that point and the focus, so the y-coordinate of the vertex must be $y = \frac{-b+b}{2} = 0$. So, the vertex of the parabola given by $f(x)$ is $(a, 0)$.

If $g(x)$ were a translation of $f(x)$, as is the case for choices A, C, and D, the vertices of $f(x)$ and $g(x)$ would differ. Since the vertex of the graph of $g(x)$ is $(a, 0)$, none of those choices represent the correct response. However, if $g(x) = -f(x)$, the vertices of the graphs of both functions would be the same; therefore, this represents a possible relation between the two functions.

92. C: When a figure is reflected twice over non-parallel lines, the resulting transformation is a rotation about the point of intersection of the two lines of reflection. The two lines of reflection $y = x + 2$ and $x = 0$ intersect at (0,2). So, $\Delta A''B''C''$ represents a rotation of ΔABC about the point (0,2). The angle of rotation is equal to twice the angle between the two lines of reflection when measured in a clockwise direction from the first to the second line of reflection. Since the angle between the lines or reflection measures 135°, the angle of rotation which is the composition of the

two reflections measures 270°. All of these properties can be visualized by drawing ΔABC, $\Delta A'B'C'$, and $\Delta A''B''C''$.

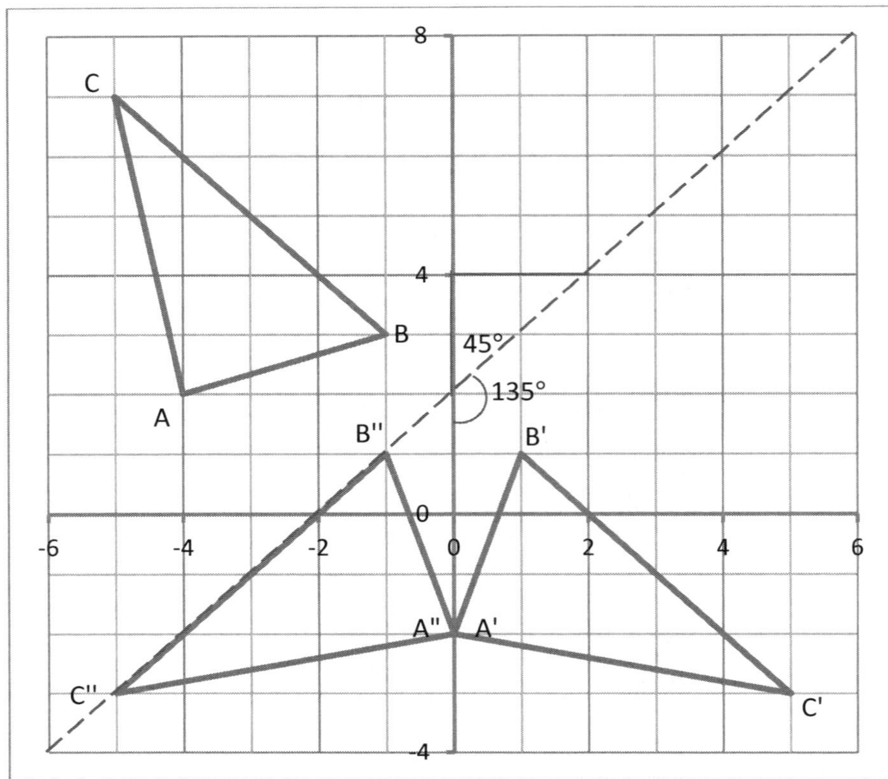

93. B: All regular polygons have rotational symmetry. The angle of rotation is the smallest angle by which the polygon can be rotated such that it maps onto itself; any multiple of this angle will also map the polygon onto itself. The angle of rotation for a regular polygon is the angle formed between two lines drawn from consecutives vertices to the center of the polygon. Since the vertices of a regular polygon lie on a circle, for a regular polygon with n sides, the angle of rotation measures $\frac{360°}{n}$.

Number of sides of regular polygon	**Angle of rotation**	**Angles ≤ 360° which map the polygon onto itself**
4	$\frac{360}{4} = 90°$	$90°, 180°, 270°, 360°$
6	$\frac{360}{6} = 60°$	$60°, 120°, 180°, 240°, 300°, 360°$
8	$\frac{360}{8} = 45°$	$45°, 90°, 135°, 180°, 225°, 270°, 315°, 316°$
10	$\frac{360}{10} = 36°$	$36°, 72°, 108°, 144°, 180°, 216°, 252°, 288°, 324°, 360°$

94. A: Since the y-coordinates of points P and Q are the same, line segment $\overline{PQ}$ is a horizontal line segment whose length is the difference in the x-coordinates a and c. Because the length of a line cannot be negative, and because it is unknown whether $a > c$ or $a < c$, $PQ = |a - c|$ or $|c - a|$. Since the x-coordinates of Q and Q' are the same, line segment $\overline{P'Q}$ is a vertical line segment whose length is $|d - b|$or $|b - d|$. The quadrilateral formed by the transformation of $\overline{PQ}$ to $\overline{P'Q'}$ is a parallelogram. If the base of the parallelogram is $\overline{PQ}$, then the height is $\overline{P'Q}$ since $\overline{PQ} \perp \overline{P'Q}$. For a parallelogram, $A = bh$, so $A = |a - c| \cdot |b - d|$.

95. B: Since $\tan B = \frac{opposite}{adjacent} = \frac{b}{a}$, choice A is incorrect.

$\cos B = \frac{adjacent}{hypotenuse}$. The hypotenuse of a right triangle is equal to the square root of the sum of the squares of the legs, so $\cos B = \frac{adjacent}{hypotenuse} = \frac{a}{\sqrt{a^2+b^2}}$. Rationalize the denominator: $\frac{a}{\sqrt{a^2+b^2}} \cdot \frac{\sqrt{a^2+b^2}}{\sqrt{a^2+b^2}} = \frac{a\sqrt{a^2+b^2}}{a^2+b^2}$. Choice B is correct.

$\sec B = \frac{hypotenuse}{adjacent} = \frac{\sqrt{a^2+b^2}}{a}$, and $\csc B = \frac{\sqrt{a^2+b^2}}{b}$, so choices C and D are incorrect.

96. C: Find the missing angle measures in the diagram by using angle and triangle properties. Then, use the law of sines to find the distance y between the window and the wife's car: $\frac{60}{\sin 15°} = \frac{y}{\sin 45°}$, so $y = \frac{60 \sin 45°}{\sin 15} \approx 163.9$ ft. Use this number in a sine or cosine function to find x: $\sin 30° \approx \frac{x}{163.9}$, so $x \approx 163.9 \sin 30° \approx 82$. Therefore, the man's wife is parked approximately 82 feet from the building.

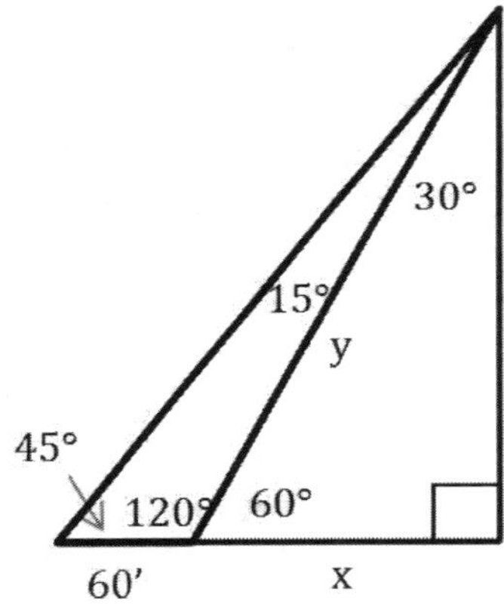

Alternatively, notice that when the man is looking down at a 45-degree angle, the triangle that is formed is an isosceles triangle, meaning that the height of his office is the same as the distance from the office to his car, or x + 60 feet. With this knowledge, the problem can be modeled with a single equation:

$$\frac{x+60}{x} = \tan 60° \quad or \quad x = \frac{60}{\tan 60° - 1}$$

97. A: The reference angle for $-\frac{2\pi}{3}$ is $2\pi - \frac{2\pi}{3} = \frac{4\pi}{3}$, so $\tan(-\frac{2\pi}{3}) = \tan\left(\frac{4\pi}{3}\right) = \frac{sin\left(\frac{4\pi}{3}\right)}{\cos\left(\frac{4\pi}{3}\right)}$. From the unit circle, the values of $\sin\left(\frac{4\pi}{3}\right)$ and $\cos\left(\frac{4\pi}{3}\right)$ are $-\frac{\sqrt{3}}{2}$ and $-\frac{1}{2}$, respectively. Therefore, $\tan(-\frac{2\pi}{3}) = \frac{-\frac{\sqrt{3}}{2}}{-\frac{1}{2}} = \sqrt{3}$.

98. D: On the unit circle, $\sin\theta = \frac{1}{2}$ when $\theta = \frac{\pi}{6}$ and when $\theta = \frac{5\pi}{6}$. Since only $\frac{5\pi}{6}$ is in the given range of $\frac{\pi}{2} < \theta < \pi, \theta = \frac{5\pi}{6}$.

99. C: Use trigonometric equalities and identities to simplify. $\cos\theta\cot\theta = \cos\theta \cdot \frac{\cos\theta}{\sin\theta} = \frac{\cos^2\theta}{\sin\theta} = \frac{1-\sin^2\theta}{\sin\theta} = \frac{1}{\sin\theta} - \sin\theta = \csc\theta - \sin\theta$.

100. B: The trigonometric identity $\sec^2\theta = \tan^2\theta + 1$ can be used to rewrite the equation $\sec^2\theta = 2\tan\theta$ as $\tan^2\theta + 1 = 2\tan\theta$, which can then be rearranged into the form $\tan^2\theta - 2\tan\theta + 1 = 0$. Solve by factoring and using the zero product property:

$$\tan^2\theta - 2\tan\theta + 1 = 0$$

$$(\tan\theta - 1)^2 = 0$$

$$\tan\theta - 1 = 0$$

$$\tan\theta = 1.$$

Since $\tan\theta = 1$ when $\sin\theta = \cos\theta$, for $0 < \theta \leq 2\pi$, $\theta = \frac{\pi}{4}$ or $\frac{5\pi}{4}$.

101. A: Since the graph shows a maximum height of 28 inches above the ground, and since the maximum distance from the road the pebble reaches is when it is at the top of the tire, the diameter of the tire is 28 inches. Therefore, its radius is 14 inches. From the graph, it can be observed that the tire makes 7.5 rotations in 0.5 seconds. Thus, the tire rotates 15 times in 1 second, or $15 \cdot 60 = 900$ times per minute.

102. C: The dashed line represents the sine function (x), and the solid line represents a cosine function $g(x)$. The amplitude of $f(x)$ is 4, and the amplitude of $g(x)$ is 2. The function $y = \sin x$ has a period of 2π, while the graph of function $f(x) = a_1 \sin(b_1 x)$ has a period of 4π; therefore, $b_1 = \frac{2\pi}{4\pi} = 0.5$, which is between 0 and 1. The graph of $g(x) = a_2\cos(b_2 x)$ has a period of π, so $b_2 = \frac{2\pi}{\pi} = 2$.

103. B: The graph of $f(x)$ is stretched vertically by a factor of 4 with respect to $y = \sin x$, so $a_1 = 4$. The graph of $g(x)$ is stretched vertically by a factor of two and is inverted with respect to the graph of $y = \cos x$, so $a_2 = -2$. Therefore, the statement $a_2 < 0 < a_1$ is true.

104. A: The graph to the right shows the height h in inches of the weight on the spring above the table as a function of time t in seconds. Notice that the height is 3 in above the table at time 0 since the weight was pulled down two inches from its starting position 5 inches above the table. The spring fluctuates 2 inches above and below its equilibrium point, so its maximum height is 7 inches above the table. The graph represents a cosine curve which has been inverted, stretched vertically

by a factor of 2, and shifted up five units; also, the graph has been compressed horizontally, with a period of 1 rather than 2π. So, the height of the weight on the spring as a function of time is $h = -2\cos(2\pi t) + 5$.

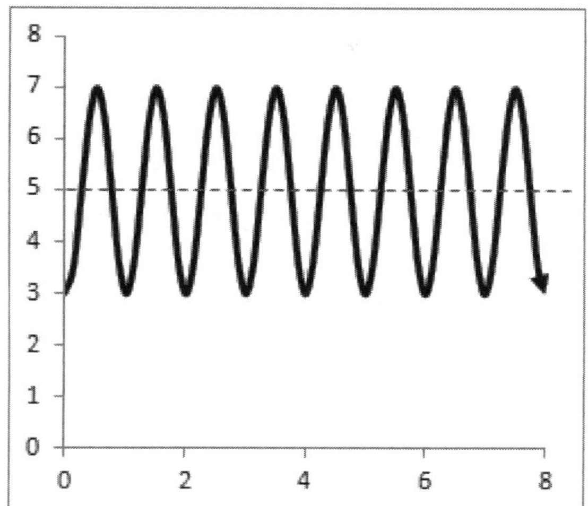

105. C: Since evaluating $\frac{x^3+3x^2-x-3}{x^2-9}$ at $x = -3$ produces a fraction with a zero denominator, simplify the polynomial expression before evaluating the limit:

$$\frac{x^3+3x^2-x-3}{x^2-9} = \frac{x^2(x+3)-1(x+3)}{(x+3)(x-3)} = \frac{(x+3)(x^2-1)}{(x+3)(x-3)} = \frac{(x+1)(x-1)}{x-3}$$

$$\lim_{x\to -3} \frac{(x+1)(x-1)}{x-3} = \frac{(-3+1)(-3-1)}{-3-3} = -\frac{8}{-6} = -\frac{4}{3}.$$

106. B: To evaluate the limit, divide the numerator and denominator by x^2 and use these properties of limits: $\lim_{x\to\infty} \frac{1}{x} = 0$; the limit of a sum of terms is the sum of the limits of the terms; and the limit of a product of terms is the product of the limits of the terms.

$$\lim_{x\to\infty} \frac{x^2+2x-3}{2x^2+1} = \lim_{x\to\infty} \frac{\frac{x^2}{x^2}+\frac{2x}{x^2}-\frac{3}{x^2}}{\frac{2x^2}{x^2}+\frac{1}{x^2}} = \lim_{x\to\infty} \frac{1+\frac{2}{x}-\frac{3}{x^2}}{2+\frac{1}{x^2}} = \frac{1+0-0}{2+0} = \frac{1}{2}.$$

107. B: Evaluating $\frac{|x-3|}{3-x}$ when $x = 3$ produces a fraction with a zero denominator. To find the limit as x approaches 3 from the right, sketch a graph or make a table of values.

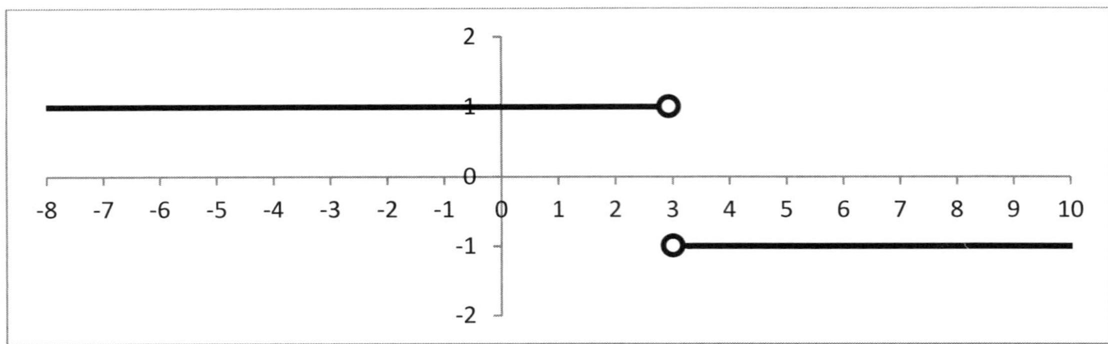

The value of the function approaches –1 as x approaches three from the right, so $\lim_{x\to3^+} \frac{|x-3|}{3-x} = -1$.

108. C: The slope of the line tangent to the graph of a function f at $x = a$ is $f'(a)$. Since $f(x) = \frac{1}{4}x^2 - 3$, $f'(x) = 2\left(\frac{1}{4}\right)x^{(2-1)} - 0 = \frac{1}{2}x$. So, the slope at x = 2 is $f'(2) = \frac{1}{2}(2) = 1$.

109. D: The definition of the derivative of f at 2, or $f'(2)$, is the limit of the difference quotient $\lim_{h\to0} \frac{f(2+h)-f(2)}{h}$. Rather than find the limit, simply evaluate the derivative of the function at x = 2:

$$f(x) = 2x^3 - 3x^2 + 4$$
$$f'(x) = 6x^2 - 6x$$
$$f'(2) = 6(2)^2 - 6(2)$$
$$f'(2) = 12$$

110. D: To find the derivative of $y = e^{3x^2-1}$, use the Chain Rule. Let $u = 3x^2 - 1$. Thus, $y = e^u$, and $\frac{dy}{du} = e^u$. Since $\frac{dy}{dx} = \frac{dy}{du} \cdot \frac{du}{dx}$, and since $\frac{du}{dx} = 6x$, $\frac{dy}{dx} = e^{3x^2-1} \cdot 6x = 6x\, e^{3x^2-1}$.

111. C: To find the derivative of $y = \ln(2x + 1)$, use the Chain Rule. Let $u = 2x + 1$. Thus, $y = \ln u$, and $\frac{dy}{du} = \frac{1}{u}$. Since $\frac{dy}{dx} = \frac{dy}{du} \cdot \frac{du}{dx}$, and since $\frac{du}{dx} = 2$, $\frac{dy}{dx} = \left(\frac{1}{2x+1}\right)(2) = \frac{2}{2x+1}$.

112. A: If $\lim_{x\to a^+} f(x) = \lim_{x\to a^-} f(x)$, then $\lim_{x\to a^+} f(x) = \lim_{x\to a^-} f(x) = \lim_{x\to a} f(x)$. Otherwise, $\lim_{x\to a} f(x)$ does not exist. If $\lim_{x\to a} f(x)$ exists, and if $\lim_{x\to a} f(x) = f(a)$, then the function is continuous at a. Otherwise, f is discontinuous at a.

113. A: To find the second derivative of the function, take the derivative of the first derivative of the function:

$$f(x) = 2x^4 - 4x^3 + 2x^2 - x + 1$$

$$f'(x) = 8x^3 - 12x^2 + 4x - 1$$

$$f''(x) = 24x^2 - 24x + 4.$$

114. A: The critical points of the graph occur when $f'(x) = 0$.

$$\begin{aligned} f(x) &= 4x^3 - x^2 - 4x + 2 \\ f'(x) &= 12x^2 - 2x - 4 \\ &= 2(6x^2 - x - 2) \\ &= 2(3x - 2)(2x + 1) \\ 0 &= 2(3x - 2)(2x + 1) \\ 3x - 2 &= 0 \quad 2x + 1 = 0 \\ x &= \frac{2}{3} \quad x = -\frac{1}{2} \end{aligned}$$

If $f''(x) > 0$ for all x in an interval, the graph of the function is concave upward on that interval, and if $f''(x) < 0$ for all x in an interval, the graph of the function is concave upward on that interval. Find the second derivative of the function and determine the intervals in which $f''(x)$ is less than zero and greater than zero:

$$f''(x) = 24x - 2$$

$$24x - 2 < 0 \quad 24x - 2 > 0$$

$$x < \frac{1}{12} \quad x > \frac{1}{12}$$

The graph of f is concave downward on the interval $\left(-\infty, -\frac{1}{12}\right)$ and concave upward on the interval $\left(-\frac{1}{12}, \infty\right)$. The inflection point of the graph is $\left(\frac{1}{12}, f\left(\frac{1}{12}\right)\right) = \left(\frac{1}{12}, \frac{359}{216}\right)$. The point $\left(\frac{2}{3}, f\left(\frac{2}{3}\right)\right) = \left(\frac{2}{3}, \frac{2}{27}\right)$ is a relative minimum and the point $\left(-\frac{1}{2}, f\left(-\frac{1}{2}\right)\right) = \left(-\frac{1}{2}, 3\frac{1}{4}\right)$ is a relative maximum.

115. D: The velocity v of the ball at any time t is the slope of the line tangent to the graph of h at time t. The slope of a line tangent to the curve $h = -16t^2 + 50t + 3$ is h'.

$$h' = v = -32t + 50$$

When $t = 2$, the velocity of the ball is $-32(2) + 50 = -14$. The velocity is negative because the slope of the tangent line at $t = 2$ is negative; velocity has both magnitude and direction, so a velocity of -14 means that the velocity is 14 ft/s downward.

116. B: The manufacturer wishes to minimize the surface area A of the can while keeping its volume V fixed at $0.5\text{ L} = 500\text{ mL} = 500\text{ cm}^3$. The formula for the surface area of a cylinder is $A = 2\pi rh + 2\pi r^2$, and the formula for volume is $V = \pi r^2 h$. To combine the two formulas into one, solve the volume formula for r or h and substitute the resulting expression into the surface area formula for r or h. The volume of the cylinder is 500 cm^3, so $500 = \pi r^2 h \rightarrow h = \frac{500}{\pi r^2}$. Therefore, $A = 2\pi rh + 2\pi r^2 \rightarrow 2\pi r\left(\frac{500}{\pi r^2}\right) + 2\pi r^2 = \frac{1000}{r} + 2\pi r^2$. Find the critical point(s) by setting the first derivative equal to zero and solving for r. Note that r represents the radius of the can and must therefore be a positive number.

$$\begin{aligned} A &= 1000r^{-1} + 2\pi r^2 \\ A' &= -1000r^{-2} + 4\pi r \end{aligned}$$

$$0 = -\frac{1000}{r^2} + 4\pi r$$
$$\frac{1000}{r^2} = 4\pi r$$
$$1000 = 4\pi r^3$$
$$\sqrt[3]{\frac{1000}{4\pi}} = r$$

So, when r≈4.3 cm, the minimum surface area is obtained. When the radius of the can is 4.30 cm, its height is $h \approx \frac{500}{\pi(4.30)^2}$≈8.6 cm, and the surface area is approximately $\frac{1000}{4.3} + 2\pi(4.3)^2 \approx 348.73\ \text{cm}^2$. Confirm that the surface area is greater when the radius is slightly smaller or larger than 4.3 cm. For instance, when r=4 cm, the surface area is approximately 350.5 cm^2, and when r=4.5 cm, the surface area is approximately 349.5 cm^2.

117. C: Partitioned into rectangles with length of 1, the left Riemann sum is 20+25+28+30+29+26+22+16+12+10+10+13=241 square units, and the right Riemann sum is 25+28+30+29+26+22+16+12+10+10+13+17=238 square units.

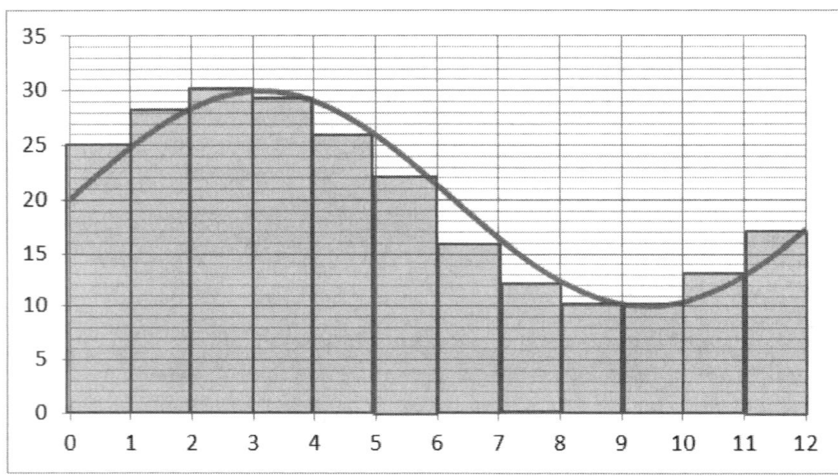

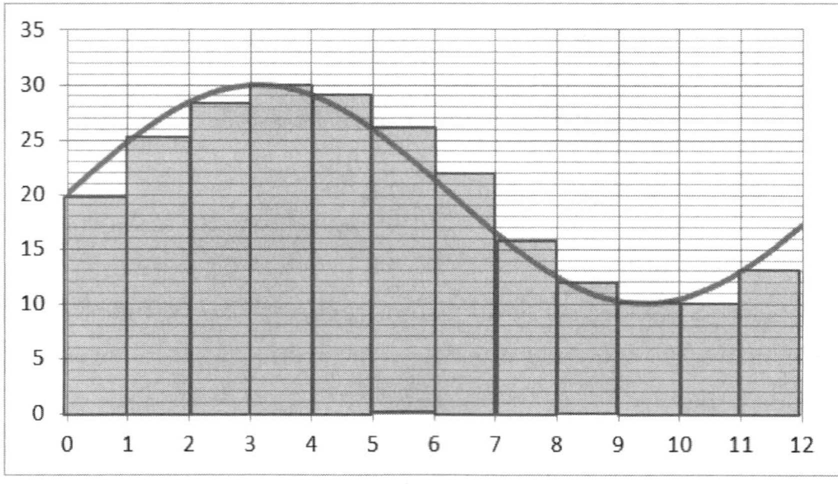

118. B: The area under curve $f(x)$ is $\int_1^2 \frac{1}{x} = [\ln(2)] - [\ln(1)] \approx 0.69$.

119. A: $\int 3x^2 + 2x - 1 = \frac{3}{2+1}x^{2+1} + \frac{2}{1+1}x^{1+1} - x + c = x^3 + x^2 - x + c$.

120. B: To calculate $\int 3x^2 e^{x^3}\,dx$, let $u = x^3$. Since $du = 3x^2 dx$, $\int 3x^2 e^{x^3}\,dx = \int e^u\,du \to e^u + c \to e^{x^3} + c$.

121. B: Find the points of intersection of the two graphs:

$$x^2 - 4 = -x + 2$$

$$x^2 + x - 6 = 0$$

$$(x + 3)(x - 2) = 0$$

$$x = -3 \quad x = 2$$

The finite region is bound at the top by the line $y = -x + 2$ and at the bottom by $y = x^2 - 4$, so the area is between the graphs on [-3,2], and the height of the region at point x is defined by $[(-x + 2) - (x^2 - 4)]$. Thus, the area of the region is

$$A = \int_{-3}^{2} [(-x + 2) - (x^2 - 4)]dx$$

$$= \int_{-3}^{2} (-\mathrm{x}^2 - \mathrm{x} + 6\,)\,dx$$

$$= \left[-\frac{1}{3}(2)^3 - \frac{1}{2}(2)^2 + 6(2)\right] - \left[-\frac{1}{3}(-3)^3 - \frac{1}{2}(-3)^2 + 6(-3)\right]$$

$$= \left[-\frac{8}{3} - 2 + 12\right] - \left[9 - \frac{9}{2} - 18\right] = \frac{22}{3} - \left(-\frac{27}{2}\right) = \frac{125}{6}$$

122. C: The acceleration a of an object at time t is the derivative of the velocity v of the object at time t, which is the derivative of the position x of the object at time t. So, given the velocity of an object at time t, $x(t)$ can be found by taking the integral of the $v(t)$, and $a(t)$ can be found by taking the derivative of $v(t)$.

$x(t) = \int v(t)dt = \int(12t - t^2)dt = 6t^2 - \frac{1}{3}t^3 + c$. Since the position of the car at time 0 is 0, $v(0) = 0 = 6(0)^2 - \frac{1}{3}(0)^3 + c \to 0 = 0 - 0 + c \to c = 0$. Therefore, $x(t) = 6t^2 - \frac{1}{3}t^3$.

$a(t) = v'(t) = 12 - 2t$.

Find the time at which the acceleration is equal to 0: $0 = 12 - 2t \to t = 6$. Then, find $x(6)$ to find the position of the car when the velocity is 0: $6(6)^2 - \frac{1}{3}(6)^3 = 216 - 72 = 144$.

123. D: To draw a box-and-whisker plot from the data, find the median, quartiles, and upper and lower limits.

Stem	Leaves
3	6 7 9 9
4	2 3 8 8 9
5	0 1 1 1 5 7
6	0 0 1 2 3

Key
$3|6 = 36$

The median is $\frac{50+51}{2} = 50.5$, the lower quartile is $\frac{22+23}{2} = 22.5$, and the upper quartile is $\frac{57+60}{2} = 58.5$. The box of the box-and-whisker plot goes through the quartiles, and a line through the box represents the median of the data. The whiskers extend from the box to the lower and upper limits, unless there are any outliers in the set. In this case, there are no outliers, so the box-and-whisker plot in choice A correctly represents the data set.

To draw a pie chart, find the percentage of data contained in each of the ranges shown. There are four out of twenty numbers between 30 and 39, inclusive, so the percentage shown in the pie chart for that range of data is $\frac{4}{20} \cdot 100\% = 20\%$; there are five values between 40 to 49, inclusive, so the percentage of data for that sector is $\frac{5}{20} \cdot 100\% = 25\%$; $\frac{6}{20} \cdot 100\% = 30\%$ of the data is within the range of 50-59, and $\frac{5}{20} \cdot 100\% = 25\%$ is within the range of 60-69. The pie chart shows the correct percentage of data in each category.

To draw a cumulative frequency histogram, find the cumulative frequency of the data.

Range	**Frequency**	**Cumulative frequency**
30-39	4	4
40-49	5	9
50-59	6	15
60-69	5	20

The histogram shows the correct cumulative frequencies.

Therefore, all of the graphs represent the data set.

124. B: A line graph is often used to show change over time. A Venn diagram shows the relationships among sets. A box-and-whisker plot displays how numeric data are distributed throughout the range. A pie chart shows the relationship of parts to a whole.

125. B: In choice A, the teacher surveys all the members of the population in which he is interested. However, since the response is voluntary, the survey is biased: the participants are self-selected

rather than randomly selected. It may be that students who have a strong opinion are more likely to respond than those who are more neutral, and this would give the teacher a skewed perspective of student opinions. In choice B, students are randomly selected, so the sampling technique is not biased. In choice C, the student uses convenience sampling, which is a biased technique. For example, perhaps the student is in an honors class; his sampling method would not be representative of the entire class of eleventh graders, which includes both students who take and who do not take honors classes. Choice D also represents convenience sampling; only the opinions of parents in the PTA are examined, and these parents' opinions may not reflect the opinions of all parents of students at the school.

126. A: Nominal data are data that are collected which have no intrinsic quantity or order. For instance, a survey might ask the respondent to identify his or her gender. While it is possible to compare the relative frequency of each response (for example, "most of the respondents are women"), it is not possible to calculate the mean, which requires data to be numeric, or median, which requires data to be ordered. Interval data are both numeric and ordered, so mean and median can be determined, as can the mode, the interval within which there are the most data. Ordinal data has an inherent order, but there is not a set interval between two points. For example, a survey might ask whether the respondent whether he or she was very dissatisfied, dissatisfied, neutral, satisfied, or very satisfied with the customer service received. Since the data are not numeric, the mean cannot be calculated, but since ordering the data is possible, the median has context.

127. A: The average number of male students in the 11th and 12th grades is 125 $\left(\text{calculated as } \frac{131 + 119}{2}\right)$. The number of Hispanic students at the school is 10% of 1219, which is 122 students (rounded up from 121.9). The difference in the number of male and female students at the school is $630 - 589 = 41$, and the difference in the number of 9th and 12th grade students at the school is 354 - 255 = 99.

128. C: 52% of the student population is white. There are 630 female students at the school out of 1219 students, so the percentage of female students is $\frac{630}{1219} \cdot 100\% \approx 52\%$. The percentages rounded to the nearest whole number are the same.

129. D: 131 of 283 eleventh graders are male. Given that an 11th grader is chosen to attend the conference, the probability that a male is chosen is $\frac{\text{number of males}}{\text{number of 11th graders}} = \frac{131}{283} \approx 0.46$. Note that this is **NOT** the same question as one which asks for the probability of selecting at random from the school a male student who is in eleventh grade, which has a probability of $\frac{131}{1219} \approx 0.11$.

130. A: The range is the spread of the data. It can be calculated for each class by subtracting the lowest test score from the highest, or it can be determined visually from the graph. The difference between the highest and lowest test scores in class A is 98-23=75 points. The range for each of the other classes is much smaller.

131. D: 75% of the data in a set is above the first quartile. Since the first quartile for this set is 73, there is a 75% chance that a student chosen at random from class 2 scored above a 73.

132. C: The line through the center of the box represents the median. The median test score for classes 1 and 2 is 82.

Note that for class 1, the median is a better representation of the data than the mean. There are two outliers (points which lie outside of two standard deviations from the mean) which bring down the average test score. In cases such as this, the mean is not the best measure of central tendency.

133. D: Since there are 100 homes' market times represented in each set, the median time a home spends on the market is between the 50th and 51st data point in each set. The 50th and 51st data points for Zip Code 1 are six months and seven months, respectively, so the median time a house in Zip Code 1 spends on the market is between six and seven months (6.5 months), which by the realtor's definition of market time is a seven-month market time. The 50th and 51st data points for Zip Code 2 are both thirteen months, so the median time a house in Zip Code 2 spends on the market is thirteen months.

To find the mean market time for 100 houses, find the sum of the market times and divide by 100. If the frequency of a one-month market time is 9, the number 1 is added nine times (1·9), if frequency of a two-month market time is 10, the number 2 is added ten times (2·10), and so on. So, to find the average market time, divide by 100 the sum of the products of each market time and its corresponding frequency. For Zip Code 1, the mean market time is 7.38 months, which by the realtor's definition of market time is an eight-month market time. For Zip Code 2, the mean market time is 12.74, which by the realtor's definition of market time is a thirteen-month market time.

The mode market time is the market time for which the frequency is the highest. For Zip Code 1, the mode market time is three months, and for Zip Code 2, the mode market time is eleven months.

The statement given in choice D is true. The median time a house spends on the market in Zip Code 1 is less than the mean time a house spends on the market in Zip Code 1.

Time on market	Frequency for Zip Code 1	Frequency for Zip Code 2	Time·Frequency for Zip Code 1	Time·Frequency for Zip Code 1
1	9	6	9	6
2	10	4	20	8
3	12	3	36	9
4	8	4	32	16
5	6	3	30	15
6	5	5	30	30
7	8	2	56	14
8	8	1	64	8
9	6	3	54	27
10	3	5	30	50
11	5	7	55	77
12	4	6	48	72
13	2	6	26	78
14	3	5	42	70
15	1	3	15	45
16	2	2	32	32
17	2	3	34	51
18	1	5	18	90
19	0	6	0	114
20	2	4	40	80
21	1	5	21	105
22	1	4	22	88
23	0	3	0	69
24	1	5	24	120
SUM	100	100	738	1274

134. C: The probability of an event is the number of possible occurrences of that event divided by the number of all possible outcomes. A camper who is at least eight years old can be eight, nine, or ten years old, so the probability of randomly selecting a camper at least eight years old is $\frac{\text{number of eight-, nine-, and ten-year old campers}}{\text{total number of campers}} = \frac{14+12+10}{12+15+14+12+10} = \frac{36}{63} = \frac{4}{7}$.

135. B: There are three ways in which two women from the same department can be selected: two women can be selected from the first department, or two women can be selected from the second department, or two women can be selected from the third department.

The probability that two women are selected from Department 1 is $\frac{12}{103} \times \frac{11}{102} = \frac{132}{10506}$, the probability that two women are selected from Department 2 is $\frac{28}{103} \times \frac{27}{102} = \frac{756}{10506}$, and the probability that two women are selected from Department 3 is $\frac{16}{103} \times \frac{15}{102} = \frac{240}{10506}$. Since any of these is a discrete possible outcome, the probability that two women will be selected from the same department is the sum of these outcomes: $\frac{132}{10506} + \frac{756}{10506} + \frac{240}{10506} \approx 0.107$, or 10.7%.

	Department 1	**Department 2**	**Department 3**	**Total**
Women	12	28	16	56
Men	18	14	15	47
Total	30	42	31	103

136. B: The number of students who like broccoli is equal to the number of students who like all three vegetables plus the number of students who like broccoli and carrots but not cauliflower plus the number of students who like broccoli and cauliflower but not carrots plus the number of students who like broccoli but no other vegetable: $3 + 15 + 4 + 10 = 32$. These students plus the numbers of students who like just cauliflower, just carrots, cauliflower and carrots, or none of the vegetables represents the entire set of students sampled: $32 + 2 + 27 + 6 + 23 = 90$. So, the probability that a randomly chosen student likes broccoli is $\frac{32}{90} \approx 0.356$.

The number of students who like carrots and at least one other vegetable is $15 + 6 + 3 = 24$. The number of students who like carrots is $24 + 27 = 51$. So, the probability that a student who likes carrots will also like at least one other vegetable is $\frac{24}{51} \approx 0.471$. The number of students who like cauliflower and broccoli is $4 + 3 = 7$. The number of students who like all three vegetables is 3. So, the probability that a student who likes cauliflower and broccoli will also like carrots is $\frac{3}{7} \approx 0.429$.

The number of students who do not like carrots, broccoli, or cauliflower is 23. The total number of students surveyed is 90. So, the probability that a student does not like any of the three vegetables is $23/90 \approx 0.256$.

137. C: Since each coin toss is an independent event, the probability of the compound event of flipping the coin three times is equal to the product of the probabilities of the individual events. For example, $P(HHH) = P(H) \cdot P(H) \cdot P(H)$, $P(HHT) = P(H) \cdot P(H) \cdot P(T)$, etc. When a coin is flipped three times, all of the possible outcomes are HHH, HHT, HTH, HTT, THH, THT, TTH, and TTT. Since the only way to obtain three heads is by the coin landing on heads three times,

$$P(three\ heads) = P(HHH) = P(H)P(H)P(H).$$

Likewise,

$$P(no\ heads) = P(T)P(T)P(T).$$

Since there are three ways to get one head,

$$\begin{aligned} P(one\ head) = P(HTT) + P(THT) + P(TTH) &= P(H)P(T)P(T) + P(T)P(H)P(T) + P(T)P(T)P(H) \\ &= P(H)[(3P(T)^2], \end{aligned}$$

And since there are three ways to get two heads,

$$P(two\ heads) = P(HHT) + P(HTH) + P(THH)$$
$$= P(H)P(H)P(T) + P(H)P(T)P(H) + P(T)P(H)P(H) = P(H)^2[3P(T)]$$

Use these properties to calculate the experimental probability P(H):

30 out of 100 coin tosses resulted in three heads, and $P(three\ heads) = P(H)P(H)P(H) = P(H)^3$. So, experimental P(H) can be calculated by taking the cube root of $\frac{30}{100}$. $\sqrt[3]{0.3} \approx 0.67$.

Similarly, $P(no\ heads) = P(T)P(T)P(T) = \frac{4}{100}$. $P(T) = \sqrt[3]{0.04} \approx 0.34$. $P(H) + P(T) = 1, P(T) = 1 - P(H)$. Thus, $P(H) = 1 - P(T) \approx 0.66$.

Notice that these calculated values of P(H) are approximately the same. Since 100 is a fairly large sample size for this kind of experiment, the approximation for $P(H)$ ought to consistent for the compiled data set. Rather than calculating $P(H)$ using the data for one head and two heads, use the average calculated probability to confirm that the number of expected outcomes of one head and two head matches the number of actual outcomes.

The number of expected outcomes of getting one head in three coin flips out of 100 trials $100\{0.665[3(1 - 0.665)^2]\} \approx 22$, and the expected outcome getting of two heads in three coin flips out of 100 trials three flips is $100\{0.665^2[3(1 - 0.665)]\} \approx 44$. Since 22 and 44 are, in fact, the data obtained, 0.665 is indeed a good approximation for P(H) when the coin used in this experiment is tossed.

138. D: A fair coin has a symmetrical binomial distribution which peaks in its center. Since choice B shows a skewed distribution for the fair coin, it cannot be the correct answer. From the frequency histogram given for the misshapen coin, it is evident that the misshapen coin is more likely to land on heads. Therefore, it is more likely that ten coin flips would result in fewer tails than ten coin flips of a fair coin; consequently, the probability distribution for the misshapen coin would be higher than the fair coin's distribution towards the left of the graph since the misshapen coin is less likely to land on tails. Choice A shows a probability distribution which peaks at a value of 5 and which is symmetrical with respect to the peak, which verifies that it cannot be correct. (Furthermore, in choice A, the sum of the probabilities shown for each number of tails for the misshapen coin is not equal to 1.) The distribution for the misshapen coin in choice C is skewed in the wrong direction, favoring tails instead of heads, and must therefore also be incorrect. Choice D shows the correct binomial distribution for the fair coin and the appropriate shift for the misshapen coin.

Another way to approach this question is to use the answer from the previous problem to determine the probability of obtaining particular events, such as no tails and no heads, and then compare those probabilities to the graphs. For example, for the misshapen coin, P(0 tails)=P(10 heads) $\approx (0.67)^{10}$, or 0.018, and the P(10 tails) $\approx (0.33)^{10}$, which is 0.000015. For a fair coin, P(0 tails)=$(0.5)^{10}$=P(0 heads). To find values other than these, it is helpful to use the binomial distribution formula $({}_nC_r)p^r q^{n-r}$, where n is the number of trials, r is the number of successes, p is the probability of success, and q is the probability of failure. For this problem, obtaining tails is a success, and the probability of obtaining tails is $p = 0.33$ for the misshapen coin and $p = 0.5$ for the fair coin; so, $q = 0.67$ for the misshapen coin and $q = 0.5$ for the fair coin. To find the probability of, say, getting three tails for ten flips of the misshapen coin, find $({}_nC_r)p^r q^{n-r} = ({}_{10}C_3)(0.33)^3(0.67)^7 = \frac{10!}{3!7!}(0.33)^3(0.67)^7 \approx 0.261$. The calculated probabilities match those shown in choice C.

139. C: When rolling two dice, there is only one way to roll a sum of two (rolling a 1 on each die) and twelve (rolling 6 on each die). In contrast, there are two ways to obtain a sum of three (rolling a 2 and 1 or a 1 and 2) and eleven (rolling a 5 and 6 or a 6 and 5), three ways to obtain a sum of four (1 and 3; 2 and 2; 3 and 1) or ten (4 and 6; 5 and 5; 6 and 4), and so on. Since the probability of obtaining each sum is inconsistent, choice C is not an appropriate simulation. Choice A is acceptable since the probability of picking A, 1, 2, 3, 4, 5, 6, 7, 8, 9, or J from the modified deck cards of cards is equally likely, each with a probability of $\frac{4}{52-8} = \frac{4}{44} = \frac{1}{11}$. Choice B is also acceptable since the computer randomly generates one number from eleven possible numbers, so the probability of generating any of the numbers is $\frac{1}{11}$.

140. C: The number 00 represents the genotype aa. The numbers 11, 12, 21, and 22 represent the genotype bb.

28 93 97 37 92 00 27 21 87 13 62 63 10 31 55 09 47 07 54 88 38 88 10 98 34 01 45 14 34 46 38 61
93 22 37 39 57 03 93 50 53 16 28 65 81 60 21 12 13 10 19 91 04 18 49 01 99 30 11 16 00 48 04 63
59 24 02 42 23 06 32 52 19 18 94 94 46 63 87 41 79 39 85 20 43 20 15 03 39 33 77 45 66 77 70 92
25 27 68 71 89 35 98 55 85 47 60 97 12 92 53 44 45 41 51 22 09 23 81 33 04 35 43 48 32 80 36 95
64 56 34 74 55 37 64 84 51 50 25 99 51 94 19 46 10 44 17 25 75 52 47 35 70 65 08 50 98 09 02 24
30 59 00 03 21 40 30 86 16 53 91 28 17 97 58 75 76 73 83 54 40 54 13 38 36 67 74 80 63 12 41 27
96 61 66 05 60 69 96 15 56 82 57 31 83 26 24 78 42 76 49 56 06 57 78 67 02 96 40 82 29 14 07 29
62 90 31 08 26 71 61 18 22 84 23 33 49 29 90 07 08 05 14 59 72 86 44 69 68 99 06 11 95 43 72 58
28 93 97 37 92 00 27 21 87 13 62 61 15 31 55 09 47 07 54 88 38 88 10 98 34 01 45 14 34 46 38 61
93 22 37 39 57 03 93 50 53 16 28 65 81 60 21 12 13 10 19 91 04 18 49 01 99 30 11 16 00 48 04 63
59 24 02 42 23 06 32 52 19 18 94 94 46 63 87 41 79 39 85 20 43 20 15 03 39 33 77 45 66 77 70 92
25 27 68 71 89 35 98 55 85 47 60 97 12 92 53 44 45 41 51 22 09 23 81 33 04 35 43 48 32 80 36 95
64 56 34 74 55 37 64 84 51 50 25 99 51 94 19 46 10 44 17 25 75 52 47 35 70 65 08 50 98 09 02 24
30 59 00 03 21 40 30 86 16 53 91 28 17 97 58 75 76 73 83 54 40 54 13 38 36 67 74 80 63 12 41 27
96 61 66 05 60 69 96 15 56 82 57 31 83 26 24 78 42 76 49 56 06 57 78 67 02 96 40 82 29 14 07 29
62 90 31 08 26 71 61 18 22 84 23 33 49 29 90 07 08 05 14 59

There are six occurrences of 00, so the experimental probability of getting genotype aa is 6/500 = 0.012. There are 21 occurrences of 11, 12, 21, and 22, so the experimental probability of getting genotype bb is 21/500=0.042. The experimental probability of either getting genotype aa or bb is 0.012+0.042=0.054. Multiply this experimental probability by 100,000 to find the number of individuals expected to be homozygous for either allele in a population of 100,000. $0.054 \cdot 100{,}000 = 5{,}400$. Notice that this is higher than the expected number based on the theoretical probability. Since the allele frequencies are in a ratio of 1:2:7, the theoretical probability of getting either aa or bb is $\frac{1}{10} \cdot \frac{1}{10} + \frac{2}{10} \cdot \frac{2}{10} = \frac{5}{100} = 0.05$. Based on the theoretical probability, one would expect 5,000 members of a population of 100,000 to be homozygous for a or b.

141. D: A score of 85 is one standard deviation below the mean. Since approximately 68% of the data is within one standard deviation of the mean, about 32% (100%-68%) of the data is outside of one standard deviation within the mean. Normally distributed data is symmetric about the mean, which means that about 16% of the data lies below one standard deviation below the mean and about 16% of data lies above one standard deviation above the mean. Therefore, approximately 16% of individuals have IQs less than 85, while approximately 84% of the population has an IQ of at least 85. Since 84% of 300 is 252, about 252 people from the selected group have IQs of at least 85.

142. C: There are nine ways to assign the first digit since it can be any of the numbers 1-9. There are nine ways to assign the second digit since it can be any digit 0-9 EXCEPT for the digit assigned in

place 1. There are eight ways to assign the third number since there are ten digits, two of which have already been assigned. There are seven ways to assign the fourth number, six ways to assign the fifth, five ways to assign the sixth, and four ways to assign the seventh. So, the number of combinations is $9 \cdot 9 \cdot 8 \cdot 7 \cdot 6 \cdot 5 \cdot 4 = 544{,}320$.

Another way to approach the problem is to notice that the arrangement of nine digits in the last six places is a sequence without reputation, or a permutation. (Note: this may be called a partial permutation since all of the elements of the set need not be used.) The number of possible sequences of a fixed length r of elements taken from a given set of size n is permutation ${}_nP_r = \frac{n!}{(n-r)!}$. So, the number of ways to arrange the last six digits is ${}_9P_6 = \frac{9!}{(9-6)!} = \frac{9!}{3!}$ =60,480. Multiply this number by nine since there are nine possibilities for the first digit of the phone number. $9 \cdot {}_9P_6 =$ 544,320.

143. B: If each of the four groups in the class of twenty will contain three boys and two girls, there must be twelve boys and eight girls in the class. The number of ways the teacher can select three boys from a group of twelve boys is ${}_{12}C_3 = \frac{12!}{3!(12-3)!} = \frac{12!}{3!9!} = \frac{12 \cdot 11 \cdot 10 \cdot 9!}{3!9!} = \frac{12 \cdot 11 \cdot 10}{3 \cdot 2 \cdot 1}$ =220. The number of ways she can select two girls from a group of eight girls is ${}_8C_2 = \frac{8!}{2!(8-2)!} = \frac{8!}{2!6!} = \frac{8 \cdot 7 \cdot 6!}{2!6!} = \frac{8 \cdot 7}{2 \cdot 1}$ =28. Since each combination of boys can be paired with each combination of girls, the number of group combinations is $220 \cdot 28 = 6{,}160$.

144. B: One way to approach this problem is to first consider the number of arrangements of the five members of the family if Tasha (T) and Mac (M) must sit together. Treat them as a unit seated in a fixed location at the table; then arrange the other three family members (A, B, and C):

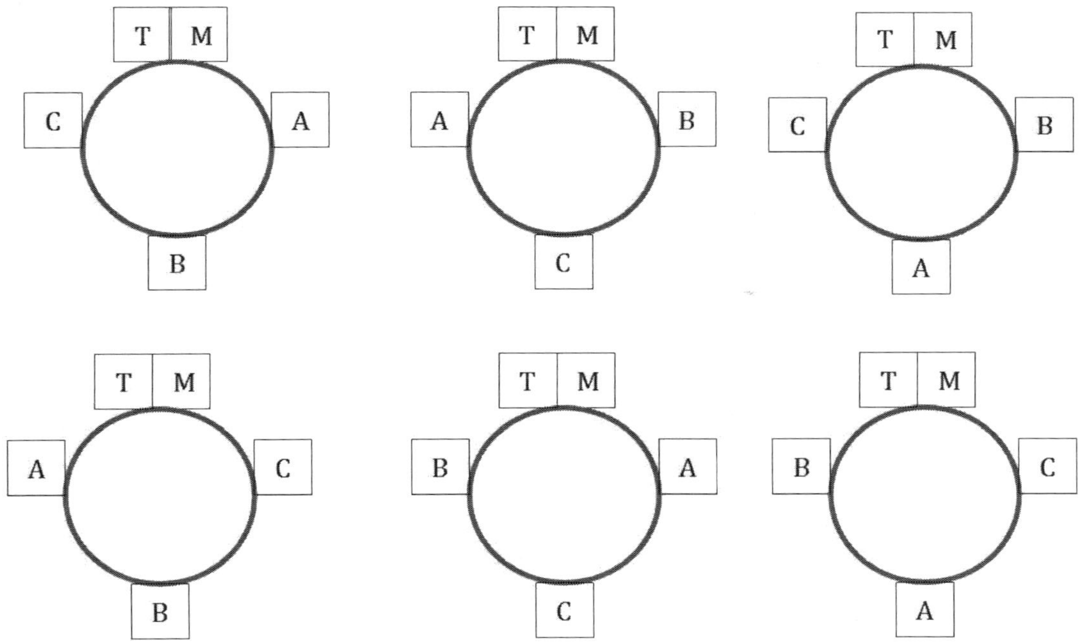

There are six ways to arrange four units around a circle as shown. (Any other arrangement would be a rotation in which the elements in the same order and would therefore not be a unique arrangement.) Note that there are $(n-1)!$ ways to arrange n units around a circle for $n > 1$.

Of course, Mac and Tasha are not actually a single unit. They would still be sitting beside each other if they were to trade seats, so there are twelve arrangements in which the two are seated next to one another. In all other arrangements of the five family members, they are separated. Therefore, to find the number of arrangements in which Tasha and Mac are not sitting together, subtract twelve from the possible arrangement of five units around a circle: $(5-1)!-12=12$.

145. A: The recursive definition of the sequence gives the first term of the series, $a_1=-1$. The definition also defines each term in the series as the sum of the previous term and 2. Therefore, the second term in the series is $-1+2=1$, the third term in the series is $1+2=3$, and so on.

n	a_n
1	-1
2	1
3	3

The relationship between n and a_n is linear, so the equation of the sequence can be found in the same way as the equation of a line. The value of a_n increases by two each time the value of n increases by 1.

n	$2n$	a_n
1	2	-1
2	4	1
3	6	3

Since the difference in $2n$ and a_n is 3, $a_n=2n-3$.

n	$2n-3$	a_n
1	2-3	-1
2	4-3	1
3	6-3	3

146. B: The series is an infinite geometric series, the sum of which can be found by using the formula $\sum_{n=0}^{\infty} ar^n=\frac{a}{1-r}, |r|<1$, where a is the first term in the series and r is the ratio between successive terms. In the series 200+100+50+25+ ..., $a=200$ and $r=\frac{1}{2}$. So, the sum of the series is $\frac{200}{1-\frac{1}{2}}=\frac{200}{\frac{1}{2}}=400$.

147. A: The sum of two vectors is equal to the sum of their components. Using component-wise addition, $\boldsymbol{v}+\boldsymbol{w}=(4+(-3),3+4)=(1,7)$. To multiply a vector by a scalar, multiply each component by that scalar. Using component-wise scalar multiplication, $2(1,7)=(2\cdot 1,2\cdot 7)=(2,14)$.

148. A: First, subtract the two column matrices in parentheses by subtracting corresponding terms.

$$\begin{bmatrix} 2 & 0 & -5 \end{bmatrix}\left(\begin{bmatrix} 4-3 \\ 2-5 \\ -1-(-5) \end{bmatrix}\right)=\begin{bmatrix} 2 & 0 & -5 \end{bmatrix}\begin{bmatrix} 1 \\ -3 \\ 4 \end{bmatrix}$$

Then, multiply the matrices. The product of a 1×3 matrix and a 3×1 matrix is a 1×1 matrix.

$$\begin{bmatrix} 2 & 0 & -5 \end{bmatrix}\begin{bmatrix} 1 \\ -3 \\ 4 \end{bmatrix} = [(2)(1) + (0)(-3) + (-5)(4)] = [-18]$$

Note that matrix multiplication is NOT commutative. The product of the 3x1 matrix $\begin{bmatrix} 1 \\ -3 \\ 4 \end{bmatrix}$ and the 1x3 matrix $\begin{bmatrix} 2 & 0 & -5 \end{bmatrix}$ is the 3x3 matrix $\begin{bmatrix} 2 & 0 & -5 \\ -6 & 0 & 15 \\ 8 & 0 & -20 \end{bmatrix}$.

149. B: The table below shows the intersections of each set with each of the other sets.

Set	{2,4,6,8,10,12,...}	{1,2,3,4,6,12}	{1,2,4,9}
{2,4,6,8,10,12,... }	{2,4,6,8,10,12,...}	{2,4,6,12}	{2,4}
{1,2,3,4,6,12}	{2,4,6,12}	{1,2,3,4,6,12}	{1,2,4}
{1,2,4,9}	{2,4}	{1,2,4}	{1,2,4,9}

Notice that {2,4} is a subset of {2,4,6,12} and {1,2,4}. So, the intersection of {1,2,4,9} and the even integers is a subset of the intersection of the even integers and the factors of twelve, and the intersection of the set of even integers and {1,2,4,9} is a subset of the intersection of {1,2,4,9} and the factors of twelve. So, while it is not possible to determine which set is A and which is B, set C must be the set of factors of twelve: {1,2,3,4,6,12}.

150. D: Use a Venn diagram to help organize the given information. Start by filling in the space where the three circles intersect: Jenny tutored three students in all three areas. Use that information to fill in the spaces where two circles intersect: for example, she tutored four students in chemistry and for the ACT, and three of those were students she tutored in all three areas, so one student was tutored in chemistry and for the ACT but not for math. Once the diagram is completed, add the number of students who were tutored in all areas to the number of students tutored in only two of the three areas to the number of students tutored in only one area. The total number of students tutored was 3+2+2+1+3+2+1=14.

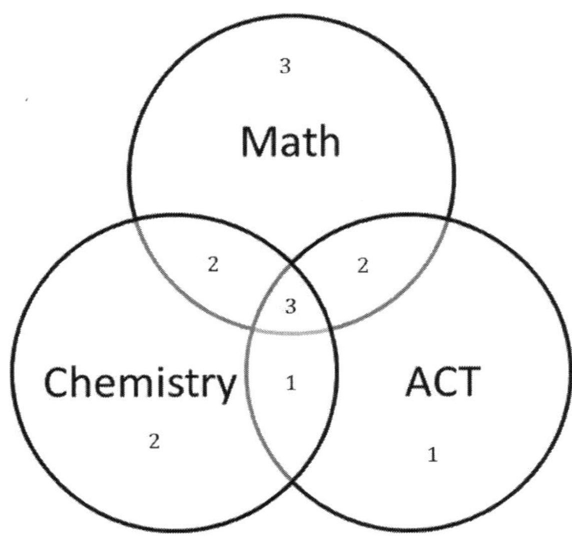

How to Overcome Test Anxiety

Just the thought of taking a test is enough to make most people a little nervous. A test is an important event that can have a long-term impact on your future, so it's important to take it seriously and it's natural to feel anxious about performing well. But just because anxiety is normal, that doesn't mean that it's helpful in test taking, or that you should simply accept it as part of your life. Anxiety can have a variety of effects. These effects can be mild, like making you feel slightly nervous, or severe, like blocking your ability to focus or remember even a simple detail.

If you experience test anxiety—whether severe or mild—it's important to know how to beat it. To discover this, first you need to understand what causes test anxiety.

Causes of Test Anxiety

While we often think of anxiety as an uncontrollable emotional state, it can actually be caused by simple, practical things. One of the most common causes of test anxiety is that a person does not feel adequately prepared for their test. This feeling can be the result of many different issues such as poor study habits or lack of organization, but the most common culprit is time management. Starting to study too late, failing to organize your study time to cover all of the material, or being distracted while you study will mean that you're not well prepared for the test. This may lead to cramming the night before, which will cause you to be physically and mentally exhausted for the test. Poor time management also contributes to feelings of stress, fear, and hopelessness as you realize you are not well prepared but don't know what to do about it.

Other times, test anxiety is not related to your preparation for the test but comes from unresolved fear. This may be a past failure on a test, or poor performance on tests in general. It may come from comparing yourself to others who seem to be performing better or from the stress of living up to expectations. Anxiety may be driven by fears of the future—how failure on this test would affect your educational and career goals. These fears are often completely irrational, but they can still negatively impact your test performance.

Review Video: 3 Reasons You Have Test Anxiety
Visit mometrix.com/academy and enter code: 428468

Elements of Test Anxiety

As mentioned earlier, test anxiety is considered to be an emotional state, but it has physical and mental components as well. Sometimes you may not even realize that you are suffering from test anxiety until you notice the physical symptoms. These can include trembling hands, rapid heartbeat, sweating, nausea, and tense muscles. Extreme anxiety may lead to fainting or vomiting. Obviously, any of these symptoms can have a negative impact on testing. It is important to recognize them as soon as they begin to occur so that you can address the problem before it damages your performance.

Review Video: 3 Ways to Tell You Have Test Anxiety
Visit mometrix.com/academy and enter code: 927847

The mental components of test anxiety include trouble focusing and inability to remember learned information. During a test, your mind is on high alert, which can help you recall information and stay focused for an extended period of time. However, anxiety interferes with your mind's natural processes, causing you to blank out, even on the questions you know well. The strain of testing during anxiety makes it difficult to stay focused, especially on a test that may take several hours. Extreme anxiety can take a huge mental toll, making it difficult not only to recall test information but even to understand the test questions or pull your thoughts together.

Review Video: How Test Anxiety Affects Memory
Visit mometrix.com/academy and enter code: 609003

Effects of Test Anxiety

Test anxiety is like a disease—if left untreated, it will get progressively worse. Anxiety leads to poor performance, and this reinforces the feelings of fear and failure, which in turn lead to poor performances on subsequent tests. It can grow from a mild nervousness to a crippling condition. If allowed to progress, test anxiety can have a big impact on your schooling, and consequently on your future.

Test anxiety can spread to other parts of your life. Anxiety on tests can become anxiety in any stressful situation, and blanking on a test can turn into panicking in a job situation. But fortunately, you don't have to let anxiety rule your testing and determine your grades. There are a number of relatively simple steps you can take to move past anxiety and function normally on a test and in the rest of life.

Review Video: How Test Anxiety Impacts Your Grades
Visit mometrix.com/academy and enter code: 939819

Physical Steps for Beating Test Anxiety

While test anxiety is a serious problem, the good news is that it can be overcome. It doesn't have to control your ability to think and remember information. While it may take time, you can begin taking steps today to beat anxiety.

Just as your first hint that you may be struggling with anxiety comes from the physical symptoms, the first step to treating it is also physical. Rest is crucial for having a clear, strong mind. If you are tired, it is much easier to give in to anxiety. But if you establish good sleep habits, your body and mind will be ready to perform optimally, without the strain of exhaustion. Additionally, sleeping well helps you to retain information better, so you're more likely to recall the answers when you see the test questions.

Getting good sleep means more than going to bed on time. It's important to allow your brain time to relax. Take study breaks from time to time so it doesn't get overworked, and don't study right before bed. Take time to rest your mind before trying to rest your body, or you may find it difficult to fall asleep.

Review Video: The Importance of Sleep for Your Brain
Visit mometrix.com/academy and enter code: 319338

Along with sleep, other aspects of physical health are important in preparing for a test. Good nutrition is vital for good brain function. Sugary foods and drinks may give a burst of energy but this burst is followed by a crash, both physically and emotionally. Instead, fuel your body with protein and vitamin-rich foods.

Also, drink plenty of water. Dehydration can lead to headaches and exhaustion, especially if your brain is already under stress from the rigors of the test. Particularly if your test is a long one, drink water during the breaks. And if possible, take an energy-boosting snack to eat between sections.

Review Video: How Diet Can Affect your Mood
Visit mometrix.com/academy and enter code: 624317

Along with sleep and diet, a third important part of physical health is exercise. Maintaining a steady workout schedule is helpful, but even taking 5-minute study breaks to walk can help get your blood pumping faster and clear your head. Exercise also releases endorphins, which contribute to a positive feeling and can help combat test anxiety.

When you nurture your physical health, you are also contributing to your mental health. If your body is healthy, your mind is much more likely to be healthy as well. So take time to rest, nourish your body with healthy food and water, and get moving as much as possible. Taking these physical steps will make you stronger and more able to take the mental steps necessary to overcome test anxiety.

Review Video: How to Stay Healthy and Prevent Test Anxiety
Visit mometrix.com/academy and enter code: 877894

Mental Steps for Beating Test Anxiety

Working on the mental side of test anxiety can be more challenging, but as with the physical side, there are clear steps you can take to overcome it. As mentioned earlier, test anxiety often stems from lack of preparation, so the obvious solution is to prepare for the test. Effective studying may be the most important weapon you have for beating test anxiety, but you can and should employ several other mental tools to combat fear.

First, boost your confidence by reminding yourself of past success—tests or projects that you aced. If you're putting as much effort into preparing for this test as you did for those, there's no reason you should expect to fail here. Work hard to prepare; then trust your preparation.

Second, surround yourself with encouraging people. It can be helpful to find a study group, but be sure that the people you're around will encourage a positive attitude. If you spend time with others who are anxious or cynical, this will only contribute to your own anxiety. Look for others who are motivated to study hard from a desire to succeed, not from a fear of failure.

Third, reward yourself. A test is physically and mentally tiring, even without anxiety, and it can be helpful to have something to look forward to. Plan an activity following the test, regardless of the outcome, such as going to a movie or getting ice cream.

When you are taking the test, if you find yourself beginning to feel anxious, remind yourself that you know the material. Visualize successfully completing the test. Then take a few deep, relaxing breaths and return to it. Work through the questions carefully but with confidence, knowing that you are capable of succeeding.

Developing a healthy mental approach to test taking will also aid in other areas of life. Test anxiety affects more than just the actual test—it can be damaging to your mental health and even contribute to depression. It's important to beat test anxiety before it becomes a problem for more than testing.

Review Video: Test Anxiety and Depression
Visit mometrix.com/academy and enter code: 904704

Study Strategy

Being prepared for the test is necessary to combat anxiety, but what does being prepared look like? You may study for hours on end and still not feel prepared. What you need is a strategy for test prep. The next few pages outline our recommended steps to help you plan out and conquer the challenge of preparation.

Step 1: Scope Out the Test

Learn everything you can about the format (multiple choice, essay, etc.) and what will be on the test. Gather any study materials, course outlines, or sample exams that may be available. Not only will this help you to prepare, but knowing what to expect can help to alleviate test anxiety.

Step 2: Map Out the Material

Look through the textbook or study guide and make note of how many chapters or sections it has. Then divide these over the time you have. For example, if a book has 15 chapters and you have five days to study, you need to cover three chapters each day. Even better, if you have the time, leave an extra day at the end for overall review after you have gone through the material in depth.

If time is limited, you may need to prioritize the material. Look through it and make note of which sections you think you already have a good grasp on, and which need review. While you are studying, skim quickly through the familiar sections and take more time on the challenging parts. Write out your plan so you don't get lost as you go. Having a written plan also helps you feel more in control of the study, so anxiety is less likely to arise from feeling overwhelmed at the amount to cover. A sample plan may look like this:

- Day 1: Skim chapters 1–4, study chapter 5 (especially pages 31–33)
- Day 2: Study chapters 6–7, skim chapters 8–9
- Day 3: Skim chapter 10, study chapters 11–12 (especially pages 87–90)
- Day 4: Study chapters 13–15
- Day 5: Overall review (focus most on chapters 5, 6, and 12), take practice test

Step 3: Gather Your Tools

Decide what study method works best for you. Do you prefer to highlight in the book as you study and then go back over the highlighted portions? Or do you type out notes of the important information? Or is it helpful to make flashcards that you can carry with you? Assemble the pens, index cards, highlighters, post-it notes, and any other materials you may need so you won't be distracted by getting up to find things while you study.

If you're having a hard time retaining the information or organizing your notes, experiment with different methods. For example, try color-coding by subject with colored pens, highlighters, or post-it notes. If you learn better by hearing, try recording yourself reading your notes so you can listen while in the car, working out, or simply sitting at your desk. Ask a friend to quiz you from your flashcards, or try teaching someone the material to solidify it in your mind.

Step 4: Create Your Environment

It's important to avoid distractions while you study. This includes both the obvious distractions like visitors and the subtle distractions like an uncomfortable chair (or a too-comfortable couch that makes you want to fall asleep). Set up the best study environment possible: good lighting and a comfortable work area. If background music helps you focus, you may want to turn it on, but otherwise keep the room quiet. If you are using a computer to take notes, be sure you don't have any other windows open, especially applications like social media, games, or anything else that could distract you. Silence your phone and turn off notifications. Be sure to keep water close by so you stay hydrated while you study (but avoid unhealthy drinks and snacks).

Also, take into account the best time of day to study. Are you freshest first thing in the morning? Try to set aside some time then to work through the material. Is your mind clearer in the afternoon or evening? Schedule your study session then. Another method is to study at the same time of day that you will take the test, so that your brain gets used to working on the material at that time and will be ready to focus at test time.

Step 5: Study!

Once you have done all the study preparation, it's time to settle into the actual studying. Sit down, take a few moments to settle your mind so you can focus, and begin to follow your study plan. Don't give in to distractions or let yourself procrastinate. This is your time to prepare so you'll be ready to fearlessly approach the test. Make the most of the time and stay focused.

Of course, you don't want to burn out. If you study too long you may find that you're not retaining the information very well. Take regular study breaks. For example, taking five minutes out of every hour to walk briskly, breathing deeply and swinging your arms, can help your mind stay fresh.

As you get to the end of each chapter or section, it's a good idea to do a quick review. Remind yourself of what you learned and work on any difficult parts. When you feel that you've mastered the material, move on to the next part. At the end of your study session, briefly skim through your notes again.

But while review is helpful, cramming last minute is NOT. If at all possible, work ahead so that you won't need to fit all your study into the last day. Cramming overloads your brain with more information than it can process and retain, and your tired mind may struggle to recall even previously learned information when it is overwhelmed with last-minute study. Also, the urgent nature of cramming and the stress placed on your brain contribute to anxiety. You'll be more likely to go to the test feeling unprepared and having trouble thinking clearly.

So don't cram, and don't stay up late before the test, even just to review your notes at a leisurely pace. Your brain needs rest more than it needs to go over the information again. In fact, plan to finish your studies by noon or early afternoon the day before the test. Give your brain the rest of the day to relax or focus on other things, and get a good night's sleep. Then you will be fresh for the test and better able to recall what you've studied.

Step 6: Take a practice test

Many courses offer sample tests, either online or in the study materials. This is an excellent resource to check whether you have mastered the material, as well as to prepare for the test format and environment.

Check the test format ahead of time: the number of questions, the type (multiple choice, free response, etc.), and the time limit. Then create a plan for working through them. For example, if you have 30 minutes to take a 60-question test, your limit is 30 seconds per question. Spend less time on the questions you know well so that you can take more time on the difficult ones.

If you have time to take several practice tests, take the first one open book, with no time limit. Work through the questions at your own pace and make sure you fully understand them. Gradually work up to taking a test under test conditions: sit at a desk with all study materials put away and set a timer. Pace yourself to make sure you finish the test with time to spare and go back to check your answers if you have time.

After each test, check your answers. On the questions you missed, be sure you understand why you missed them. Did you misread the question (tests can use tricky wording)? Did you forget the information? Or was it something you hadn't learned? Go back and study any shaky areas that the practice tests reveal.

Taking these tests not only helps with your grade, but also aids in combating test anxiety. If you're already used to the test conditions, you're less likely to worry about it, and working through tests until you're scoring well gives you a confidence boost. Go through the practice tests until you feel comfortable, and then you can go into the test knowing that you're ready for it.

Test Tips

On test day, you should be confident, knowing that you've prepared well and are ready to answer the questions. But aside from preparation, there are several test day strategies you can employ to maximize your performance.

First, as stated before, get a good night's sleep the night before the test (and for several nights before that, if possible). Go into the test with a fresh, alert mind rather than staying up late to study.

Try not to change too much about your normal routine on the day of the test. It's important to eat a nutritious breakfast, but if you normally don't eat breakfast at all, consider eating just a protein bar. If you're a coffee drinker, go ahead and have your normal coffee. Just make sure you time it so that the caffeine doesn't wear off right in the middle of your test. Avoid sugary beverages, and drink enough water to stay hydrated but not so much that you need a restroom break 10 minutes into the test. If your test isn't first thing in the morning, consider going for a walk or doing a light workout before the test to get your blood flowing.

Allow yourself enough time to get ready, and leave for the test with plenty of time to spare so you won't have the anxiety of scrambling to arrive in time. Another reason to be early is to select a good seat. It's helpful to sit away from doors and windows, which can be distracting. Find a good seat, get out your supplies, and settle your mind before the test begins.

When the test begins, start by going over the instructions carefully, even if you already know what to expect. Make sure you avoid any careless mistakes by following the directions.

Then begin working through the questions, pacing yourself as you've practiced. If you're not sure on an answer, don't spend too much time on it, and don't let it shake your confidence. Either skip it and come back later, or eliminate as many wrong answers as possible and guess among the remaining ones. Don't dwell on these questions as you continue—put them out of your mind and focus on what lies ahead.

Be sure to read all of the answer choices, even if you're sure the first one is the right answer. Sometimes you'll find a better one if you keep reading. But don't second-guess yourself if you do immediately know the answer. Your gut instinct is usually right. Don't let test anxiety rob you of the information you know.

If you have time at the end of the test (and if the test format allows), go back and review your answers. Be cautious about changing any, since your first instinct tends to be correct, but make sure you didn't misread any of the questions or accidentally mark the wrong answer choice. Look over any you skipped and make an educated guess.

At the end, leave the test feeling confident. You've done your best, so don't waste time worrying about your performance or wishing you could change anything. Instead, celebrate the successful completion of this test. And finally, use this test to learn how to deal with anxiety even better next time.

Review Video: 5 Tips to Beat Test Anxiety
Visit mometrix.com/academy and enter code: 570656

Important Qualification

Not all anxiety is created equal. If your test anxiety is causing major issues in your life beyond the classroom or testing center, or if you are experiencing troubling physical symptoms related to your anxiety, it may be a sign of a serious physiological or psychological condition. If this sounds like your situation, we strongly encourage you to seek professional help.

How to Overcome Your Fear of Math

The word *math* is enough to strike fear into most hearts. How many of us have memories of sitting through confusing lectures, wrestling over mind-numbing homework, or taking tests that still seem incomprehensible even after hours of study? Years after graduation, many still shudder at these memories.

The fact is, math is not just a classroom subject. It has real-world implications that you face every day, whether you realize it or not. This may be balancing your monthly budget, deciding how many supplies to buy for a project, or simply splitting a meal check with friends. The idea of daily confrontations with math can be so paralyzing that some develop a condition known as *math anxiety*.

But you do NOT need to be paralyzed by this anxiety! In fact, while you may have thought all your life that you're not good at math, or that your brain isn't wired to understand it, the truth is that you may have been conditioned to think this way. From your earliest school days, the way you were taught affected the way you viewed different subjects. And the way math has been taught has changed.

Several decades ago, there was a shift in American math classrooms. The focus changed from traditional problem-solving to a conceptual view of topics, de-emphasizing the importance of learning the basics and building on them. The solid foundation necessary for math progression and confidence was undermined. Math became more of a vague concept than a concrete idea. Today, it is common to think of math, not as a straightforward system, but as a mysterious, complicated method that can't be fully understood unless you're a genius.

This is why you may still have nightmares about being called on to answer a difficult problem in front of the class. Math anxiety is a very real, though unnecessary, fear.

Math anxiety may begin with a single class period. Let's say you missed a day in 6th grade math and never quite understood the concept that was taught while you were gone. Since math is cumulative, with each new concept building on past ones, this could very well affect the rest of your math career. Without that one day's knowledge, it will be difficult to understand any other concepts that link to it. Rather than realizing that you're just missing one key piece, you may begin to believe that you're simply not capable of understanding math.

This belief can change the way you approach other classes, career options, and everyday life experiences, if you become anxious at the thought that math might be required. A student who loves science may choose a different path of study upon realizing that multiple math classes will be required for a degree. An aspiring medical student may hesitate at the thought of going through the necessary math classes. For some this anxiety escalates into a more extreme state known as *math phobia*.

Math anxiety is challenging to address because it is rooted deeply and may come from a variety of causes: an embarrassing moment in class, a teacher who did not explain concepts well and contributed to a shaky foundation, or a failed test that contributed to the belief of math failure.

These causes add up over time, encouraged by society's popular view that math is hard and unpleasant. Eventually a person comes to firmly believe that he or she is simply bad at math. This belief makes it difficult to grasp new concepts or even remember old ones. Homework and test grades begin to slip, which only confirms the belief. The poor performance is not due to lack of ability but is caused by math anxiety.

Math anxiety is an emotional issue, not a lack of intelligence. But when it becomes deeply rooted, it can become more than just an emotional problem. Physical symptoms appear. Blood pressure may rise and heartbeat may quicken at the sight of a math problem – or even the thought of math! This fear leads to a mental block. When someone with math anxiety is asked to perform a calculation, even a basic problem can seem overwhelming and impossible. The emotional and physical response to the thought of math prevents the brain from working through it logically.

The more this happens, the more a person's confidence drops, and the more math anxiety is generated. This vicious cycle must be broken!

The first step in breaking the cycle is to go back to very beginning and make sure you really understand the basics of how math works and why it works. It is not enough to memorize rules for multiplication and division. If you don't know WHY these rules work, your foundation will be shaky and you will be at risk of developing a phobia. Understanding mathematical concepts not only promotes confidence and security, but allows you to build on this understanding for new concepts. Additionally, you can solve unfamiliar problems using familiar concepts and processes.

Why is it that students in other countries regularly outperform American students in math? The answer likely boils down to a couple of things: the foundation of mathematical conceptual understanding and societal perception. While students in the US are not expected to *like* or *get* math, in many other nations, students are expected not only to understand math but also to excel at it.

Changing the American view of math that leads to math anxiety is a monumental task. It requires changing the training of teachers nationwide, from kindergarten through high school, so that they learn to teach the *why* behind math and to combat the wrong math views that students may develop. It also involves changing the stigma associated with math, so that it is no longer viewed as unpleasant and incomprehensible. While these are necessary changes, they are challenging and will take time. But in the meantime, math anxiety is not irreversible—it can be faced and defeated, one person at a time.

False Beliefs

One reason math anxiety has taken such hold is that several false beliefs have been created and shared until they became widely accepted. Some of these unhelpful beliefs include the following:

There is only one way to solve a math problem. In the same way that you can choose from different driving routes and still arrive at the same house, you can solve a math problem using different methods and still find the correct answer. A person who understands the reasoning behind math calculations may be able to look at an unfamiliar concept and find the right answer, just by applying logic to the knowledge they already have. This approach may be different than what is taught in the classroom, but it is still valid. Unfortunately, even many teachers view math as a subject where the best course of action is to memorize the rule or process for each problem rather than as a place for students to exercise logic and creativity in finding a solution.

Many people don't have a mind for math. A person who has struggled due to poor teaching or math anxiety may falsely believe that he or she doesn't have the mental capacity to grasp mathematical concepts. Most of the time, this is false. Many people find that when they are relieved of their math anxiety, they have more than enough brainpower to understand math.

Men are naturally better at math than women. Even though research has shown this to be false, many young women still avoid math careers and classes because of their belief that their math abilities are inferior. Many girls have come to believe that math is a male skill and have given up trying to understand or enjoy it.

Counting aids are bad. Something like counting on your fingers or drawing out a problem to visualize it may be frowned on as childish or a crutch, but these devices can help you get a tangible understanding of a problem or a concept.

Sadly, many students buy into these ideologies at an early age. A young girl who enjoys math class may be conditioned to think that she doesn't actually have the brain for it because math is for boys, and may turn her energies to other pursuits, permanently closing the door on a wide range of opportunities. A child who finds the right answer but doesn't follow the teacher's method may believe that he is doing it wrong and isn't good at math. A student who never had a problem with math before may have a poor teacher and become confused, yet believe that the problem is because she doesn't have a mathematical mind.

Students who have bought into these erroneous beliefs quickly begin to add their own anxieties, adapting them to their own personal situations:

I'll never use this in real life. A huge number of people wrongly believe that math is irrelevant outside the classroom. By adopting this mindset, they are handicapping themselves for a life in a mathematical world, as well as limiting their career choices. When they are inevitably faced with real-world math, they are conditioning themselves to respond with anxiety.

I'm not quick enough. While timed tests and quizzes, or even simply comparing yourself with other students in the class, can lead to this belief, speed is not an indicator of skill level. A person can work very slowly yet understand at a deep level.

If I can understand it, it's too easy. People with a low view of their own abilities tend to think that if they are able to grasp a concept, it must be simple. They cannot accept the idea that they are capable of understanding math. This belief will make it harder to learn, no matter how intelligent they are.

I just can't learn this. An overwhelming number of people think this, from young children to adults, and much of the time it is simply not true. But this mindset can turn into a self-fulfilling prophecy that keeps you from exercising and growing your math ability.

The good news is, each of these myths can be debunked. For most people, they are based on emotion and psychology, NOT on actual ability! It will take time, effort, and the desire to change, but change is possible. Even if you have spent years thinking that you don't have the capability to understand math, it is not too late to uncover your true ability and find relief from the anxiety that surrounds math.

Math Strategies

It is important to have a plan of attack to combat math anxiety. There are many useful strategies for pinpointing the fears or myths and eradicating them:

Go back to the basics. For most people, math anxiety stems from a poor foundation. You may think that you have a complete understanding of addition and subtraction, or even decimals and percentages, but make absolutely sure. Learning math is different from learning other subjects. For example, when you learn history, you study various time periods and places and events. It may be important to memorize dates or find out about the lives of famous people. When you move from US history to world history, there will be some overlap, but a large amount of the information will be new. Mathematical concepts, on the other hand, are very closely linked and highly dependent on each other. It's like climbing a ladder – if a rung is missing from your understanding, it may be difficult or impossible for you to climb any higher, no matter how hard you try. So go back and make sure your math foundation is strong. This may mean taking a remedial math course, going to a tutor to work through the shaky concepts, or just going through your old homework to make sure you really understand it.

Speak the language. Math has a large vocabulary of terms and phrases unique to working problems. Sometimes these are completely new terms, and sometimes they are common words, but are used differently in a math setting. If you can't speak the language, it will be very difficult to get a thorough understanding of the concepts. It's common for students to think that they don't understand math when they simply don't understand the vocabulary. The good news is that this is fairly easy to fix. Brushing up on any terms you aren't quite sure of can help bring the rest of the concepts into focus.

Check your anxiety level. When you think about math, do you feel nervous or uncomfortable? Do you struggle with feelings of inadequacy, even on concepts that you know you've already learned? It's important to understand your specific math anxieties, and what triggers them. When you catch yourself falling back on a false belief, mentally replace it with the truth. Don't let yourself believe that you can't learn, or that struggling with a concept means you'll never understand it. Instead, remind yourself of how much you've already learned and dwell on that past success. Visualize grasping the new concept, linking it to your old knowledge, and moving on to the next challenge. Also, learn how to manage anxiety when it arises. There are many techniques for coping with the irrational fears that rise to the surface when you enter the math classroom. This may include controlled breathing, replacing negative thoughts with positive ones, or visualizing success. Anxiety interferes with your ability to concentrate and absorb information, which in turn contributes to greater anxiety. If you can learn how to regain control of your thinking, you will be better able to pay attention, make progress, and succeed!

Don't go it alone. Like any deeply ingrained belief, math anxiety is not easy to eradicate. And there is no need for you to wrestle through it on your own. It will take time, and many people find that speaking with a counselor or psychiatrist helps. They can help you develop strategies for responding to anxiety and overcoming old ideas. Additionally, it can be very helpful to take a short course or seek out a math tutor to help you find and fix the missing rungs on your ladder and make sure that you're ready to progress to the next level. You can also find a number of math aids online: courses that will teach you mental devices for figuring out problems, how to get the most out of your math classes, etc.

Check your math attitude. No matter how much you want to learn and overcome your anxiety, you'll have trouble if you still have a negative attitude toward math. If you think it's too hard, or just have general feelings of dread about math, it will be hard to learn and to break through the anxiety. Work on cultivating a positive math attitude. Remind yourself that math is not just a hurdle to be cleared, but a valuable asset. When you view math with a positive attitude, you'll be much more likely to understand and even enjoy it. This is something you must do for yourself. You may find it helpful to visit with a counselor. Your tutor, friends, and family may cheer you on in your endeavors. But your greatest asset is yourself. You are inside your own mind – tell yourself what you need to hear. Relive past victories. Remind yourself that you are capable of understanding math. Root out any false beliefs that linger and replace them with positive truths. Even if it doesn't feel true at first, it will begin to affect your thinking and pave the way for a positive, anxiety-free mindset.

Aside from these general strategies, there are a number of specific practical things you can do to begin your journey toward overcoming math anxiety. Something as simple as learning a new note-taking strategy can change the way you approach math and give you more confidence and understanding. New study techniques can also make a huge difference.

Math anxiety leads to bad habits. If it causes you to be afraid of answering a question in class, you may gravitate toward the back row. You may be embarrassed to ask for help. And you may procrastinate on assignments, which leads to rushing through them at the last moment when it's too late to get a better understanding. It's important to identify your negative behaviors and replace them with positive ones:

Prepare ahead of time. Read the lesson before you go to class. Being exposed to the topics that will be covered in class ahead of time, even if you don't understand them perfectly, is extremely helpful in increasing what you retain from the lecture. Do your homework and, if you're still shaky, go over some extra problems. The key to a solid understanding of math is practice.

Sit front and center. When you can easily see and hear, you'll understand more, and you'll avoid the distractions of other students if no one is in front of you. Plus, you're more likely to be sitting with students who are positive and engaged, rather than others with math anxiety. Let their positive math attitude rub off on you.

Ask questions in class and out. If you don't understand something, just ask. If you need a more in-depth explanation, the teacher may need to work with you outside of class, but often it's a simple concept you don't quite understand, and a single question may clear it up. If you wait, you may not be able to follow the rest of the day's lesson. For extra help, most professors have office hours outside of class when you can go over concepts one-on-one to clear up any uncertainties. Additionally, there may be a *math lab* or study session you can attend for homework help. Take advantage of this.

Review. Even if you feel that you've fully mastered a concept, review it periodically to reinforce it. Going over an old lesson has several benefits: solidifying your understanding, giving you a confidence boost, and even giving some new insights into material that you're currently learning! Don't let yourself get rusty. That can lead to problems with learning later concepts.

Teaching Tips

While the math student's mindset is the most crucial to overcoming math anxiety, it is also important for others to adjust their math attitudes. Teachers and parents have an enormous influence on how students relate to math. They can either contribute to math confidence or math anxiety.

As a parent or teacher, it is very important to convey a positive math attitude. Retelling horror stories of your own bad experience with math will contribute to a new generation of math anxiety. Even if you don't share your experiences, others will be able to sense your fears and may begin to believe them.

Even a careless comment can have a big impact, so watch for phrases like *He's not good at math* or *I never liked math.* You are a crucial role model, and your children or students will unconsciously adopt your mindset. Give them a positive example to follow. Rather than teaching them to fear the math world before they even know it, teach them about all its potential and excitement.

Work to present math as an integral, beautiful, and understandable part of life. Encourage creativity in solving problems. Watch for false beliefs and dispel them. Cross the lines between subjects: integrate history, English, and music with math. Show students how math is used every day, and how the entire world is based on mathematical principles, from the pull of gravity to the shape of seashells. Instead of letting students see math as a necessary evil, direct them to view it as an imaginative, beautiful art form – an art form that they are capable of mastering and using.

Don't give too narrow a view of math. It is more than just numbers. Yes, working problems and learning formulas is a large part of classroom math. But don't let the teaching stop there. Teach students about the everyday implications of math. Show them how nature works according to the laws of mathematics, and take them outside to make discoveries of their own. Expose them to math-related careers by inviting visiting speakers, asking students to do research and presentations, and learning students' interests and aptitudes on a personal level.

Demonstrate the importance of math. Many people see math as nothing more than a required stepping stone to their degree, a nuisance with no real usefulness. Teach students that algebra is used every day in managing their bank accounts, in following recipes, and in scheduling the day's events. Show them how learning to do geometric proofs helps them to develop logical thinking, an invaluable life skill. Let them see that math surrounds them and is integrally linked to their daily lives: that weather predictions are based on math, that math was used to design cars and other machines, etc. Most of all, give them the tools to use math to enrich their lives.

Make math as tangible as possible. Use visual aids and objects that can be touched. It is much easier to grasp a concept when you can hold it in your hands and manipulate it, rather than just listening to the lecture. Encourage math outside of the classroom. The real world is full of measuring, counting, and calculating, so let students participate in this. Keep your eyes open for numbers and patterns to discuss. Talk about how scores are calculated in sports games and how far apart plants are placed in a garden row for maximum growth. Build the mindset that math is a normal and interesting part of daily life.

Finally, find math resources that help to build a positive math attitude. There are a number of books that show math as fascinating and exciting while teaching important concepts, for example: *The Math Curse; A Wrinkle in Time; The Phantom Tollbooth;* and *Fractals, Googols and Other Mathematical Tales.* You can also find a number of online resources: math puzzles and games, videos that show math in nature, and communities of math enthusiasts. On a local level, students can compete in a variety of math competitions with other schools or join a math club.

The student who experiences math as exciting and interesting is unlikely to suffer from math anxiety. Going through life without this handicap is an immense advantage and opens many doors that others have closed through their fear.

Self-Check

Whether you suffer from math anxiety or not, chances are that you have been exposed to some of the false beliefs mentioned above. Now is the time to check yourself for any errors you may have accepted. Do you think you're not wired for math? Or that you don't need to understand it since you're not planning on a math career? Do you think math is just too difficult for the average person?

Find the errors you've taken to heart and replace them with positive thinking. Are you capable of learning math? Yes! Can you control your anxiety? Yes! These errors will resurface from time to time, so be watchful. Don't let others with math anxiety influence you or sway your confidence. If you're having trouble with a concept, find help. Don't let it discourage you!

Create a plan of attack for defeating math anxiety and sharpening your skills. Do some research and decide if it would help you to take a class, get a tutor, or find some online resources to fine-tune your knowledge. Make the effort to get good nutrition, hydration, and sleep so that you are operating at full capacity. Remind yourself daily that you are skilled and that anxiety does not control you. Your mind is capable of so much more than you know. Give it the tools it needs to grow and thrive.

Thank You

We at Mometrix would like to extend our heartfelt thanks to you, our friend and patron, for allowing us to play a part in your journey. It is a privilege to serve people from all walks of life who are unified in their commitment to building the best future they can for themselves.

The preparation you devote to these important testing milestones may be the most valuable educational opportunity you have for making a real difference in your life. We encourage you to put your heart into it—that feeling of succeeding, overcoming, and yes, conquering will be well worth the hours you've invested.

We want to hear your story, your struggles and your successes, and if you see any opportunities for us to improve our materials so we can help others even more effectively in the future, please share that with us as well. **The team at Mometrix would be absolutely thrilled to hear from you!** So please, send us an email (support@mometrix.com) and let's stay in touch.

If you'd like some additional help, check out these other resources we offer for your exam:
http://MometrixFlashcards.com/TExES

Additional Bonus Material

Due to our efforts to try to keep this book to a manageable length, we've created a link that will give you access to all of your additional bonus material.

Please visit http://www.mometrix.com/bonus948/texesmath7-12 to access the information.